FLORENTINE CODEX

Florentine Codex

General History of the Things of New Spain

FRAY BERNARDINO DE SAHAGÚN

Florentine Codex

neral History of the Things of New Spain

FRAY BERNARDINO DE SAHAGÚN

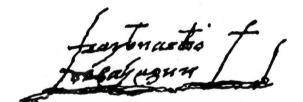

FLORENTINE CODEX

Book 10 – The People

Translated from the Aztec into English, with notes and illustrations

By

CHARLES E. DIBBLE
UNIVERSITY OF UTAH

ARTHUR J. O. ANDERSON
SCHOOL OF AMERICAN RESEARCH

IN THIRTEEN PARTS

PART XI

Chapter heading designs are from the Codex

Published by
The School of American Research and The University of Utah

Monographs of The School of American Research and The Museum of New Mexico
Santa Fe, New Mexico

Number 14, Part XI   1961

Published and distributed by
The University of Utah Press
Salt Lake City, Utah 84112

CONTENTS

THE TENTH BOOK WHICH TREATETH OF THE GENERAL
HISTORY, IN WHICH ARE TOLD THE DIFFERENT
VIRTUES AND VICES WHICH WERE OF THE
BODY AND OF THE SOUL, WHOSOEVER
PRACTISED THEM

LIST OF ILLUSTRATIONS

BOOK X

following page 62

BOOK TEN -- THE PEOPLE

Libro decimo de los vicios y virtudes

desta gente indiana y de los miembros

de todo el cuerpo interiores y

esteriores y de las enfer

medades y medicinas

contrarias y de las

nationes que a esta

tierra an venido

a poblar

De los vícíos y vírtudes desta gente

THE TENTH BOOK[1] WHICH TREATETH OF THE GENERAL HISTORY, IN WHICH ARE TOLD THE DIFFERENT VIRTUES AND VICES WHICH WERE OF THE BODY AND OF THE SOUL, WHOSOEVER PRACTISED THEM.

INIC MATLACTLI AMOSTLI, ITECHPA TLATOA IN HISTORIA GENERAL: IN VNCAN MOTENEOA IN NEPAPAN VIRTUES QUALTIUANI, IECTIUANI: IOAN IN NEPAPAN TLATLACULLI IN TONACAIOTICA CHIOALO IOAN IN ICA TOIOLLO I ÇAÇO AQUIQUE QUICHIOA

First Chapter. Here are told the inherent qualities, the nature, of those related through lineage.

Inic ce capitulo vncan moteneoa in imiuhcatiliz in iieliz in iehoantin tlacamecaiotica miximati

FATHER — ONE'S FATHER[2]

TATLI, TETA,

One's father [is] the source of lineage, the beginning of lineage. [He is] the sincere one. One's father [is] diligent, solicitous, compassionate, sympathetic; a careful administrator [of his household].[3] He rears, he teaches people; he rears, he teaches others. He advises, he admonishes one. He is exemplary; he leads a model life.[4] He stores up for himself; he stores up for others. He cares for his assets; he saves for others. He is thrifty — he saves for the future, teaches thrift, looks to the future. He regulates, distributes with care, establishes order.

in teta tlacamecaionelhoaiutl, tlacamecaiopeuhcaiutl, in qualli yiollo teta yiel: tlaceliani, moiolitlacoani, motequipachoani, cuexane, teputze, macoche. Tlacazcaltia, tlacauapaua, teizcaltia, teizcalia, tenonotza, tenotza, tenemiliztia, coiauac tezcatl quitemanilia in necoc xapo quitequechilia in tomauac ocutl, in hapocio, motetzontia, tetetzontia, tlapachoa, tetlapachilhuia, monepacholtia, monemachtia, tenepacholtia, veca tlachia, tetlamachia, tlatlalia, tlatecpana

One's bad father [is] lazy, incompassionate,[5] negligent, unreliable. He is unfeeling, neglectful of duty, untrustworthy; a shirker, a loafer, a sullen worker.

In teta tlaueliloc, tlatziuhqui amo moiolitlacoani, tlanemmatini, tlaxiccauani, hatle quiiolitlacoa, tlateputzcaoa, tlaxiccaoa, tlaquelmati, monēcaoa tlaqueliecoa

1. A grant by the National Science Foundation to Charles E. Dibble and a fellowship awarded Arthur J. O. Anderson by the John Simon Guggenheim Memorial Foundation have been of great benefit and help in their work. The translators acknowledge their profound gratitude to these Foundations. Book X, which is of varied content, measurably expands the total number of Nahuatl words. Many chapters are mainly descriptive; the one on the parts of the body (Chap. 27), while it reflects the native concepts as to the human body, is perhaps of most interest for its lists of terms. Under such circumstances, the translation of parts of Book X requires somewhat more literal treatment than appears to be necesary in other books. In the opening chapters, differences between Nahuatl and English in kinship terminology occasionally require repetition of the English kinship term.

2. In the "Memoriales con Escolios," *Academia de la Historia MS*, which can be found in Francisco del Paso y Troncoso, ed.: *Historia general de las cosas de Nueva España por Fray Bernardino de Sahagún: edición parcial en facsímile de los códices matritenses en lengua mexicana* (Madrid: Hauser y Menet, 1905), Vol. VI, a note on p. 199 reads: "*El hijo del señor dice a su padre nopiltzintzin, nopiltzintzine, la hija dizele noconetzin. notecu. totecu. notecuiyo. El hijo del principal, mercader, o oficial dice a su padre. niccauhtzin niccauhtzine. la hija dizele noconetzin. El hijo del labrador dize a su p.ᵉ notatzin. notecutzin. notecutze. tecutze. tachitze. tachietze. la hija dizele notecutzin. tecutzin. tachitzin.*"

3. *Loc. cit.*: "*Estos tres vocablos andan siempre iuntos.*"

4. Literally, "he presents one the wide mirror, the two-sided mirror; he sets up the large, clear torch." Cf. *Florentine Codex*, Book VI, cap. xliii, fol. 204r; cf. also Miguel León-Portilla: *La Filosofía Náhuatl* (Mexico: Instituto Indigenista Interamericano, 1956), pp. 72*sqq*., 275.

5. *Hamoyolitlacoani* in "Memoriales con Escolios."

MOTHER — ONE'S MOTHER[6]

One's mother has children; she suckles them. Sincere, vigilant, agile, [she is] an energetic worker — diligent, watchful, solicitous, full of anxiety. She teaches people; she is attentive to them.[7] She caresses, she serves others; she is apprehensive for their welfare; she is careful, thrifty — constantly at work.

One's bad mother [is] evil, dull, stupid,[8] sleepy, lazy; [she is] a squanderer, a petty thief, a deceiver, a fraud. Unreliable, [she is] one who loses things through neglect or anger, who heeds no one. She is disrespectful, inconsiderate, disregarding, careless; she castigates;[9] she causes disregard of conventions, she shows the way — leads the way — to disobedience;[10] she expounds nonconformity.

ONE'S CHILD — ONE'S CHILD[11]

One's child; [that is,] the legitimate child, the child born within the household, the child born within the habitation, the spiritually acceptable child.

The secret child, the bastard; the bastard, the child of a slave, the slave's child.

One's good son[12] [is] obedient, humble, gracious, grateful, reverent. [He is] one who shows reverence, who obeys, humbles himself, is thankful, shows appreciation, resembles [father or mother] in body and character, [and] in way of life.

One's bad son [is] perverse, wicked, rebellious; a vile brute — mad, deranged, disobedient; one who ignores commands; a fool, lewd, gaudy, vain, untrained; a dunce who accepts not, who receives not the counsel of mother [and] father. Training, teachings, reprimands, corrections go in one ear and out the other. He belittles; he is disrespectful, bold, defiant, agitated, impetuous, rash, fitful.

ONE'S DAUGHTER[13] — ONE'S DAUGHTER[14]

One's daughter: the daughter [is] untouched, pure, a virgin. The good daughter[15] [is] obedient, honest,

NANTLI, TENAN,

in tenan pilhua chichiua in qualli yiollo cochiçani tzicuictic, mopopoxani yiel, ixtoçoani, yiollo ymac ca, miçauiani, tlacauapaua, tecemmati, [tececemmati] texoxocoiomat teca mochiua, teca miçauia hatlaixcaua momotzoloa, motlatlaça

In tenan tlaueliloc, in amo qualli, tlacanexquimilli, xolopitli, tonalcochqui, maxixilopauax, tlanẽpopoloani, tetlaixpachilhuiani, tetlanaualchichiuiliani, tetlanaualpolhuiani, tlaxiccauani, tlatlatziuhcauani, tlatlauelcauani, aquen tema haquen temati, haquen motecuitlauia, hateca muchiua, hatle ipan tlachia, teatoiauia, tetepexiuia, teixpopoiotilia tochin maçatl yiuui quiteittitia, quitetoctia patlauac vtli quitenamictia

TEPILTZIN TECONEUH,

in tepiltzin tlaçopilli, calitic cunetl chanecaconetl teuiotica tepiltzin

Ichtacaconetl, calpan pilli, calpan conetl, mecaconetl mecapilli

In qualli tepiltzin, tlatlacamati, mocnomatini, mocnotecani, tlatlaçocamatini tlamauiztiliani, tlamauiztilia, tlatlacamati, mocnoteca, mocnopilmati, mocnelilmati, tequixtia, tenemiliztoca, tetlaieiecalhuia.

In tlaueliloc tepiltzin tlatlaueliloc, çan tlatlaueliloc, tzontetl, iollochico, iollotlaueliloc, cuexcochcoyoc, hatecacqui, tlamaxaqualoani, ixtotomac, hiciccala, topal, chamatl, hatlanonotzalli, tequixolopitli, hamo cana, hamo quicui in naiutl, in taiutl. Centlapal quiça centlapal calaqui in inacazco in tlacazcaltiloni, in tlacauapaualoni in atl cecec tzitzicaztli, hatle ipan tlachia, aiac quimacaci, hicicatinemi, neneciuhtinemi, ixtotomaua, tlailiuizuia, tlaxcoloa, tlatlaxcoloa

TEICHPUCH TECUNEUH,

yn tecuneuh yn ichpuchtli, quiztica, macitica vel nelli ichpuchtli in iectli in qualli, in qualli ichpuchtli,

---

6. In *ibid.*, p. 200, a note reads: "El hijo del principal dize a su madre nopiltzintzin. nopiltzintzine. la hija dizele noconetzin. notecu. totecu. El hijo del pilli mercader, o oficial dize a su madre niccauhtzin. niccauhtzine. la hija dizele noconetzin. notecutzin. El hijo del labrador dize a su madre nonãtzine, nonãtze. pitze. pitzetzine. pitzetze. tecitztze. tecitzine. notecitze. la hija dizele, nonãtzin. pitzin."

7. *Tecemmati* is followed by *tececemmati* in *ibid.*

8. Cf. *Florentine Codex*, Book VI, cap. xliii, fol. 208r.

9. Cf. Andres de Olmos, in *Grammaire de la langue nahuatl ou mexicaine* (Paris: Imprimerie Nationale, 1875), p. 213.

10. Cf. Florentine Codex, Book VI, cap. xliii, fol. 209v.

11. See *supra*, n. 2; kinship terms vary with the person speaking, not with the person spoken to.

12. *Tepiltzin* may be translated as "one's child" or "one's son"; *teconeuh* as "one's child" or "one's daughter" (female speaking).

13. *Teichpuch*: "hija o moça o virgen" in "Memoriales con Escolios," p. 202.

14. Female speaking.

15. In "Memoriales con Escolios," *yn yectli yn qualli ychpuchtli*.

2

intelligent, discreet, of good memory, modest, respectful, revered, well reared, well taught, well trained, well instructed, prudent, chaste, circumspect.[16]

One's daughter [who is] bad, evil, perverse, [is] full of vice,[17] dissolute, proud; a whore, she is showy, pompous, gaudy of dress, garish; she is a loiterer, given to pleasure; a courtesan, given to amusement, always vicious, crazed, besotted.

THE CHILD — THE CHILD

The small boy of noble descent,[18] who imitates his elders, [is] well reared.

The small girl, the little girl, [is] delicate, kind, beautiful, good.

The oldest daughter, the first-born, one's first-born, the first daughter, one's beloved first-born. One's second daughter, one's beloved second daughter. The third daughter, the beloved third daughter. The last daughter, the youngest daughter, the beloved last daughter.

The good noble[19] boy, the [good] noble girl [are] diligent, solicitous, active, agile, discreet, considerate, tractable, obedient [children] who cheerfully obey commands.

The bad boy [is] lazy, indolent, sluggish; a lump of flesh with two eyes; a confused, stupid imbecile who understands things backwards, who does things backwards; rude, dull, pilfering, agitated; a fool, restless, full of affliction.

UNCLE — ONE'S UNCLE

One's uncle [is] the provider for those who are orphaned, the entrusted one, the tutor, the manager, the provider of support; the one who takes charge, who directs.

One's good uncle [is] kind; [he is] one who serves, [who cares for people, who cares for things,][20] who is solicitous; [he is] a caretaker, a guardian, loyal, respectful, just — a server of others, a pitier of others.

One's bad uncle [is] a dissipator, an alienator of people; he squanders, dissipates, wastes his possessions; he hates, despises, detests one.

ONE'S AUNT

One's aunt [is] a provider for [her nieces and nephews]. One's good aunt [is] merciful, of good

tecacqui, mimati, tlacaqui, mozcalia, iollo timalli, yxtilli imacaxtli, tlanonotzalli, tlazcaltilli, tlauapaualli, tlamachtilli tlanemachtilli, chipauacanemilice, mimattzintli

Tecuneuh in amo qualli in amo iectli, in tlaueliloc, teuhio tlaçollo, cuecuech, cuecuel, ciuatlaueliloc, mihimati, moquequecimmati, moieiecquetza, muchichiua, apan vpan nemi, auilnemi, auilquiztinemi, mahauiltia, ahauiltzoncaloa, cuecuenocini, iuinti.

PILTONTLI, CONETONTLI

oquichpiltontli, tetzon teizti, tequixti, quixtilpilli, quixtilconetl,

in ciuapiltõtli, conetzintli cocotzin, tepitzin, chontzin, quaqualtzin.

Tepi, tiacapan, teiacapan, iacapantli tiacapantzin, teicu, teicutzin, tlaco, tlacocua, tlacotzin, xoco, xocoiutl, xocotzin.

In qualli in tlacatl oquichpiltõtli, ciuapiltontli yiel yiehel, yitzqui, tzicuictic, yolizmatqui, uel monotza, notzaloni, tecacqui, tlatlacamatquit.

In piltontli tlaueliloc cuitlatzul quitemmatqui, hetic, xocopatic, haoompa xolopitli nextecuili, haompa eeua, oolpatlacheua, cocopichcholoa, tompux poxaqua, iolpoliuhqui, iollotlaueliloc, hanenqui, teupoliuhqui

TLATLI, TETLA,

in tetla, ytech necaualoteuani, itech necahualoni, tenice, machice, mamale, naoatile.

yn qualli tetla ycnoio, teca muchioani [motecuitlauiani, tlamocuitlauiani] tlaceliani, tlapiani, tepiani, itech netlacaneconi, mauhqui, tlamauhcachiuani, teca muchiua, teca tlaocuya.

Tetla amo qualli tlaauilizittani, teauilizittani, tlaauilquixtia, tlaauilizitta, tlaauilpoloa, tecocolia, tetlailitta, tlatelchiua.

TEAUI,

yn teaui mamale yn qualli teaui tlaocullo in iiollo, icnoio, tepan tlatoani, tehiceliani, tlaçotli in iiollo, te-

---

16. *Mimatcatzintli* in *ibid.*
17. *Teuhio, tlaçollo — esta lleno de poluo, y de estiercol;* cf. *Florentine Codex,* Book VI, cap. xliii, fol. 201*v.*
18. Cf. *infra,* Chap. 5.
19. Cf. *ibid.*
20. "Memoriales con Escolios" adds *motecuitlauiani, tlamocuitlauiani,* here enclosed in brackets.

memory, kind; an intercessor, solicitous, of noble birth, loving. She admires others, cares for them, is solicitous of others.

One's bad aunt is savage, rude, vicious, tempestuous, pouting, sullen. She is peevish; she looks at one with hate, with ill-will; she is disdainful, spiteful.

NEPHEW (NIECE) [MALE SPEAKING][21] — ONE'S NEPHEW (NIECE)

A nephew (niece) has an uncle [or] an aunt. [He is] an orphan — parentless — who serves in another's house, a servant; one who lives with others.

The good nephew (niece) [is] obliging, willing, resourceful, judicious, considerate, circumspect, far-sighted, thoughtful.

The bad nephew (niece) [is] a liar, a teller of falsehoods, a prevaricator, a fabricator, an evil talker, two-faced, a thief, a mocker, inquisitive, inconsistent, indecisive, wavering, demented, corrupt. He mocks, lies, becomes drunk, bears tales; he is a traitor, a spy.

ONE'S NEPHEW (NIECE) [FEMALE SPEAKING]

A nephew (niece) [is] tractable, teachable, meritorious of castigation.[22]

One's good nephew (niece) [is] exemplary, a follower of the good example of others, respectful. He sweeps the streets, serves,[23] cleans the house, places things in order, arranges things, carries things,[24] accepts reprimands patiently.

One's evil nephew (niece) [is] one who flees, who runs away. Lazy, [he is] a sleeper, a constant sleeper, a heavy sleeper, a dreamer, a drowser — one who goes about falling asleep, who wanders about drowsing. He hides himself, takes cover, pilfers, works with deceit, practises petty thievery.

ONE'S GRANDFATHER — GRANDFATHER

One's grandfather [is] hardened, lean, white-haired, white-headed. He becomes impotent, childish.

The good grandfather [is] an adviser, an indoctrinator. He reprimands one, beats one with nettles, teaches one prudence, discretion.

tlaçotlani, tetlaçotla motecuitlauia, teca motequipachoa

Teaui in atlacatl iollococole, iollocuicuitla, qualaxpul, temputzpul, tempilopul, tenxiquipil, haitloc monequi, tetlauelitta, tequalancaitta, tetlailitta, haiel teitta

MACHTLI, TEMACH,

ym machtli tlaua, auiua ycnotl, tlacnocaualli, tetloc tenauac nemini, tetlan nenenqui tetlan nenqui.

In qualli machtli ateilhuiliztli, çan ce ynacaz, hamamachtiliztli, tlachixcatzintli, vel monotzcatzintli, julteutl, tlaiolteouia tlanemilia

Machtli in aqualli iztlacatini, yztlaccoxoc, yztlacatl, tlapiquini, iollocamachal, necoc tene, ichtequi, tlaquequeloani, yztlaccomoc, yztatl in iiollo, iztlactli yn iiollo. Auel ca yiollo, iollococoxqui, iolloitlacauhqui, tlaquequeloa, yztlacati, tlauana, tetlatolçaçaca tetlanencati tetlanenqui.

TEPILO, PILOTL,

notzaloni, machtiloni, quauitl tetl atl cecec tzitzicaztli toctiloni.

Qualli tepilo, tenemiliztocani, tetech mixcuitiani tlaxtilia ochpana, tlachpana, tlacuicui chicotlanauac tlateca, tlateca, tetloc tenauac mocalaquia

Tepilo in auel ca yiollo, choloani, teixpanpaeuani, cuitlaçotlac, cochini, cochmimil, cochipilotl, cochiztli, cochiztecatl cochipichi, cochiaiatli, motlatia, minaia tlainaia tlanaualchiua tlaixpachoa

TECUL, CULLI,

yn tecul, chicauac, pipinqui, tzoniztac, quaiztac, otlatziuh aoc quen ca yiollo, oteut.

Qualli culli, tenonotzani, teizcaliani, tealceceuia, tetzitzicazuia, teixtoma, tenacaztlapoa.

---

21. Corresponding Spanish text: *"De vna manera llaman los hõbres a sus sobrinos y de otra manera los llaman las mugeres: los hõbres dizen, al sobrino, nomach: y las mugeres dizen al sobrino, nopilo, nopilpotzin. . . . vn vocablo vsan los hombres para dezir sobrino, que es machtli, y otro vocablo vsan las mugeres, que es tepilo o pilotl."*

22. Lit., "one who is strengthened by the stick, the rock, cold water, the nettle." Cf. Rémi Siméon: *Dictionnaire de la langue nahuatl ou mexicaine* (Paris: Imprimerie Nationale, 1885), *toctia;* also Olmos, *op. cit.,* p. 217 (*Riñole o corrigole de palabra*).

23. *Tlachpana, tlacuicui: Florentine Codex,* Book VI, cap. xliii, fol. 207r — *"Varrere y amontonare el estiercol. Por metaphora dizen esto: los que se ofrecen a servir y obedecer en la casa de dios o en la casa de los señores."*

24. In "Memoriales con Escolios," *tlauica.*

4

The bad grandfather [is] negligent, of misspent days and nights; of no fame, of no renown. A luxurious old man, he is decrepit, senile.

Culli aqualli tlaauilmatini, onen oiouac, onen oncalac, yn tonatiuh, atle yteiio atle itoca, auilueue, auilueueti teupilueueti.

GRANDMOTHER — ONE'S GRANDMOTHER

One's grandmother has noble descendants.[25]

The good grandmother [is] a reprimander, a leader of an exemplary life, a counselor.

The bad grandmother [is] a stupid old woman, a leader of others into darkness, a bad example. She misleads, she deludes one; she places one in danger, she leads one into difficult places. She introduces one into the forest, the cliff, the desert, the water's current, the crag.

CITLI TECI,

in teci tzone, izte, yxquamule, tentzone, yxuiua, cacamaio, tzicueuallo, vitzio, auaio.

Yn qualli citli quauitl tetl quitetoctiani, tehutequiani teixtlamachtiani.

Amo qualli citli xolopihilama, tetlaiouaian aquiani teuuitiliani teuuitilia, tlaixpopoiotilia, tlaouicanaquia ouican tlauica, quauitl texcalli, ixtlauatl, atoiatl, tepexitl quitenamictia

THE GREAT-GRANDFATHER

[He is] decrepit, in his second childhood.

The good great-grandfather [is] of exemplary life,[26] of fame, of renown. His good works remain written in books. He is esteemed, he is praised. He leaves a good reputation, a good example.[27]

The bad great-grandfather [is] forgotten,[28] worthy of being detested, cursed, ridiculed; worthy after death of complaints, worthy of murmurs in his absence. There are ridicule, spitting, anger because of him.

ACHTONTLI,

aoc quimati ueue, oppa piltontli.

In qualli achtontli, tlillo tlapallo, teio, tocaie, hecauhio, amuxtli, tlacuilolli, teneuallo, itolo, tzonteconacocuiua, xijutl, octacatl, quitecauilia.

Achtontli tlaueliloc, xomolli caltechtli, tlaioualli, telchiualoni, haioni, yca tlatelchiualoni, mictlampa ontelicçaloni, teputzcomoniloni, ica tlatelchiualo, chichalo tlaqualania

THE GREAT-GRANDMOTHER

One's great-grandmother [is] decrepit, childish in her old age.

The good great-grandmother [is] worthy of praise, deserving of gratitude. She is accorded glory, acclaim by her descendants. She is the founder, the beginner [of her lineage].

The bad great-grandmother [is] detestable, unworthy of mention by name; she arouses nausea, loathing, anger, wrath.

VELTIUHTLI

teueltiuh: yiellelacic ilama, aoc quimati ilama,

Qualli ueltiuhtli iecteneualonj, tlaçocamachoni, itech netlamilo, ytech netzatzilo, tlacapeualtia, tlacatzintia.

Amo qualli ueltiuhtli, tequalani, acaconj, tetlaelti, tetlatultia, tequalania, tetlauelcujtia

GREAT-GREAT-GRANDPARENT

The great-great-grandparent [is] one who trembles with age, a cougher, a totterer. He has reached extreme old age.

The good great-great-grandparent [is] the originator of good progeny. He started, began, sowed [a good progeny]; he produced off-shoots.[29]

MINTONTLI,

in mintontli viuixcani, totolcani, chûchupunini, oacic ueuetla ylamatla.

Qualli mintontli iecnelhuaiotl tlatzintia tlapeualtia, mopixoa mocacamaiotia.

---

25. Cf. Chap. 5, *infra.*, and *Florentine Codex*, Book VI, cap. xliii, fol. 203r.

26. Olmos, *op. cit.*, p. 223 (*Partiose dexando de si memoria por las buenas obras o hazañas que hizo y buen exemplo*).

27. Cf., however, *ibid.*, p. 227 (*Vino a poner nueua doctrina, o vino a fundar de nueuo*).

28. *Xomolli, caltechtli, tlaioualli*: cf. *Florentine Codex*, Book VI, cap. xliii, fol. 215r.

29. Cf. *infra*, Chap. 5.

The bad great-great-grandparent [is] a vile old person, a despicable originator of progeny. He left [his own] ruined, destitute.

The grandchild

[He is] beloved, a noble descendant,[30] one's descendant, a jewel, a precious feather. He resembles his own in appearance and works.

The good grandchild [is] a living likeness, an image [of his people]. He provides fame and glory; he buds, he blossoms.

The bad grandchild [is] a prodigal, a spendthrift, a squanderer — a tarnisher, a besmircher of the honor of his own; perverse, dejected, miserable; a yielder before evil. He shows no concern but for himself, lives completely for himself, governs his own conduct, intercedes for himself, judges himself, needs no one. He is proud, self-indulgent, a law unto himself.

In tlaueliloc mintōtli tlahelueue, tlaçolnelhuaiutl, tlatlacoteua, tlateopouhteoa

Ixuiuhtli,

tepiltzin, tetzon, teizti, tentzontli, ixquamulli, teuitzio, teauaio, tetzicueoallo, tecacamaio, tenecauhca, cozcatl, quetzalli, tequixti.

In qualli, ixuiuhtli, tepatillo teixiptla, tlateiotia tlatauhcaiotia, xotla cueponi.

In ixuiuhtli tlaueliloc tlaauilquixtiani tlanenpopoloani tlaixpoloani, tlateuhiotiani, tlatlaçollotiani, tlacamicqui, yiellelacic yiolacic, quimaxilti tlaueliloc, haiac quiiocoia, moceniocoia, motqui momama, motlatalhuia, ça motlatzontequilia, haiac connenequi, mocecocamati, mocnauia, motlatlalilia

---

30. *Ibid.*

{Second Chapter, concerning the]¹ degrees of affinity.

FATHER-IN-LAW — FATHER-IN-LAW
OF A DECEASED PERSON

The father-in-law [is] one who has a son-in-law, a daughter-in-law, grandchildren; who sought — who gained — a woman for his son; who has affinal relatives, who gives his daughter in marriage—who gives a woman in marriage.

The good father-in-law [is] one who loves, who provides for, the married couple; who intercedes for them, who embraces them.

The bad father-in-law [is] a sower of discord among his affinal relatives, a divider, a scatterer of others. He is withdrawn, stingy, avaricious.

MOTHER-IN-LAW — MOTHER-IN-LAW
OF A DECEASED PERSON

[She is] one who has a son-in-law, a daughter-in-law, grandchildren, affinal relatives.

The good mother-in-law [is] one who guards, who deals kindly, who watches and waits. She stands guard; she cares for others.

The bad mother-in-law [is] one who rejoices, delights in the misfortune of others, who alienates people, who is disloyal.

THE FATHER OF THE PARENTS-IN-LAW

[He has] noble descendants. The good father of the parents-in-law [is] a worker, a possessor of wealth, a possessor of goods. The bad father of the parents-in-law [is] poor, miserable, useless. He lives in want, endures fatigue, suffers affliction suffers torment in his heart [and] in his body.

THE MOTHER OF THE PARENTS-IN-LAW

[She has] children, grandchildren. The good mother of the parents-in-law [is] an aged, honored woman deserving of love, veneration, reverence. The bad mother of the parents-in-law [is] one who leaves

---

GRAdo de AFinidad

MONTATLI MICCAMONTATLI

im mõtatli, mone, cioamone, cioatlanqui cioatlani. Ixuioa, vexiue, vexioa, tlaocchutiani, teocchutiani.

In qualli montatli tetlaçotlani, techantlaliani, temacochoani temalcochuani.

In amo qualli in tlaueliloc montatli, tetzalan tenepantla motecani, texexeloani, temomoiauani, aitloc monequi, tzotzocati, teuieuacati.

MONNANTLI, MICCAMONNÃTLI,

mone, cioamone, ixuioa, vexioa vexiue.

In qualli monnantli, tlapiani, tlamalhuiani tlachieni, tetlachialiani, tlapia motecuitlauia.

Amo qualli monnantli, teca auiani teca paquini teauilizittani hacemelle.

MONCULLI,

tzone, izte: qualli monculli, tlaiecole, axcaoa, tlatquioa In amo qualli monculli, motolinia icnotlacatl, nentlacatl, quihiiouia, quiciaui, toneoa, chichinaca, in iiollo, in inacaio

MONCITLI,

cozque, quetzale: qualli moncitli, yecilama, tlaçotlaloni, mauhcaittoni, imacaxtli. In tlaueliloc moncitli, teca moquauitequini, mopatoani, quinmoncauiliteoa in itechpa quiça

---

1. No chapter heading is provided in the Nahuatl column. The Spanish has "Capitulo segundo de los grados de afinjdad."

debts for her heirs, who assumes debts indiscriminately. She leaves debts to her descendants.

THE SON-IN-LAW

[He is] married, has a spouse, [is] exempt from the priesthood, [is] a mature youth.

The good son-in-law [is] one who reveres, venerates, respects, esteems, loves [his parents-in-law].

The bad son-in-law [is] a fool. Covetous,[2] he steals. He is given to pleasure; he lives in concubinage.

THE DAUGHTER-IN-LAW

The daughter-in-law [is] the woman asked in marriage, the requested one, a legitimate wife.

The good daughter-in-law [is] a sparing talker who does not return evil words; patient; a receiver of reprimands calmly, composedly. She loves, regales, appeases others.

The bad daughter-in-law [is] a ready answerer, envious, enraged, wrathful, furious, violent, raging, envious, quarrelsome, unboundedly furious.

BROTHER-IN-LAW[3] [MALE SPEAKING]

One's brother-in-law [is] kind, gentle; a provider, a worker, a craftsman; benign, candid.

The bad brother-in-law [is] evil of tongue, impudent, contentious, wrangling.[4]

BROTHER-IN-LAW[5] [FEMALE SPEAKING]

[He is] one who has a brother-in-law, a sister-in-law, a mother-in-law, a father-in-law, kinsmen.

The bad brother-in-law is one who lives in concubinage with his sister-in-law, who lives in concubinage with his mother-in-law. He is covetous.

SISTER-IN-LAW [MALE SPEAKING]

One's sister-in-law [is] a woman who has older brothers, older sisters, younger brothers.

The good sister-in-law [is] gentle, helpful, peacemaking — constantly peacemaking.

The bad sister-in-law sows discord.

SISTER-IN-LAW[6] [FEMALE SPEAKING]

One's sister-in-law [is] a woman with relatives — someone's older sister, someone's younger sister; a pleasant young woman.

MONTLI

monamicti, namique, mocauhqui tlapaliui.

In qualli montli, tlamauiztiliani, tlaimacazqui, tlaxtiliani, tlaixtiliani, tetlaçotlani.

In tlaueliloc montli, ixtotomac, maçol tlamaçoloa, auilnemi, momecatia

CIOAMONTLI,

in cioamontli, cioatlantli, tlaitlantli, techanecauh.

In q̄lli cioamontli, amo naoatl, amo tenanquiliani, tlapaccaihiiouiani, tlapaccaceliani, itech quipachoani, in quauitl in tetl, tetlaçotla, tetlacauiloa, tlaiolceuia.

Amo qualli cioamontli, chachalcani, moxicoani, çomalcuitla, iollocuicuitla, tlauele qualane, iellele, moxicoani, qualani moçoma, tlaueia,

TEXTLI,

tetex ioliamanqui, iolceuhqui, motlaecultiani, tlaayni, toltecatl, tlatlacatl, tlacamelaoac

In tlaueliloc textli tencoauitl, atenaquiliztli tenichtic tentlâpâltic

VEPOLLI OQUICHTLI,

texe, vepole monnane, montaôa, tlacaiooa,

In amo qualli vepolli, tlauepoloa mouepolhuia, momonnauia tlamatataca.

VEPOLLI CIOATL:

in teuepol oquichtioa icue, mamale, tlamamale.

In qualli uepolli tlatlacatl, tepaleuiani teceuiani, tececeuiani.

In amo qualli uepolli techalania

VEZOATLI,

teuezui, tecotonca, teuiltecca, teueltiuh, teiccauh, teicu, tepi, tepiton.

---

2. Cf. *Florentine Codex*, Book VI, cap. xlii, fol. 186*v*.

3. *Textli: cuñado de varon* (Alonso de Molina: *Vocabulario de la Lengua Mexicana* [Julio Platzmann, ed.; Leipzig: B. G. Teubner, 1880]).

4. Cf. Olmos, *op. cit.*, p. 217 (*Parlero, chismoso de mala lengua*).

5. *Vepolli*: brother-in-law or sister-in-law (female speaking). The gender of the person spoken of is determined by the addition of *oquichtli* for the male and *ciuatl* for the female.

6. *Vezoatli: cuñada de muger* (Molina, *op. cit.*).

The good sister-in-law [is] a gracious speaker, just, honest, modest.

The bad sister-in-law works with deceit, is importunate.

OLDER BROTHER

One's older brother [is] a carrier, a taker, a bearer of all the burdens [of his father's household]; one who counsels [his younger brothers], who prepares them for the work of men.

One's bad older brother scatters, disperses them.

STEPFATHER

[He is] one who has stepchildren, who adopts children; one who provides support, who works steadily, who accepts his stepchildren as his own.

The bad stepfather [is] one who desires, wishes, yearns for the death [of his stepchildren].

STEPMOTHER

The stepmother [is] one who has stepchildren.

The good stepmother [is] one who is gracious, who loves, who is merciful [to her stepchildren].

The bad stepmother [is] sad, hateful, rancorous, impatient. She looks at one with anger; she foretells the worst for one.

STEPCHILD — STEPCHILD [FEMALE SPEAKING]

The stepchild [is] an orphan, one whose mother [or] father has died. The good stepchild [female speaking] — the stepchild — [is] reserved, one who hangs his head in humility. He shows respect, reverence.

The bad stepchild [is] fitful, demanding. He is furious, he defames, murmurs against, belittles others.

In qualli uezoatli tlatlatlauhtiani, iecnemi velnemi mimatcanemi

In amo qualli vezoatli, tlanaoalchioa, tlauhchioa

TETIACHCAUH,

teachcauh, teteachcauh, teach, tecemitquini, tecenuilanani, tecēmamani, teixtlamachtiani, tetetzaoani.

In amo qualli tetiachcauh tececenmana temomoiaoa

TLACPATATLI,

tlacpauitequini, motepiltzintiani, tetlanaquini, amo tlatziuhcanequini, tlacpauitecqui

In amo qualli tlacpatatli, temiquiztemachiani, temiquitlanini, temiquitlani, temiquiztemachia.

CHAOANANTLI,

in chaoanantli tlacpauitecqui.

In qualli chaoanātli, tepaccaittani, tetlaçotlani, tetlaoculiani.

In tlaueliloc chaoanantli, ixcococ, yhiio, vel iollococole, cocole, çan niman aiel teittaz temaiecoa

TLACPAUITECTLI, CHAOACONETL,

yn tlacpauitectli, tlacnocaoalli, ycnotl, nanmicqui, tâmicqui. In qualli chaoaconetl, in tlacpauitectli, mopiloani, toloani, tlaxtilia, tlaimacaci.

In tlaueliloc, tlacpauitectli, tlatlaxcoloani, monenequini, moçoma, tlachicoitoa, tlateputzitoa, teixco nemi.

[Third Chapter.]¹ Age differences.

THE OLD MAN

The revered old man, the aged man [is] white-haired, white-headed, hardened with age, aged, ancient, experienced, a successful worker.

The good old man [is] famous, honored, an adviser, a reprehender, a castigator, a counselor, an indoctrinator. He tells, he relates ancient lore; he leads an exemplary life.²

The bad old man [is] a fabricator, a liar, a drunkard, a thief; decrepit, feeble; a gaudy old man, a luxurious old man, an old fool, a liar. He invents falsehoods.

THE OLD WOMAN

The revered old woman, the noble old woman [is] one who never abandons the house, who is covered with ashes, who guards [the home].

The good old woman [is] a supervisor, a manager, a shelter.³

The bad old woman [is] one who is forgotten.⁴ She deceives, she dishonors one.

THE NOBLE MAN OF MIDDLE AGE⁵

The middle-aged man [is] strong, powerful, energetic.

The good middle-aged man [is] a doer, a worker — agile, active, solicitous.

The bad noble man of middle age [is] lazy, negligent, slothful, indolent, sluggish, idle, languid, a lump of flesh, a lump of flesh with two eyes, a thief. He absconds; he is a petty thief; he kills one by treachery; he steals from one.

THE MIDDLE-AGED WOMAN⁶

The middle-aged woman [is] a parent, with sons, with daughters, with a husband; married, wise.

Differencias de las Edades

VEUE,

ueuentzin, ueuetlacatl tzoniztac, quaiztac, chicaoac, uecauhtlacatl, uecauitz, tlaztlacole tlaiecole.

In qualli ueue, tenio, mauizio, tenonotzale alcececaoa tzitzicace, tlatole, teizcaliani, quiteilhuia quiteneoa in uecauhiotl, quitemanilia in coiaoac tezcatl in necoc xapo, quitequechilia in tomaoac ocutl in apocio.

Yn tlaueliloc ueue tlapiquini, iztlacatini, tlaoanqui ichtecqui, teupilueue, xoxoloueue, topalueue, auilueue totonpotlaueue, iztlacatini, tlapiqui.

ILAMA,

ilamatzin, ilamatlacatl, caliollutl, tlacpeoalli, tlapixqui.

In qualli ilamatzin, tenotzani, tetzatziliani, tlauilli, ocutl, tezcatl xiutl, octacatl.

Amo qualli ilama xomulli, tlaiooalli caltechtli, mixtecomatl, teca mocaiaoa, teauilquistia

YIOLLOCO OQUICHTLI TIACAUH:

in iiolloco oquichtli, chicaoac tlapaltic popuxtic.

In qualli yiolloco oquichtli tlaaini, tlatequipanoani, motzomocoani, tzomoctic yieel.

In tlaueliloc yiolloco oquichtli, tlatziuhqui, quitemmatqui, cuitlananaca, cuitlaçoçotlac, quitlatzcopic, cuitlatzcocopictli, cuitlatzol, tlacamimil tlacamimilli. Ichtecqui, tlainaia tlaixpachoa, teichtacamictia, tetlacuicuilia.

IOLLOCO CIOATL:

in iiolloco cioatl pilhua, telpuche, ichpuche, namique monamicti, ixtlamati.

---

1. No chapter division is provided in the Nahuatl column except the notation "Differencias de las Edades." The Spanish column has "Capitulo tercero" but no further identification.

2. Cf. *supra*, Chap. 1, n. 4.

3. Cf. *Florentine Codex*, Book VI, cap. xliii, fol. 204r, and Olmos, *op. cit.*, p. 211 (*Padre, madre . . . que son o estan como arbol de amparo*) and p. 227 (see *supra*, Chap. 1, n. 27).

4. Cf. *supra*, Chap. 1, n. 28.

5. Corresponding Spanish text: "*Mancebos.*" "Memoriales con Escolios," p. 215, n. 1, reads: "*tiacauh en este lugar no q̃ere dezir hõbre diestro ẽ la guerra. sino hõbre noble de media edad.*"

6. Corresponding Spanish text: "*Muger moça*" — "*La muger de media edad.*"

The good middle-aged woman [is] a skilled weaver, a weaver of designs, an artisan, a good cook, a preparer of good food. She weaves designs, she works, she is diligent.

The bad middle-aged woman [is] foolish, stupid, useless, worthless, dumb. She works to no avail; she squanders.

THE MATURE MAN[7]

The mature man [is] resolute, stout-hearted, wise, sharp-witted, discreet.

The good mature man [is] a worker, a sage, a willing worker — one who works willingly. He works energetically; he is resolute; he is a steadfast worker.

The bad mature man [is] uncoöperative, irresponsible; he is impetuous; he acts without consideration.

THE MATURE WOMAN[8]

The mature woman [is] respected, revered, dignified — a woman of the home. She works; she never rests; she is active, hardy.

The bad mature woman lives in wickedness — a courtesan, a whore. She is a whore, a tramp; she goes about in gaudy dress, drunk, besotted.

THE YOUTH[9]

The youth [is] a good man, a genteel man, pleasing of appearance, goodly, active, agile, energetic, witty; a story-teller.

The good-hearted youth [is] obedient, happy, peaceful, careful, diligent. He obeys, works, lives in chastity [and] modesty.

The bad youth goes about becoming crazed;[10] [he is] dissolute, mad; he goes about mocking, telling tales, being rude, repeating insults.

THE MAIDEN[11]

The good woman [is] modest, pure, pleasing of appearance, honest. [She is] one's daughter [female speaking] — one's daughter [male speaking]. She is not the subject of ridicule.

The virtuous maiden [is] reserved, jealous of her virtue, chaste, continent, just, pious, pure of heart. She guards herself, guards her honor; she is jealous of her virtue; [she is] not to be ridiculed.

In qualli yiolloco cioatl, tlatecoa, tlamachchiuhqui tultecatl, iecaoa, iectlaçle, tlamachchioa, tlatequipanoa yieelti

In tlaueliloc yiolloco cioatl, tlacaxolopitli, totompotla, nenquizqui, nenpoliuhqui, nenenpotla, nenquiça, tlanenquixtia

OMACIC OQUICHTLI:

in omacic oquichtli, iollotetl, iollotlacoaoac ixtlamati, ixe, iollo, mozcalia.

In qualli omacic oquichtli, tlatequipanoani, tlanemiliani, tlaoquichuiani, tlaoquichuia, motzomocoa, acomolpia, acomotetziloa.

In tlaueliloc omacic oquichtli, tlaixtomaoani, mocitl, momociuia, tlaixtomaoa.

OMACIC CIOATL:

in omacic cioatl ixtilli, imacaxtli, haquequelli, cioaiutl ixcoca, tlatequipanoa, hamo teteca, motlatlaça, motlapaloa

In tlaueliloc omacic cioatl, tlauelilocanemi auilquizqui, auiiani, auiianiti, hanemi, topalnemi, xocomictinemi, iuintitinemi.

TELPUCHTLI:

in telpuchtli, iectlooquichtli: qualloquichtli, qualnezqui, qualtepul, tzomuctic, tzicuictic popuxtli, camanale, tlaquetzale

In uelca yiollo telpuchtli, tlatlacamatini, paccanemini, iocuxcanemini, hatlaquelmatini yiel, tetlacamati, tlatequipanoa, chipaoacanemi, mimatcanemi.

In tlaueliloc telpuchtli, mixitl, tlapatl, nanacatl, muchiuhtinemi, cuecuech, iollotlaueliloc, tlaquequelotinemi, tlaquetztinemi, tlaxocotinemi, camanalotinemi

ICHPUCHTLI,

iectli cioatl timalli cioatl, chipaoac, qualnezqui mimati, teconeuh, teichpuch haquequelli.

In qualli yiollo ichpuchtli mocuiliani, motlaçotlani, mopiani, mopixqui, iecnemilice, qualnemilice, iollochipaoac, mopia, momaluia motlaçotla, hamo quequeloloani

---

7. "Hombre de perfecta edad" (ibid.).

8. "Muger de perfecta edad" (ibid.).

9. "Mancebillo" and "mancebo" (ibid.).

10. Cf. Florentine Codex, Book VI, cap. xliii, fol. 209r.

11. Corresponding Spanish text: "Moçuela," "donzella."

The bad maiden [is] one who yields herself to others — a prostitute, a seller of herself, dishonored, gaudy. She goes about shamelessly, presumptuously, conspicuously washed and combed, pompously.

THE BOY[12]

The boy [is] delicate; he has a mother, a father; [he is loved as] an only boy, an only child; [he is] a younger brother [or] an older brother. [He is] teachable, tractable — one who can be directed.

The good-hearted boy [is] obedient, intelligent, respectful, fearful; one who bows in reverence. He bows in reverence, obeys, respects others, is indoctrinated.

The bad boy [is] always inhuman, incorrigible, disloyal, corrupt, perverse. He flees constantly; [he is] a thief; he lies; he does evil, is perverse.

THE INFANT[13]

[It is] delicate. The good infant [is] healthy,[14] polished, clean, beautiful, without blemish. It grows, develops, grows stronger, ages,[15] increases in size. The bad infant [is] unfit, without resistance to sickness, full of sickness, hare-lipped, lacking an arm, a leg, blemished. It sickens, becomes very sick, dies.

THE CHILD[16]

[It is] small. The good child [is] happy, laughing, joyful, rejoicing. It becomes happy, it laughs, it jumps about; it becomes joyful, amused. The bad child [is] one which cries, which is enraged, violent. It becomes enraged; it cries.

THE LITTLE CHILD[17]

The little child [is] one which cries, which is suckled. The good little child brings happiness [and] joy. It is suckled, it becomes bigger, it grows. The bad little child causes trouble, worry. [It is] full of scabies; it has scabies; [it is] full of sores.

BABY[18]

The suckling baby, the tender one, or the one within [the womb].

In tlaueliloc ichpuchtli motemacani, motetlaneuhtiani, monamacani, haquetzqui, topal momixiuitinemi, motlapauitinemi, tlaaltilnemi, cuecuechotinemi

PILTONTLI,

in piltontli, celic, nane, taoac, cemoquichtli, centeconetl, teiccauh, teach, machtiloni, notzaloni, titlanoni.

In qualli yiollo piltontli, tetlacamatini, tlacaquini, temauhcaittani, mauhqui, mopechtecani, mopechteca, tetlacamati, temauhcaitta, momachtia.

In tlaueliloc piltontli, çã niman uel hatlacatl, hatlacaquizqui, hacemelle iolloitlacauhqui, tlaueliloti, chocholoa ichtequi, iztlacati, tlatlaculchioa tlaueliloti.

CONETONTLI

chonequiztli. In qualli conetontli, haqã quenami, tetzcaltic, chipactic, tlacamelaoac, tlacanezquj, mozcaltia, mooapaoa, papatlaca, patlani, mana In haiectli conetontli hacemelle haõmanamic, teupoliuhqui, tenqua, xocotonqui, matzicul, hitlacauhqui, mococoa, tlanaui, mjqui.

PILPIL,

tepiton. In qualli pilpil papaquini ueuetzcani, ahauile, cecele, papaqui, ueuetzca, chocholoa, ahauia, paqui. In tlauelilocapil chucani, moçomani, iollococole, moçoma choca

CONEPIL,

in conepil chucani, chichini. In qualli conepil tepapaquilti, aahauile, chichi, motoma, mozcaltia. In aqualli conepil, tetequipacho, tetlaoculti, moca çaoatl, çaoati, papalani.

CONETL,

chichiltzintli atzintli anoço hititl

---

12. "Muchacho" (ibid.)

13. "Niño o njña," "infante, o infanta" (ibid.).

14. The remainder of the Nahuatl text is also found in the *Real Academia de la Historia MS*, in *op. cit.*, Paso y Troncoso, Vol. VIII (hereafter cited and referred to as *Acad. Hist. MS*.). For *haqã* read *hacã* as in *Acad. Hist. MS*.

15. A marginal note in *ibid*. reads: "*papatlaca propiamēte quiere dezir rebolear: patlani bolar: por methaphora quieren dezir crescer y enbarnescer en el cuerpo.*" See also Olmos, *op. cit.*, p. 232 (*yuhqui yequin timoyeecoa inic tipapatlantinemiz*).

16. Corresponding Spanish text: "*njño de cinco, o seys años.*" The *Acad. Hist. MS*, in n. 19, translates as *niño pequeño*.

17. *Niño de cinco o seys años o menos* in the *Acad. Hist. MS*.

18. Notations in the "Primeros Memoriales" of the *Real Palacio MS*. (Vol. VI of the Paso y Troncoso ed.), p. 145, may indicate age levels applying to these terms: *piltõtli. maviltia tlaololoa tzatzi — conetõtli quin otlacat ayamo vel chichi — piltzintli ayamo tlacaq' ayamo quimati — conetzintli ayamo tlachia amo temauhcaitta.*

Fourth Chapter, in which are mentioned the works, the nature, and the honors of the nobles.

THE NOBLE PERSON[1]

A noble person [is] great, superior of lineage, wonderful, revered. He merits respect; [he is] due obedience.

The good noble person [is] loving, merciful, compassionate; he loves others, benefits others, merits respect.

The bad noble person is oppressive, arouses fear, demands reverence, causes fear and trembling, implants fright, causes a tumult.

THE RULER

The ruler [is] a shelter[2] — fierce, revered, famous, esteemed; well reputed, renowned.

The good ruler [is] a protector; one who carries [his subjects] in his arms, who unites them, who brings them together. He rules, takes responsibilities, assumes burdens. He carries [his subjects] in his cape; he bears them in his arms. He governs; he is obeyed. [To him] as shelter, as refuge, there is recourse. He serves as proxy, as substitute.

The bad ruler [is] a wild beast, a demon of the air, a demon, an ocelot, a wolf — infamous, deserving of being left alone, avoided, detested as a respecter of nothing, savage, revolting. He terrifies with his gaze; he makes the earth rumble; he implants, he spreads fear. He is wished dead.

THE MAGISTRATE[3]

The magistrate [is] a judge, a pronouncer of sentences, an establisher of ordinances, of statutes. [He is] dignified, fearless, courageous, reserved, stern-visaged.

The good magistrate [is] just: a hearer of both sides,[4] an examiner of both sides, a listener to all factions, a passer of just sentences, a settler of quarrels, a

---

Inic naui capitulo, vncan moteneoa: in intequiuh, in inieliz ioã in inmauizio, in mauiztique tlaca.

TLACATL,

in tlacatl uei uecapan, mauiztic, imacaxtli, tlamauhtia, tlacamachoni.

In qualli tlacatl, tetlaçotlani, teicnoittani, tlaocullo, tetlaçotla, teicnelia, tlamauhtia

In amo qualli tlacatl tetequipacho, temauhti imacaxtlaqui, tlauiuiiotza tlaiçauia, mauiztli quiteca comontli quitlaça

TLATOANI:

in tlatoani ceoallo hecauhio, malacaio, puchotl, aueuetl, tequaio, imacaxio, tleio, mauizio, teio, tocaiô.

In qualli tlatoani, cuexane, teputze, macoche, temacochoani, tecentlaliani, teololoani, tlatocati, tlatqui, tlamama, tecuexanoa temacochoa, tlapachoa, tlacamacho, iceoallotitlan, yiecauhiotitlan necalaquilo teuiuiti, tepatilloti.

In tlaueliloc tlatoani, tequani tzitzimitl, coleletli ocelutl, cuitlachtli machoni, tlalcauiloni, yixpãpaieooani telchioaloni, hatle ipan ittoni, iollococole, ixcococ, ixtleio tlamamauhtia, tlalli quitetecuinia mauiztli quiteca, mauiztli quitlaça miquitlano

TECUTLI.

Jn tecutli tlatzontequini tlatzontecqui, tlatlaliani, tetlatlaliliani, haquequelli, ixtleio, ixtequaio, teixmauhti, ihiio.

In qualli tecutli melaoac, mecoc tlacaquini, necoc tlatlachiani, nouiãpa tlacaquini, melaoacatlatzontequini, tenepantla quiçani, amo teixittani, aiac quima-

---

1. Corresponding Spanish text: *"la persona generosa o de gran linaje."*

2. *Ibid.:* *"las excellentias del señor Rey o emperador: obispo, o papa: ponense por uja de methaphora. ceoallo, hecauhio, quiere dezir, cosa que haze sombra: porque el mayor ha de hazer sombra a sus subditos: malacayo: cosa que tiene gran circujto, en hazer sombra, porque el mayor ha de amparar a todos chicos y grãdes. puchotl: es vn arbol que haze grã sombra y tiene muchas ramas. aueuetl es de la mjsma manera, porque el señor ha de ser semejante a estos arboles dõde todos sus suditos se amparẽ."* Cf. also Olmos, *op. cit.,* p. 211 (*Padre, madre, señor, capitan, gouernador que son o estan como arbol de amparo*).

3. *"El senador"* in corresponding Spanish text.

4. Read *necoc.*

shower of no favor. He fears no one; he passes just sentences; he intercedes in quarrels; he shows no bias.

The bad magistrate [is] a shower of favor, a hater of people, an establisher of unjust ordinances, an accepter of bribes, an issuer of corrupt pronouncements, a doer of favors [with partiality]. He does favors [with partiality]; he establishes unjust ordinances.

THE NOBLE[5]

The noble [is] virtuous, noble of birth, noble in way of life, humble, serious, modest, energetic, esteemed, beloved, benign, good, candid, good of heart, just, chaste, wise, prudent.

The bad noble [is] a fool, irresponsible, presumptuous, evil in his talk, crazy, perverted: a revolting noble, a gluttonous noble. He becomes drunk; he is rude; he goes about telling tales; he becomes addicted to drunkenness; he molests people. He goes about mocking; he goes about drunk.

THE NOBLE[6]

The noble [is] esteemed, highly esteemed, noble of birth. All people [have] his esteem. [He is] no one's dog. [He is] tranquil, peaceful. He esteems, admires, shows reverence for things. He compliments others; he speaks graciously to them.

The bad, the evil noble [is] inconsiderate, indiscreet, stupid. He does things backwards. [He is] a spreader of hate — furthermore, impetuous, detestable. He causes nausea; he makes one angry. He causes loathing; he is disrespectful to others.

THE ESTEEMED NOBLE[7]

[He is like] a precious green stone, a bracelet of fine turquoise, a precious feather. [He is] an esteemed noble, a youngest child — one who deserves to be treated with tenderness, with care. [He is] a sensitive person, not unclean, not besmirched; a fortunate noble.

The good esteemed noble [is] illustrious, lovable, cherishable, respectable. [He is] one who loves, who respects others — who does not affront others, who does not offend them; who lives at peace. He provides harmony, establishes peace. What he says, mentions, repeats, composes,[8] is all wholesome, good, honorable.

caci, melaoacatlatzontequi, nepãtla quiça amo tlaixitta.

In tleueliloc teuctli, teixittani, tecocoliani, tlachicotlaliani, motlaxtlauiani, tençulpotoniloni, tlauhchioani, tlauhchioa, tlachicotlalia

PILLI.

in pilli yeciollo, tlaçotli, in iiollo, piltic in inemiliz, tolole, malcoche, mimatqui, mocxiiehecoani, tlaçotli, tlaçoio, tlatlacatl iectli qualli, tlacamelaoac, uel ca in iiollo, iecnemilice, chipaoacanemice tlamatini mimatini.

In tlaueliloc pilli, ixtotomac, mocitl, topal, iollocamachal, quatlaueliloc, iollocuecuech, tlahelpilli, tlacaçulpilli, miuintia, tlaxocoa tlaquetztinemi, yuintiliztli quimana, teamana, tlaquequelolotinemi miuintîtinemi

TECPILLI.

Jn tecpilli tlaçotli, uel tlaçotli, tlaçotli yn iiollo, muchi tlacatl itlaço, aiac itzcuin iuiiaio, iocuxcaio, tlatlaçotla, tlamauiçoa, tlamauiztilia, tepepetla, tetlatlatlauhtia.

In tlaueliloc in amo qualli tecpilli, iliuiz tlacatl, hamozcalia xolopitli, oholpatlacheoa, motlauelmaiauini, ca çan ie motequitlaçani, tequalani, tetlahelti, tequalania, tetlaheltia, teuic eoa

TLAÇOPILLI,

chalchiuitl, maquiztli teuxiuitl, quetzalli tlaçotli, tlaçotitlacatl, xocoiutl, malhuiloni, tlamaluilli, chonequiztli, hatzoio, hateuhio, uel quiztica tepiltzin.

In qualli tlaçopilli, mauiztililoni, tlaçotlaloni, pialoni, tlamauiztiliani, tetlaçotlani, temauhcaittani amo teixcoieoani, amo teixconemini, iocuxcanemini, tlaiuiianchioa, tlaiuiiantlalia, muchi iectli, muchi qualli, muchi mauiztic in quitoa, in quiteneoa in quitenquixtia, in que.

---

5. *"La persona noble o de linaje"* in *ibid.*

6. *"El uerdadero cavallero"* in *ibid.*

7. *"El que es Jll.° o generoso"* in *ibid.*

8. Read *q̃va* as in *Acad. Hist. MS.*

The evil esteemed noble [is] troubled; his speech, his life, his bearing are reprehensible. He disturbs; he causes trouble. His speech [is] twisted, incoherent, disorganized, stupid. He is diffident; he causes trouble.

In amo iectli tlaçopilli aiuiiaio, quauhio, teio, in itlatol, in inemiliz, in iieliz, teaman, tetequipacho, ixcultic in itlatol, hanaoatl, tonquimil, tonpotla texiuhtlati, tetequipacho

Fifth Chapter.[1] Here are mentioned the honored nobles.[2]

THE NOBLE[3]

The noble has a mother, a father. He resembles his parents.[4] [He is] an only man, an only child, an older brother, a younger brother, a first born, a second child, [or] a youngest child. He has an older sister, a younger sister; he has a grandfather, a grandmother. [He is] esteemed, lovable, everywhere desirable, everywhere lovable, good of lineage; not to be neglected, not to be ignored. [He is] one to share things with.

The good noble [is] obedient, coöperative; a follower of the ways [of his parents], a discreet worker; attentive, willing. He is willing; he obeys; he follows the ways [of his parents]; he resembles his father; he becomes his father's successor,[5] he assumes his lot.

The bad noble [is] mad, a vile brute — wicked, perverted, foolish, revolting; a vile child. He lives in vice; he defames his reputation.

THE NOBLE GRANDCHILD[6] [is] wonderful, worthy of admiration.

The good noble grandchild [is] wise, inquiring, inquisitive. He makes inquiries, searches; he deliberates.

The bad noble [grandchild is] haughty, presumptuous, covetous — a greedy noble, an inflated noble[7] . . . He is presumptuous; he deludes himself; he pretends to be well known.

ONE OF NOBLE LINEAGE[8]

The one of noble lineage [is] a follower of the exemplary life, a taker of the good example of others; a seeker, a follower of the exemplary life.[9]

The good one of noble lineage [is] a student, teachable, indoctrinated. He follows the exemplary life. He offers, he sets forth the exemplary life.[10]

Injc macujlli capitulo vncan moteneoa in maviztique tepilhoan

TEPILTZIN:

in tepiltzin, nane, tate taoa, tequixti, cemoquichtli centeconetl, teach, teiccauh, iacapantli, tlacoeoa, xocoiutl ueltioa, iccaue, cule, cioa, tlaçotli, tlaçotlaloni, neneconi, tlatlaçotlaloni, teiolloimecaio, aixcaoaloni, axiccaoaloni, tlaxexeluiloni.

In qualli tepiltzin tetlacamatini, tecacqui, tenemiliztocani, tlamauhcachioani, tlamauhcaittani, tlaiollocopauiani, tlaiollocopauia, tetlacamati, tenemiliztoca, tequistia, teixiptlati, tepatilloti, tetonaleoa.

In tlaueliloc tepiltzin, iollotlaueliloc, iollochico iollonecuil, iollocuecuech, tlacaxolopitli, tlahelpul, tlahelconepul tlaueliloti, tlaauilquixtia

TEIXUIUH, mauiztic, mauiçoloni.

In qualli teixuiuh, tlanemiliani, tlatlanini tlatemoani, tlatlani, tlatemoa, tlanemilia.

In tlaueliloc mopoani, atlamatini, ihicol, ihicopil, popoçapil, totoliztli, totolictli, ac çan momati, mihineoa, machicanequi.

TETZON.

In tetzon, ocutl tlauilli quitocani, tezcatl itech mixcuicuitiani, tlilli tlapalli, quitemoani quitocani.

In qualli tetzon momachtiani, mixtlamachtillani momachtia tlilli tlapalli quitoca tezcatl ocutl tlauilli quimana quiquetza.

---

1. The Nahuatl chapter heading appears in the Spanish column, under the Spanish chapter heading.
2. In the absence of a definitive study of Aztec social structure, it is preferable here to recognize only the two-fold division of Aztec society into commoners (*maceualli*) and nobles (*pilli*). Hence in Chap. 5 the various Nahuatl terms are translated as "noble," sometimes with a qualifying adjective. In the *Acad. Hist. MS*, fols. 112–114, opposite each new term for "noble," Sahagún has written, *otra manera de nobles.* See Alfonso Caso, *Instituciones Indígenas Precortesianas* (Mexico: Instituto Nacional Indigenista, 1954), Vol. VI, p. 21.
3. "*El hidalgo*" in the corresponding Spanish text.
4. Ibid.: "*correspõde a los suyos, en gesto o en obras.*"
5. Lit., "he becomes someone's picture, someone's image." Cf. *Florentine Codex,* Book VI, cap. xliii, fol. 203*v.*
6. Corresponding Spanish text: "*El que desciende de personas nobles.*"
7. *Acad. Hist. MS:* pôpocapil.
8. Lit., "one's hair." Cf. *Florentine Codex,* Book VI, cap. xliii, fol. 203*r.* Corresponding Spanish text: "*La persona noble de buen linage.*"
9. See *Florentine Codex,* Book VI, cap. xliii, fol. 213*v.*
10. Cf. chap. i, n. 4 (*supra*).

The bad one of noble lineage [is] a scandalizer, a flatterer — a drinker, besotted, drunk. He goes about becoming crazed;[11] he goes about eating *Datura stramonium* and mushrooms. He becomes vain, brazen.

In tlauelliloc tetzon tetlapololtiani, tlaixmamate-loani, iuintitl, tlaoanqui xocomicqui, mixitl, tlapatl, nanacatl muchiuhtinemi, quiquatinemi, moquatlaça, haquetza.

[ANOTHER] OF NOBLE LINEAGE[12]

The one of noble lineage speaks eloquently; [he is] soft-spoken, virtuous, deserving of gratitude.

The good one of noble lineage [is] one who addresses others gently, who allows people to live in harmony. He lives in quiet, in peace — withdrawn.

The bad one of noble lineage [is] proud, brazen. He consumes his inner substance; he acts superior; he becomes brazen, presumptuous.

TEIZTI:

in teizti, tecpillatoa, iocuxcatlatole, ieciollo tlaçoca-machoni

In qualli teizti, teiocuxcanotzani teiocuxcanemitia, tlamatcanemi, iuian nemi, mopilotinemi

In tlaueliloc teizti, cuecuenotl, haquetzqui, eltecue-tlan, cuecuenoti haquetza, hatlamati.

[ANOTHER] OF NOBLE LINEAGE[13]

The one of noble lineage [is] noble of heart, gentle of words, righteous of life.

The good one of noble lineage [is] compassionate, solicitous of others. He speaks calmly, peaceably; he is just.

The bad one of noble lineage [is] disputatious, obstinate, prolix, unresponsive. He becomes insistent, he responds not, he disputes, chatters, gibbers; [he is] a ceaseless speaker.

TEIXQUAMUL:

in teixquamul, tecpiliollo, iectlatole, iecnemilice

In qualli teisquamul, teca tlaocuiani, teca motequi-pachoani, matca tlatoa yuian tlatoa iecnemi

In tlaueliloc teixquamul, chachalacani tenquauitl, tlatolueiac, hatenaquiliztli motenquauhtilia amo tena-quillani chachalaca tlatetoa popoloca, atenpoztequini

[ANOTHER] OF NOBLE LINEAGE[14]

The one of noble lineage [is] discreet, well reared, well taught, well instructed.

The good one of noble lineage [is] an adviser, an indoctrinator, a presenter to others of the exemplary life; he is a shelter, an enlightener. He illuminates for others, guides them, takes the lead.

The bad one of noble lineage [is] a scandalizer, a deceiver, a sower of discord, a spreader of trouble, a causer of riots, a braggart. He brags of his exploits, sows discord, spreads trouble.

TENTZONTLI, TETENTZON:

in tetētzon mozcalia, tlanonotzalli, tlazcaltilli tla-machtilli

In qualli tentzontli, tenonotzani, teizcaliani, qualli iectli machiutl quitetlaliliani, xiutl octacatl, tlilli tla-palli, tezcatl ocutl, iectli machiutl, tetlauilia, tetlanex-tilia, teiacana, tlaiacana

In tlaueliloc tentzontli, tetlapololtiani, teixcuepani, techalaniani tetlâ motecani, tlacomoniani, mochacha-maoani, mochachamaoa techalania, tetla moteca.

[ANOTHER] OF NOBLE LINEAGE[15]

The one of noble lineage [is] moderate, observing.

The good one of noble lineage [is] energetic, inquiring, inquisitive. He makes inquiries, searches, shares; he scratches the earth with a thorn.[16]

TEUITZIO:

in teuitzio, tlaixieiecoani, tlaixtlaxiliani.

In qualli teuitzio, mocxiiehecoani, tlatlanini, tlate-moani, tlâtlani, tlatemoa, tlaxeloa, vitztica tlatataca.

---

11. Cf. chap. iii, n. 10 (*supra*); *mixitl, tlapatl, nanacatl* are taken as applying to *quiquatinemi* as to *muchiuhtinemi.*

12. Lit., "one's nails." Corresponding Spanish text: "*La persona de buena ralea.*"

13. Lit., "one's eyebrows." *Ibid.*: "*La perso [sic] de buen solar.*"

14. Lit., "one's beard." *Ibid.*: "*La persona de solar.*"

15. Lit., "one's spine." "Memoriales con Escolios," p. 208: "*persona que procede de otro como la spina en ello en que nasce.*" Corresponding Spanish text: "*La persona de estima.*"

16. The phrase *vitztica tlatataca* might also be translated, "he provides for his heirs." Bernardino de Sahagún: *Historia general de las cosas de Nueva España* (Angel María Garibay K., ed.; Mexico: Editorial Porrúa, S.A., 1956; hereafter referred to as Sahagún, Garibay ed.), III, p. 40, writes:

The bad one of noble lineage [is] unconsidering, debauched; a talker of nonsense, a belittler. He out-talks others, spreads rumors, acts without considera-tion, spreads scandal.

[ANOTHER] OF NOBLE LINEAGE[17] [is] one who fasts, starves his entrails, abstains, parches his lips.

The good one of noble lineage [is] an attendant upon others, a server of food, a provider of nourish-ment. He sustains one, he serves food, he provides comfort, he provides solace.

The bad one of noble lineage [is] miserly, nig-gardly, avaricious . . . , intemperate, gluttonous. He eats to excess; he is an intemperate eater. He is miserly, stingy, grasping.

[ANOTHER] OF NOBLE LINEAGE[18]

The one of noble lineage wishes no praise; [he is] a concealer, a hider, a coverer of himself; an enterer into caves; a burier, a belittler of himself.

The good one of noble lineage [is] one who mag-nifies, praises, exalts, commends [the things of others]. He praises, speaks well of, [and] does honor to [the things of others].

The bad one of noble lineage [is] one who brags of his noble lineage, who boasts of his noble estate, who gloats without reason over his nobility, who calls himself a noble, who lifts his head in pride, who dis-parages the things of others. He shows no respect, glorifies no one, belittles others, gloats without reason over his nobility.

[ANOTHER] OF NOBLE LINEAGE[19] [is] gentle, kind. The good one of noble lineage [is] a consoler, an animator of others, an indoctrinator, a comforter, a stimulator, an inspirer. He consoles, animates, com-forts another.

The bad one of noble lineage [is] rough, bristly, revolting, bitter — one who looks at others with ill-will, who is overcome with hate, who mocks, who scoffs at others. He scoffs at others, ridicules them, looks at them with ill-will.

In tlaueliloc teuitzio tlailiuizuiani, chochopoctli, tla-tolchôchopoc tlatolcampax, tlatoltepapanaui, tlatol-mocuicuitlaui tlailiuizuia tlatolmocuicuitlauia

TEAUAIO, moçaoani, mocuitlaxcolçaoani, tlaqualiz-caoani, motenoatzani.

In qualli teaoaio tetlamacani, tetlaqualtiani, teihiio-cuitiani, teihiiocuitia, tetlaqualtia teacotlaça, teiolloiz-calia.

In tlaueliloc teaoaio, tzotzoca, teuieh, tlatlametl, co-litli, xixicui, moxuitiani, moxuitia, xixicuinti, tzotzo-cati, momotzoloa, molpilia

TETZICUEOALLO:

in tetzicueoallo, amihtollani, minaiani, motlatiani motlapachoani, tlallancalaquini, motlaltocani, motlal-pachuani.

In qualli tetzicueoallo, tlauecapanoani, tlaiectene-oani, tlachamaoani, tlaiecitoani, tlaiecteneoa tlaqual-itoa, tlamauiziotia.

In tlaueliloc tetzicueoallo tlauicoloani, tetech atla-matini, mopilnequini, mopilitoani, mixacocuini tla-papatzaoani, aontepoa, atetletilia, atle ipan tlachia, mopilnequi.

TETLAPANCA, iolceuhqui, ioliamanqui.
In qualli tetlapanca teiollaliani, techicaoani, teoapa-oani, teiollotlapaltiliani, haco tetetziloani, haco teil-piani teiollalia, techicaoa, teiollotlapaltilia

In tlaueliloc tetlapanca, tequâquâ, auaio, ixcococ, chichic yiollo, tequalancaittani, tlatlauelpoloani, ic tlaqueloani, teca tlatelchioani, teca tlatelchioa, itla-quel quichioa tlatlauelpoloa

"decían cuando las enterraban: 'Aquí habemos plantado uitztli yietl, de aquí nacerá la comida y bebida de nuestros hijos y nietos; no se perderá.' Querían decir que por virtud de aquellas ofrendas sus hijos, y nietos habían de ser prósperos en este mundo." Cf. also Charles E. Dibble and Arthur J. O. Anderson: Florentine Codex, Book IX, "The Merchants" (Santa Fe: School of American Research and University of Utah, 1959), p. 40.

17. Lit., "one's thorn." "Memoriales con Escolios," loc. cit.: "persona que procede de otro como la spina en ello en que nasce." Corresponding Spanish text: "La persona noble, que desciende de buenos."

18. Lit., "one's chip." "Memoriales con Escolios," loc. cit.: "quebradura de la piedra que se labra o nieto o hijo." Corresponding Spanish text: "La persona que viene de buen tronco."

19. Lit., "one's fragment." Cf. tlapani, to break off. "La persona que viene de limpia sangre" in ibid.

[Another] of noble lineage[20]

The one of noble lineage [is] one's treasure, one's jewel, one's noble child; a descendant of nobles; one's child.

The good one of noble lineage [is] a mourner for the dead, a doer of penances, a gracious speaker; devout, godly, desirable, wanted, memorable.

The bad one of noble lineage [is] ungrateful, forgetful. [He is] one who goes about content, always satisfied, continually amusing himself. [Toward his benefactors] his heart hardens like rubber, like metal. [To his friends] he shows himself hard as river boulders, hard as rock, [although] he goes about content, rejoicing in his heart.

[Another] of noble lineage[21]

The one of noble lineage [is] dignified, courteous, well disposed, good-hearted, steadfast.

The good one of noble lineage ennobles one; he shows one how to be a noble;[22] he takes the place of the ruler — speaks for him. He shows honor to others; he admires, he does honor to the things of others.

The bad one of noble lineage [is] a debaser, a disparager of things; contemptuous of others, arrogant, bragging. He brags of himself, disparages the work of others, creates disorder, glories over his lineage, extols his own virtues.

Teezio:

in teezio tenecauhca, teoxiio, tetlapallo, tetech quizqui, tepiltzin, teconeuh.

In qualli teezio, miccaoatini, tlamaceoani, tlatlatlauhtiani, tlateumatini, teuio, neconi, temoloni, ilnamiconi.

In tlaueliloc teezio icnopillaueliloc tlalcaoani, pactinemini, papactinemini, mehellelquixtihtinemini, oolquiz, otepuzquiz yn iiollo, atlan tetl, tepuztetl oquimolloti, pactinemi, moielpaquiltia

Tetlapallo:

in tetlapallo piltic tecpiltic, tlacamelaoac, uel ca yiollo, iolteutl.

In qualli tetlapallo tepiltilia, tepilnextia, tetlatocatilia, tetlatocuitia, temauiziotia tlamauizoa, tlamauiziotia

In tlaueliloc tetlapallo tlamaceoalquistiani, tlapâpatzaoani, moteicxipepechtiani, macçâmatini, chamatl mochamaoa, tepapatzaoa tlapapatla, motlacamecaiopoa, moiehoaitoa

---

20. Lit., "one's blood." *"La persona que desciende de buena sangre"* in *ibid.*

21. Lit., "one's color." *"La persona notable"* in *ibid.*

22. Read *tetlatocaitoa* as in the *Acad. Hist. MS.*

22

Sixth Chapter, which telleth of the men, the valiant men.[1]

BRAVE MAN[2]

The brave man [is] tall, very tall, small, fat, thin, very fat, very thin, somewhat like a stone pillar, moderately capable, good of appearance. The brave man [is] an eagle [or] ocelot warrior, scarred, painted, courageous, brave, resolute.

The good, the true brave man [is] one who stands as a man, who is firm of heart, who charges, who strikes out at [the foe]. He stands as a man, he rallies, he takes courage; he charges, he strikes out at the foe. He fears no one, none can meet his gaze.

The bad brave man [is] one who leads others to destruction by his deception, who secretly puts one in difficulty; who visits others' houses; who yells; who slays others viciously, who treacherously forsakes one, who swoons with terror. He becomes frightened, he swoons with terror, he secretly puts one in difficulty.

THE VALIANT MAN[3]

[In] the valiant man [are] invincibility, robustness, unconquerability. [He is] powerful, rugged, strong.[4]

The good valiant man [is] one who excels others —a victor, a conqueror, a taker of captives. He is reckless; he destroys, he charges the foe; he takes captives; he besieges, he sweeps away [the foe]. He glorifies himself, he glorifies [his exploits].

The bad valiant man [is] vainglorious,[5] a boaster that he is an eagle warrior, an ocelot warrior, a brave warrior. He pretends to be a brave warrior; he brags of himself, he boasts that he is a brave warrior.

THE SHORN ONE[6]

The shorn one [is] of many [virtues]. He is a bulwark, furious in war; a rabid, a vigorous warrior; a great leader.

The good shorn one [is] a skirmisher, an aggressor, who hurls himself to his death; a vanquisher, a

Inic chiquacen capitulo, itechpa tlatoa in oquichtin in tiacahoa.

OQUICHTLI:

in oquichtli quauhtic quauhticapul: tetepito, tomaoac, pitzaoac, totomacpul, pipitzato, çan uel temimiltic, çan uel ipā quitquiticac, uel ipani. In oquichquauhtli ocelutl, nexeoac, cuicujliuic iollotlapaltic iollotepitztic iollotetl.

In qualli in nelli oquichtli moquichquetzani, iollochichic tetopeoani, teuitequini, moquichquetza moiollochichilia motlapaltilia tetopeoa teuitequi, aiac quimacaci aiac iixco tlachia.

In tlaueliloc oquichtli tenaoalpoloani, tetlanaoaltequiliani, tecacalaquini tlaoio, teauilmictiani texiccaoani, mauhcaçonequini, momauhtia, mauhcaçonequi tetlanaoaltequilia.

TIACAUH:

in tiacauh, aixco eoaliztli, atlauitequiztli, apeoaltiliztli, tlapaltic, chicactic chicaoac

In qualli tiacauh tepanauiani, tepeoani, tlalpoloani, tlamani, atlatlamati, tlalpoloa, tetopeoa, tlama temaololoa, teochpaoazuia motimaloa, tlatimaloa

In tlaueliloc tiacauh mochaoani, moquauhitoani, moceloitoani, moquichitoani, moquichnenequini mochamaoa, moquichitoa.

QUACHIC:

in quachic centetzontli, iaotenamitl, iaotlaueliloc tlahiloquichtli, uei oquichtli, uei tiacauh

In qualli quachi micalini milacatzoani, momiccatlaçani tlacemoliniani, teochpaoazuiani quimalaca-

---

1. Concerning terminology (*oquichtli, tiacauh*, etc.), cf. *supra*, chap. v, n. 2; also Dibble and Anderson, *op. cit., passim*; esp. Book IX, p. 47, n. 10.

2. *Oquichtli*: cf. Olmos, *op. cit.*, p. 216. Corresponding Spanish text: "*varones fuertes.*"

3. *Ibid.*: "*El hombre valiente, que se dize tiacauh.*"

4. *Ibid.*: "*es invencible, robusto, recio, y fuerte: . . . nunca buelue atras, nj tiene en nada los fieros.*"

5. *Mochaoani: mochamaoani* in the *Acad. Hist. MS.*

6. Corresponding Spanish text: "*hombre, o varon fuerte.*"

sweeper away [of the foe]. He encircles [the foe]; he turns them back. He instils courage, he instils pride. He is unchallenged; no man meets his gaze. He remains firm; he stands up against one.

The bad shorn one [is] an avoider of battle — dainty, delicate of body, self-indulgent, afraid, fearful, cowardly. He retreats — he is afraid; he acts like a woman — he is effeminate; he instils cowardice; he causes riots.

THE VALIANT WARRIOR[7]

The valiant warrior wears his hair over the back of his head; he has his lip pendant,[8] ear plugs, war devices, shield, war club.

The good valiant warrior [is] a sentinel, a strategist, a tracker, a seeker of roads [to the foe], a skirmisher, a taker of captives. He commands respect; he spreads — implants — fear; he terrorizes; he takes captives; he is reckless.

The bad valiant warrior [is] unreliable – one who sleeps at his post, who leads into ambush, who causes death through neglect. He is afraid of war, timid; he is cowardly in his retreat.

THE COMMANDING GENERAL, THE GENERAL[9]

The commanding general, as well as the general, the military governor, the ruling general: his office [is] warfare. [He is] the maneuverer of troops — a courageous warrior,[10] one whose mission is to go to his death.

The good commanding general, [or] general, [is] able, prudent, a holder of vigil, a maneuverer of forces. He devises the strategy; he declares, he assumes the responsibility of war. He distributes, he supervises the arms; he distributes, commands, supervises the provisioning. He lays out, he searches out the roads [to the foe]; he tracks [them]. He establishes the war huts, the prisons, the market places in enemy lands. He places the sentries, posts the chosen ones, stations the spies, the hidden ones, the concentrated ones. He interrogates them; he discovers the places where the enemy will approach.

The stupid commanding general, [or] general, causes trouble, causes death, leads one into danger.

choa tecuepa tlaoquichtilia, tlacuenotilia, itech atlamacho, aiac iixco tlachia pepechteuhtlateca, tequequezteoa

In tlaueliloc quachic iaotzintopolto nacamalhuiani, nacatlaçotlani momalhuiani mauhq̄ in iiollo mauhqui, mauhcatlacatl, tlatzinquistia, momauhtia, tlacioatlamachtia, tlacioatilia tlamauhcaçonequiltia, tlacomonia

TEQUIOA:

in tequioa quatzone in cacaoa, nacoche tlauize chimale, quaue.

In qualli tequioa iaotlachiani, tlanemiliani tlacxitocani, hutemoani, micalini, tlamani, tlamauhtia, mauiztli quitlaça mauiztli quiteca, tlaiçauia tlama atlatlamati

In tlaueliloc tequioa, tlaxicaoani, tlacochcaoani, tlaouicanuicani, tlaauilmictiani, iaomâmaui cuecuechca in iiollo itzimiquizmaui

TLACATECCATL, TLACOCHCALCATL,

in tlacateccatl in ioan tlacochcalcatl quauhtlato, quauhtlatoani, teuatl tlachinolli itequiuh, iaotecani uei quauhtli uei ocelutl, uel xocoztic, uel tencoztic, uel cuicuiliuhqui, miquiztequitini.

In qualli tlacateccatl tlacochcalcatl mozcaliani, mimatini ixtoçoani tlatecpanani, quiiiocoia, quipitza, quimamali in teuatl, in tlachinolli, tlauizteca, tlauiztlatoa hitacateca, hitacatzatzi, hitacatlatoa, huteca, hutemoa, tlacxitoca, quitlalia in iaoxacalli in quauhcalli in iaotianquiztli quimana in iaotlapixque cana in tlapepentli quintecpana in tlatlacaanque in mopachoq̄ in tetzaoac, tetlatoltia, quittilia in campa uel iaz toiaouh

In xolopitli tlacateccatl tlacochcalcatl, tlaouitilia, tlamictia, atoiatl tepexitl quiteittitia.

7. *Ibid.*: "El maestre de campo."

8. Read *teçacava.*

9. *Ibid.*: "capitan general" (for *tlacateccatl tlacochcalcatl*).

10. Cf. Olmos, *loc. cit.*

Seventh Chapter. Here is told the way of life of the goldcasters and the featherworkers.

THE CRAFTSMAN

The craftsman [is] well instructed, [he is] an artisan. There were many of them.[1]

The good craftsman [is] able, discreet, prudent, resourceful, retentive. The good craftsman [is] a willing worker, patient, calm. He works with care, he makes works of skill; he constructs, prepares, arranges, orders, fits, matches [materials].

The stupid craftsman [is] careless — a mocker, a petty thief, a pilferer. He acts without consideration; he deceives, he steals.

THE FEATHERWORKER [is] accomplished, ingenious.

The good featherworker [is] imaginative, diligent; meritorious of confidence, of trust. He practises the featherworkers' art; he glues, he arranges [the feathers]. He arranges different colors, takes measurements, matches [feathers].

The bad featherworker [is] a hypocrite, a destroyer of good work — heedless of others, dull, uncouth.[2] [He is] stupid, torpid. He can do nothing; he harms, damages, wastes [feathers].

THE GOLDWORKER, THE GOLDCASTER

The goldcaster [is] a possessor of knowledge, of information.[3] [He is] the final processor, the processor of works of skill.

The good goldworker [is] skilled of hand, observant, careful in his work — a purifier [of gold]. He is observant; he purifies [gold], works suitably — correctly. He beats out new designs;[4] he melts, he pours [the gold]; he forms the charcoal [mold];[5] he casts, he liquefies [the gold]; he places [the heated mold] on the sand.

The bad goldworker [is] one who lets ashes enter — swirl — [into the gold. He is] a pilferer, a robber of part [of the gold], a thief, a looter; one who slips

Inic chicome capitulo vncã moteneoa in innetlaiecoltiliz in teocuitlapitzque ioã in amanteca

TOLTECATL:

in toltecatl tlamachtilli, toli, centzon, aman

In qualli toltecatl, mozcaliani, mozcalia, mimati, moiolnonotzani tlalnamiquini In qualli toltecatl tlaiollopauiani, tlapaccachioani, tlaiuianchioani, tlamauhcachioa toltecati tlatlalia, tlahimati, tlaiocoia tlauipana, tlapopotia, tlananamictia

In xolopitli toltecatl, tlailiuizuiani teca mocacaiaoani, tlaixpachoani, iixco quiçani tlailiuizuia teca mocaia ichtequi

AMANTECATL, hacic, ixe, iollo.

In qualli amantecatl, tlanemiliani, iiel, itech netlacaneconi, netlacauiloni, amantecati, tlaçaloa, tlauipana, tlatlatlapalpoa, tlatlalpoa tlananamictia.

In tlaueliloc amantecatl: tlaixpaniani, tlapâpanquani, motexictiani iolloquimilli totolin iitic cochticac, tenitzintli miccatzintli, atle ueli, tlatlacoa, tlahitlacoa tlanenpoloa

TEUCUITLAOA, TEUCUITLAPITZQUI:

in teucuitlapitzqui, tlaiximatini, tlaiximatqui, tlatlaliani tlatoltecatlaliani

In qualli teucuitlaoa momahimati, tlaixtlaxiliani, tlaixieiecoani tlachipaoani tlaixtlaxilia, tlachipaoa, tlapanitia tlaipantilia, tlanextzotzona tlaatilia, tlatoiaoa tlatecullalia, tlapitza, tlapatia, tlaxaltema

In tlaueliloc teucuitlaoa tlanexaquiani tlanexmoloniani tlaixpachoani, ichtequini tlamachicoluiani, matzinallotl tzinaca tlanexaquia, tlanexmolonia

---

1. Read *oman*, as apparently in *Acad. Hist. MS.* Corresponding Spanish text: *"primero es aprendiz, y despues es maestro de muchos officios, y de tantos que del se puede dezir que el es omnis homo."*

2. Lit., "his heart is covered, a bird is sleeping inside."

3. *Ibid.:* *"conocedor del buē metal."*

4. *Ibid.:* *"sabe . . . hazer planchuelas o tejuelos de oro, o de plata."*

5. Cf. *ibid.* *"sabe hazer moldes de carbon."*

his hand under. . . . He introduces ashes [into the gold]; he allows ashes to swirl into it.

THE COPPERCASTER, THE COPPERFINISHER

The coppercaster [is] dexterous, wiry, energetic, strong.

The good coppercaster is wise, honest, discreet, imaginative, adroit; [he is] one who outlines in black, who etches, who throws [his arm about in beating copper]. He etches, outlines in black; he beats, he casts the copper. He blows the fire, places the charcoal, cuts [the copper] — cuts it into strips.

The bad coppercaster [is] a fabricator of lies, lazy, languid, weak, feeble. [He is] one who lets the work disintegrate, who adulterates [the copper], who works in haste. He works in haste, adulterates [the copper], wastes it.

THE LAPIDARY

The lapidary [is] well reared, well advised; a counselor, informed in his art; an abrader, a polisher; one who works with sand; who glues [mosaic] with thick glue, works with abrasive sand, rubs [stones] with fine cane, makes them shine. He makes them shine.

The good lapidary [is] a creator of works of skill. [He is] adroit, a designer of works of skill, a gluer [of mosaics of stone]. They are glued. He creates, he designs works of skill. He grinds down, he polishes, he applies abrasive sand [to stones]. He rubs them with fine cane; he makes them shine; he glues [mosaics of stone], of turquoise. He cuts [stones], cuts them into pieces, grinds them down, cuts them into triangles, forms designs of them.

The bad lapidary [is] one who scrapes [the stones], who roughens them; who raises a clattering din. [He is] stupid, bird[-like]. He scrapes [the stones]; roughens, shatters, pulverizes, ruins, damages them; raises a clattering din.

TEPUZPITZQUI, TEPUZTECAC:

In tepuzpitzqui matlatlâpaliui ichtic pupuxtli chicaoac

In qualli tepuzpitzqui, ixtlamati, mimati, muzcalia tlanemiliani, tlahimatini, tlâtliloani, tlatlatlilhuiani, maiauini, tlatlâtlilhuia, tlâtliloa, tlatetzotzona, tepuzpitza tlepitza tecultema, tlatequi, tlatzooalcotona.

In tlaueliloc tepuzpitzq̄ tlapiquini tlatziuini cuitlatzol iaiâcapil, iaiaqui tlatlaoiotiani, tlatlanellotiani, tlaciuhcachioani, tlaciuhcachioa tlatlanelotia, tlanachcatlaça.

TLATECQUI:

in tlatecqui, tlanonotzalli, nonotzqui, nonotzale, tlaiximatini, tlachiquini, tlapetlaoani tlaxaluiani, tlatzinacancuitlaujani, tlateuxaluiani, tlaquetzalotlauiani, tlaiottouiani tlaiottoui.

In qualli tlatecqui: tlatoltecatlaliani, tlaimatini tlatoltecaicuiloani, tlaçaloani, tlaçalo, tlatoltecatlalia, tlatoltecaicuiloa, tlachiqui, tlapetlaoa, tlateuxaluia tlaquetzalôtlauia, tlaiottohuia tlaçaloa, tlateuxiuhçaloa, tlatequi tlatetequini, tlachichiqui, tlachiquinaltequi, tlatlamachtlalia

In tlaueliloc tlatecqui: tlateteçoani, tlachachaquachoani tlatetecuitzoani, xolopitli, totoli: tlateteçoa, tlachachaquachoa tlatlapana tlatextilia, tlatlacoa tlaitlacoa, tlâtlatetecuitzoa

26

Eighth Chapter, in which are mentioned other ways of gaining a livelihood, such as [the work of] carpenters and the stone cutter.

THE CARPENTER — the woodcutter, the axe-wielder, the feller of trees, splitter [of wood], chopper [of wood], topper [of trees]; the cutter, the trimmer of branches, the user of the wedge.

The good carpenter [is] one who uses the plumb; who is resourceful; who uses the cord, marks with lines — uses the cord to mark lines. He straightens [the lumber], evens the edges; planes them, polishes them; makes the edges match; cuts, cuts into parts; carves them; sets in the uprights, joins the beams, forms the recesses, fits [the beams] together firmly; cuts mortises — makes them; hollows out [the wood], lays the wood, covers the beams, makes grooves, carves pillars, drives nails. He works carefully, skillfully; he sculptures in wood, carves it, smooths the surface, fits the wood, saws it, lashes it, forms tenons, forms recesses.

The bad carpenter [is] one who breaks [the work] into pieces, who raises a clattering din; who is a nonchalant worker, a mocker; uncoöperative, wasteful, squandering. He squanders, he wastes. He dismembers [the work] — breaks it up. He forms crooked objects; he cuts them crooked.

THE STONE CUTTER, THE STONE BREAKER

The stone cutter [is] one who works with a wedge; who throws, who swings [the arm about in his work] — wiry, powerful, energetic. [He is] a stone cutter, a good builder.

The good stone cutter is honest, discreet, resourceful, moderate, successful. He is of skilled hands, able hands, accomplished [after the manner of] Tula. He quarries, breaks [the rocks]; pecks, smooths them; tumbles, breaks them from the [cliff's] surface; forms the corner stone; places, fits [the stones] well; abrades them; pounds, hammers them; splits them with a wedge, marks them with black; forms curved stone — cuts it. He carves out habitations in the rock; sculptures in stone, carves it; forms works of artifice, of

Inic chicuei capitulo, vncã moteneoa, in oc centlamantli ic motlaiecoltia: in iuhqui iehoanti quauhxinque ioã tetzotzonqui

TLAXINQUI, quauhxinqui tlatepuzuiani quauhtlaçani tlaxeloani, tlatzaianani, tlatzontequini, tlatequini, tlamatepeoani, tlatlatlilhuiani

In qualli quauhxinqui, tlaixuiani, tlanemiliani, tlamecaniani, tlatlilaniani, tlamecatiliniani, tlamelaoa, tlatenmelaoa: tlachichiqui, tlatetzcaloa, tlatēneneuilia, tlatequi, tlatetequi, tlacuicui, tlaquauhtoca, tlaoapalaquia, tlacallotia, tlacacalteuhtlalia, tanâxima, tanachioa, petlacalchioa, quauhtema, tlaoapaltzaqua, tlaoacaloa, q̃uhtemimilxima, tlatepuzmina, tlanematcachioa, tlatlâmachia, quauhtlacuiloa, tlacuicuiloa, tlaixpetlaoa, tlauelteca tlaxotla, tlatlalpia, tlaquauhiotia, tlacallotia

In aqualli tlaxinqui tlapapaiaxoani, tlatetecuitzoani, tlaquelchioani, teca mocaiaoani, teca moquauitequini, tlaixpoloani, tlanenpoloani tlanenpoloa, tlaixpoloa tlateteitza tlaxaxamatza, tlanenecuillalia, tlanecuilxima

TETZOTZONQUI, TETLAPANQUI:

In tetzotzonqui, tlatlatlilhuiani, maiauini, matlapaliui, ichtic, tlapaltic, pupuxtli, tlaximani, tlaiectlaliani.

In qualli tetzotzõqui mimati mozcalia, tlaixtlaxiliani, tlaixieiecoani, tlaipantiliani momaimati, uel maie, hacic tolla, tetlapana, tlatlapana, tlaixpetlaoa, tlaquaquaui, tlaixtepeoa, tlaixtlaça, tlanacaztia, tlaiectlalia, tlaiecteca, tlachichiqui, tetzotzona, tlatzotzona, tlatlâtlilhuia, tlâtliloa, tlauitoloa, tlauitoliuhcaxima, oztocalxima, tetlacuiloa, tlatlacui, tlaamantecatlalia, tlatoltecatlalia tlatlamachia, tlatlâmachtontoquia, tlaqueninmachtlalia, calquetza, callacuiloa, tlacalicuiloa tlamachiotia, mocalimati, callamati, tlatlalana tlate-

skill; labors with dexterity, with dexterous judgment;[1] he makes things of all sorts — he builds a house; draws, sketches a house; draws plans, devises a house, projects house plans; digs a trench, provides footings, builds up a foundation; establishes the corners, provides the house with corners; forms the walls, builds the terrace,[2] provides the exterior surfacing, treats the exterior circumference,[3] provides a thin surfacing, puts in the hearth, builds the smoke hole, improves it with clay, makes a storage place. He works as a stone cutter.[4]

The bad, the evil stone mason [is] of lame, feeble arm; a crooked cutter, a crooked builder: a mocker — as if [he were] a builder of curved, leaning [walls]. He mocks people, builds crooked, builds with mud.

toca caltetzonteca, tlanacaztia tlacalnacaztia, tlaçaloa, tlapantlaça, tlacaltentia, tlaanauhtia tlaamaiotia, tlatlecallotia, tlapuchquiiaoaiotia, tlaçoquiqualtia, tlaeltzaqua, tetzotzoncati.

In tlaueliloc in aqualli tetzotzonqui, macuetlauic macuetlauhqui, tlanenecuilximani tlanenecuillaliani, teca mocacaiaoa iuhqui tlaçoquiquetzani, tlateputzoquistiani, tlaaquetzaltiani, teca mocacaiaoa, tlanecuillalia tlaçoquiquetza

THE MASON

The mason [is] one who makes mortar, who adds water, who spreads [the mortar] flat; who smooths, polishes, burnishes the surface; who whitewashes. He whitewashes; he thins [the mortar] with water. He flattens the surface; he burnishes it; he moistens it.

The bad mason [is] feeble, stupid. [He is] one who makes a shattering din, who gouges, who roughens the surface. He makes the surface coarse, uneven, lumpy.

TLAQUILQUI:

in tlaquilqui, tlapatlani, tlatoiaoani, tlaxtlananj tlacalaniani, tlacacalaniani, tlapetzoani, tlâquilini: tlaquili, tlatoiaoa, tlaxtlaoa, tlapetzoa, tlachapania

In amo qualli tlâquilqui xoxolotl, nenpotla, tlacocomotzoani, tlaoaoacaloani, tlaixteçonoani: tlachachaquachoa, tlaxixipochua, tlaxixiquipiloa.

THE SCRIBE

The scribe: writings, ink [are] his special skills.[5] [He is] a craftsman, an artist, a user of charcoal, a drawer with charcoal; a painter who dissolves colors, grinds pigments, uses colors.

The good scribe is honest, circumspect, far-sighted, pensive; a judge of colors, an applier of the colors, who makes shadows, forms feet, face, hair. He paints, applies colors, makes shadows, draws gardens, paints flowers, creates works of art.

The bad scribe [is] dull, detestable, irritating — a fraud, a cheat. He paints without luster, ruins colors, blurs them, paints askew — acts impetuously, hastily, without reflection.

TLACUILO:

in tlacuilo, tlilli, tlapalli, tlilatl, ialuil, toltecatl tlachichiuhqui, tlatecullaliani, tlateculaniani, tlatlilani, tlilpatlac, tlapaltecini tlapallaliani.

In qualli tlacuilo: mîmati iolteutl, tlaiolteuuiani, moiolnonotzani, tlatlapalpoani, tlatlapalaquiani, tlaceoallotiani, tlacxitiani, tlaxaiacatiani, tlatzontiani: tlacuiloa, tlatlapalaquia, tlaceoallotia, suchitlacuiloa, tlasuchiicuiloa, toltecati.

In amo qualli tlacuillo: iolloquiquimil, tequalani, texiuhtlati, tenenco, tenenenco, tlaticeoa, tlatlapalmictia, tlatlaiooallotia, tlanenecuillalia, tlaxolopicachioa, tlaciuhcachioa tlaixtomaoa

THE SINGER

The singer [is] one who cries out, who utters clear sounds. He sings in full voice, in falsetto; [he is] one who holds a note, who raises [the voice], who lowers

CUICANI:

in cuicani tzatzini naoatini, tlatomaoa, tlapitzaoa: motiliniani, tlaâcoquistiani, tlatemohuiani, tlatlaliani, tlaiocoiani tlapiquini tlaçaloani.

---

1. Read *tlatlamachtzontequia* as in the *Acad. Hist. MS.*

2. The term appears to be *tlaxantlaça* in *ibid.*

3. If derived from *tlanauhtli,* reference would be to interior coating. Cf. Rémi Siméon, *op. cit.*

4. In the *Acad. Hist. MS,* the passage reads *tlaamayotia. tlaçoquiqualtia. tepâteca. tlapuchq̃auayotia. tlatlecallotia. tlaeltzaqua. tlaqu[auh?]-callotia. tetzotzôcati.*

5. Read *ioluil.*

it; who composes, who sets to music, originates [songs], gives them form.

The good singer [is] of sound voice. Good, sound [is] his voice; well rounded [are] his words. [He is] of good, sharp memory, keeping the songs in mind; retentive, not forgetful. He sings, cries out, enunciates clearly; [he sings] with well-rounded voice, in full voice, in falsetto. [He sings] softly; he tempers his voice, accompanies judiciously, gives the pitch, lowers [the voice], raises it. He reduces it to medium; he uses it moderately. He practises; he improves his voice. He composes, sets to music, originates [songs]. He sings songs, sings others' songs, provides music for others, instructs others.

The bad singer [is] hoarse, husky, coarse-voiced; crude, dull, heartless, unintelligent. He revolts me; he is fraudulent, vainglorious, arrogant. [He is] haughty, foolish, obstinate, avaricious, indigent, envious, absconding. He grunts,[6] sounds husky, makes one's ears ring; he is restless, forgetful, violent, indigent; he absconds,[7] he brags; he is presumptuous, vain.[8]

THE WISE MAN[9]

The wise man [is] exemplary.[10] He possesses writings; he owns books. [He is] the tradition, the road; a leader of men, a rower, a companion, a bearer of responsibility, a guide.

The good wise man [is] a physician, a person of trust, a counselor; an instructor worthy of confidence, deserving of credibility, deserving of faith; a teacher. [He is] an adviser, a counselor, a good example; a teacher of prudence, of discretion; a light, a guide who lays out one's path, who goes accompanying one. [He is] reflective, a confessor, deserving to be considered as a physician, to be taken as an example. He bears responsibility, shows the way, makes arrangements, establishes order. He lights the world for one;[11] he knows of the land of the dead; he is dignified, unreviled.[12] He is relied upon, acclaimed by his descendants, confided in, trusted—very congenial. He reassures, calms, helps. He serves as a physician; he makes one whole.

In qualli cuicani iectozque qualli iectli chipaoac in itozqui temimiltic in itlatol iollo, tlaiollo, tlapiani tlalnamiquini atlalcauhqui. Cuica, tzatzi, naoati, tlatemimiloa, tlatomaoa, tlapitzaoa, tlaiamania, tlaiamanilia, tlanematcauica, tlatozquitia, tlatemouia, tlaacocui, tlatlanepantlaquistia, tlatlacoitta, tlaieiecoa motozcaiectia, tlatlalia, tlaiocoia, tlapiqui, tlaeua, tlacuiqueoa, tecuicatia temachtia.

In amo qualli cuicani: nanaltic hiçaoaccon, hiçaoac tepetla, iollo micqui iollo azcacoaloc atle iiollo quimati, çaçan nechmoquixtili, motlamachitocani, mochachamaoani chamatl, mopoani, quatlaueliloc, quacuecuech teuie tzotzoca, moxicoani, tlainaiani: nanal, çaçaoaca tlanacaztititza, tlaamana, tlalcaoa, iolpoliui, tzotzocati, tlinaia mopoa, atlamati, moquatlaca

TLAMATINI:

in tlamatini tlauilli ocutl, tomaoac ocutl apocio, tezteatl, coiaoac tezcatl, necoc xapo, tlile, tlapale, amuxoa, amoxe, tlilli, tlapalli, utli, teiacanqui, tlanelo, teuicani, tlauicani, tlaiacanqui

In qualli tlamatini: ticitl piale machiçe, temachtli temachiloni neltoconi, neltoquiztli, temachtiani, tenonotzani, teixtlamachtiani, teixcuitiani, teixtomani, tenacaztlapoani, tetlauiliani, teiacanani tehutequiliani, itech pipilcotiuh, tetezcahuiani, teiolcuitiani, neticiuiloni, neixcuitiloni, tlauica, tlahutlatoctia, tlatlalia, tlatecpana, cemanaoac tlauia tepan mictlan onmati, aquequelti, haxixicti, itech nechicaoalo, itech netzatzililo, temachilo, itech netlacaneco, itech tlaquauhtlamacho, tlaiolpachiuitia, tepachiuitia, tlapaleuia ticiti, tepatia

---

6. Read *nanalca* as in *ibid.*

7. Read *tlainaia* as in *ibid.*

8. Read *moquatlaça* as in *ibid.*

9. Cf. León-Portilla, *op. cit.*, pp. 73*sqq.* Corresponding Spanish text: *"El sabio."* Gloss in *Acad. Hist. MS: sabios o phylosophos.*

10. Cf. Chap. 1, n. 4. The term apparently written *tezteatl* in the *Florentine Codex* is read *tezcatl* as in the *Acad. Hist. MS.*

11. *Acad. Hist. MS: topan.*

12. Cf. *Aiac xictli in tlalticpac* in Book VI, fol. 184*v* of the *Florentine Codex.*

The bad wise man [is] a stupid physician, silly, decrepit, [pretending to be] a person of trust, a counselor, advised. [He is] vainglorious; vainglory is his; [he is] a pretender to wisdom . . . , vain — discredited.[13] [He is] a sorcerer, a soothsayer, a medicineman, a remover of intrusive objects from people.[14] A soothsayer, a deluder, he deceives, confounds, causes ills, leads into evil; he kills; he destroys people, devastates lands, destroys by sorcery.

In amo qualli tlamatini xolopiticitl, xolopitli, teupilpul, piale, nonotzale nonotzquj tlanjtz tlanitze, motlamachitocani, pancotl chamatl, atoiatl, tepexitl, xomulli, caltechtli, tlaiooalli, naoalli tlapouhqui, ticitl, tetlacuicuili, tlapouhqui, teixcuepani, teca mocaiaoani, teixpoloa, tlaohuitilia, tlaohuicanaquia, tlamictia, tepoloa, tlalpoloa, tlanaoalpoloa

THE PHYSICIAN

The physician [is] a curer of people, a restorer, a provider of health.

The good physician [is] a diagnostician, experienced — a knower of herbs, of stones, of trees, of roots. He has [results of] examinations, experience, prudence. [He is] moderate in his acts. He provides health, restores people, provides them splints, sets bones for them, purges them, gives emetics, gives them potions; he lances, he makes incisions in them, stitches them, revives them, envelopes them in ashes.

The bad physician [is] a fraud, a half-hearted worker, a killer with his medicines, a giver of overdoses, an increaser [of sickness]; one who endangers others, who worsens sickness; who causes one to worsen. [He pretends to be] a counselor, advised, chaste. He bewitches; he is a sorcerer, a soothsayer, a caster of lots, a diagnostician by means of knots.[15] He kills with his medicines; he increases [sickness]; he seduces women; he bewitches them.

TICITL:

in ticitl tepatiani, tlapatiani tlapaleuiani.

In qualli ticitl tlanemiliani, tlaiximatini, xiuhiximatqui, teiximatqui, quauhiximatqui, tlaneloaioiximatqui, tlaieiecole, tlaztlacole, iztlacole, tlaixieiecoani, tlapaleuia, tepatia tepapachoa, teçaloa, tetlanoquilia, tlâçotlaltia, tetlaitia, tlaitzmina, texotla, tehitzoma, teeoatiquetza, nextli teololoa

In tlaueliloc ticitl: ic tlaqueloani, itlaquelh quichioani tepâmîctiani, tepaixuitiani, tlaouitiliani, teouitiliani, tlatlanalhuiani, tetlanaluiani, nonotzale: nonotzqui, pixe, suchioa naoalli, tlapouhqui, tlapoani mecatlapouhqui, tepamictia, tlaouitilia, tepixuia, tesuchiuia

---

13. Cf. León-Portilla, *op. cit.*, p. 80, for an analysis of the figure of speech.

14. Or "public robber"; see Siméon, *op. cit.* See also Angel Ma. Garibay K.: "Paralipómenos de Sahagún," *Tlalocan*, II, 3 (1947), p. 241 (*Tetlacuicuiliqui*).

15. Eduard Seler, *Gesammelte Abhandlungen zur Amerikanischen Sprach- und Altertumskunde* (J. Eric S. Thompson and Francis B. Richardson, tr. and ed.; Cambridge: Carnegie Institution of Washington, 1939), II, Pt. 1, pp. 53–4: "The diviner twisted a rope together into a kind of knot and then drew it quickly. If the knot came out easily, then he said the patient would recover, but if he only made the knot tighter, . . . the patient would die." See also Garibay, *loc cit.*

Ninth Chapter, which telleth of the enchanters, the sorcerers, the magicians.

THE SORCERER[1]

The sorcerer [is] a wise man, a counselor, a person of trust — serious, respected, revered, dignified, unreviled, not subject to insults.

The good sorcerer [is] a caretaker, a man of discretion, a guardian. Astute, he is keen, careful, helpful; he never harms anyone.

The bad sorcerer [is] a doer [of evil], an enchanter. He bewitches women; he deranges, deludes people; he casts spells over them; he charms them; he enchants them; he causes them to be possessed. He deceives people; he confounds them.

THE SOOTHSAYER, THE READER OF THE DAY SIGNS[2]

The soothsayer is a wise man, an owner of books [and] of writings.

The good soothsayer [is] one who reads the day signs for one; who examines, who remembers [their meaning]. He reads the day signs; he brings them to one's attention.

The bad [soothsayer is][3] a deceiver, a mocker, a false speaker, a hypocrite — a diabolical, a scandalous speaker. He disturbs, confounds, beguiles, deceives others.

THE POSSESSED ONE[4]

The possessed one [is] one who transforms himself, who assumes the guise of an animal. [He is] a hater, a destroyer of people; an implanter of sickness, who bleeds himself over others,[5] who kills them by potions — who makes them drink potions; who burns wooden figures of others.[6] [Hence there is] poverty, [there is] hunger in his home; his fate, his lot [is] affliction. [He is] poor, miserable, useless, destitute.

Inic chicunaui capitulo, intechpa tlatoa in tetlachiuiani: in nanahoalti, in texixicoani.

NAOALLI:

in naoalli tlamatini, nonotzale, piale, hacemelle ixtilli, imacaxtli, haquequelli, axictli, aixcoeoaliztli

In qualli naoalli: tlapiani, tlaiollotl, tlapixqui: itzqui, itztica, tlapia, tlapaleuia, aiac quen quichioa.

In tlaueliloc naoalli: tlachioale, tetlachiuiani suchioa, teiolmalacacho, teixcuepa, tetlanonochilia, texoxa, tetlachiuia tetlacatecolouia, teca mocaiaoa tetlapololtia

TLAPOUHQUI TONALPOUHQUI:

in tlapouhqui ca tlamatini, amuxe tlacuilole

In qualli tlapouhqui tetonalpouiani, tlacxitocani, tlalnamiquini, tonalpoa, tetlalnamictia

In tlaueliloc tlacateculotl: teiztlacauiani, teca mocacaiaoani, iztlacatlatole, naoallatole, tlacatecolotlatole, tetlapololtiliztlahtole, tetlapololti, tetlapololtia, teiztlacauia teca mocaiaoa

TLACATECULUTL:

in tlacateculotl mocuepani naoale, tecocoliani, tepoloani, tecocollaliliani, tepan mîçoni, tepâmictiani tepâitiani, teeuillotlatiani alcecec quiquiztoc ehecatl moteteuilacachoa in ichan cococ teopouhqui iilhuil inemac, motolinia, icnotlacatl nentlacatl, ahommonamiqui in iquechtlan, in iquezpan cocotontinemi, tlaciaui quihiiouia ompa onquiça in tlalticpac tetlacateculouia tepoloa, teeuillotlatia tepã mîço tenaoalpoloa,

---

1. Cf. George Foster: "Nagualism in Mexico and Guatemala," *Acta Americana*, II, 1–2 (1944), pp. 85*sqq*.
Corresponding Spanish text: "*El naoalli propriamente se llama bruxo, que de noche espanta a los hombres y chupa a los njños.*" Cf. also Dibble and Anderson, *op. cit.*, IV, p. 42, n. 5.

2. Refer to *ibid., passim*.

3. Judging by the section which follows, *tlapouhqui* is intended in this passage.

4. Corresponding Spanish text: "*El hombre que tiene pacto con el demonjo, se transfigura en diuersos anjmales.*"

5. Cf. Garibay, *op. cit.*, II, 3 (1946), p. 169 and p. 174, n. 23.

6. Seler, *op. cit.*, p. 56, citing Sahagún: "the sorcerer dresses up the wooden image to represent a corpse and *burns it at night on the funeral pile* at the same time offering sacrificial gifts" (italics are in the original). Cf. Dibble and Anderson, *op. cit.*, pp. 43 and 69–70 for a fuller description.

He goes about in tatters.[7] He is fatigued; he lives in want, in extreme privation.[8] He causes one to be possessed; he destroys people, he burns wooden figures of them; he bleeds himself over others, destroys them by deception, depresses their hearts. He turns himself into a dog, a bird, a screech owl, an owl, a horned owl.[9]

THE ATTORNEY

The attorney [is] an agent, an intercessor, an appealer, an offerer of rebuttals, a proclaimer, a deputy, a drawer of recompense.

The good attorney [is] a discreet person. He is discreet, able, astute, diligent, constant, unflagging, sharp-tongued, contentious, wrangling, ingenious, persevering, audacious, unyielding, persistent, dignified, solicitous, careful of things. He is solicitous; he is careful of things. He offers rebuttals; he appeals, he pleads. He bows in reverence; he humbles himself. He ensnares; he accuses. He solicits things; he shouts; he is daring, compulsive; he misleads one; he contends, emerging victorious, triumphant; he is aggressive. He collects tribute; he collects tribute for one. He consumes a tenth of it — he draws recompense.

The bad attorney [is] one who takes things from others by fraud. [He is] a persistent beggar, an excessively importunate one; [he is] one who spirits things away by deceit, who travels the road with cunning. He is a hypocrite — lazy, lukewarm, negligent, deceiving, two-faced, inconstant, squandering, dumb, mute. He is a hypocrite; he distracts; he deceives one; he takes things from others by fraud.

THE SOLICITOR; HE [WHO] SOLICITS

The solicitor [is] one who wanders here and there, who is restless, who arranges.[10]

The good solicitor [is] diligent, agile. [He is] impulsive, impetuous, over-hasty, solicitous. [He goes] without his food, without his sleep. He solicits with sympathy, with constant sympathy. He goes about troubled, fearful. He does things of his own volition; he works energetically.

The bad solicitor [is] a shirker, a loafer, a pusher who blinds one, distracts one, lulls one to sleep in order to rob him; who destroys by sorcery, removes by stealth, accepts bribes; who makes corrupt pro-

teiollopachoa chichi totoli, chiquatli, chichtli, teculotl mocuepa.

TEPANTLATO:

in tepantlato tepaleuiani tetlocpaicani, tetlacuepiliani, tetlananquililiani, tlatzatzitiani, teixiptla, tepatillo motlaxtlauiani.

In qualli tepantlato: mozcaliani mozcalia mîmati, itzqui iiel, amo xiuhtlatiani auetzini tenquauitl, tenichtic, tentlapaliui, iollo, iollotetl, ixquauitl, amo tlaçalmatqui, amo quequetzani, aquequelli, tlaceliani, tlamocuitlauiani, tlacelia tlamocuitlauia, tlananquilia, tlacuepa, tlaitlani mopechteca, mocnoteca, tlatzouia tetlatzouilia, tlaciuitia, tzatzi, motlapaloa, motlaquauhicxitia, tecuepa, micali, tepanauia, tlapanauia, teelpan tequechtlã onmoquetza, tlacalaquia, tetlacalaquilia, tlamatlacqua, motlaxtlauia.

In amo qualli tepantlato tetlanaoalcuiliani tlamatatacani, cenca tlauhchioani, tlanaoaluicani, tlanaoalhutlatoctiani, tlaixpania, tlatziuhqui, tlaquelchioani, tlaauilmatini teca mocaiaoani, necoc tene, necoc tlachia, tlanachcatlaçani, motẽtzaqua monontilia, tlaixpania, tlaixneccocoloa, teca mocaiaoa, tetlanaoalcuicujlia

TLACIUITIANI, TLACIUITI:

in tlaciuitiani, auic uetzini mocuecuetzoani, ontlaluitoni.

In qualli tlaciuitiani, iiel, tzicuictic, ixcultic, motequitlaçani, motequimaiauini, tlaceliani, aitlaqualiz, aicochiz quimati: motequipachoa, motetequipachoa, xoq̃chpaniuhtinemi, mauhqui tlaiollocopauia, motzomocoa

In tlaueliloc tlaciuitiani: tlaquêquelmatini, moquequetzani, moquequeçanani, teixtlapaiaoalochtiani, tlaixneccocoloani tecochtlaçani, tlanaoalpoloani, tlanaoaluicani, teca motlaxtlahuiani, tẽçolpotoniloni, tem-

7. Lit., "he goes with rags on his neck, his hips."
8. Cf. *Florentine Codex*, Book VI, *fol*. 189r.
9. Garibay, *op. cit*., p. 174, n. 22: *"se convierte en lechuza, en mochuelo, en buho."*
10. Read *ontlaliani*; cf. *Acad. Hist. MS*, which, however, is difficult to decipher.

nouncements; who is bribed — who lets his tongue be silenced. He is bribed; he makes corrupt pronouncements. He eats [at the expense of] both sides, both parties. He strips both sides. He sells one's goods without one's knowledge. A thief, a liar, he blinds others; he leads one, he shows one the way to the water's current, the rocky crag; he takes one to the forest, to the craggy places; he gets one into a thicket.

pacholoni, tenpachioazuiloni, tenpacholo, tençolpotonilo, necoc tlaqua, necoc tequa, necoc tlatziquimoloa teteputznamaca ichtecqui, iztlacati, teixpopoiotilia, atlauhtli, texcalli quitetoctia, quiteittitia, quauhtla, texcalla tecalaquia, tequauixmatlatilia.

Tenth Chapter, in which is mentioned gaining a living by tailoring and by weaving.

THE TAILOR

The tailor [is] a fitter, a skilled man, a cutter, a trimmer — a practiser of tailoring.

The good tailor is able, discreet; a careful worker, skilled of hand — of craftsman's hands; sharp-witted, meditative, resourceful, dedicated, persevering. He sews; he sews pieces together; he turns hems, he rolls hems; he finishes the edges. He makes a firm stitch; he sews firmly. He is just, trustworthy. He makes [the clothing] fit well; he fits it to persons; he makes it suit them. He applies designs; he works designs; he embellishes it; he sews on designed ornaments; he applies all manner of things. He chooses the best for people; he makes ready for them.

The bad tailor [is] a mocker, a ridiculer, a thief, a stealthy robber, a petty thief who keeps things for himself; a hasty worker, a sewer of insubstantial cloth, a tangler [of thread]. He tangles [thread]; he bastes; he stitches crooked; he tangles things. He defrauds one; he claims not to spoil things. He is demanding of things; he demands of one. [He is] stingy, thieving, grasping. He pilfers.

THE SPINNER[1]

The spinner, the spindle-user [is] one who unravels well, who unsews.[2]

The good spinner [is] one who forms a thread of even thickness, who stretches it delicately. She[3] puts it in her lap. She fills the spindle, stretches [the thread] about the spindle, winds the thread into a ball — with her hand she takes it; she shapes it into a skein. She is persevering and diligent; she works delicately.

The bad spinner [is] a spinner of lumpy thread, of uneven thread, a puller of threads — one who extends them loosely, who twists them poorly. She twists them poorly, spins knots, extends [the thread] loosely, forms it unevenly. [She is] useless of hand, overbold, weak of body, dull; she is lazy; she constantly drops things.

Inic matlactli capitulo, vncan moteneoa: inic motlaecoltia, tlatzomaliztli, ioan hiquitiliztli.

TLATZONQUI:

in tlatzonqui, tlatlaliani, tlaimatini: tlatecqui, tlatequini tlatzomani

In qualli tlatzonqui: mimati mozcalia tlamauhcachioani, momaimati, matoltecatl, ixe, iollo, moiolpoani moiolnonotzani, tlacẽmatini, tlacemanani, tlatzoma, tlaçaloa, tlatencuepa, tlatẽmimiloa, tenquatonoa, tlatepitzço, tlatepitzitzoma, melaoac, itech netlacaneco, tlapanitia, tepanitia, tepantia, tlatlamachotia, tlatlamachia, tlaiecchioa, tlatlamachtzõtoquia, tlaquecimachtlalia, tetech momictia, tetech mocencaoa

In tlaueliloc tlatzonqui: teca mocacaiaoani, teca mauiltiani, ichtequini, tlanaoalchioani, tlaixpachoani, motlacauiani, tlaciuhcachioani, tlapoxaoacahitzomani, tlapapaçoni, tlapapaço tlacuecueço, tlaneneculiço tlapapaçoloa, tetetemachia, amo nenpolollani, tlamatataca tematataca, amo cotontlani, ichtequi, matzinalloti, tlainaia.

TZAUHQUI:

in tzauhqui, tlamalacacho, tlaiectoniani, tlatotiani.

In qualli tzauhqui: tlatemimiloani tlacelicaanani, tlacuetia, tlamalacatema, tlamalacaania, tlaololoa, tlamacuia, tlamacuicui, tlacemana, tlacẽmati, tlacelia.

In aqualli tzauhqui: totolontzaoani, tlaxixipochuani, tlatatacaloani, tlapoxaoacaanani, tlacotziloani: tlacotziloa, totolontzaoa, tlapoxaoacaana, tlachachapania, macuecuetlauhqui, cuitlachpel, cuitlatznaca, hetipâtic quitenmati, mapipixauia.

---

1. See *infra*, chap. xxix, n. 50.
2. Read *tlatontiani* as in *Acad. Hist. MS*.
3. Corresponding Spanish text and illustration infer a male spinner; some of the Nahuatl terminology, however, implies a female.

THE WEAVER [is] one who warps, presses the treadle with her feet, puts the weft in place, provides the heddle. [She is] a possessor of heddle leashes, a provider of heddle leashes.[4]

The good weaver [is] one who presses down [what she weaves], beats it, picks [the thread] with a thorn; who weaves loosely, weaves tightly. She makes it tight, compresses it, beats it down; she warps, provides the heddles, provides the leashes; she places the template — inserts it; she puts the weft in place — extends it; she twists [the thread]. She weaves; she directs others in weaving.

The bad weaver [is] lazy, indolent — a nonchalant, sullen worker; a deceiver. She mauls [her weaving; she is] one who makes gouges in it with her thorn, cuts it in her impatience, makes it look like a corncob; who makes it loose — weaves loosely — is a loose weaver. She works nonchalantly, sullenly; she mocks one. A thief, she pilfers.

HIQUITQUI, tetecac: tlatelicçani, paciotemani, moxiotiani, quâtzone, moquatzontiani.

In qualli hiquitqui: tlatetepachoani, tlauitequini. mouitzcuini, tlaatcaiquitini, tlatilaoani, tlatilaoa, tlapachoa, tlatzotzona, teteca, tlaxiotia, tlaquatzoma, tlaoctacatia, tlaoctacaiotia, paciotema, mana, tlailacatzoa, hiquiti tehiquitilia.

In amo qualli hiquitqui: tlatziuhqui, quitẽmati, tlaquelchioani, tlaqueliecoani, teca mocaiaoani, tlamatzoltilia, tlauitzacaloani, tlanequallocotonani, tlaoiazcopinani, tlapoxaoacachioani, tlapoxaoacahiquitqui, tlapoxaoacahiquitini, tlaqueliecoa, tlaquechchioa, teca mocaiaoa ichtecqui tlainaia

---

4. Ibid.: "El texedor, o la texedora, hurde, y pone en el telar la ordiambre: y moeue las primjderas con los pies: y juega de la lãçadera, y pone la tela en los lizos."

Eleventh Chapter, which telleth of the the vicious, the perverse, such as bawds or pimps.

THE DERANGED MAN, THE MADMAN

The deranged man is perverse, sick, sickly, poor. The deranged man goes about drinking crude wine; he goes about besotted; he is possessed. He gives offense; he is oppressive, disrespectful; he meets no one's gaze; he scatters hatred; he spreads hatred.

THE LEWD YOUTH

The lewd youth is a madman. He goes about drinking crude wine — a drunkard, foolish, dejected; a drunk, a sot. He goes about eating mushrooms. He goes about demented. [He is] restless, dissolute, shameless, presumptuous, lewd, tattling, wicked; a vile brute — brazen. He is impudent; he consumes his inner substance. [He is] vain, proud, debauched; a pleasure seeker, a libertine — revolting, filthy, vicious, a keeper of mistresses; a talker. He lives in concubinage; he is given to pleasure.

THE OLD WHOREMONGER

The old whoremonger [is] fameless, nameless; a libertine, a brainless old man — senile, feeble, decrepit. He is reviled; he becomes decrepit, senile, feeble, perverted.

THE PROCURER

The procurer [is like a] mouse; [he is] a beguiler, a windbag, an enticer, a seducer, a seducer with words, a wheedler, a tempter. He entices one, he tempts one; he strings out lengthy discourses; he converses deceitfully, he ensnares one.

THE PERVERT

The pervert [is] of feminine speech, of feminine mode of address. [If a woman, she is] of masculine speech, of masculine mode of address; [she has] a vulva, a crushed vulva, a friction-loving vulva. [He is] a corrupter, a deranger; one who deprives one of his reason. She rubs her vulva on one; she perverts, confuses, corrupts one.

THE SODOMITE[1] [is] an effeminate — a defilement, a corruption, filth; a taster of filth, revolting, perverse,

Inic matlactli oce capitulo, intechpa tlatoa: in atlacacemeleque, in amo tlacamelaoaque, in iuhque tetlatlaquechilique in anoço tetlatlanochilique

IOLPOLIUHQUI, IOLLOTLAUELILOC:

in iolpoliuhqui, ca tlacamicqui, cocuxqui, cocoxcatzintli, motolinia. In iolpoliuhqui xoxouhcaoctli quitinemi, mixitl, tlapatl quiquatinemi, itech quineoa, teca momotla, teca motepachoa aiac quimacaci, aiac iixco tlachia, motlahellaça, motlahelmaiaui

TELPUCHTLAUELILOC:

in telpuchtlaueliloc ca iollotlaueliloc, xoxouhcaoctli quitinemi, miuintiani, quatlaueliloc, iiellelacic, xocomicqui, tlaoanqui, monanacauitinemi mumixiuitinemi, anenqui, cuecuech, cuecuechtli, topal, hiciccala, iollocamachal, iollonecuil, iollochico, haquetzqui, haquetztzana, eltecuetla, cuecuenotl, cuecuenociuhqui auilnenqui, mauiltiani, auilnemini, auilquizqui, tlahello, cuitlaio, teuhio, tlaçollo, mecaoa, notzale momecatia, auilnemi.

VEUETLAUELILOC:

in ueuetlaueliloc, atle itenio, atle itoca, auilquizqui, auilueue teupilueue, xôxoloueue, teupilpul, auilquiça, auilueueti, teupilti xôxoloti, tlacamiccati.

TETLANOCHILIANI:

in tetlanochili quimichi tensuchitl, hecatlatole, tecoconauiani, suchioa, tetensuchiuiani, tetensuchitzotzonanii tepauiani: tecoconauia, tepauia, hecamecatl quiteca, tenaoalnotza tetlachichiuilia

SUCHIOA:

in suchioa cioatlatole, cioanotzale, oquichtlatole, oquichnotzale, pixe, pixtlatexe, pixtlaxaqualole, teiollocuepani, teiolmalacachoani, tenanacauiani, tepixuia, tesuchiuia, teixmalacachoa, teiolcuepa.

CUILONI, chimouhqui, cuitzotl itlacauhqui, tlahelli, tlahelchichi, tlahelpul, tlacamicqui, teupoliuhqui

---

1. Corresponding Spanish text: "sodometico paciente."

full of affliction. [He merits] laughter, ridicule, mockery; [he is] detestable, nauseating. Disgusting, he makes one acutely sick. Womanish, playing the part of a woman, he merits being committed to flames, burned, consumed by fire. He burns; he is consumed by fire. He talks like a woman, he takes the part of a woman.

THE MURDERER, THE MURDERER OF PEOPLE

The murderer [is] cruel, a dog at heart — a dog indeed. [He is] a hater of people, a trouble-maker, a killer, a spy, a tempter. Daring, he is rash, brutal, disorderly. He bears false witness; he accuses people; he hates, slanders, calumniates, libels them. He strikes, he charges at them; he kills, he leaves his mark on them. He is a demon of the air — a demon. He sheds blood.

THE TRAITOR

The traitor is a gossip. [He is] excrement, dung. He sows discord among people. He excites revolt, he causes turmoil. He makes one swallow falsehoods. He spits in one's mouth. Hot-tempered, he arouses passions, causes riots, stirs rebellion.[2]

THE STORY TELLER [is] pleasing, witty, charming — skilled, adroit in speech.

The good story teller [is] mild, pleasing of speech, flowery of speech; amusing, a conversationalist, gentle of words. His language is delicate, sweet, pleasing. [He is] elegant, soft-spoken.

The bad story teller [is] incoherent, misrepresenting, vile-tongued – of evil tongue. He tells indecent stories; he speaks lewdly, vainly; he is shameless.

THE BUFFOON

The buffoon [is] uncouth, daring, proud, perverse; a drunk, a sot, a libertine.

The good buffoon [is] mild, pleasing, delicate; of flowery, mellifluous speech; an agreeable speaker.

The bad buffoon [is] detestable—of detestable face — insolent,[3] evil-tongued, incoherent, foolish. He misconstrues. Lacking coherence, irritating, he arouses irritation. He is rude, [even though] he provides recreation, makes people laugh, amuses them, dances — dances continuously.

THE THIEF

The thief [is] poor, miserable, useless, full of affliction, undone, niggardly, hungry, miserable, glutton-

auilli, camanalli, netopeoalli, tequalani, tetlahelti, teuiqueuh, teiacapitztlaheltí, cioaciuhqui, mocioanenequini, tlatiloni, tlatlani, chichinoloni, tlatla, chichinolo, cihcioatlatoa, mocioanenequi.

IAUTL: TEIAOUH:

in iautl iollocococ, itzcuintli in iiollo, uel chichi, tecocoliani, tetoliniani, temictiani, motepachiuiani: moteiêieicultiani, neneciuhqui, neneciui, mitonia, mâmana, tetlatoleuia, teteixpauia, tecocolia, tetlapiquia, tetlâtlapia, tetlatolchichiuilia, teuitequi, tetopeoa, temictia, tenezcacaoa, tzitzimitl, coleletli, quinoquia in eztli in tlapalli.

NECOC IAUTL:

in necoc iautl, ca chiquimuli, xistli, cuitlatl, tetzalan, tenepantla, moteca, tenetechieoa, techalania, iztlactli, tequalactli, quitetololtia, tecamac chichicha, tlatolli itlaqual, tlacomonia, tlaacomana tlaconeoa

TLAQUETZQUI, auile camanale tentlamache, tentoltecatl, camatoltecatl.

In qualli tlaquetzqui: tlatoluelic, tlatolauiiac, tensuchitl, çaçanile, tlatole iectlatole, camasuchioa: suchitl uelic auiac itlatol, tecpillatole, iamancatlatole.

In amo qualli tlaquetzqui: tlatolchochopoc, tlatolcampax, tenquappol, tenquauitl, tlahellaquetza, tlahellatoa, auillatoa amo mamati.

TETLAUEUETZQUITI:

in tetlaueuetzquiti ixquauitl, ixtlapaliui, ixtitilac, tlacamicqui, xocomicqui, tlaoanqui, auilquizqui.

In qualli tetlaueuetzquiti: tlatoluelic, tentlamache, camasuchitl, tensuchitl, camasuchihecacal, tenuelic

In amo qualli, tetlaueuetzquiti, tequalani, ixtequalani chalchalpul tenquauitl, chochopoctli, aoompa, aompa heeoa, chochopuc, chichincal, chîchîncalehoa, cocopichcholoa, tlaellelquistia, tetlaueuetzquitia, teauiltia, maceoa, mamâceoa

ICHTECQUI:

in ichtecqui motolinia icnotlacatl, nentlacatl, cococ, teupouhqui, côcotoc, mômotz, apiztli, icnoiutl, apiz-

---

2. Read tlaçoneua.
3. Acad. Hist. MS: chachalpul.

ous, corrupt, prying. He makes plans, spies, breaks through the walls of one's house, fishes things out with his hand. He pants; his heart flutters. He slavers; his mouth waters. He steals; he makes off with things by trickery. He practises petty theft; he pilfers.

THE DANCER WITH A DEAD WOMAN'S FOREARM; THE DANCER WITH THE FOREARM

One who dances with a dead woman's forearm is advised.[4] [He is] a guardian [of secret rituals]; a master of the spoken word, of song. [He is] one who robs by casting a spell, who puts people to sleep; [he is] a thief. He dances with a dead woman's forearm; he robs by casting a spell, causing people to faint, to swoon. He heaps together, he carries away all the goods. He bears the maize bin on his back; he carries it in his arms. [While his victims sleep] he dances, beats the two-toned drum, sings, leaps about.

THE HIGHWAYMAN

The highwayman [is] a beast, furious, savage, violent, pitiless, merciless, bitter-hearted, revolting, inhuman. He waylays one, ambushes one, seizes one by stealth, awaits one on the road; he beats one, wounds one on the head, bruises one on the head, kills one by treachery, ambushes one, tricks one to his destruction.

teutl, iollo itlacauhq̄ iztlaccomoc: tlanemilia, tlaztlacoa, tecalxapotla, tlamachicoluia, nenêciui, iolcapani, tlaztlaqui, quihiztlaqui, ichtequi, tlanaoachioa, tlaixpachoa, tlainaia

TEMACPALITOTI: MACPALITOTI:

Jn temacpalitoti, ca notzale, piale, tlatole, cuique, tecochtlaçani, tecochtecani, ichtecqui: temacpalitotia tecochtlaça, teiolmictia, teçotlaoa, tlacemololoa, tlacemitqui cuezcomatl quimama quinapaloa mitotia, tlatzotzona, cuica chocholoa

TEICHTACAMICTI:

in teichtacamictiani, tequani, tlauele, iollococole, qualane, aicnoio, aicnohoa, iollochichic, ixcococ, atlacacemelle, motepachiuia, tetlallauia, tenahoalana, teuchia, teuitequi, tequatepitzinia, tequatlâtlilhuia, tepoiomictia, tetlanaoaltequilia, tenaoalpoloa

---

4. *Ibid.: nonotzale.*

Twelfth Chapter, which telleth of some of the works, some of the ways of gaining a livelihood of those such as merchants or workers of the soil.

THE MAN WHO HAS BECOME RICH; THE RICH MAN

The rich man is discreet, able, diligent, reflective, resourceful, deliberating, constantly deliberating, sharp-witted; provided with drink and food; possessing wealth, possessing goods.

The good rich man [is] kind, compassionate, merciful, pious. [He is] a caretaker, a kindly dealer, an admirer of things. He takes care of things, deals kindly, profits; he provides an increase, he makes a profit; he is thoughtful, resourceful. He reflects.

The bad, the evil rich man [is] a waster of his possessions, a prodigal, a spendthrift, a squanderer, a dissipator of his possessions. [He is] parsimonious, niggardly, greedy, constantly greedy; a thrifty one, avaricious, mundane; a stingy one. He squanders, he wastes; he squanders his possessions, he dissipates them. He is greedy, mean, thrifty, avaricious. He barters, lends at usury, charges interest, realizes his increase at others' expense, is demanding of others.

THE FARMER

The farmer [is] strong, hardy, energetic, wiry, powerful.

The good farmer, the [good] field worker [is] active, agile, diligent, industrious: a man careful of things, dedicated — dedicated to separate things; vigilant, penitent, contrite. [He goes] without his sleep, without his food; he keeps vigil at night; his heart breaks. He is bound to the soil;[1] he works — works the soil, stirs the soil anew, prepares the soil; he weeds, breaks up the clods, hoes, levels the soil, makes furrows, makes separate furrows, breaks up the soil. He sets the landmarks, the separate landmarks;[2] he sets the boundaries, the separate boundaries; he stirs the soil anew during the summer; he works [the soil] during the summer; he takes up the stones;[3] he digs furrows; he makes holes; he plants, hills, waters, sprinkles;[4] he broadcasts seed; he sows beans, pro-

Inic matlactli omome capitulo: intechpa tlatoa in itla intequiuh, ca in itla innetlaecoltiliz vnca, in iuhque puchteca, in anoço tlalchiuhque

MOCUILTONO, MOCUILTONOA:

In mocuiltonoa, mozcalia, mimati, iiel, moiolpoani, moiolnonotzani tlanemiliani, tlanenemiliani, ixe, iollo, aoa, tlaquale, axcaoa tlatquioa.

In qualli mocuiltonoa icnoio, icnoa, tetlaoculiani, teicnoittani, tlapiani, tlamalhuiani, tlamauiçoani: tlapia, tlamalhuia, tlamauiçoa, tlamixiuitia, tlaixtlapana, tlanemilia, moiolnonotza, moiolpoa.

In amo qualli, in tlaueliloc mocuiltonoa, tlaauilpoloani, tlaauilquistiani, tlanenpoloani, tlanenquistiani, tlaauilicittani, tzotzoca, teuie, motzol, mômotz, momotzoloani, tlatlametl, tlaixoa, atle quitemacani: tlanenquixtia, tlanenpoloa, tlaauilquixtia, tlaauilicitta, teuieoacati, tzotzocati, momotzoloa, tlatlameti, tetlatlacuiltia tetech tlaixtlapana, tetech tlamieccaquistia, tetech tlamixiuitia, tematâtaca

TLALCHIUHQUI:

in tlalchiuhqui, chicaoac, vapaoac, popuxtli, ichtic, tlapaltic.

In qualli tlalchiuhquj, milchiuhqui: tzomoctic, tzicuictic, iiel, tlaceliani, tlamocuitlauiani, tlacēmatini, tlacecenmatini, cochiçani, moiolitlacoani, moiolcocoani, aicochiz, aitlaqualiz, quimati, acochiztlj quimochioaltia tlatlatzcotoni in iiollo, oltlaluitotoc, tlatequipanoa, tlaay, çacamoa, elimiqui, tlaxiuhtlaça, tlateuhchioa, tlapopuxoa, tlaixteca, tlacuenteca, tlacuecuenteca, tlamolonia, tlaxotla, tlaxoxotla, tlaquaxochquetza, tlaquaquaxochquetza, xopançacamoa, tlaxopanchioa, tlâtiana, tlacuemitaca, tlatacaxtlalia, toca, tlapotzallalia, atoca, quauhtoca, tlapixoa, hetlaça, tlatzotzopitza, tlatzotzoputza, tlatacaxtlaloa, tlatlaluia, tlaxilotlapana, tlacincuecuextlaça ohoapuztequi, oacui, xilotzaiana, cacamatzaiana, tlaâquetzaltia, tlacotzana, miiaoacui, elocui, tlacinpoztequi, pixca, tlaxipeoa, tla-

---

1. *Acad. Hist. MS: ōtlalvitoc.*
2. Read *tlalxotla, tlalxoxotla.*
3. Read *tlâteana.*
4. *Acad. Hist. MS: quiauhtoca.*

vides holes for them — punches holes for them, fills in the holes; he hills [the maize plants], removes the undeveloped maize ears, discards the withered ears, breaks off the green maize stalks, thins out the green maize stalks, breaks off the undeveloped maize ears, breaks off the nubbins, harvests the maize stalks, gathers the stubble; he removes the tassels, gathers the green maize ears, breaks off the ripened ears, gathers the maize, shucks the ears, removes the leaves,[5] binds the maize ears, binds the ears [by their shucks], forms clusters of maize ears, makes necklaces of maize ears. He hauls away [the maize ears]; he fills the maize bins; he scatters [the maize ears]; he spreads them; he places them where they can be reached. He cuts them, he dismembers them. He shells them, treads on them, cleans them, winnows them, throws them against the wind.

The bad farmer [is] a shirker, a lukewarm worker, a careless worker; one who drops his work, lazy, negligent, mad, wicked, noisy, coarse, decrepit, unfit — a field hand, nothing but a field hand; a glutton — one who gorges himself; nothing but a beggar — stingy, avaricious, greedy, niggardly, selfish. . . . He is lazy, negligent, listless; he works unwillingly; he does things listlessly.

THE HORTICULTURIST

The horticulturist [is] a planter of seeds, a broadcaster of seeds; a tree-planter, a planter; an uprooter of plants; a worker of the soil, a breaker up of the soil; . . . .

The good horticulturist [is] a careful worker, a calm worker — diligent, solicitous, careful of things, dedicated, able; a knower of books, a reader of the day signs, of the months, of the years.

THE POTTER

The potter is wiry, active, energetic.

The good potter [is] a skilled man with clay, a judge of clay — thoughtful, deliberating; a fabricator, a knowing man, an artist. He is skilled with his hands.

The bad potter [is] silly, stupid, torpid.

THE MERCHANT

The merchant is a seller, a merchandiser, a retailer; [he is] one who profits, who gains; who has reached an agreement on prices; who secures increase, who multiplies [his possessions].

zoaiotlaca, ochoa, tlaochoa, tlaochollalia, mocincozcatia tlaçaca, tlacuezcomatema, tlapixoa, tlachaiaoa, tlaxioania tlatequi, tlapuztequi, tlacotona tlauitequi, tlaquequeça, tlaacana tlahecaquetza, tlahecamotla

In amo qualli tlalchiuhqui: tlaquelmatini, tlaquelchioani, tlatēmatini, aontlaecoani, tlatziuhqui, quitenmatqui, iollo tlaueliloc, tlaueliloc, têtecuinpul têtêtlapul, xoxolopul, aompa heêoa millacatl, tequimillacatl, xixicui, tlaquani, tequitlani, tzotzoca, tlâtlametl, motzol, atlaixcauhquj, amo cotontlani, auel in macequi, iê uel in me, tlatziui, tlatziuhcaoa tlaquelmati, tlaquehecoa, tlaquelchioa

QUILCHIUHQUI:

in quilchiuhqui tlatocani, tlapixoani, quauhtocani, tlaaquiani, tlaani, elimiquini, tlamoloniani, tlacoçolteuhtlaliani.

In qualli quilchiuhqui, tlanêmâtcachioani, tlaiuiachioani, iiel, tlâceliani, tlamocuitlauiani, tlacenmatini, mozcaliani, amoxmatini, tonalpoani, metztlapoani xippoani.

ÇUQUICHIUHQUI:

in çuquichiuhqui, ichtic, popuxtic, popuxtli

In qualli çoquichiuhqui: tlaliximati, tlaliztlacoani, moiolnonotzani, tlanemiliani, tlatlaliani, tlâtlama toltecatl, momaimati.

In amo qualli çoquichiuhquj, xolopitli, nextecuili, miccatzintli

PUCHTECATL:

in puchtecatl ca tlanamacani, tlanamacac, tlanecuilo, tlaixtlapanqui, tlaixtlapanani, tlatennonotzani, tlamixitiani, tlapilhoatiani.

---

5. Read *tlazoaiotlaça*.

The good merchant [is] a follower of the routes, a traveler [with merchandise; he is] one who sets correct prices, who gives equal value. He shows respect for things; he venerates people.

The bad merchant [is] stingy, avaricious, greedy. [He is] thrifty, grasping, deceiving; [he is] a misrepresenter of things to others; [he is] evil-tongued, one who becomes insistent, who over-praises things, who exaggerates things; [he is] a usurer, a profiteer, a thief, a misrepresenter, a liar — dog-like, deceitful, profiting excessively. Filth is his drink, his food. He deceives people; he deceives about things. He comes to an agreement on prices – he cheats, he wheedles, he makes people desire things — makes them desire many things, makes them covet things; he displays, he extends a cape for one.

In qualli puchtecatl, tlaotlatoctiani, tlanênemitiani, çan tlaipantiliani, tlanamictiani, tlaimacazqui teimacazqui.

In amo qualli puchtecatl: tzotzoca, teuie, motzol, momotzoloani, molpiliani teca mocaiaoani, tetlaixcuepiliani, tenquauitl, motenquauhtiliani, tlachamaoani, tlachachamaoani, tetech tlaixtlapanani, tetech tlamieccaquixtiani, ichtecqui, tlaixcuepani, iztlacatini, chichiio, tenqualacio, tzoneoaio, teuhio, tlaçollo iiauh, itlaqual, teca mocaiaoa, tlaztlacauia, tlatennonotza, tentlamati, tetensuchitzotzona, tetlanectia, tetlanenectia, tetlaeleuiltia, tetlaçouilia, tlaçooa.

Thirteenth Chapter, which telleth of the noblewomen.

A NOBLEWOMAN[1]

A noble person [is] wonderful, revered, esteemed, respected; a shelter.[2]

The good noblewoman [is] a protector[3] — one who loves, who guards people. She protects, loves, guards one.

The bad noblewoman [is] violent, furious, savage, revolting — a respecter of no one. She respects no one; she belittles, brags, becomes presumptuous; she takes things in jest and keeps them; she appropriates things; she deceives herself.

[ANOTHER] NOBLEWOMAN[4]

The noblewoman [is] esteemed, lovely — an esteemed noble, respected, revered, dignified.

The good noblewoman [is] a protector. She shows love, she constantly shows love. She loves people. She lives as a noblewoman.

The bad noblewoman [is] savage, wrathful, spiteful, hateful, reserved; [she is] one who is enraged, unjust, disturbed, troubled. She becomes troubled, disturbed, enraged, over-demanding.

[ANOTHER] NOBLEWOMAN[5]

The noblewoman [is] one who merits obedience; [she is] honorable, of high standing — to be heeded. A modest woman, a true woman, accomplished in the ways of women, she is also vigorous,[6] famed, esteemed, fierce, stern.

The good noblewoman is venerable, respectable, illustrious, famed, esteemed, kind, contrite. [She is] one who belittles no one, who treats others with tenderness.

The bad noblewoman [is] wrathful, an evildoer. [She is] one who is overcome with hatred — pugnacious, revolting, hateful — who wishes to trouble, who wishes to cause worry; irresponsible, irritable, excitable — one who is disturbed. She becomes dis-

Inic matlactli omei capitulo: intechpa tlatoa in cioapipilti

TLACATL:

in tlacatl mauiztic, mauizio, imacaxtli, ixtilli, pochutl, aueuetl, ceoallo, ecauhio, malacaio.

In qualli tlacatl: tepan quiçoani in iahaz in icuitlapil, tetlaçotlani, tepiani: tepan quiçoa in iahaz in icuitlapil, tetlaçotla, tepia.

In amo qualli tlacatl: qualane, tlauele, iollococole, ixcococ, atle ipan teittani: atle ipan teitta, atle ipan tlachia, ōmopoa, hatlamati, monelchioa, moneltoca, moztlacauia.

CIOAPILLI:

in cioapilli, tlaçotli, tlaçotzintli, tlaçotitlacatl, ixtilli, imacaxtli, aquêquelli.

In qualli cioapilli: cuexane, teputze, malcoche, mamaloace, motetlâçotilia, motetlâtlaçôtilia, tetlaçotla, cioapilti.

In amo qualli cioapilli: iollococole, iollocuicuitla, aiiel teittani, ellele, teixmauhti, moçomani, çomalcuitla, mamanani motequjpachoani, motequipachoa, mamana, moçoma monenequi.

TOTECUIOCIHOATL:

tocioatecuio tlacamachoni, tlacamachiztli, caquiztli, caconi, timalli cioatl, nelli cioatl, acic cioatlan, niman nima pilli, tleio mauizio tequaio ihiio.

In qualli tocioatecuio, ixtilli, ixtililoni, mauiztililoni, teio, mauizio, icnoio, icnotlamatini, aiac itzcuin, tepêpetlani.

In amo qualli totecuiocioatl: iollocuicuitla, tlatlauelchioani, tlatlauelpoloani, ixtleio, ixcococ, ihiio, amamātlani, amotequipachollani, mocitl, popoçuctli, iolpopoçuctic, mamanani: mamana, motequipachoa tlatlauelchioa, tlatlauelpoloa.

---

1. Corresponding Spanish text: "*La muger noble.*"
2. Cf. chap. iv, *supra,* n. 2.
3. Lit., "one who spreads her wings, her tail feathers over one."
4. Corresponding Spanish text: "*La muger hidalga.*"
5. *Ibid.:* "*La señora que mantiene familia.*"
6. *Acad. Hist. MS: ateupilli.*

turbed, troubled; she does evil; she becomes overwrought with hatred.

[ANOTHER] NOBLEWOMAN[7]

The noblewoman [is] a protector, meritorious of obedience, revered, worthy of being obeyed; a taker of responsibilities, a bearer of burdens — famed, venerable, renowned.

The good noblewoman [is] patient, gentle, kind, benign, hard-working, resolute, firm of heart, willing as a worker, well disposed, careful of her estate. She governs, leads, provides for one, arranges well, administers peacefully.

The bad noblewoman [is] one who is rash, who is fitful. She incites riots; she arouses fear, implants fear, spreads fear; she terrorizes [as if] she ate people. She impels flight — causes havoc — among people. She squanders.

[ANOTHER] NOBLEWOMAN[8]

The noblewoman [is] a woman ruler, governor, leader — a provider, an administrator.

The good woman ruler [is] a provider of good conditions, a corrector, a punisher, a chastiser, a reprimander. She is heeded, obeyed; she creates order; she establishes rules.

The bad noblewoman [is] unreliable, negligent, overbearing — one who mistreats others. She is overbearing; she mistreats one, is given to vice, drinking, drunkeness. She leads one into danger; she leads, she introduces one into error. She is troubled; she confounds one.

THE MAIDEN[9]

The maiden is noble, a noble among nobles, a child of nobility. [She is one] from whom noble lineage issues, or she is of noble birth, worthy of being loved, worthy of preferred treatment.

The good maiden is yet a virgin, mature, clean, unblemished, pious, pure of heart, benign, chaste, candid, well disposed. She is benign; she loves; she shows reverence; she is peaceful; she bows in reverence; she is humble, reserved; she speaks well, calmly.

The bad maiden [is] a descendant of commoners — a belittler, a rude person, of lowly birth. She acts like a commoner; she is furious, hateful, dishonored, dissolute, given to carnal pleasure, impetuous.

CIOATECUTLI:

in cioatecutli macuche, teputze, mamale, tlacamachoni, imacaxtli, tlaiecultiloni, tlatquini, tlamamani, tenio, tocaie, tocaio.

In qualli cioatecutli, tlapaccaihiiouiani, iolceuhqui, ioliamanqui, tlâtlacatl, quiihiiouiani, iollotetl, iollochichic, tlaoquichuiani, aeltzoio, tlapacho, tepachoa, tlaiacana, tenemitia, tlauelmanitia, iuian iocuxca tlauica.

In amo qualli cioatecutli: tlaxcoloani, tlâtlaxculoani, tlacomonia, tlamauhtia, mauiztli quiteca, mauiztli quitlaça, tlaiçauia, tequa, tepan motlaloa, texaxamatza, tlaixpoloa.

TLATOCACIOATL:

in tlatocacioatl, ca cioatlatoani, tepachoani, teiacanani, tetlataluiani, tlanaoatiani.

In qualli cioatlatoani: tlauelmâmanitiani, atl cecec, tzitzicaztli quitecani quitlaçani, tealcececaui, tetzitzicazui, caco, nepechtequililo, tlatecpana, naoatillalia.

In amo qualli tlatocacioatl: tlaxiccaoani, tlacochcaoani, tlaetiliani, tlacianmictiani: tlaetilia, tlacianmictia, auillotl, iuiniotl, iuintiliztli, quimana, atoiatl tepexitl quiteittitia, quauitl texcalli quiteittitia, quitenamictia, motlapololtia, tetlapololtia

TOCHPUCHTZIN:

in tochpuchtzin, ca pilli, ca tecpilli, tecpilpan tlacatl, tecpilconetl, pillacamecaiutl itech quizqui, anoço in tlaçotli iiollo, in tlaçotlaloni, in maluiloni.

In qualli tochpuchtzin: ca oc quiztica, macitica, atzoio, ateuhio, qualnemilice, chipaoaca iollo, tlatlacatl, tlacatl, tlacamelaoac, aeltzoio, tlatlacati, tetlaçotla, tlaimacaci, iocuxcanemi, mopechteca, mocnomati, mopiloa: uellatoa, matcatlatoa

In amo qualli tochpuchtzin: momaceoalquixtianj, teixconemini, teixcoeoani, momaceoalquixtia, maceoalti, itzcuinti, motlaheloa, mauilquixtia, mauiloa, auilnemi, tlatlacanequi

---

7. Corresponding Spanish text: "*La muger principal.*"
8. *Ibid.:* "*La señora principal.*"
9. *Ibid.:* "*La infanta, o la donzella generosa.*"

The girl, the little girl[10]

The little girl is a noble, an esteemed noble, a descendant of nobles.

A good little girl[11] [is] of good, clean life — a guardian of her honor. [She is] self-respecting, energetic, deliberating, reflective, enterprising. She is self-respecting, energetic, patient when reprimanded, humble.

The bad little girl [is] an evil talker, a belittler — inconsiderate, perverse, impetuous, lewd. She shows disrespect; she detests, she shows irreverence, she belittles, she presumes.

The maiden[12]

The maiden [is] of the nobility — courteous, loved, esteemed, beloved.

The good maiden [is] loving, pleasing, reverent, respectful, retiring. She is pleasing, appreciative, admiring of things.

The bad maiden [is] corrupt, incorrigible, rebellious — a proud woman, shameless, brazen, treacherous, stupid. She is inconsiderate, imbecile, stupid; she brings dishonor, disgrace.

[Another] noblewoman[13]

The noblewoman — the courteous, illustrious noble.

The good noblewoman [is] a child of lineage, of noble lineage. She brings fame to others, honors her birthright, causes one to be proud of her.

The bad noblewoman [is] a gluttonous noble, a noble completely dishonored, of little value — a fool, impudent — a consumer of her inner substance, a drunkard. She shows concern for none but herself; she lives completely for herself; she governs her own conduct, assumes her own burdens; she is disrespectful.

[Another] noblewoman[14]

The noblewoman [is] esteemed — an esteemed noble, a legitimate child.

The good noblewoman [is] one who is exemplary, who follows the ways of her parents, who gives a good, sound example. She is of the chosen; she is one of the chosen few.

Conetl conetzintli:

in conetzintli, ca tecpilli, tlaçopilli, pilli, tetechcopa quioquixti.

In qualli conetzintzili: qualli iectli in inemiliz, momaluiani, mixmaluiani, mocxiieiecoani, tlanemiliani, mocuepani, moieiecoani, mixmaluia, mocxiieiecoa, tetloc tenaoac mocalaquia, toloa.

In amo qualli conetzintli: iollocamachal tlatolcampax, iliuiztlacatl, mitoniani, momociuiani, hicciccala, teixco teicpac eoa, atlamauhca itta, atlaimacaci, atle ipā tlachia, atlatlamati.

Teichpuch:

in teichpuch pilpan pouhqui, tecpiltic, tlaçotic, tlaçotli, tlaçoio.

In qualli teichpuch: tlatlaçotlani, tlatlaçomatini, tlaimacacini, tlamauhcaittani, mauhcaio, tlatlaçomati, mocnelilmati, tlamauiçoa.

In amo qualli teichpuch: iolloitlacauhqui, auel monotza, tzõtetl, cioacuecuel, cuecuechtli cuecuetol, tlacapuiutl, tlacaxolopitli, ihiliuizti, xôxoloti, xolopiti, mauilquixtia, auilquiça

Tetzon:

in tetzon tecpiltzintli tecpilli.

In qualli tetzon: quixtilconetl, quixtilpilli, teteiotia, tlatonaleoa, tetzonteconacocui.

In amo qualli tetzon: tlacaçolpilli, ça ça molui pilli, ça ça ie pilli, ixtotomac, haquetztzana, eltecuetlan, miuintiani, aiac quiiocoia, moceniocoia, motqui momama, aontepoa

Teizti:

in teizti tlaçotli, tlaçopilli tlaçoconetl.

In qualli teizti, tenemiliztocani, tetlaieiecaluiani, qualli iectli machiutl, tlapepenani, tlacecenquixtiani

---

10. *Ibid.*: *"La donzella delicada."*
11. Read *conetzintli.*
12. *Ibid.*: *"La hija de claro."*
13. *Ibid.*: *"La hija noble de buen linage."*
14. *Ibid.*: *"La muger de buena ralea."* Cf. chap. v, *supra*, n. 12.

The bad noblewoman [is] one who degrades herself, who lives in filth and corruption — detestable, slobbering, false. She degrades herself, brings herself to ruin, hurls — places — herself in filth and corruption.

[ANOTHER] NOBLEWOMAN[15]

The noblewoman is a descendant of noble ancestors; [she is] of noble rearing.

The good noblewoman [is] tranquil, quiet, peaceful, modest, dignified. She honors, she respects all people. She shows respect, consideration, veneration.

The bad noblewoman [is] daring, overbearing toward others — a scatterer, a spreader of hatred. She scatters hatred, shows effrontery, is rude, becomes brazen, lifts her head in pride, exhibits vanity.

[ANOTHER] NOBLEWOMAN[16]

The noblewoman is of noble rearing — a meritorious noble.

The good noblewoman is peaceful, kind, gentle.

The bad noblewoman [is] inflated; a consumer of her inner substance, decrepit. She is presumptuous; she acts in haste; she is impetuous.

[ANOTHER] NOBLEWOMAN[17]

The noblewoman [is] the child of nobles, a true noble. She is worthy thereof. She realizes the estate of nobility; she participates in and is suited to it.

The bad noblewoman [is] common, dull — descended from commoners, irritating. She brags; she presumes; she understands things backwards; she does things backwards; she causes irritation.

[ANOTHER] NOBLEWOMAN[18]

The noblewoman [is] completely good, just, pure, respectable.

The good noblewoman [is] one who humbles herself, who bows in reverence. Gracious, kind, she is benign, persuasive; she bows in reverence; she is humble, appreciative.

The bad noblewoman [is] untrained, deranged, disobedient, pompous. She goes about dissolute, brazen. She is gaudy; she goes about in gaudy raiment — rude, drunk.

---

15. *Ibid.*: "*La donzella de buen solar.*" Cf. chap. v, n. 13.
16. *Ibid.*: "*La muger noble de buena estima.*" Cf. chap. v, n. 15.
17. *Ibid.*: "*La muger descendiente de nobles.*" Cf. chap. v, n. 17.
18. *Ibid.*: "*La muger noble de solar conocido.*" Cf. chap. v, n. 14.

In amo qualli teizti, mauilquixtiani, cuitlatitlan tlaçoltitlan inemia, tlaelittoni, moca chichitl iztlacio, tenqualacio, mauilquixtia, mopôpoloa, cuitlatitlan tlaçoltitlan motlaça maquia.

TEIXQUAMUL:

in teixquamul ca necauhcaiutl, tecpiltontli.

In qualli teixquamul: matcatlacatl, matcaio, iocuxcaio, iocuxqui, piltic, muchi tlacatl imauiz, muchi tlacatl iixtil, tlaixtilia, tlaxtilia, tlamauiztilia

In amo qualli teixquamul: teca momotlani, teca motepachoani, motlahellaçani, motlahelmaiauini, motlaellaça, teca momotla, teixco eoa, aquetza, mixacocui, quimopantlaxilia.

TEUITZIO:

in teuitzio: ca tecpilpil, icnotecpilli.

In qualli teuitzio: ca iocuxcatlacatl, ioliamanqui, iolceuhqui

In amo qualli teuitzio: elpoxcauhqui, eltecuetlan iellellacic, atlatlamati, amotlatlamatchioa, motequimaiaui.

TEAOAIO:

in teaoaio, tecpilpil, nell in piltic, quitquiticac in pillutl tlapanitia, quicui, ipaniti

In amo qualli teaoaio: maceoaltic, tetecuintic, maceoalquizqui, chincal, mopoa, atlamati, aompa ieheoa, oholpatlacheoa, chichincaleoa.

TETENTZON:

in tetentzon: uel ipã qualli, iectli, chipaoac, moxtic

In qualli tetentzon: mocnotecani, mopechtecani, icnotl, icnotzintli tlatlacati, tetlatlacauiloa, mopepechteca, môcnomati moôcnelilmati.

In tlaueliloc tetentzon, atlanonotzalli, cuexcochcoioc, atecacqui, cuecuechoa, cuecuechnemi, aquetznemi, topalti, totopalnemi, tlaxocotinemi, miuintitinemi.

[ANOTHER] NOBLEWOMAN[19]

The noblewoman:[20] through her is nobility engendered. [She is] of the nobility.

The good noblewoman [is] retiring, submissive, humble,[21] desirous of no praise.

The bad noblewoman [is] boastful, vainglorious, desirous of being known. She is vainglorious, desirous of being known; she boasts, brags, boasts.

[ANOTHER] NOBLEWOMAN[22]

The noblewoman is famed, venerable, esteemed, honored.

The good noblewoman [is] one who weeps, who is compassionate, concerned; one who admires, who shows veneration, who reveres things, who reveres people. She shows understanding of the poor; she reveres things;[23] she reveres people.

The bad noblewoman [is] proud, ..., inflated; she acts superior....

[ANOTHER] NOBLEWOMAN[24]

The noblewoman [is] of noble heart, of nobility.

The good noblewoman [is] of elegant speech, soft-spoken — a gentle person, peaceful, refined. She speaks with elegance; she acts with refined modesty.

The bad noblewoman [is] like a field worker — brutish, a great field worker, a great commoner; a glutton, a drinker, an eater — a glutton, incapable, useless, time-wasting....

[ANOTHER] NOBLEWOMAN[25]

The noblewoman [is] of nobility, belongs to the order of rulers, comes from rulership whether she is legitimate or a bastard child.

The good noblewoman [is] one who is bashful, ashamed [of evil], who does things with timidity, who is embarrassed [by evil]. She is embarrassed [by evil]; she works willingly, voluntarily.

The bad noblewoman [is] infamous, very audacious, stern, proud, very stupid,[26] brazen, besotted, drunk. She goes about besotted; she goes about demented; she goes about eating mushrooms..

TETZICUEUHCA, TETZICUEOALLO:

in tetzioallo, tepal motlacatili, pilpan pouhqui.

In qualli tetzicueoallo: motocani, mopopoloani, moxiuhtlapachoa, amitollani

In amo qualli tetzicueoallo: pancotl, mochachamaoani, machicanequini, mochachamaoa, machicanequi, mocinoa, mocicinoa, mocinoa.

TETLAPANCA:

in tetlapanca, ca tẽio, tocaie, mauiztic, mauizço.

In qualli tetlapanca: chocani, tlaocoiani, moteupoani, tlamauiçoani, tlamauiztiliani, tlaimacazqui, teimacazqui: quimati in icnoiotl, tlaimaci, teimacaci

In amo qualli tetlapanca: cuecuenotl, comoz, popoçac, cuecuenoti, mocomoçoa

TEEZIO:

in teezio, tecpiliollo, tecpillo.

In qualli teezio: tecpillatole, iamancatlatole, iamancatlacatl, iuiianio, iocuxqui, tecpillatoa, tlaiocuxcachioa.

In tlaueliloc teezio, millacatic, itzcuintic, tequimillacatl, tequimaceoalli, xixicuin, atlini tlaquani, tlaqualxixicuin, xiuhnel, xiuixcul, atle ueli, nentlacatl, nenqui, tetl popoxiuhteuh.

TETLAPALLO:

in tetlapallo, pilli tlatocapan pouhqui, tlatocaiutl itech quizqui, anoço uel tepiltzin anoço calpan tepiltzin.

In qualli tetlapallo: pinaoani, pinauizio, tlapinauizchioani, momamatini: momamati, tlaiollocacopauia, tlaiollocati.

In amo qualli tetlapallo: amo pinaoani, ixquappol, ixtepul, ixtitilacpul, ictenopaltilacpul, ixcepocpol, tlaoanqui, xocomicqui, mixitl, tlapatl quiquatinemi, momixiuitinemi, monanacauitinemi.

---

19. *Ibid.*: "*La muger de buena parentela.*" Cf. chap. v, n. 18.
20. Read *tetzicueuallo.*
21. Lit., "she buries herself, destroys herself, covers herself with foliage."
22. Corresponding Spanish text: "*La muger que desciende de buenos.*" Cf. chap. v, n. 19.
23. Read *tlaimacaci.*
24. Corresponding Spanish text: "*La muger noble de limpia sãgre.*" Cf. chap. v. n. 20.
25. *Ibid.*: "*La muger de noble sangre.*" Cf. chap. v, n. 21.
26. *Acad. Hist. MS: ixtenopaltilacpol.*

[ANOTHER] NOBLEWOMAN[27]

The noblewoman is a noble, a noble ruler, an esteemed noble — esteemed, lovely, worthy of being loved, worthy of preferred treatment, worthy of veneration, deserving of honor, enjoying glory; good, modest, respected, self-respecting. [She is like something] white — refined; like a pillar; like a wooden beam, slender, of medium stature. [She is] valiant, having valor, bravery, courage. [She is] esteemed, famed, precious, beautiful.

THE GOOD NOBLEWOMAN

The good noblewoman, the beloved noblewoman [is] highly esteemed, good, irreproachable, faultless, dignified, brave; [like] a quetzal feather, a bracelet, a green stone, a turquoise. Very much hers are goodness, humanity, humaneness, the human way of life, excellence, modesty, the fullness of love. Completely hers are the sources of goodness, of grace, of humaneness as to body and soul.[28] [She is] perfect, faultless.

The bad noblewoman [is] bad, wicked, evil, ill, incorrigible, disloyal, full of affliction, quite besmirched, quite dejected. [She is] haughty, presumptuous, arrogant, unchaste, lewd, debauched. She is given to drunkenness, to drinking; she goes about being rude; she goes about telling tales. [She is] vain, petty, given to bad conduct; a drunkard, savage, torpid, [like] a foreigner, an imbecile — stupid, feeble..., ...; she is oblivious of what all know of her.[29] [She is] a sleepy-head, a dried-out sleepy-head, an oversleeping woman; a pervert, a perverted woman, perverse.

TEIXUIUH, IXUIUHTLI:

in teixuiuh, ca pilli, tecpilli, tlaçopilli, tlaçotli, tlaçotzintli, tlaçotlaloni, maluiloni, mauiztililoni, mauhcaittoni, mauiztli, qualli iectli: timalli ixtilli, moxtic, teztic, tetzcaltic, temimiltic, oapaltic, piaztic ipan qualli, colotic, ixtleio, ixtequaio, ixmauizio, mauizio, tleio, tlatlaçochioalli, tlaiecchioalli

In qualli teixuiuh,

in qualli toxuiuh, toxuiuhtzin: uellaçotli in iiollo iectli qualli, atle iiâioca, acan ca iiaioca, aquequelli, tequaio, quetzalli maquiztli, chalchiuitl, teuxiuitl, muchi itech cenca in qualli in tlacaiutl, in tlacanezcaiutl, in tlacanemoani, in tlaçoiutl, in tlacanemiliztli, tlaçotlanqui, itech cenquizca ca: in qualtiani, in iqualnezca, in itlacanezca tonacaio, ioan in ianima, cenquizqui, hacitica.

In amo qualli toxuiuhtzin: tlaueliloc, tlauelilocapul, aiectli, aiecpul, atlacaquizqui, acemelle, teupoliuhqui, uel hitlacauhqui, uel iiellelacic, mopoani, atlamatini, mopancoani, aquetzqui, auilli, auilnenqui, iuintiztli quimana, iuiniutl quimana, tlaxocotinemi, tlaquetztinemi, xacan, xacampa, xocomicqui, tlaoanqui, tenitl, pinotl, chontal, xolopitli, nextecuilli, xoxolotl, xolonquatl, nextli tlaxiquipilquetzalli ipan ontlatelicçalli, ixnex, ixnextiacapan, poxaquatl, poxaquatlacectli, poxaquacioatl, suchicioatl, tlacamiccacioatl tlacamicqui

---

27. Corresponding Spanish text: *"La muger de buen parentesco."* The term usually is translated *nieto* or *nieta.*

28. *Acad. Hist. MS: yoan y̆ anima.*

29. See *Florentine Codex,* Book VI, cap. xliii, fol. 188*v.*

Fourteenth Chapter, which telleth of the nature, the condition of the common women.

THE ROBUST WOMAN

The robust woman, the middle-aged woman [is] strong, rugged, energetic, wiry, very tough[1]—exceedingly tough, animated, vigorous; a willing worker, long-suffering.

The good robust woman [is] pious, chaste, careful of her honor; not unclean; unblemished; one who is irreproachable — like a bracelet, like a green stone, like fine turquoise.

The evil robust woman [is] belittling and offensive to others — belittling to others; disgusting. She is ill bred, incompatible; she does not work in calm; she acts fitfully,[2] without consideration; she is impetuous.

THE MATURE WOMAN

The mature woman [is] candid.

The good mature woman [is] resolute, firm of heart; constant — not to be dismayed; brave, like a man; vigorous, resolute; persevering — not one to falter; a steadfast, resolute worker. She is long-suffering; she accepts reprimands calmly — endures things like a man. She becomes firm — takes courage. She is intent. She gives of herself. She goes in humility. She exerts herself.

The bad mature woman [is] thin, tottering, weak — an inconstant companion, unfriendly. She annoys others, chagrins them, embarrasses, shames, oppresses one. Extremely feeble, impatient, chagrined, exhausted, fretful, she becomes impatient, loses hope, becomes embarrassed — chagrined. She goes about in shame; she persists in evil. Evil is her life. She lives in vice.

THE WEAVER OF DESIGNS

The weaver of designs is one who concerns herself with using thread, who works with thread.

The good weaver of designs is skilled — a maker of varicolored capes, an outliner of designs, a blender of colors, a joiner of pieces, a matcher of pieces, a person of good memory. She does things dexterously.

Inic matlactli onnaui capitulo: intechpa tlatoa, in inieliz, in imiuhcatiliz, in cioa in atle, intẽio

CIOATLAPALIUI:

in cioatlapaliui, iollococioatl, chicaoac, oapaoac, popuxtli, ichtic, ichpalala ichpalalatic, iollotlapaliui, oquichiollo, tlaoquichuiani, tlapaccaihiiouiani.

In qualli cioatlapaliui: qualnemilice, mopiani, momaluiani, atzoio, ateuhio, atle itech quimaxitilillani, maquiztic, chalchiuhtic, teuxiuhtic.

In tlaueliloc cioatlapaliui: teixco teicpac nemini, teixco nemini, teuiqueoani, amo tlacachioa, amo tlatlacateca, atlatlamachchioa, tlaxtlacoloa, tlaixtomaoa, tlailiuizuia

QUAUHCIOATL:

in quauhcioatl, tlacamelaoac.

In qualli quauhcioatl: iollotetl, iollochichic, iolchichic, amo cuetlaxoani oquichtini, oquichiollo, tepitziollo, tlacemanani, auetzini, aco molpiani, aco motetziloani, tlapaccaihiiouia, tlapaccacelia, tlaoquichuia, tlatepitzuia, moiolchichilia, oalixtetẽmotzoloa, quioalmocotonilia, quioalcotona in iollo oalmocentlanqua, mellaquaoa

In amo qualli quauhcioatl: ûiuixqui, iaiaquî, iaiacatontli, ateuiui, atetlapalo, texiuhtlati, teellelaxiti, tepinocuiti tepinoquetz, tetequipacho, uiuixcatontli, moxiuhtlatiani, mellelaxitiani, ciãmiquini, mociauhcanequini, moxiuhtlatia, mopatla, pinocui, mopinoquetza, pinonemi, aqualli, aiectli quimauiltia, aiectli inemiliz, tlaueliloti

TLAMACHCHIUHQUI:

in tlamachchiuhqui: ca icpatl quimauiltiani, icpachiuhqui.

In qualli tlamachchiuhqui: ca mimati, tlatlapalpoani, tlatlilaniani, tlapoiaoani, tlananamictiani, tlapopotiani, iollo, tlatlamachia, tlamachchioa, tlapepena, tlatzotzona, tlatentia, tlatozquitia, tlatlacouite-

---

1. *Acad. Hist. MS: ichpâtic.*

2. Read *tlâtlaxcoloa*, as in *ibid*.

She weaves designs. She selects. She weaves tightly. She forms borders. She forms the neck. She uses an uncompressed weave. She makes capes with the ball-court and tree design.[3] She weaves loosely — a loose, thick thread. She provides a metal weft. She forms the design with the sun on it.

The bad weaver of designs is untrained — silly, foolish, unobservant, unskilled of hand, ignorant, stupid. She tangles [the thread]; she harms [her work] — she spoils it. She ruins things scandalously; she scandalously ruins the surface of things.

THE SPINNER

The spinner [is] one who combs, who shakes out [the cotton].

The good spinner [is] one who handles things delicately,[4] who forms an even thread. [She is] soft, skilled of hand — of craftsman's hands. She puts [the thread] in her lap; she fills the spindle; she makes a ball [of thread]; she takes it into her hand — winds it into a skein in her hands. She triples [the thread]. She spins a loose, thick thread.

The bad spinner pulls [threads], leaves lumps, moistens what she grasps with her lips, twists incompletely. [She is] useless — of useless hands, negligent, slothful, neglectful — a neglectful one, lazy.

THE SEAMSTRESS

The seamstress is one who uses the needle,[5] a needle worker. She sews; she makes designs.

The good seamstress [is] a craftsman, of craftsman's hands, of skilled hands — a resourceful, meditative woman. She makes designs; she sews.

The bad seamstress [is] one who bastes, who tangles [thread]. She tangles [thread]; she bastes; she tangles the sewing. She deceives one; she ridicules one.

THE COOK

The cook is one who makes sauces, who makes tortillas; who kneads [dough]; who makes things acid, who leavens. [She is] wiry, energetic. [She is] a maker of tortillas — a tortilla-maker; she makes them disc-shaped, thin, long. . . . She makes them into balls; twisted tortillas — twisted about chili; she uses grains of maize. She makes tamales — meat tamales; she makes cylindrical tortillas; she makes thick, coarse ones. She dilutes sauces; she cooks; she fries; she makes juices.

qui, tlatlachquauhiotia, tlaatcaiquiti, tlapotoncaiotia, tlateputzpaciotia tonatiuh õmani quichioa.

In amo qualli tlamachchiuhqui: amozcalia, xolopitli, aoompa, atlachia, amo maimati, poxaquatl, nextecuili, tlapapaçoloa, tlatlacoa, tlaitlacoa, tlatetzappoloa, tlaixtetzappoloa.

TZAUHQUI:

in tzauhqui, tlapochinqui, tlauitecqui.

In qualli tzauhqui: tlaceliani, tlatemimiloani, maiamanqui, momaimati, matoltecatl, tlacuetia, tlamalacatema, tlaolooloa, tlamacuia tlamacuicui, tlaeilia, potoncatzaoa.

In amo qualli tzauhqui: tlatatacaloa, tlaxixipochoa, tlatenqualacana, tlacotziloa, macuetlauic, macuecuetlauhqui aiiel, cuitlananaca, quitẽmati, quitẽmatitl, tlatziuhqui

TLATZONQUI:

in tlatzonqui, ca tlauitzmollauiani, tlaixaquiani tlatzoma, tlacuicuiloa.

In qualli tlatzonqui: toltecatl, matoltecatl, momaimati, moiolnonotzani, tlaiolpoani, tlacuicuiloa tlatzoma

In amo qualli tlatzonqui: tlacuecueçoni, tlapapaçoloani, tlapapaçoloa, tlacuecueço, tlapapazço, teca mocaiaoa, teca mauiltia.

TLAQUALCHIUHQUI:

in tlaqualchiuhqui, ca mulchiuhqui, ca tlaxcalchiuhqui, tlaxaqualoani, tlaxocoliani, tlaxocotextlaliani, ichtic, popuxtic, tlaxcaloani, tlaxcalo, tlaiaiaoaloa, tlacanaoa, tlamemelacoa, tlaxcalxocuichca, tlamatzoa, tlailacatzoa, tlachililacatzoa, tlatlaoiotia, tamaloa nacatamaloa, tlaxcalmimiloa, quauhtlaqualoa, moloa, tlapaoaci, tlatetzoionia, patzcaloa.

---

3. Siméon *op. cit.* (citing Clavijero) describes this as the costume of military officers in the court.
4. Read *tlacelicaanani*, as in *Acad. Hist. MS.*
5. Read *tlauitzmallouiani;* cf. *ibid.*

52

The good cook is honest, discreet; [she is] one who likes good food — an epicure, a taster [of food. She is] clean, one who bathes herself; prudent; one who washes her hands, who washes herself; who has good drink, good food.

The bad cook [is] dishonest, detestable, nauseating, offensive to others — sweaty, crude, gluttonous, stuffed, distended with food — much distended, acquisitive. As one who puts dough into the oven, she puts it into the oven. She smokes the food; she makes it very salty, briny; she sours it. She is a field hand — very much a field hand, very much a commoner.

THE PHYSICIAN

The physician [is] a knower of herbs, of roots, of trees, of stones; she is experienced in these. [She is] one who has [the results of] examinations; she is a woman of experience, of trust, of professional skill: a counselor.

The good physician is a restorer, a provider of health, a reviver, a relaxer — one who makes people feel well, who envelopes one in ashes. She cures people; she provides them health; she lances them, she bleeds them — bleeds them in various places, pierces them with an obsidian lancet. She gives them potions, purges them, gives them medicine. She cures disorders of the anus. She anoints them; she rubs, she massages them. She provides them splints; she sets their bones — she sets a number of bones. She makes incisions, treats one's festering, one's gout, one's eyes. She cuts [growths from] one's eyes.

The bad physician [pretends to be] a counselor, advised, a person of trust, of professional knowledge. She has a vulva, a crushed vulva, a friction-loving vulva. [She is] a doer of evil. She bewitches — a sorceress, a person of sorcery, a possessed one. She makes one drink potions, kills people with medications, causes them to worsen, endangers them, increases sickness, makes them sick, kills them. She deceives people, ridicules them, seduces them, perverts them,[6] bewitches them, blows [evil] upon them, removes an object from them, sees their fate in water, reads their fate with cords, casts lots with grains of maize, draws worms from their teeth. She draws paper — flint — obsidian — worms from them; she removes these from them. She deceives them, perverts them, makes them believe.

In qualli tlaqualchiuhqui: ca mimati, mozcalia, tlauelmatini, tlauelicamatini, tlaieiecole chipaoac, maltiani, mimatini, momatequiani, mopapacani, iecaoa, iectlaquale.

In amo qualli tlaqualchiuhqui: amihimati, tequalani, tetlahelti, teiolitlaco, tzotzocuitlapol, têtenexpol, xixicuinpol, tlaquaxi, tlaquaxiquipol, tlaquaxixiquipol, iztlaccomoc, tlatexquetzani, tlatexquetza, tlapoquiialia, tlaztaquauhtilia, tlaztachichilia, tlaxocolia, millacatl, tequimillacatl, tequimaceoalli.

TICITL:

in ticitl, xiuiximatini tlaneloaioiximatini, quauhiximatini, teiximati, tlaiximatqui, tlaieiecole, tlaztlacole, piale, machice nonotzale.

In qualli ticitl: ca tepatiani, tlapaleuiani, teeoatiquetzani, teiamaniani, teneuelmachitiani, nextli, teololoani, tepatia, tepaleuia, teitzmina, teço teçoço, teihitzaquia, tetlaitia, tetlanoquilia tepamaca, tetzinana, teuça, tematoca, temamatoca, tepapachoa, teçaloa, teçaçaloa texotla tepalancapatia, tecoaciuizpatia, teixpatia, teixtequi.

In amo qualli ticitl, nonotzale, nonotzqui, piale, machice, pixe, pixtlatexe, pixtlaxaqualole, tlachioale, suchioa, naoalli, naoale, tlacateculotl, tepaitia, tepamictia, tetlanaluia, teuuitilia tlauuitilia, tlacocolizcuitia, tlamictia, teca mocaiaoa, teca mauiltia, tepixuia, tesuchiuia, texoxa teipitza, tetlacuicuilia, atlan teitta, mecatlapoa tlaolli quichaiaoa, tetlanocuilana, amatl, tecpatl, itztli, ocuilin, tetech cana, tetech quiquixtia, teixcuepa, teiolcuepa, tetlaneltoctia

---

6. Variant translation is possible; cf. *supra,* chap. xi, "The pervert."

Fifteenth Chapter, which telleth of the different kinds of evil women.

THE HARLOT; THE CARNAL WOMAN

The carnal woman is an evil woman who finds pleasure in her body; who sells her body — repeatedly sells her body; an evil young woman [or] an evil old woman, besotted, drunk — very drunk, much besotted; dejected, perverse; [like] a sacrificial victim, a bathed slave, a captive; full of affliction, mortal.

She consumes her inner substance — a brazen, a proud, a dissolute woman of debauched life; a fraud — gaudy, fastidious, vain, petty. [She is] oblivious of what all know her to be: a petty old woman, a free yielder of herself, a whore from the brothel, a deflowered one, a lascivious old woman; of itching buttocks — an old woman of itching buttocks; an aged woman, a flabby old woman, a filthy one; a filthy old dog who brings herself to ruin like a dog.

She parades; she moves lasciviously; she is pompous. Wheresoever she seduces, howsoever she sets her heart [on one], she brings him to ruin. She makes herself beautiful; she arrays herself; she is haughty. She appears like a flower, looks gaudy, arrays herself gaudily; she views herself in a mirror — carries a mirror in her hand. She bathes; she takes a sweat bath; she washes herself; she anoints herself with *axin* — constantly anoints herself with *axin*.[1] She lives like a bathed slave,[2] acts like a sacrificial victim; she goes about with her head high — rude, drunk,[3] shameless — eating mushrooms. She paints her face, variously paints her face; her face is covered with rouge, her cheeks are colored, her teeth are darkened — rubbed with cochineal. [Half] of her hair falls loose, half is wound about her head.[4] She arranges her hair like horns.

She goes about haughtily, shamelessly — head high, vain, filthy, given to pleasure. She lives in vice.

---

1. *Acad. Hist. MS: maxpetzoa.*
2. *Ibid.: tlatlaatilnemi* and *moteumiccanênequi* are added.
3. *Ibid.: motlapavitinemi* is added.
4. Cf. corresponding Spanish text.

Inic castolli capitulo: intechpa tlatoa, in iuh tlatlamãtiticate in cioatlaueliloque

AUIANI, AUILNENQUI:

in auiiani, ca cioatlaueliloc, inacaio ic mauiltiani, nacanamacac, nanacanamacac, ichpuchtlaueliloc, ilamatlaueliloc, tlaoanq̃, xocomicqui, tequixocomicqui, tequitlaoanqui, iellelacic, tlacamicqui, suchimicqui, tlaaltilli, teumicqui, teupoliuhqui, miccatzintli,

eltecuetlan, cuecuetol, cioacuecuel, cioacuecuech, cuecuetznemitl, ixtimalpol, topal topalala, xacan xacampa, ixnex tiacapan, xacampailama, iliuizmotecamacani, motetlatlaneuhtiani, cuicuixoch, ilamaioio, tzincuecuetzoc, tzincuecuetzoc ilama, capaxilama, tlahelpol, tlahelchichipol, motzcuinpoloani,

moiecoa, moioma, moquecinmachmati, caninmach quimati, queninmach momati, quipolotlali, moieiecquetza, moiecchichioa, mocecenmati, mosuchiquetza, motopalquetza, motopalchichioa, motezcauia, matezcauia, maltia, motema, mopapaca, maxpetzcoa, maxixipetzcoa, tlaaltilnemi, mosuchimiccanenequi, aquetztinemi, tlaxocotinemi miuintitinemi momixiuitinemi, monanacauitinemi, moxaoa, moxaxaoa, mixtlapaloatzaluia, mocacantlapaluia, motlamiaoa, motlannochezuia, itzon quiquequemi, mochicoaxtlaoa, motzotzõquaquauhtia,

mocuecueloa, cuecuetznemi, aquetztinemi, moquatlaztinemi, tlaelnemi, auilnemi, teuhtica tlaçoltica milacatzotinemi,

She perfumes herself, casts incense about her, uses rose water. She uses the *poyomatli* herb.[5] She chews chicle — she clacks chicle. She lives on the water — in the streets; she goes about disgracing the streets,[6] frequenting the market place, as if a part of the market place.

She promenades; she goes about pushing. She pushes; she insults; she goes about insulting; she goes about constantly merry, ever on the move, wandering here and there, never coming to repose, unquiet, restless, flighty. Her heart is constantly throbbing; she follows the wide road, goes the way of the rabbit, the deer.

She is a pretender, a fraud. She waves her hand at one, gestures with her head, makes eyes at one, closes one eye at one, winks, beckons with her head, summons with the hand, turns her face. She laughs — goes about laughing; she vomits — vomits constantly; she drinks wine; she is drunk — she constantly drinks wine. She is covetous; she becomes wealthy. She woos; she wishes to be coveted; she makes herself desirable. She goes about making a fool of one — deceiving one. She is importunate. She is a procuress; she goes about procuring, selling persons, providing prostitutes, corrupting others.

THE SCANDALOUS WOMAN

The scandalous woman is an adulteress, a practiser of adultery. [She merits] laughter, ridicule, sneers, mockery. She is nameless, fameless — [as if] dead, deceased. [She is] a bearer of bastards, an aborter. No one deals with her. She commits adultery; she practises adultery. She cheats, deceives, blinds [her husband].

THE HERMAPHRODITE

The hermaphrodite is a detestable woman, a woman who has a penis,[7] a [virile] arrow, testes; who takes female companions, female friends; who provides herself with young women, who has young women. She has man's body, man's build, man's speech. She goes about like a man. She is bearded, she has fine body hair, she has coarse body hair. She has carnal relations with other women; she takes female companions. She never desires a husband; she hates, detests men exceedingly; she scandalizes.

mopopochuia, miiiemotla mosuchialia, mopoiomauia, tzicquaqua, motzictlatlatza, apan upan nemi, utli quimatilitinemi, tlatianquiçoa, tianquiztli quiuiuiltectinemi,

mahantinemi, moquêquêçantinemi, moquêqueçana, tlaquequeloa, tlaquequelotinemi, papactinenemi, auic iauh, auic iâtinemi atzintlaltechpachiui, tzinquauhquechiloc, iollocholotica, cholotoc, iollotetecuicatica, quitoca in patlaoac vtli, in tochin maçatl iiuui,

ixtimal, ixtimalpol, temaneloa, teixnotza, teicopiluia, teixcapitzuia, teixcapitzaluia, teixtlaxilia, temanotza, mixtlaça, uetzca, uetzcatinemi, mosuchtia, mususuchtia, tlaoana, xocomiqui, tlatlaoana, motlanênequiltia, motlanenectia, motenectia, motenenectia, tetlanectia, teiztlacauitinemi, teca mocaiauhtinemi, tlauhchiuhtinemi, tetlanochilia, tetlanochilitinemi, tenamaca, tetzinnamaca, tetlaixcuepilia.

TETZAUHCIOATL:

in tetzauhcioatl, ca tetlaxinqui tepaniani, auilli camanalli, uetzquiztli, netopeoalli, aoc tle itoca, aoc tle itenio, omic, omomiquili, ichtacapiloa, motlatlaxiliani, açazce quimixnamictia, tetlaxima, tepan iauh, teixtzacutlaxilia, teixtzacupepechoa, teixpepechoa.

PATLACHE:

In patlache: ca tlahelcioatl, cioatl xipine tepule, choneoa, mioa, ateoa, mocioapotiani, mocioaicniuhtiani, mocicioapiltiani, cicioapile, oquichnacaio, oquichtlaque, ôoquichtlatoa, ôoquichnenemi, tetentzone, tomio, tzôtzoio, tepatlachuia, mocioaicniuhtia, aic monamictiznequi, cenca quincocolia aiel quimittaz in oquichti, tlatetzauia

---

5. Cf. *Florentine Codex*, Book XI, fol. 196*v*: *poiomasuchitl: iehoatl in jtecomaio cacaoasuchitl: qujtoa teiolcuep, teiolmalacachoa, teiollochololti....*

6. Read *quimamatilitinemi*, as in *Acad. Hist. MS.*

7. *Tepule, choneoa*: possibly synonymous; *choneoa* might be read *çoneua* (it erects).

THE PROCURESS; [THE WOMAN] WHO PROCURES

The procuress is verily a demon. [The devil] truly dwells within her, truly hides within her. Hers is truly the disguise of the demon of the air, of the devil. The deceiver is really the eyes, the ears — the messenger — of the devil, of the demon of the air.

This aforementioned one [is] a deceiver, a perverter, a provoker, a deranger, a corrupter, a destroyer of others. [She is] flowery of speech, gentle of words, mellifluous of speech; an agreeable talker, mild softspoken. Her language [is] delicate, sweet, pleasing. [She is] adroit, skilled in speech. [She is] a fraud who lulls one with words,[8] who wheedles. She entices one; [she is] a cajoler, a spell-casting robber,[9] ...,[10] who converses deceitfully, ruins by sorcery, performs trickery. She strings out lengthy discourses, converses deceitfully,[11] wheedles; she lulls one with words; she deranges, provokes, perverts, corrupts, mocks one; she induces one — induces one with deceit; she robs one by casting a spell; she cajoles one.

TETLANOCHILI, TETLANOCHILIANI:

in tetlanochili, ca uel tlacateculotl, ca uel iitic nemi, uel quimonaoaltia, uel inaoal in tzitzimitl, in coleletli, in teiztlacauiani, uel iix, uel inacaz, uel ititlan in diablo, in tzitzimitl.

Inin tlanotzqui: teiztlacauiani, teiolcuepani, teiollochololtiani, teiolmalacachoani, tetlacuepiliani, teioltzicuinalti, tensuchitl, camasuchitl, camasuchiecacal, tenuelic, tlatoluelic, tlatoliamanqui, suchitl uelic auiiac itlatol, camatoltecatl, tentoltecatl, tentlamatini, tetencoxouiani tetensuchitzotzonani, tecoconauia, tecochtecani, tecochtlacani, tetamooalchalpoloani, tenaoalnotzani, tenaoalpoloani, tetlanaoaltequiliani, hecamecatl quiteca: tenaoaltza, tetensuchitzotzona, tetencoxouia, teiolmalacachoa, teiollochololtia, teiolcuepa, tetlacuepilia, teca mocacaiaoa, tecoconauia, tenaoalcoconauia, tecochtlaça, tecochteca.

---

8. Read *tetencoçouiani*.

9. *Acad. Hist. MS: tecochtlaçani*.

10. Perhaps to be read *tetenaualchalpoloani*.

11. *Acad. Hist. MS: tenavalnotza*.

Sixteenth Chapter, which telleth of gainers of livelihoods such as the merchants.

THE MERCHANT[1]

The merchant [is] a vendor, a seller, a practiser of commerce, a watcher of the market place. He watches the market place; [he is] a watcher of merchandise in the market place.

The good merchant [is] a maker of profits, a securer of increase, a multiplier [of his possessions] — one who holds fast [to the profits. He is] a straightforward dealer, honest, reliable. He is god-fearing, devout. He negotiates contracts, he makes agreements, he helps others.

The bad merchant [is] a deceiver, a conspirer, a confusing dealer, a liar, an ignorer of others, a practiser of trickery, an illicit trafficker. He tricks others, practises usury, demands excessive interest.

THE SLAVE DEALER, THE BATHER OF SLAVES

The bather of slaves [is] a leading merchant. He excels [all others]; his wealth[2] is [as] possessor of slaves. He is rich — rich in possessions. [He is] acknowledged by our lord — a friend of our lord.

The good bather of slaves [is] a conserver of his resources, a guardian of his assets, a caretaker; a devout man, admiring, grateful [to our lord]. He takes the top, the lead in merchantry. He conserves his resources; he admires, he is devoted [to our lord].

The bad bather of slaves [is] rapacious, predaceous; prodigal, wasteful, . . . He squanders his possessions; he dissipates, he wastes his possessions. . . . He is self-indulgent, avaricious, stingy.

THE HEAD MERCHANT, THE PRINCIPAL MERCHANT IN FOREIGN PARTS, THE DISTINGUISHED TRADER

The head merchant — and the other titles — is a ruler of merchandising, of trading; a leader of merchants, a ruling merchant. He governs merchandising; he directs trading; [he is as] the mother, the father of merchantry.

Inic caxtolli oce capitulo: intechpa tlatoa, in motlaiecoltiani, in iuhque puchteca

PUCHTECATL:

in puchtecatl, ca tlanamacani, tiamiquini, tianquiçoani, tianquiço, tlatianquiçoani.

In qualli puchtecatl tlaixtlapanani, tlamixiuitiani, tlapiloatiani, molpiliani, melaoacatlatoani, tlatolmelaoac, melaoac in iiollo, teuimacaci, teutl in iiollo, tlanamaca, tlatennonotza, tlatentotoca, tenanamiqui.

In amo qualli puchtecatl: teca mocaiaoani, tlatentotocani, tlatenpâpatlani, iztlacatini, motexictiani, texicoani, tepoiouiani, texixicoa, tlaixtlapana tetech tlamieccaquistia.

TECOANI, TEALTIANI:

in tealtiani, puchtecaiacatl, tlapanauia, tlacaoa, in innecuiltonol, mocuiltonoa, motlamachtia, totecuio itlaiximach, totecuio iicniuh.

In qualli tealtiani: molpiliani, tlapachoani, tlapiani, tlateumatini, tlamauiçoani, tlatlaçocamatini, quimiiaoaiotia, quiiacapitzaoa, in puchtecaiotl, molpilia, tlamauiçoa tlateumati.

In amo qualli tealtiani, mapach, mapachpol: macpalcocoioc, macpalcocoiocpol. cioapaiatl, cioapaiapol, tlaauilquixtia, tlaauilicitta, tlaauilpoloa, tlatollantilia, mocnauia, tlatlameti, tzotzocati.

PUCHTECATZINTLI PUCHTECA TLAILOTLAC, ACXOTECA.

In puchtecatzintli ioan in oc cequi tocaitl: ca puchtla, ca puchtecapan, acxotla tecutli tlato, puchtecaiacatl, puchtecatlatoani, puchtlan tlapachoa, acxotlan tlatoa, puchtlan tenan, teta.

---

1. Cf. chap. xii, *supra*.
2. Read *inecuiltonol*.

The good ruler of merchandising, of trading [is] the real mother, the real father of the common people. [He is] a protector, a shelter, a refuge; a place of shelter,[3] a place of refuge. He becomes a mother, a father; he is made a mother, a father; he is respected, venerated; he becomes a leader, a peer; he becomes a governor in merchantry. He consigns, he entrusts wares to others. Wares are consigned, marketed,[4] sold. He is obeyed. He supervises, manages, governs; he bestows, he extends his exhortations; he extends his motherliness, his fatherliness; he castigates.

The bad ruler of merchants [is] importunate, demanding, unreliable, negligent. He hides, he conceals motherliness [and] fatherliness.

The vanguard merchant

The vanguard merchant is a merchant, a traveler, a transporter of wares, a wayfarer, a man who travels with his wares.

The good vanguard merchant [is] observing, discerning. He knows the road, he recognizes the road; he seeks out the various places for resting, he searches for the places for sleeping, the places for eating, the places for breaking one's fast. He looks to, prepares, finds his travel rations.

The bad vanguard merchant [is] uncouth, crude, rude, dull. He goes to no purpose when he goes; he travels the road to no purpose.[5] Obstinate, impetuous, blind, ignorant of the road, he is unobserving, careless. He encounters the gorges, the cliffs; he leads people into the forests, the grass lands; he plunges them into thickets.

The seller of green stones; the man [with] the basket

The seller of green stones is a lapidary, a polisher — a man who rubs [green stones] with a piece of fine cane, who makes them shine; who abrades them — thins them.

The good seller of green stones is of experience, of great wisdom. He sells the different stones — fine turquoise; green stones; emerald-green jade; blue obsidian; the very smoky fine turquoise; the transparent, the herb-green, the deep green jewels of green stone. He sells, he deals in jet, in pearls, in opals. He finds, he identifies all the different precious stones,

In qualli puchtla acxotla tecutli tlato: uel tena, uel teta, aaze, cuitlapile, cuexane, teputze, mamaloace, puchotl, aueuetl, ceoallo, iecauhio, iceoallotitlan, iiecauhiotitlan, calacoa, nanchioalo, tachioalo, nenantilo, netatilo, iixco iicpac tlachialo, acouic tlalchiuic itto, tlaiacatia, tlamiiaoaiotia in puchtla, petlati icpalti, tetlatquitia, tetech tlapiloa, tlatquilolo, tianquililo, tlanamaquililo, tlacamacho, tenotza, tetzatzitia, tepachoa, itlatol concauhtoc contlaztoc, inaio, itaio contlaztoc, alcecec, tzitzicaztli quauitl tetl quicaoa.

In amo qualli puchtecatlato: tlauhchioani, tlamatatacani, tlaxiccaoani, tlacochcaoani, quinaia, quitlatia in naiutl in taiutl.

Oztomecatl:

in oztomecatl, ca puchtecatl, nenemini, tlaotlatoctiani, nenenqui, tlanenemitiani.

In qualli oztomecatl tlaixtlaxiliani, tlaixuiani, ômati, ûiximati, quixtlaxilia in cecen neceuiliztli, quixtlaxilia in cochioaia, in tlaqualoia, in netlacauiloia, quixtlaxilia quimati, quipantilia in itacatl.

In amo qualli oztomecatl: tenitl, otomitl, tompotla, tlacanexquimilli, ça ça ie iauh in ie iauh, ca çan ie utlatoca, motequitlaçani, motequimaiauini, ixpopoiotl, aûiximati, atlaixtlaxilia, atlaixieiecoa, atlauhtli, texcalli quinamiqui, quimottitia, quauhtla çacatla calaqui, quauixmatlati.

Chalchiuhnamacac, tanapã tlacatl.

In chalchiuhnamacac ca tlatecqui, tlapetlaoani, tlaquetzalotlauiani, tlaiottouiani tlachiquini, tlacanaoani.

In qualli chalchiuhnamacac: ca tlaiximatini, tlâtocâmatini, nepapan tetl in quinamaca, in teuxiuitl, in chalchiuitl, in quetzalitztli, in matlalitztli, in uel popoca teuxiuitl, in atic in quiltic, in xopaleoac, chalchiuhtli maquiztli, quinamaca quitenamaquiltia, in teutetl in epiollotli, in uitzitziltetl muchi quitta, muchi quiximati, in nepapan tlaçotetl in maquiztetl, qui-

3. Cf. *supra*, Chap. 3, n. 3.

4. *Acad. Hist. MS: tlatquililo, tianquilo.*

5. For *ca çan*, read *ça çan*, as in *Acad. Hist. MS.*

the jewels. He seeks out stones such as the clear, the very green, the transparent, the common ones. He assesses them as to their properties.[6]

The bad seller of green stones [is] a deceiver, vindictive, deluding — one who treats the surface of stones, who [fraudulently] embellishes stones. The damaged stones, those of common rock, the worthless ones he increases in price, declares to be costly. He wheedles; he deceives with words.

The seller of cast metal objects, of necklaces, of bracelets, of golden bracelets

The seller of cast metal objects is a possessor of gold.

The good seller of cast metal objects [is] respectful, venerating; a man who adjusts,[7] who accommodates the price. [He is] god-fearing. He sells shield-shaped necklaces, shrimp necklaces, golden bracelets.

The bad seller of cast metal objects, the [bad] possessor of gold [is] a deceiver — a man who shines up, who rubs an unguent over — who cleans up — the metals. He deceives; he deludes; he is vindictive; he blinds; he dulls. He haggles; he becomes insistent, importunate.

The feather seller

The feather seller is a feather worker, a merchant — the man [with] the basket.

The good feather seller [is] a gentle worker — one who esteems [his wares], who is dedicated. He sells various feathers — precious feathers; he sells fine green feathers,[8] chili-green feathers, those curved at the tip, the feathers of young birds. He sells [feathers] of the trogonorus, the troupial,[9] the blue cotinga.[10]

The bad feather worker [is] a [fraudulent] embellisher of feathers, a treater of feathers with glue.[11] He sells old, worn feathers, damaged feathers. He dyes feathers; he dyes those which are faded, dirty, yellow, darkened, smoked.

The exchange dealer, the dealer in gold

The exchange dealer is a merchant. He owns possessions, goods, gold.[12]

---

pantilia in iuh chipaoac, in iuh xopaleoac, in iuh atic tetl, in aquen nezqui quipantilia in iuh ihiio.

In amo qualli chalchiuhnamacac: teca mocaiaoani, tetlaixcuepiliani, teixcuepani, teixchioani, techichiuhqui, tepopoiutl, in ça çan ie tetl, in atle inecoca quichamaoa, quiuueitzatzitia, tetensuchitzotzona tlatencoxouia

Tlapitzalnamacac: cozcanamacac, macuexnamacac, teucuitlamacuexnamacac.

In tlapitzalnamacac, ca teucuitlaoa.

In qualli tlapitzalnamacac, teimacazqui, tlaimacazqui, tlapototiani, tlanamictiani in patiuhtli teuimacaci: chimalcozcatl, chacalcozcatl, teucuitlamacuextli, quinamaca

In amo qualli tlapitzalnamacac in teucuitlaoa, teca mocaiaoani, tlatlaoiotiani, tlaoçani tlaaltiani, teca mocaiaoa teixcuepa, tetlacuepilia, tepoiouia, teotonchioa, tlatennonotza motenquauhtilia amo tenaquillani.

Ihuinamacac:

in ihuinamacac: ca amantecatl, ca puchtecatl, tanapan tlacatl.

In qualli ihuinamacac: tlamaluiani, tlatlaçotlani, tlacēmatini, quinamaca in nepapan ihuitl, in tlaçoihuitl, quinamaca in quetzalli in chilchotic, in tzicoliuhqui in pilihuitl quinamaca in tzinitzcan, in çaquauh, in tziuhtli.

In amo qualli amantecatl: ihuichichiuhqui, ihuicalo, iuiçolli, ihuipalaxtli in quinamaca, ihuipâ, in quipa ticectic, cuitlanextic iztalectic, cuichectic, pocheoac.

Tlapatlac, teucuitlapatlac:

in tlapatlac ca puchtecatl, tlatquioa, axcaoa, teucuitle.

---

6. Cf. gloss in *Acad. Hist. MS* — *la virtud q̃ tiene.*

7. *Ibid.*: *tlapótiani.*

8. Cf. corresponding Spanish text. In *Florentine Codex*, Book XI, fol. 58v, different places on the wing are associated.

9. *Acad. Hist. MS*: *çaqua.*

10. Read *xiuhtototl*. In these terms we follow Dibble and Anderson, *op. cit.*, Book IX, *passim*. The *Florentine Codex*, *loc. cit. et sqq.*, however, identifies *tzinitzcan* as head or wing feathers.

11. *Acad. Hist. MS*: *ỹviçaçalo.*

12. *Ibid.*: *yztac teucuitle, coztic teucuitle* follow *teucuitle.*

The good exchange dealer [is] successful, sensitive. When silver coins are exchanged . . . , he is just; he gives very even weight; he does not withhold — rather, he gives good measure.

The bad exchange dealer [is] an ignorer of others, a practiser of trickery, a covetous man. He is ever desiring, ever covetous. He seizes things forcibly. He is a confusing dealer, a conspirer.

In qualli tlapatlac: çan tlaipantiliani, moiolitlacoani, in patililo tomines iztacatica, ca uel izqui, uel quinamictia in pesotli amo tle iloti, oc ie quioaltzontia

In amo qualli tlapatlac: motexixictiani, texixicoani, tematatacani, tetêtemachi, tematataca, tlatenquauhcui, tlatenpapatla, tlatentotoca.

ILLUSTRATIONS

meuh, cioatlaueliloc, cioa cueruel, cue cue toleioatl, ichpuchpil, ich puchtontli, quinuelicaton, uel ica cioatl, ichpuchtli, ichpuch= pol: ilama, ilamapol, ilanton, a uililama, anengui apan, apan nemini, atzintlaltechpachiui, v tli, quitotocatinemi, vtli quimama tiliti, tianguiz, quiuiu rectinemi, tianquiztli, quiuilo tinemi, vtli quiouocuelpachoti nemi, moiaoatinemi, remantine mi, acan chamitla, cacan uetzi, cacan cuchi, cacan tlatui, caque uetzi in iooalli, memilhuitl.

¶ Picienamacac: quinamaca picietl, xicotietl, tlalietl, quima xaqualoa: inaca quitta picietl, quiqua, Auh cequintin iztauhiatl inquipicie poa inpicietl tetech quiz, teiuinti, tetla remouilli, te ciauiz popolo.

¶ El que vende picicte mue le primero las hojas del mezela dolas con vna poca de cal, yan si mezclado, estregalo muy bien entre las manos. hazelinos hazen lo de el axenxo de la tie ra. y puesto en la boca haze desuanecer la cabeça, o emborra cha: haze tambien dizir lo co mjdo, y haze prouecho para qui tar el cansancio.

Capitulo veinte y sie te de todos los mjembros exteriores, e interio

Inic cempoalli onchicome capitulo: intechpa tlatoa incuitlaxculli, ioan inix

Page from *Florentine Codex* (Chapters 26–27)

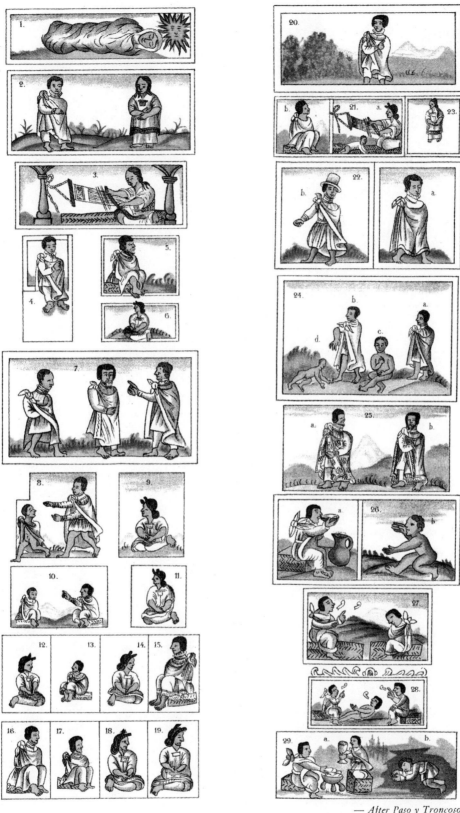

— *After Paso y Troncoso*

1. The bad, lazy mother (Chapter 1). 2. The humble child (Chapter 1). 3. The well-taught daughter (Chapter 1). 4. The bad son (Chapter 1). 5. The bad uncle (Chapter 1). 6. The good aunt (Chapter 1). 7. The good nephews (Chapter 1). 8. The evil nephew (Chapter 1). 9. the good grandmother (Chapter 1). 10. The good great-grandfather (Chapter 1). 11. The good great-grandmother (Chapter 1). 12. The mother-in-law (Chapter 2). 13. The son-in-law (Chapter 2). 14. The daughter-in-law (Chapter 2). 15. The older brother (Chapter 2). 16. The old man (Chapter 3). 17. The bad old man (Chapter 3). 18. The old woman (Chapter 3). 19. The bad old woman (Chapter 3). 20. The noble man of middle age (Chapter 3). 21. The middle-aged woman (Chapter 3). 22. The youth (Chapter 3). 23. The maiden (Chapter 3). 24. Boy, infant, child (Chapter 3). 25. The bad noble (Chapter 4). 26. The drinker (Chapter 5). 27. The well-instructed noble (Chapter 5). 28. The bad noble (Chapter 5). 29. One who enters caves (Chapter 5).

30. The noble child (Chapter 5). 31. The bad shorn one (Chapter 6). 32. One who leads others into danger (Chapter 6). 33. The goldcaster (Chapter 7). 34. The copper finisher (Chapter 7). 35, 36. The lapidary (Chapter 7). 37, 38. The carpenter (Chapter 8). 39. The carpenter (Chapter 8). 40. The stone cutter (Chapter 8). 41. The mason with plumb (Chapter 8). 42. The mason (Chapter 8). 43. The singer (Chapter 8).

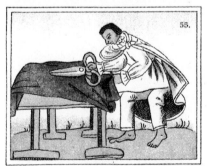

— *After Paso y Troncoso*

44. The wise man (Chapter 8). 45. The physician (Chapter 8). 46. The bad physician (Chapter 8). 47. The sorcerer (Chapter 9). 48. The bad sorcerer (Chapter 9). 49. The possessed one (Chapter 9). 50. One who turns himself into a dog, etc. (Chapter 9). 51. The good attorney (Chapter 9). 52. The bad attorney (Chapter 9). 53. The good solicitor (Chapter 9). 54. The bad solicitor (Chapter 9). 55. The tailor (Chapter 10).

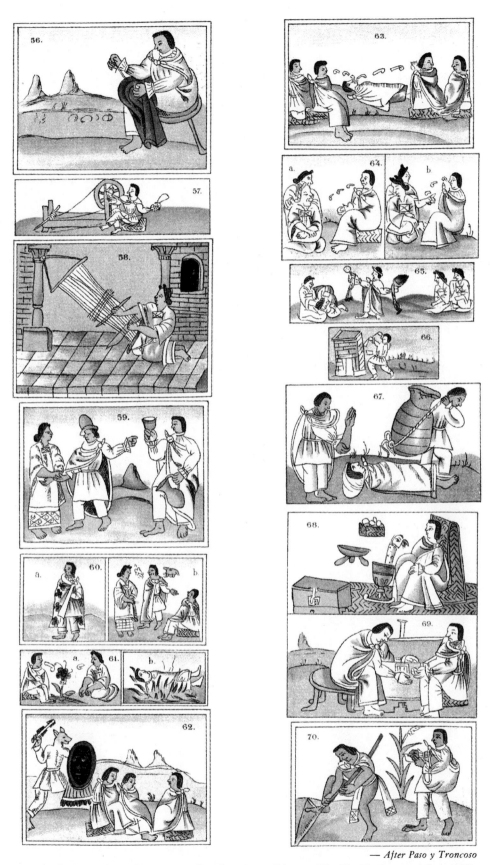

56. The bad tailor (Chapter 10). 57. The spinner (Chapter 10). 58. The weaver (Chapter 10). 59. The lewd youth (Chapter 11). 60. The procurer (Chapter 11). 61. The sodomite (Chapter 11). 62. The murderer (Chapter 11). 63. The traitor (Chapter 11). 64. The story teller (Chapter 11). 65. The buffoon (Chapter 11). 66. The thief (Chapter 11). 67. The dancer with a dead woman's forearm (Chapter 11). 68. The good rich man (Chapter 12). 69. The evil rich man (Chapter 12). 70. The good farmer (Chapter 12).

71. The bad farmer (Chapter 12). 72. The horticulturist (Chapter 12). 73. The good horticulturist (Chapter 12). 74, 75. The merchant (Chapter 12). 76–79. The noblewoman (Chapter 13). 80–89. The noblewoman (Chapter 13).

— *After Paso y Troncoso*

90–98. The noblewoman (Chapter 13). 99. The noblewoman (Chapter 13). 100. The common woman (Chapter 14). 101. The evil robust woman (Chapter 14). 102. The mature woman (Chapter 14). 103. The bad mature woman (Chapter 14). 104. The weaver of designs (Chapter 14). 105, 106. The cook (Chapter 14). 107. The harlot (Chapter 15).

— *After Paso y Troncoso*

108, 109. The harlot (Chapter 15). 110. The hermaphrodite (Chapter 15). 111. The procuress (Chapter 15). 112. The merchant (Chapter 16). 113. The bather of slaves (Chapter 16). 114. The head merchant (Chapter 16). 115. The vanguard merchant (Chapter 16). 116. The seller of green stones (Chapter 16). 117. The seller of cast metal objects (Chapter 16). 118. The feather seller (Chapter 16). 119, 120. The cape seller (Chapter 17). 121. The cacao seller (Chapter 18). 122. The maize seller (Chapter 18). 123. The bean seller (Chapter 18).

After Paso y Troncoso

124. The amaranth seed seller (Chapter 18). 125. The chili seller (Chapter 18). 126. The seller of gourd seeds (Chapter 18). 127. The seller of tamales (Chapter 19). 128. The wheat seller (Chapter 19). 129. The seller of coarse maguey fiber capes (Chapter 20). 130. The seller of palm leaf fiber capes (Chapter 20). 131. The paper seller (Chapter 21). 132. The fruit seller (Chapter 22). 133. The fisherman (Chapter 22). 134. The meat seller (Chapter 22). 135. The carpenter (Chapter 22). 136. The clay worker (Chapter 23). 137. The needle seller (Chapter 24). 138. The gathering of bitumen (Chapter 24).

139. The chicle chewer (Chapter 24). 140. *Axin* as medicine (Chapter 24). 141. The candle seller (Chapter 25). 142. The herb seller (Chapter 25). 143. The atole seller (Chapter 26). 144. The seller of fine chocolate; the salt seller (Chapter 26). 145. The chalk and limestone seller (Chapter 26). 146. The procuress (Chapter 26). 147. The prostitute (Chapter 26). 148. The tobacco seller (Chapter 26).

— *After Paso y Troncoso*

149–154. Parts of the body (Chapter 27). 155. Eye pains (Chapter 28). 156. Opacity of the eyes (Chapter 28). 157. The snuffles (Chapter 28). 158. The laceration of a lip (Chapter 28). 159. Sore lips (Chapter 28). 160. Tooth infection (Chapter 28). 161. The cleaning of the teeth (Chapter 28). 162. Swelling of the throat (Chapter 28). 163. Abscesses on the neck (Chapter 28). 164. Coughing (Chapter 28). 165, 166. Ailments of nursing women (Chapter 28). 167. Jigger fleas (Chapter 28).

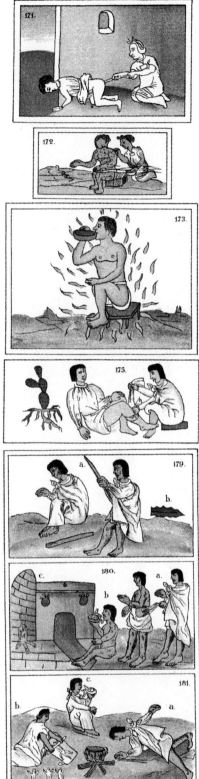

— *After Paso y Troncoso*

168. Jigger fleas (Chapter 28). 169. A constant cough (Chapter 28). 170. A bloody flux (Chapter 28). 171. Hemorrhoids (Chapter 28). 172. Pustules (Chapter 28). 173. Fever (Chapter 28). 174. Burns, cuts (Chapter 28). 175. A broken leg (Chapter 28). 176. A broken leg (Chapter 28). 177. A wrenched neck (Chapter 28). 178. A head wound (Chapter 28). 179. A club stroke (Chapter 28). 180. A lash stroke (Chapter 28). 181. A fall (Chapter 28).

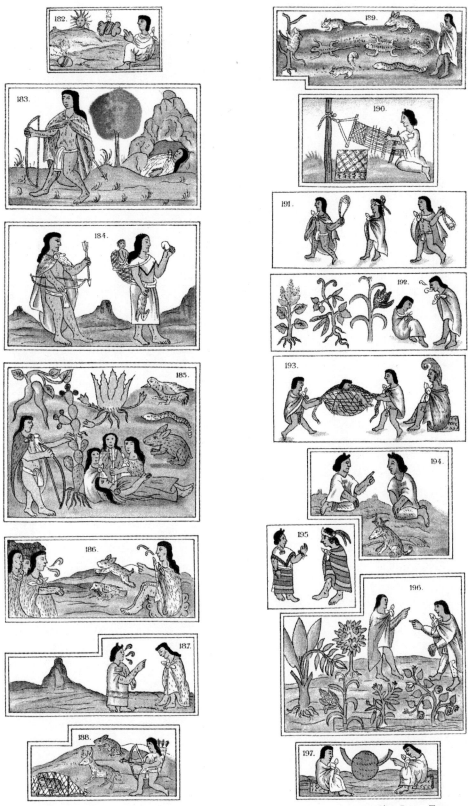

— *After Paso y Troncoso*

182. The finding of precious stones (Chapter 29). 183, 184. The Teochichimeca (Chapter 29). 185. The death of the aged (Chapter 29). 186, 187. The Otomí (Chapter 29). 188. Food of the Otomí (Chapter 29). 189. Food of the Otomí (Chapter 29). 190. The Otomí weaver (Chapter 29). 191. The Quaquata (Chapter 29). 192. The bewitching of people (Chapter 29). 193. Crushing with a net (Chapter 29). 194. The Maçauaque (Chapter 29). 195. The Totonaca (Chapter 29). 196. The Tlalhuica (Chapter 29). 197. The Tenime (Chapter 29).

Seventeenth Chapter, which telleth of the cape sellers, the people with the capes.

THE MAN WITH THE CAPES

The man with the capes is a seller of large cotton capes: one who sells them in single lots, who offers them separately; an importer, a distributor.

The good seller of large cotton capes [is] just, honest, respectful, reverent. He sells, trades, negotiates fairly. He sells the one which is good, new, strong, firm, like tough grass; thick, thin, loose-woven, smooth, sleek; of coarse thread, wide, long, dense.

The bad seller of large cotton capes [is] unconsidering — a man of little worth: bad, uncoöperative, deceiving, lying. He praises, — he wheedles one; he haggles; he strikes a bargain with one, is verbose, belittles, importunes.

He sells spoiled large cotton capes — rotten ones; spoiled capes — spurious ones, patched, smoothed, darned, falsified by sewing, treated with maize dough, washed — washed with ashes, dressed with ashes, pounded, beaten, treated with an adhesive, with [thick] atole, with ground tortillas; of loose weave, sparse, badly woven, coarse, pierced by [burnishing] stones; narrow, small, short — [like] little handbags; made of cotton waste. [He sells] capes of little value, ordinary large cotton capes; finally, at the very last follow large cotton capes of little value.

THE PRINCIPAL MERCHANT

The principal merchant is a retailer, a seller of worked capes. He sells, he finds pleasure in worked shifts,[1] fine capes, fine shifts, fine skirts.

The good principal merchant [is] just, fair; he adjusts the price. In order to deal, he seeks out that which he sells: the fresh, the new, the good, the strong, the designed — designed capes, capes to be worn; those of a weave not compressed; those of a ball-court eagle design, those with a sun design on them — provided with suns; ocelot capes — the oce-

Inic castolli omome capitulo: intechpa tlatoa, in tilmanamacaque, in tilmapan tlaca.

TILMAPAN TLACATL:

in tilmapan tlacatl, ca quachnamacac, tlacemanqui, tlacemanani, tlaquixtiani, motlaquixtiliani.

In qualli quachnamacac, melaoac, melaoacaiollo, tlamauhcaittani, tlaimacacini, yuiia, iocuxca tlanamaca, tlanamictia, tlaipantilia: in quinamaca ie in qualli, in iancuic, chicaoac, tlalichtic, xomaltic, tilaoac: canaoac, atic, xipetztic, xipetziuhqui, tetzictic, patlaoac, ueiac, tlatztic.

In amo qualli quachnamacac: iliuiztlacatl, çan molhui tlacatl, tlaueliloc, teca moquauitequini, teca mocaiaoani: iztlacatini, tetentlanenectia: tetensuchitzotzona, tlatenquauhcui, tlatennonotza, tlatentotoca, tetempapatla, tlaxixiuhtlatia.

In quinamaca quachpalan, quachpalaxtli, tilmapalan, tlachichioalli, tlachichitl, tlaixtectli, tlaixaquilli, tlapiquitzõtli, tlatexuilli, tlapactli, tlanextlatilli, tlanexquaqualatzalli, tlateuilli, tlatepitzinilli, tlatzacuuilli, atollo, tlaxcallo, tlaxcalaio, poxatic, caciltic, cacaciltic: tlatepepetlalli, tlatecocoionilli, pitzato, tepiton, titichtontli, titichpil, chitictontli, ichcacuitlaio, çan molhui tilmatli, çaçan ie õchtli quitzacuia, quicentzacuia, tlatoquilia, çan molhui quachtli.

VEICAPAN TLACATL:

in ueicapan tlacatl, ca tlanecuilo, tlâmâchtilmanamacac, tlamachuipile, mimatcatilmatli, mimatcauipilli, mimatcacueitl, in quinamaca, in quimauiltia.

In qualli veicapan tlacatl: tlacamelaoac, melaoacatlacatl, tlananamictia, inic tlanamaca, quipantilia in quinamaca, ioltica, iancuic, qualli, chicaoac, tlamachio, tlamachtilmatli: apantilmatli, tlâcouitecqui, tlachquauhio, tonatiuh onmani, tôtonatiuhio, ocelotilmatli, ocelutl, quauhtli onicac, îhuimoiaoac, tetemalacaio, suchimoiaoac, suchiteteio, susuchiteio, co-

---

1. Read *tlamachuipilli;* otherwise, the translation could be, "[he is] an owner of worked shifts."

lot, the eagle stand thereon; those with a design of scattered feathers, a design of stone discs, a scattered flower design; with flowered borders — with flowers on the border; with serpent mask designs; those painted with bloodied faces; those with a curved labret, with head pendants extending; carmine-colored capes, red capes, those with yellow flower designs; capes with the blowgun design — those with the blowgun design with flowers; netted capes, scorpion-colored netted capes; those having a border, having a trimming, having red eyelets — bordered with eyes; having fluffed, frayed borders, rolled seams, fringed borders.

The bad principal merchant is quite detested. Incorrigible, acting without consideration, he deceives the people, lies,[2] praises his wares. Those he sells are washed, renovated with ashes — old capes dressed with ashes, boiled in water; old capes, old skirts, old shifts,[3] old strips of cloth, burnished. He is full of affliction. He has little concern for capes; he has no capes. [They are] pounded, beaten, burnished — burnished with pottery, with a bone; dyed with [false] colors, added [false] colors. [For] skirts, shifts, capes he sells renovated strips of cloth raveled of end, false of sewing, mended, [false] of design, [false] of pattern.

oaxaiacaio, ixnextlacuilollo, tezçacanecuillo, tlalpiloni ontemi, nochpaltilmatli, tlauhtilmatli, suchpallasuchio, tlâcaloaztilmatli, tlacaloaz tlasuchio, tlalpilli, colotlalpilli, tenê, tlatentilli, tenchilnaoaio, tenixio, tenmolonqui, tenpoçõqui, têmimiliuhqui, tenchapanqui.

In amo qualli ueicapan tlacatl: çan niman atlamauhcaittac, âtlaimacazqui, tlailiuizuiani, uel teca mocacaiaoan iztlacati, tlachamaoa: in quinamaca tlapactli, tlanextlatilli, tlanexquaqualatzalli, tlaatlancuicatilli, tilmaçolli, cueçolli, vipilcolli canacçolli, tioa, oellelacic, aoc quimati tilmatli, aocac itilma, tlateuilli, tlatepitzinilli, tlapetzolli, tlaxicaluilli, tlaomiuilli, tlatlâtlapalhuilli, tlatlatlapalaquilli: in quinamaca cueitl, uipilli, tilmatli, canaoac, tlachichitl, tlatenquatonolli, tlatlapiquitzontli, tlatlamamanililli, tlatlatlâmachiotilli, tlatlâmachilli.

2. *Acad. Hist. MS: vel teca mocâcayava. iztlacati.*
3. Read *vipilçolli.*

Eighteenth[1] Chapter, which telleth of the cacao sellers and of those who sell grains of maize [and] dried beans.

THE CACAO SELLER, THE CACAO DEALER

The cacao seller [is] a cacao owner, an owner of cacao fields, an owner of cacao trees; or an importer, a traveler with merchandise, a traveler or retailer who sells in single lots.

The good cacao seller sells [cacao beans which are] developed, full, round — each one round; firm; each kind selected, chosen. He sells, he seeks out each kind separately. Separately, in one place, he sells the developed, the firm ones; separately the shrunken, the hollow, the broken, the shattered; separately the powdered cacao, the dust; separately the small beans like chili seeds from Tochtepec; those from Anauac separately, those from Guatemala separately, those from Coatolco separately, those from Xolteca; he sells those from Çacatollan separately — the whitish, the green, the varicolored.[2]

The bad cacao seller, [the bad] cacao dealer, the deluder counterfeits cacao. He sells cacao beans which are placed in [hot] ashes, toasted, made full in the fire;[3] he counterfeits by making the fresh cacao beans whitish; he places them in [hot] ashes — stirs them into the [hot] ashes; [then] he treats them with chalk, with chalky earth, with [wet] earth; he stirs them into [wet] earth. [With] amaranth seed dough, wax, avocado pits he counterfeits cacao; he covers this over with cacao bean hulls; he places this in the cacao bean shells. The whitish, the fresh cacao beans he intermixes, mingles, throws in, introduces, ruins with the shrunken, the chili-seed-like, the broken, the hollow, the tiny. Indeed he casts, he throws in with them wild cacao[4] beans to deceive the people.

THE SELLER OF MAIZE GRAINS

The seller of maize grains [is] a worker of the fields, a worker of the land, or a retailer.

Inic matlactli onchicuei capitulo: itechpa tlatoa, in cacaoanamacaque, ioan in tlaolli, in etl quinamaca

CACAOANAMACAC, CACAOANANAUHQUI:

in cacaoanamacac, cacaoaoa, cacaoamile, cacaoaquaue, anoço oztomecatl, tlaotlatoctiani, tlanênemiti, anoço tlanecuilo, tlacemanqui.

In qualli cacaoanamacac: in quinamaca chamaoac, tomaoac, tolontic, totolontic, tepitztic, tlacenquixtilli, tlapepentli, nononqua, tlanamaca, tlaihipantilia, nonquâ ceccan quinamaca in chamaoac in tepitztic, nonqua in patzaoac in cacaltic, in xamanqui, in xaxamanqui, nonqua in cacaoatlalli, in teuhtic, nonqua in tochtepecaiutl in chilacachtic, nonqua in anaoacaiutl, nonqua in quauhtemaltecaiutl, nonqua in coatolcaiutl, xolotecaiutl, nonqua quinamaca in çacatoltecaiutl, in ticeoac, in xoxouhqui, in suchicacaoatl.

In tlaueliloc cacaoanamacac: cacaoananauhqui, teixcuepani, cacaoachichiuh In quinamaca cacaoatl tlanexquetzalli, tlâcectli, tlatletomaoalli, quiticeoacatlapiquia, in xoxouhqui, quinexuia, quinexpopoxoa, quiticauia, quitlalticauia, quitlaluia, quitlalpopoxoa, tzooalli, xicocuitlatl, aoacaiollotli, quicacaoatlapiquia, cacaoaxipeoallotl ic quiquimiloa, cacaoacacalotl conaaquia, in ticeoac in xoxouhqui, in patzaoac, in chilacachtic, in xamanqui, in cacaltic, in quimichnacaztic, quicenneloa, quicepanneloa, quimotlaltia, itlan caquia, quicepanmictia, nel quappatlachtli itlã quitlaça, quimotlaltia, inic teca mocaiaoa.

TLAOLNAMACAC:

in tlaolnamacac, milchiuhqui, tlalchiuhqui, anoço tlanecuilo.

---

1. Normally, *inic caxtolli omei.*

2. Cf. Sahagun (Garibay ed.), I, p. 279.

3. *Acad. Hist. MS* adds *tlaatomavalli* — swollen with water.

4. Corresponding Spanish text: *"otras bastardas, que parecen ser tambien cacaos que tienen por nombre quauhpatlachtli."* Also cf. *infra,* chap. xxix, in discussion of the Olmeca.

The good seller of maize grains sells grains of maize [which are] clean, smooth, round, full, good, flawless, perfect, firm, hard; like a copper bell, like flint, like fruit pits.[5] Each [sort] he sells separately, he sells prudently; separately the white, the black, the varicolored; separately the soft, the yellow, the red. Each one separately he sells, that of Chalco, of the Matlatzinca, of Acolhuacan, of the people of the north desert lands;[6] that produced in the tropics — that of the Tlalhuica, of Tlaxcalla, of Michoacan, all ears of maize produced in the tropics. Separately he sells the soft, the spongy, the uneven. All he sells, he displays separately.

The bad seller of maize grains [is] verily uncoöperative, a deceiver. With the good grains of maize he stirs, tosses, throws in the infested, the hollow, the withered, the maize silk. He mixes in, he throws in the rotten maize grains. With that of the new harvest he mixes in, he throws in that of two years, of three years, of ten years — the moldy, the sour, the wormy, the weevil-infested. He tosses, he casts into it the mouse-gnawed maize, the maize shelled in the bin, the spoiled maize, the fetid, the bad, the stinking. The displeasing, the damaged he declares good, declares sound; he praises it; he makes it appealing, desirable to others. He places the good grains of maize over the spoiled grains — the swollen ones, enlarged in water. He sells them full of chaff, full of cobs.

THE BEAN SELLER

The bean seller is a bean owner. The good bean owner sells each kind of bean separately. Separately, in one place, he prices, sorts, selects the good beans, the new crop — the clean, the smooth, the round, the pellet-like, the very clean; the well-formed food, the so-called good bracelet, good green stone, good turquoise; that worth being stored, worth being put away in the bag, in the reed box, in the storage bin; the yellow beans, red beans, brown beans, white beans, small beans, whitish beans, small black beans, pinto beans, spotted beans, round yellow beans, large black beans, wild beans.

The bad bean seller never tells the truth; he always lies. [He is] a great liar, a congenital liar, a teller of falsehoods. He mixes the good, the precious with the spoiled, the infested beans.

In qualli tlaolnamacac: in quinamaca tlaolli, chipaoac, tetzcaltic, tolontic, tomaoac, qualli, atlê yiaioca acan ca, yiaioca, tepitztic, tlaquaoac, coioltic, tecpatic, xocollotic, tlanononquanamaca, tlaioiocanamaca, nonqua in iztac, iiauitl, in tlaolnenel, nonqua in poxaoac in coztic, in xiuhtoctli, nononqua quinamaca in chalcaiutl, in matlatzincaiutl, in aculoacaiutl, in teutlalpanecaiutl, in tonaiã muchioa, in tlaluicaiutl, in tlaxcaltecaiutl, in michoacaiutl, in ie ixquich tonaian muchioa, cintlaolli, nonqua in quinamaca in poxaoac in çonectic, in açotic muchi nonqua quinamaca, quinanamictia.

In tlaueliloc tlaolnamacac: uel teca moquauitequini, uel teca mocaiaoani. In qualli tlaolli quineloa, quiminaltia, quimotlaltia, in quaquâ, in cacaltic, in patzaoac, in tzontlaolli, quicenneloa, in tlaolpala, in amaneoa quicenneloa quimotlaltia, in õxiuhcaiutl, in exiuhcaiutl, in matlacxiuhcaiutl in puxcauhq̃ in xoiauhqui, in ocuillo, in iacatotoio quiminaltia, itla quitlaça in quimichtlaolli, in cuezcontlaolli, in tlaolpalaxtli, in tlaliiac, in cocoiac, in quipiiac, in aoc cemelle, in itlacauhqui, quiiequitoa, quiqualitoa, quichachamaoa, quitenectia, quiteeleuiltia, quisxotia, in qualli tlaolli, in tlaolpalaxtli, tlaolciaoalli, tlaatomaoalli, moca xoneoatl, moca olotl in quinamaca.

HENAMACAC.

In henamacac: ca eoâ. In qualli eoa, nononqua quinamaca in etl, nonqua ceccan quiteniotia quinamictia, quipanitia, in qualli etl in amaneoa, in chipactic, in tetzcaltic, in tolontic, in telolotic, in chipaccaltic, in uel quizqui tonacaiutl, in mitoa uel maquiztli, uel chalchiuitl, uel teuxiuitl, in tlâtiloni, in toptemaloni, in petlacaltemaloni, in cuezcomatemaloni, in ecoztli, in echichilli paletl, in iztaquetl, in epitzactli, in xaltetl, in quimichtetl, in ecuicuilli, in cuicuiletl, in ecoztapaiolli, in aiecotli, in quauecoc.

In tlaueliloc enamacac, aic nelli in quitoa, muchipa iztlacati, iztlacapul, iztlacamecapul, iztlaccoxocpul, in qualli in tlaçotetl, quineneloa, in epalaxtli, in quaqua.

---

5. *Acad. Hist. MS: xocoyollotic.*

6. Cf. Eduard Seler: *Gesammelte Abhandlungen zur Amerikanischen Sprach und Alterumskunde* (Berlin: Ascher und Co., 1902–23), VI, p. 267.

THE AMARANTH SEED[7] SELLER

The amaranth seed seller [is] an amaranth seed owner or a retailer. He sells the new crop, [or] he sells that which is two years old, three years old, etc. He sells *chicalotl*[8] [seeds], white amaranth seeds, bird amaranth seeds, bird-egg amaranth seeds, black amaranth seeds, grey amaranth seeds, colored amaranth seeds.

The bad amaranth seed seller sells the good seeds, [but] mixes in the spoiled amaranth seeds, the bitter amaranth seeds, the black, the red amaranth seeds, weed seeds, bird seeds.

The CHÍA SELLER is one who owns *chía.*

The *chía* seller sells white *chía,* blighted *chía,* the shriveled seeds, the shriveled *chía.*

The bad *chía* seller sells *chía,* [but] he throws in, he introduces weed seeds, chaff, the shriveled seeds.[9]

The CHILI SELLER [is] either . . . a worker of the fields, or a retailer. He sells mild red chilis,[10] broad chilis, hot green chilis,[11] yellow chilis, *cuitlachilli, tenpilchilli, chichioachilli.* He sells water chilis,[12] *conchilli;* he sells smoked chilis, small chilis,[13] tree chilis,[14] thin chilis, those like beetles. He sells hot chilis,[15] the early variety,[16] the hollow-based kind. He sells green chilis, sharp-pointed red chilis, a late variety,[17] those from Atzitziuacan, Tochmilco, Huaxtepec, Michoacan, Anauac, the Huaxteca, the Chichimeca. Separately he sells strings of chilis, chilis cooked in an olla, fish chilis, white fish chilis.[18]

VAUHNAMACAC:

in uauhnamacac, oâue, anoço tlanecuilo, quinamaca in amaneoa, quinamaca in oxiuhcaiutl in exiuhcaiutl, et.ª quinamaca in chicalotl, in iztac oauhtli, in totoloauhtli, in totolteoauhtli, in tezcaoauhtli, in cocotl, in nexoauhtli, in suchioauhtli.

In tlaueliloc oauhnamacac: in quinamaca in qualli, quicepanneloa in oauhpalaxtli, in chichic oauhtli in iacacolli, in iacatzotl, in polocatl, in petzicatl.

CHIENNAMACAC: ca chiane.

In chiennamacac, qujnamaca in iztac chiẽ, in aiauhchien, in coçolli, in chiencoçolli

In tlaueliloc chiannamacac: qujnamaca in chian, qujmotlaltia, itlan caquja in polocatl, in chianpolocatl, in coçolli.

CHILNAMACAC, aço colitli, mjlchiuhquj, anoço tlanecujlo, qujnamaca in texochilli in chilpatlaoac, in chilacatl, in chilcoztli, in cujtlachilli, in tenpilchilli, in chichioachilli: qujnamaca, in achilli, in côchilli, qujnamaca in pucheoac, in chiltecpin, in quauhchilli, in pitzaoac chilli, in temoltic, quinamaca in totocuitlatl chilli, in tzinquauhio, in tzincoionqui, quinamaca in chilchotl, in milchilli, in tonalchilli, in atzitzioa, in tochmilcaiutl, in oaxtepecaiutl, in michoacaiutl, in anaoacaiutl, in cuextecaiutl, in chichimecaiutl, nõqua quinamaca, in chilçolotl, in chilpaoaxtli, in chilmichi, in chilamilotl.

---

7. All varieties listed here are described and illustrated on fols. 251–252 of Book XI of the *Florentine Codex,* under the heading, "De los cenizos que comen estos naturales." *Chicalotl,* in this text, is the same as *michioauhtli,* and *cocotl* is the same as *nexoauhtli.*

Of these, Jonathan D. Sauer states: "The Indians themselves probably used the name *huauhtli* for a variety of plants, grown for different purposes. Some of the compound names may well have been restricted to particular species. *Xochihuauhtli* (flower *huauhtli*) may have meant a chenopod whose inflorescences were cooked in the bud stage as a green vegetable as is commonly done in modern Mexico. *Nexhuauhtli* (ash *huauhtli*), like the common Spanish word for chenopods, *cenizo,* probably referred to the whitish appearance of some chenopods. . . . *Michihuauhtli* (fish *huauhtli*) and *tezcahuauhtli* (mirror *huauhtli*) probably referred to light- and dark-seeded amaranths, respectively, the former with pale seeds like little fish eggs, the latter with shiny black seeds" ("The Grain Amaranths: A Survey of Their History and Classification," *Annals* of the Missouri Botanical Garden, XXXVII, November, 1950, p. 565).

8. *Chicalotl: Argemone mexicana* (Sahagún, Garibay ed., IV, p. 333), or *A. ochroleuca* Sweet. in Maxímino Martínez: *Las Plantas Medicinales de México* (México: Ediciones Botas, 1933), pp. 103sqq.

9. Corresponding Spanish text: "*las que son aparentes y dañadas, que se dizen polocatl, y coçolli, que sõ vnas semjllas, de que no se puede sacar oleo.*"

10. Francisco Hernández: *Historia de las Plantas de Nueva España* (México: Imprenta Universitaria, 1946), II, p. 432.

11. Francisco J. Santamaría: *Diccionario General de Americanismos* (Méjico: Editorial Pedro Robredo, 1942), I, p. 491.

12. Cf. *Florentine Codex,* Book XI, fol. 184r.

13. *C. frutescens* L. (Hernández, *op. cit.,* II, 435).

14. *Ibid.,* pp. 430, 435.

15. *Ibid.,* p. 431.

16. *Ibid.,* p. 432: "*se siembra en marzo.*"

17. *Loc. cit.*

18. Corresponding Spanish text may mean these in referring to some "*tocados del hielo.*"

The bad chili seller sells chili [which is] stinking, sharp to the taste, evil-smelling,[19] spoiled; waste from the chilis, late-formed chilis, chaff from the chilis. He sells chilis from wet country, incapable of burning, insipid to the taste; unformed, not yet firm, immature;[20] those which have formed as droplets, as buds.

THE TOMATO SELLER sells large tomatoes, small tomatoes,[21] leaf tomatoes, thin tomatoes, sweet tomatoes, large serpent tomatoes, nipple-shaped tomatoes, serpent tomatoes. Also he sells coyote tomatoes, sand tomatoes, those which are yellow, very yellow, quite yellow, red, very red, quite ruddy, ruddy, bright red, reddish, rosy dawn colored.

The bad tomato seller sells spoiled tomatoes, bruised tomatoes, those which cause diarrhea; the sour, the very sour. Also he sells the green, the hard ones, those which scratch one's throat, which disturb — trouble one; which make one's saliva smack, make one's saliva flow; the harsh ones, those which burn the throat, ...

THE SELLER OF GOURD SEEDS

He who sells gourd seeds, seeds from the gourd tree, sells toasted gourd seeds, those treated with maize flour, salted ones, very salty ones.

The bad seller of gourd seeds sells spoiled, stinking, bitter ones; toasted gourd seeds [which are] too salty, bitter with salt, briny.

Also [the gourd seed seller] sells cakes of gourd seeds, fried gourd seeds, gourd seeds with honey, compressed ones — honeyed, delicious, well made, very good, tasty, appetizing, savory, very savory, very pleasing.

In tlaueliloc chilnamacac: in quinamaca chilli xôiac, tetelquic, chipaoac, chilpalaxtli, chilcuitlatl, tlacpatl, chiltzontli, quinamaca chilli in âtlalticpa, in acococ, in acamatetelquic, in oc quilitl, in aia chicaoa, in amâci, in chipini in tomoliui.

TOMANAMACAC: quinamaca in xitomatl, in miltomatl, in izoatomatl, in tomapitzaoac, in tzopelic, in coaxitomatl, in chichioalxitomatl, in coatomatl, no quinamaca in coiotomatl, in xaltotomatl, in xaltomatl, coztic, cozpatic, cozpiltic, chichiltic, chilpatic, tlammilectic, tlatlacpatic, chichilpatic, tlappatic, tlauizcaltic.

In tlaueliloc tomanamacac: in quinamaca tomapalaxtli, tomapitzictli, in apitzaltic, in xocoiac, in xocopatic, no quinamaca in xoxoctetl, in chalchiuhtexoxoctli, in tetozcaoaoaço, in teiolacoman, in teiolitlaco, in teiztlaccacapatz, in teiztlacmemeialti, in tetelquic, in tozcacococ, in quecinami.

AIOACHNAMACAC:

in quinamaca in aiooachtli, quauhaiooachtli, quinamaca in aiooachtlacectli, tlatexuilli, iztaquauitl, poiec popoiec, poelpatic, poeltic.

In tlaueliloc aiooachnamacac, quinamaca in aiooachpalan, in quipiiâc, in chichic, in aiooachtlacectli, iztaquauitl, iztachichic, tlaztamictilli, iztamicqui;

no quinamaca in aiooachtlapololli, aiooachtlatzoionilli, aiooachnecu tlaquequeçalli, necutic, uelic, uel tzopatic, uel pâtic, ueltic, auiiac auixtic, auixpâtic, auixcaltic.

---

19. Read *chipayac*, as in *Acad. Hist. MS.*
20. *Ibid.*: *âyâmaci.*
21. *Lycopersicum esculentum* Mill. or *Physalis philadelphica* Lam. (Hernández, *op. cit.*, III, p. 701).

Nineteenth Chapter, which telleth of the sellers of tortillas [and of] tamales, or of those who sell wheaten bread.

THE TORTILLA SELLER, the food seller [is] an owner of tortillas or a retailer. He[1] sells meat tamales, turkey pasties, plain tamales, barbecued tamales, those cooked in an olla—they burn within; grains of maize with chili, tamales with chili, burning within; fish tamales, fish with grains of maize, frog tamales, frog with grains of maize, axolotl with grains of maize, axolotl tamales, tadpoles with grains of maize, mushrooms with grains of maize, tuna cactus with grains of maize, rabbit tamales, rabbit with grains of maize, gopher tamales: tasty — tasty, very tasty, very well made, always tasty, savory, of pleasing odor, of very pleasing odor; made with a pleasing odor, very savory. Where [it is] tasty, [it has] chili, salt, tomatoes, gourd seeds: shredded, crumbled, juiced.

He sells tamales of maize softened in wood ashes, the water of tamales, tamales of maize softened in lime — narrow tamales, fruit tamales, cooked bean tamales; cooked beans with grains of maize, cracked beans with grains of maize; broken, cracked grains of maize. [He sells] salted wide tamales, pointed tamales, white tamales, fast foods, roll-shaped tamales, tamales with beans forming a seashell on top, [with] grains of maize thrown in; crumbled, pounded tamales; spotted tamales, pointed tamales, white fruit tamales, red fruit tamales, turkey egg tamales; turkey eggs with grains of maize; tamales of tender maize, tamales of green maize, adobe-shaped tamales, braised ones; unleavened tamales, honey tamales, beeswax tamales, tamales with grains of maize, gourd tamales, crumbled tamales, maize flower tamales.

The bad food seller [is] he who sells filthy tamales, discolored tamales — broken, tasteless, quite tasteless, inedible, frightening, deceiving; tamales made of chaff, swollen tamales, spoiled tamales, foul tamales — sticky, gummy; old tamales, cold tamales — dirty and sour, very sour, exceedingly sour, stinking.

The food seller sells tortillas which [are] thick, thickish, thick overall, extremely thick; he sells thin

Inic castolli onnaui capitulo: intechpa tlatoa, in tlaxcalnamacaque: in tamalli, anoço castillan tamalli quinamaca.

TLAXCALNAMACAC, tlaqualnamacac, tlaxcale, anoço tlanecuilo: quinamaca nacatamalli, totolquimilli, icel tamalli, tlatemaltamalli, tlaconpaoaxtli, iitic mococoa, chillaio, chiltamalli, iticococ, michtamalli, michtlaoio, cueiatamalli, cueiatlaoio, axolotlaoio, axolotamalli, atepocatlaoio, nanacatlaoio, nopallaoio, tochtamalli, tochtlaoio, toçantamalli, uelic, ueltic, uelpâtic, ueltzopâtic, ueuelic, auiiac, auixtic, auixpatic, auixtzocaltic, auiialpatic, canin mach uelic, chillo, iztaio, tomaio, aiooachio, tlamatilolli, tlamatilollo, patzcallo

quinamaca, quauhnextamalli, tamalatl, in tenextamalli, in tamalpitzaoac, in xocotamalli, in epaoaxtamalli, in epaoaxtlaoio, in exixilquitlaoio, tlaoioputztic, tlaoioxixitic, popoiec tamalpatlachtli, tamalhuitzoctli ichcatamalli, tlacatlaqualli, tamalmimilli, quatecuicuilli, tlatzincuitl, tlapactamalli, tlamaquauilli, ocelotamalli, tamaluitzoctli, iztac xocotamalli, chichiltic xocotamalli, totoltetamalli, totoltetlaoio, xilotamalli, elotamalli, santamalli, tlecoiutl, iotamalli, necutamalli, xicotamalli, tlaoltamalli, aiôtamalli, tlapactamalli, miiaoatamalli.

In amo qualli tlaqualnamacac: in quinamaca tamaltzocuitlatl, tamalpinetli, papaiaxtli, acecec, acecepatic, tenenquaqua, tenentlamachti, tenenco, polocatamalli, cecepoltamalli, tamalpalan, tamaliiac, çaçalic, çaçaltic, tamalçolli, tamalcecec, cuitlaxococ xocopatic, xocopetzquauitl, iiatatl.

In tlaqualnamacac quinamaca in tlaxcalli in tilaoac, in tilactic in titilactic, in tilacpul: quinamaca, in cana-

---

1. The corresponding Spanish text opens referring to a woman *"La que es official,"* but subsequent references are to males. The illustration, however, is of a woman.

[ones] — thin tortillas,[2] stretched-out tortillas: disc-like, straight . . . , with shelled beans, cooked shelled beans, uncooked shelled beans; with shelled beans mashed;[3] chili with maize, tortillas with meat and grains of maize, folded, doubled over, doubled over and salted, doubled over with chili, wrapped with chili — chili-wrapped, gathered in the hand; ashen tortillas,[4] washed tortillas.

He sells folded tortillas, thick tortillas, coarse tortillas. He sells tortillas with turkey eggs, tortillas made with honey, pressed ones, glove-shaped tortillas, unleavened tortillas, assorted ones, braised ones, sweet tortillas, amaranth seed tortillas, gourd tortillas, green maize tortillas, adobe-shaped tortillas, tuna cactus tortillas; broken, crumbled, old tortillas; cold tortillas, toasted ones, dried tortillas, stinking tortillas.

He sells foods, sauces, hot sauces; fried [food], olla-cooked [food], juices, sauces of juices, shredded [food] with chili, with gourd seeds, with tomatoes, with smoked chili, with hot chilis, with yellow chilis, with mild red chilis, with an early variety of chili, with green chilis, with large tomatoes. [He sells] roasted [meat], barbecued meat, barbecue sauce, chili sauce, mild red chili sauce, yellow chili sauce, hot chili sauce, sauce of an early variety of chili, sauce of smoked chilis, heated [sauces], bean sauce; [he sells] toasted beans, cooked beans, mushroom sauce, sauce of small gourds, sauce of large tomatoes, sauce of ordinary tomatoes, sauce of various kinds of sorrel, avocado sauce — hot, very hot, very glistening-hot, glistening-hot, extremely glistening-hot, most hot; salted, salty, very salty, extremely salty, very salt, bitter with salt, very bitter with salt, most bitter with salt. . . .

THE SELLER OF WHEATEN BREAD [is] a flour sifter, a sieve user, a dough kneader — a worker of dough, an adder of [yeast]; a maker of loaves, of bread: a breadmaker. He sifts, he sieves [flour]; he kneads dough; he makes loaves; he puts them into the oven; he bakes them — he sets the dough [in the oven]. He sells wheaten bread [which is] clean, white, cooked, toasted, put in the fireplace, burned — much burned. The dough set in the oven [is] tasty, savory, of pleasing odor, sweet smelling, made with a pleasing odor. [Where it is tasty],[5] where it is savory, [it is] sweet;

oac, in tlaxcalnamaccac, in tlaxcalcecempacio, in iaoale, in memela in tlaxcalsucuichtli, in tlaoio, in epaoaxtlaoio, in xoxouhcatlaoio, in etlaoio, papatztic, in chillaoio tlaxcalli nacatlaoio, tlacuelpacholli, tlamatzoalli, iztatlamatzoalli, chillamatzoalli, chillailacatzolli, chililacatztli, tlamapictli, nesxotlascalli, tlapactlaxcalli,

quinamaca tlaxcalpacholli, quauhiotlaqualli, quauhtlaqualli: quinamaca in totoltetlaxcalli, necutlaxcalli, tlatepacholli, queceoatlaxcalli, iotlaxcalli, nenepanolli, tlecoiotl, tzopelic tlaxcalli, tzooallaxcalli, aiotlaxcalli, elotlaxcalli, xantlaxcalli, nochtlaxcalli, papaiaxtic, papaiaca, tlaxcalçolli, tlaxcalcecec, totopuchtli, tlaxcalquappitztli, tlaxcaliiac

Quinamaca in tlaqualli, in molli, in tlemolli, tlatetzoionilli, compaoaxtli, patzcalli, patzcalmolli, tlamatilolli, chillo, aiooachio, tomaio, pucheoacaio, chiltecpiio, chilcozio, texiochillo, totocuitlaio, chilchoio, xitomaio, tlatleoatzalli, tlatemalnacatl, tlatemalmolli, chilmolli, texiochilmolli, chilcozmolli, chiltecpinmollin, totocuitlatl molli, pucheoac chilmolli, tlatonilli, emolli, etotopochtli, epaoaxtli, nanacamolli, aionanacamolli, xitomamolli, tomamolli, xoxocoiolmolli, xocoiolmolli, aoacamolli, cococ, cocopâtic, cocopetzpatic, cocopetztic, cocopetzquauitl, cocopalalatic, poec, poieltic, poelpatic, iztaquauitl, iztapatic, iztachichic, iztachichipâtic, iztachichipalalâtic, itztõquauitl.

CAXTILLAN TLAXCALNAMACAC: tlatzetzeloani, tlatzetzeloazuiani, tlaxaqualô, tlaxaqualoani, tlatlâtlaliani, tamaloani, tlaxcaloani, tlaxcalo, tlatzetzeloa, tlatzetzeloazuia, tlaxaqualoa, tamaloa, tlatexcaltema, tlacuxitia, tlatexquetza: quinamaca in castillan tlaxcalli, chipaoac, iztac, icucic, tleoacqui, tlecaleoac, tlatlac, tlâtlatlac, tlatexquetzalli, uelic, auiiac, auixtic, auiialtic, auixtzoncaltic, cani mach uelic, tzopelic, xococ, xocopâtic, xocopetzquauitl, xocopalalatic, motexq̃.

---

2. Read *tlaxcalcanavac* as in *Acad. Hist. MS.* The *Florentine Codex* has perhaps been partly corrected here.

3. Referring to the passage beginning *in tlaoio,* cf. corresponding Spanish text; *tlaolli* is sometimes applied to any shelled seed, as well as to a dough of these seeds.

4. *Acad. Hist MS.: nexyotlaxcalli.*

5. *Ibid.: canjmmach âviyac* (here translated in brackets) is inserted.

[otherwise, it is] sour, very sour, extremely sour, spoiled....[6]

THE SELLER OF WHEAT, of Castilian grain [is] a field owner, a landowner, a field worker ..., or a retailer. He sells white wheat — clean, very white; yellow wheat, dark wheat, ordinary wheat: round, full, fat, firm, hard — like a fruit pit, like a copper bell, much like a copper bell.

[The bad seller of wheat sells] smutty, blighted, frozen, rancid, rotten, evil-smelling, stinking [wheat], full of chaff, softened. With the white, the yellow, the dark wheat he mixes, he tosses in, he throws in the smutty, the ill-formed, the frostbitten, the infested, the rancid.

THE FLOUR SELLER

The seller of Castilian flour, the flour seller is a miller, a flour grinder. He sells ground [flour] — finely ground, very finely ground, well ground, well done, very well done; clean, very clean — very clean, clean, white, very white.

The [bad] one who sells good flour adds to it the poorly ground, the broken, that spilled on the surface, the broken-up flour; the chewed up, the dirty, the dark, the rancid, the infested. He increases it with ground maize.

TRIGONAMACAC, castillantlaolnamacac, mile, tlale, michiuhqui, colicatl, colitli, anoço tlanecuilo: quinamaca in iztac trigo, chipaoac, iztacpatic: coztic trigo, iauitl trigo, ça ça ie trigo, tolontic, tomaoac, chamaoac, tepitztic, tepitzpatic, xocoioltic, coioltic, coiolpatic.

Patzaoac patzactic, patzacoacqui, xoiauhqui, palanqui, tlaliiac, quipiiac, polocaio, cecepollo: in iztac trigo, in coztic, in iauitl, in patżaoac in auelquizqui, in cemâ, in quaq̃ quicẽneloa, in xoiauhqui, quicenminaltia, ic quimotla.

TEXNAMACAC,

castillan tesnamacac, in texnamacac, ca tecini, tlatecini, in quinamaca cuechtic cuechpâtic, cuecuechpatic, cuecuechtic, axtic, axpâtic, chipaoac, chipaoactic, chipacpâtic, chipactic, iztac, iztacpatic.

In quinamaca in qualli textli quinamictia in tlaeltextli, in papaiaxtic, in tlaixtoxaoalli, in tlapapaiaxolli, in tlacacampaxolli, in catzaoac, in iauitl, in xoiauhqui, in quaqua, tlaoltextica quitlapiuia.

6. Ibid.: motexqua.

Twentieth Chapter, which telleth of the sellers of coarse maguey fiber capes and of the sellers of sandals.

THE SELLER OF COARSE MAGUEY FIBER CAPES, of maguey fiber capes, the dresser of maguey leaves in order to extract the fiber — the one who dresses them — [is] an owner of maguey fiber who toasts [the leaves], treats them with maize dough. He dresses them, scrapes them, presses out the moisture, shakes out the water, places [the fibers] over his shoulder, treats them with maize dough.

He sells capes of maguey fiber — clean ones, white, dough-treated — with dough applied, burnished with a stone, made firm. . . ; an arm wide; [like] a small cylinder; narrow and short, long, extended; thick, very thick, exceedingly thick, like a foundation [cape]. It rings like metal. [It is] of tight weave, very tight; like a pottery rattle [in sound], a maguey fiber cape which sounds like a pottery rattle; [ornamented] with the whirlpool design, as if with eyes painted; with the turkey having the mat-designed interior; with the small face; the maguey fiber cape of twisted weave; the one with broken cords, with husks outlined in black — in wide black lines, with the interior diagonal design; the cape with the ocelot design; the shiny maguey fiber one — shiny maguey fiber of fine grade.

The coarse maguey fiber capes which he sells are of loose weave — loose, picked with a thorn, trimmed with maguey spines; thick all over, of tight weave; carefully done ones, skillfully made coarse maguey fiber capes; [those made of] a single maguey fiber; white coarse maguey fiber capes, flowered coarse maguey fiber capes — those with flowers; small coarse maguey fiber capes; coarse maguey fiber capes of very thick weave; soft coarse maguey fiber capes; those of wavy design; those of sparse and loose weave — very sparse and loose ones, very sparse and loose . . . ; the coarse maguey fiber cape with nettles; the coarse maguey fiber cape . . . ; the coarse maguey fiber cape of fine quality.

THE SANDAL SELLER, THE SANDAL MAKER

The sandal seller is a sandal maker, a maker of sandals who cuts the soles, shakes out [the cords],

Inic cempoalli capitulo: intechpa tlatoa in aianamacaque, ioan in cacnamacaque.

AIANAMACAC, ichtilmanamacac tlacinqui, tlacimani, iche, tlachichinoani, tlatexuiani, tlacima tlaoaçoma, aquixtia, tlaapetla, tlatlaquechtlapauia, tlatexuia,

quinamaca ichtilmatli, chipaoac, iztac, texio, tlatexuilli, tlateuilli, tlatepitzinilli, iectilmacuitlatl, mapatlaoac, mimiltontli, titichtontli, quauhtic uecapã tilaoac, tilactic, tilacpatic, xopetlatic, calani, quauhtilactic, quauhtilacpatic, cacalachtic, ichtilmacacalachtli, axicio, ixtecuicuiliuhqui, totolîtipetlaio, ixtepitoton, ilacatziuhqui ichtilmatli, mecaio tlatlapanqui cacallo, tlilaanqui, tlilpapatlaoac, itichicoio, ocelotilmatli, ichpetztli, quetzalichpetztli:

in aiatl quinamaca tlaatcaiquittli, atic, tlauitzcuitl, tlauitzcaiaoalli, ipanocatilaoac, tlapacholli, tlanematcauilli, mimati aiatl, ce ichtli, iztac aiatl, suchaiatl, suchiaiatl, aiatôtontli, aiatotomactli, aiatepaxitli, iaiatoc, caciltic, câcacili, cacaciltic, tzitzinatl, aiatzitzicaztli, ichaiatl, pataiatl, quetzalichaiatl

CACNAMACAC, CACÇOC:

in cacnamacac, ca cacçoc, cacçoni, tlaoapaltecani, tlatzetzeloani, tlamalinqui, coiolomioa, tepuzomioa,

rolls them. He has an awl, a copper awl; he has sandal soles. He dresses [them] with leached ashes; he shakes out the water. He selects the best. He cleans [the threads], twists them using his teeth, rolls them over his hip. He stitches the sandals, sews them, applies tabs. He puts on leather straps; he braids them by hand. He adorns the sandals with flowers.

[He who] sells sandals, sells sandals of cured leather, of maguey fiber — of tight stitching, of thin stitching, of thick stitching, of tangled stitching, basted, of loose stitching; loose, straight and long, straight, shiny, not dragging — in no way dragging, with gathered tabs — tabs which are gathered, with short tabs; white, black, tawny, green, blue; with designs, with feathers, with dyed fur,[1] with the ocelot claw design, with the eagle claw design, with streamers, with the shield jewel, with the wind jewel; narrow, wide, long; large sandals, small sandals, children's sandals; tangled ones; enlarged ones; creaking, noisy, noise-making ones; distended ones.

The retailer asks an excessively high price for them. He praises them, brags of them, sells them by talking. He treats the sandals with leached ashes. The sandal owner paints old sandals, adorns them with flowers, places designs on them, provides them with thongs of cured leather.

THE MAGUEY SYRUP SELLER [is] an owner of maguey plants, a planter of maguey plants, a scraper [of maguey plants]. He heats the syrup. He extracts the syrup; he cooks it. He plants maguey; he breaks up [the plants]; he cleans the surface; he scrapes the maguey plant; he extracts syrup, cooks it — cooks it, boils it in an olla. He fills large storage jars, pours it into skin containers, cools it.

He sells thick syrup, thick, very thick, viscous — it quakes, it quivers; syrupy, sweet, savory, throat-burning, sour, very sour, watery, urine-like, briny.

The good syrup seller sells what [is] like honey, just like wild bee honey, syrup the color of boiled honey, thick syrup, white syrup, dark maguey syrup.

The evil syrup seller, when he sells syrup, damages, treats, alters it — adds roots to it, adds scrapings of maguey pith, treats it with leached ashes and water, adds a "soap tree"[2] [infusion], mallow,[3] fish amaranth seed; he waters it down — increases it with water.

cacoapale, tlanextlatia, tlaapetla, tlaichana, tlaiectia, tlatlancoluhcauia, tlamalina, cacço, tlaço, tlanacaztia, tlaixtoca, tlamaiquiti, tlacacsuchiotia,

cacnamaca: quinamaca cuetlascactli, ichcactli, tlatepitzçotl, tlacanaoacaçotl, tlatilaoacaçotl, tlapapâçotl, tlacuecuezçotl, tlapoxaoacaçotl, poxaoac, melaztic, melaoac, tetzcaltic, mauilanqui, mauilaxpol, nacazpeltic, nacazpeliuhqui nacaztitichtic, iztac, tliltic, quappachtli, xoxouhqui, texotli, tlamachcactli, hiuiio, tochomiio, ocelotetepoio, quauhtetepoio, tlalpiloniio, chimalcozcaio, ecacozcaio, pitzaoac, patlaoac, uiiac, uei cactli, cactepiton, cacconepil, papaçoltic xixipuchtic cocomotztic, têtecuintic, tetecuintli, xixicuintli.

In tlanecuilo: tlaueicatzatzitia tlachachamaoa, tlachamaoa, tempochtecati, quinextlatia in cactli, in cactioa, quicuiloa, quisuchiotia quitlamachia, in cacçolli, quicuetlaxmecaiotia.

NECUNAMACAC: meoa, metecani, tlachicqui, necutlati, necutlazqui, tlatzoioni, meteca, tlatlapana, tlaixochpana, tlachiqui, necutlaça, tlatzoionia, tlacuxitia, tlapaoaci, tlatzotzocoltema, tlacuextlaxteca, tlaceuia:

in quinamaca necutli, tetzaoac, tetzactic, tetzacpâtic, chapantica, ioiolcatica, uiiontica, necutic, tzopelic, auiiac, tozcacococ, xococ, xocopâtic, atic, axixtic, iztaiotic.

In qualli necunamacac: in iuhqui necutli, çan iuhqui quinamaca in quauhnecutli, in necutlatlatilli, in necutetzaoac, iztac necutli, tliltic necutli.

In tlaueliloc necunamacac: in quinamaca necutli, quitlacoa, quichichioa, quipatia, quitlanellotia, ca quimetzallotia, quinexaiouia, quiquaoalaoacaiotia, quitlalalalaoacaiotia, quimichioauhiotia, caiotia, caquechia.

1. Cf. *infra,* chap. xxi, n. 10.
2. Emily Walcott Emmart: *The Badianus Manuscript* (Baltimore: The Johns Hopkins Press, 1940), p. 317; unident.
3. Cf. corresponding Spanish text.

THE COTTON SELLER

The cotton seller is a field owner, a cotton field owner, a cotton owner; [he is] a worker of the soil, a planter of cotton, or an importer, or a retailer.

The cotton which he sells [is] round, fat, full-bodied, double-bodied.[4] The good cotton, the precious, the irrigated land variety, comes from irrigated lands. That which comes from the hot countries follows. Also that which comes from the west follows. Finally comes that which comes from the desert lands, from the north. That which is like the Totonac variety — tree cotton — comes last of all.

Separately the good man sells these. And he adjusts their prices. Separately he sells the yellow, separately the broken, the stretched.

The bad cotton seller takes some cotton from each section;[5] he fluffs the cotton with a needle; into each cotton boll he introduces [other cotton]; he fluffs it with a needle.

THE SELLER OF WRINKLED CHÍA

The wrinkled *chía* seller [is] an owner of *chía*, of *chía* fields, of wrinkled *chía*. [He is] one who rubs it between his hands, who cleans it. Separately he sells the Chontal variety, the [kind which] comes from Oztoman, the Tlaluica variety, the Itziocan variety. Separately he sells the white, the hard, separately the unformed, the black, the curdling, the unthreshed, the green, the smutty.

THE SELLER OF PALM LEAF FIBER CAPES, the maker of palm leaf fiber capes [is] a traveler [or] a retailer [dealing in] palm leaf fiber capes of two arm lengths, plain ones,[6] the kind which tie on, diagonal capes, the kind to wrap about one, to cover one, to sleep in, to cover one over; small plain ones,[7] narrow and short ones — those which are narrow and short; pounded — much pounded, of tight weave, made to fit well; mended, darned, washed — washed in the water of leached ashes; the kind in which to dress up for market, the stiff edged kind, the broken kind, the jointed kind; very shiny palm leaf fiber capes, ordinary palm leaf fiber capes; going last of all, following, the loosely woven, the loose, of loose weave, the netlike.

ICHCANAMACAC:

in ichcanamacac, ca mile, ichcamile, ichcaoa, tlachiuhqui, ichcatocani, anoço oztomecatl, anoço tlanecuilo,

in quinamaca ichcatl, iaoaliuhqui, nânatztic, nacaio, ontlaca: in qualli ichcatl, in tlaçotli, amilpanecaiotl, amilpampa uitz quitoquilia in tonalixcopa uitz: oc ceppa quioalcatoquilia in tonatiuh icalaquiampa uitz, tlatzacuia, in teutlalpampa vitz, in mictlampa uitz: in iuhqui totonacapanecaiotl, quicentzacuia in quauhichcatl:

nononqua quinamaca in qualli tlacatl: auh quinamictia in ipatiuh, nonqua quinamaca in coioichcatl, nonq̄ in xamanqui, in uilanqui.

In tlaueliloc ichcanamacac: quinacazana in ichcatl, ichcaçoço, in ichcacacallotl quinacazaquia, quiçoço.

CHIENTZOTZOLNAMACAC:

in chientzotzolnamacac: chieme, chienmille, chientzotzole, tlamatiloani, tlaiectiani, nononqua quinamaca in chontalcaiotl, in oztoman uitz, in tlaluiccaiotl, in itziocaiutl, nonqua quinamaca in iztac in tepitztic, nonqua in poxaoac, in iauitl, in papachcani, in amo tlapanani, in xoxoctic, in patzactic.

Icçotilmanamacac, icçotilmachiuhqui, tlanenemiti, tlanecuilo icçotilmaommatl, cemanqui, netlalpililli, ixtlapaltilmatli, neolololoni, nequentiloni, cochioani, nequimiloloni, cemācatontli, titichtontli, titichpil, tlateuilli, tlateteuilli, tlatepitzinilli, tlatequaltilli, tlachichitl, tlaixaquilli, tlapactli, tlanextlatilli, tlatiamicchichioalli, tēnquauhio, popuztecqui, uiuiltecqui, icçotilmaxixipetztli, ça ça ie icçotilmatli, tlatzacuia tetocatiuh, poxâtic, uixaltic cacaciltic matlatic.

---

4. *Ibid.*: "*los capullos de algodon . . . son buenos, gordos, redondos, y llenos de algodon.*"

5. *Acad. Hist. MS: quinânacazana.*

6. *Ibid.: cemmanqui.*

7. *Ibid.: cemmancatontli.*

Twenty-first Chapter, which telleth of those who sell[1] colors, rabbit hair [material], and gourd bowls.

THE DISPLAYER OF WARES ON A LARGE BASKET[2] is a seller of colors, of various colors, of dyes; a man who piles [small baskets of color] on a large basket. He sells dried pigment, bars of cochineal pigment, cochineal mixed with chalk or flour, [pure] cochineal; light yellow, sky blue pigment; chalk, lampblack, dark blue pigment; alum, *axin,* chicle, bitumen-mixed chicle, red ochre; *tlilxochitl,*[3] *mecaxochitl,*[4] *uei nacaztli,*[5] *teonacaztli;*[6] opossum,[7] opossum tail; small herbs, small roots; bitumen, resin, copal; *nacazcolotl,*[8] *quimichpatli;*[9] a blue coloring made from blossoms; sulfate of copper, iron pyrites.

Inic cempoalli oce capitulo intechpa tlatoa in tlapalli in tochomitl ioan in xicalli, quinama

CHIQUIPPANTLACATL: ca tlapalnamacac, nepapan tlapalnamacac, pâcanamacac, chiquiuhtetecpich, quinamaca tlapaloatzalli, tlaquaoac tlapalli, tlapalnextli, nocheztli, çacatlaxcalli texotli, tetiçatl, tlilli, tlaceuilli, tlalxocotl, axi, tzictli, tlaaxnelolli, tlauitl, tlilsuchitl, mecasuchitl uei nacaztli, teunacaztli, tlaquatl, tlaquacuitlapilli, xiuhtotonti tlaneloatotonti, chapopôtli, tecupalli, copalli, nacazcolotl, quimichpatli, matlalin, tlaliiac, apetztli.

THE SELLER OF RABBIT-HAIR [MATERIAL][10]

The seller of rabbit-hair [material] is a dyer, a user of dyes, a dyer [of material] in many colors. [Sometimes he is] a user of faded colors, who dresses [the material] with ashes. He sells the good rabbit-hair [material] — well prepared, harmonious, not dulled with ashes. He sells it in red, yellow, sky blue, light green, dark blue, tawny, dark green, flower yellow, blue-green, [carmine],[11] rose, brown. [With these] he dyes, he provides the colors.

TOCHOMINAMACAC:

in tochominamacac, ca tlapã, tlapani, tlatlatlapalpoani, tlatlapalquistiani, tlanextlatiani, tlanextlati: quinamaca in qualli tochomitl, in uel quizqui, in amo quauhtlatlac in amo nexmicqui: quinamaca in chichiltic, in coztic, in texotli, in quiltic, in mouitli, in quappachtli, in iapalli, in suchipalli, in quilpalli, [noch]palli tlaztaleoalli, camiltic, tlapa tlatlapalaquia

THE SELLER OF GOURD BOWLS

The seller of gourd bowls is an owner of gourd· bowls, a dealer in gourd bowls, a retailer. [He is a

XICALNAMACAC:

· in xicalnamacac, ca xicale, xicalnanauhqui, tlanecuilo, tlapochquiiotlaçani, tlaôçac, tlatzotlani, tlacuilo:

---

1. Read *quinamaca.*

2. Corresponding Spanish text: *"El que vende las colores que pone encima de vn cesto grande . . . cada genero de color ponelo, en vn cestillo encima del grande."*

3. *Tlilxochitl: Vanilla planifolia* (Santamaría, *op. cit.,* III, p. 188).

4. *Mecaxochitl: Piper amalago* L. (*ibid.,* II, p. 265).

5. *Uei nacaztli: Cymbopetalum penduliflorum* (Dunal) Baill. (Emmart, *op. cit.,* p. 315).

6. *Teonacaztli:* same as *uei nacaztli,* according to Emmart, *loc. cit.* In Sahagún (Garibay ed.), IV, pp. 336, 356, *uei nacaztli* is *Chiranthrodendron pentadactylon* Lan., and *teonacaztli* is *Cymbopetalum penduliflorum.*

7. Identification of mammals is based mainly on Martin del Campo: "Ensayo de interpretación del Libro de la Historia General de las Cosas de Nueva España, de Fray Bernardino de Sahagún," III, "Los Mamíferos," *Anales del Instituto de Biología,* XII, I (1941), pp. 489–506, and Bernardo Villa R.: "Mamíferos Silvestres del Valle de México," *Anales del Instituto de Biología,* XXIII, Nos. 1, 2 (1952), pp. 269–492. In personal communication Dr. Stephen D. Durrant, Professor of Zoology at the University of Utah, has supplied English names. In some cases he has supplied the current taxonomy. — *Tlaquatl, tlaquatzin: Didelphis marsupialis californica* Bennet, Villa., *op. cit.,* p. 308.

8. *Nacazcolotl: Caesalpina corierea,* according to Sahagún, *op. cit.,* p. 344; gall nuts (Spanish text).

9. *Quimichpatli:* in Martínez, *op. cit.,* p. 182 (*quimixpatli*), *Buddleia sessiliflora* H. B. K.; Santamaría, *op. cit.,* II, p. 551, *Sebadilla officinarum* Gray.

10. *Tochomitl:* rabbit hair (Molina, *op. cit.;* Rémi Siméon, *op. cit.*). Corresponding Spanish text heads this section *"El que es tintorero"* and describes variously dyed wool. In Santamaría, *op. cit.,* III, p. 191, *tochomite* is *especie de estambre de lana de colores;* in his *Diccionario de Mejicanismos* (Méjico: Editorial Porrúa, S. A., 1959), p. 1064, a citation from Trens (*Méjico de antaño,* 145) refers to *lanas hiladas y torcidas.* Elsewhere we have seen some justification for translating *tochomitl* as rabbit fur, or as dyed fur.

11. *Acad. Hist. MS: nochpalli.*

worker] who removes the [gourd's] bumps,[12] who burnishes, varnishes, paints them. He sells gourds with raised [designs], with stripes, with lines, scraped, rubbed with *axin,* rubbed with [the powdered] fruit pits [of the yellow sapote tree],[13] smoked, treated with oils. He sells Guatemalan gourd vessels. He sells gourds for gourd rattles — white, yellow, light colored, black; with cotton. He sells gourd bowls — polished gourd bowls, burnished, varnished; painted gourd bowls from Mexico, from Acolhuacan, from Uexotzinco, from Tlaxcalla, from Anauac; from the Totonaca, Huaxteca, Tlalhuica, Itzteyocan, Michoacan regions. [He sells them] round, cylindrical, flat-based, pointed-based, circular, constricted; with legs, feet, handles, spouts; [he sells] small pitchers, [ordinary] pitchers, vessels for drinking water, drinking vessels, atole vessels, shallow gourd bowls, gourd bowls for washing the hands, bowls for cacao, gourd jars. He sells web-like [gourds], strainers, pouring vessels, water sprinklers; he retails gourd bowls, travels with gourd bowls, imports gourd bowls. He burnishes gourd bowls.

THE PAPER SELLER — the paper beater, the paper importer — sells coarse paper, bark paper, maguey fiber paper. He sells Castilian paper. He sells [paper which is] clean, white, very clean, very white; thin, thin overall; web-like; wide, long, thick — thick overall; rough, crumpled, torn, blotched, rotten, yellowed. He sells paper, he makes it, he beats it.

THE SELLER OF LIME

The seller of lime [is] a shatterer of rocks, a burner of limestone, a slaker of lime. He places the limestone in the oven, places the firewood, sets the fire, burns the limestone, cools the oven, slakes the lime, carries the lime on his back. He sells limestone rock, slaked lime — lime which is slaked. He sells good lime, "raven stone" [14] — fired, cooked, white, very white. He sells earth like calcareous tufa; [lime] with calcareous tufa [or] with earth used to mix with lime.[15] [He sells] cooked calcareous tufa.

in quinamaca pochquioxicalli, tlaoaoantli, tlaoaoanalli, tlachictli, tlaaxuilli, tlapizuilli, pizio, tlapocheoalli, tlachiaoalli: quinamaca in aiotectli quauhtemaltecaiotl, quinamaca, aiacachtecaiutl, iztac, coztic, ticeoac, tliltic, ichcaio: quinamaca in xicalli, tlaxicalteuilli, tlaoçalli, tlatzotlanilli, xicallacuilolli, mexicaiotl, acoloacaiutl, uexotzincaiutl, tlaxcaltecaiutl, anaoacaiutl, totonacaiutl, cuextecaiutl, tlaluiccaiutl, itztecaiutl michoacaiutl: ololtic, mimiltic, pechtic, apechtli, teololtic, patztic xopiltic, icxe, vicollo, piazio xicalûicolli, xicalapilolli, atlioani, tlaioani, tzôoacalli, xicalpechtli, nematequilxicalli, achioalxicalli, xicaltecomatl, xicalnamaca peiotl, amatlatl, achachaiactli, atzetzeloaztli, xicalnecuiloa, xicalotlatoctia, xicaloztomecati, xicaloça

AMANAMACAC, amauitecqui, amaoztomecatl: quinamaca in quaoamatl, in texamatl, in ichamatl, quinamaca in castillā amatl, quinamaca chipaoac, iztac, chipactic, chipacpatic, chipaccaltic, aztatic, canaoac, cacanactic, peiotic, patlaoac, uia tilaoac, tilactic, titilactic, chachaquachtic, tetecuitztic, papaiaxtic, chichicauhqui, palanqui, coztic, amanamaca, amachioa, amauitequi.

TENEXNAMACAC:

in tenexnamacac, tetlapanqui, tenextlati, tenexmoloni, tlatexcaltema, tlatlequauhiotia, tlatlemina, tenextlatia, texcalceuia, tenexmolonia tenexmama, quinamaca tenextetl, molonqui, tlamolonilli, quinamaca in tenextli, qualli, in cacalotetl, tlatlatilli, tlacuxitilli, iztac, iztacpâtic: quinamaca in tepetlatlaltic, in tepetlaio, in tlaltenexio, in tepetlatl, tlacuxitilli.

---

12. *Pochquiotl:* this term is not in the vocabularies. Some possibilities as to meaning are suggested *infra,* chap. xxvii, § 12, and in *Florentine Codex,* Book XI, fols. 120*v*, 215*r*, 216*v*.

13. Cf. corresponding Spanish text.

14. *Cacalotetl:* cf. *Florentine Codex,* Book XI, fol. 236*r* — *chipaoac, cuechtic, tetzcaltic, tetzcalpatic, tenextlatilonj.*

15. *Ibid.,* fol. 229*v:* *çan tlalli in xamjtl, in tliltic, in iztac . . . in jquac oiccucic . . . moneloa in tenextli.*

Twenty-second Chapter, which telleth of the fruit sellers and the food sellers.

THE MAN WITH THE FRUIT

The fruit seller [is] a fruit owner. He carries fruit upon his back — transports it. [He is] a retailer. He plants trees; he puts trees into [the ground]. He picks fruit — he picks, harvests, produces fruit.

He sells tender maize stalks, green maize, tender maize ears; tamales of green maize, tortillas of green maize, mixed foods; green maize ears parched [or] fried; sweet tortillas; tamales; tamales of uncooked ground maize; rabbit with toasted maize; glove-shaped tortillas;[1] pressed tortillas; pressed tortillas with honey added; toasted maize with honey, pinole with honey, gourd seeds fried in honey; *chia* fried in honey; tortillas made of gourd; tamales, tamales of tender maize; tortillas of tender maize, tortillas made with tuna cactus fruit, tuna cactus fruit tamales; gourds, cooked gourds, gourds cut in pieces, boiled gourds, baked gourds; *chayote*,[2] sweet potatoes, *jícamas*,[3] manioc; *tlalcamotli*,[4] *tolcimatl*,[5] *cacomitl*,[6] *cacapxon*;[7] anonas, sapotas, yellow sapotas, green sapotas, black seeded sapotas,[8] *tetlapotl*;[9] plums — red ones, yellow ones, large-pitted ones; *tlacolxocotl*;[10] guavas; *tejocotes*;[11] American cherries — large ones, small ones. He sells tuna cactus fruit, [those which are] yellow, red, white, slightly reddened, purple centered, purple, round, large, sweet centered, sour, sweet; [he sells] tomatoes; the fruit of *atlitlilatl*;[12] of *atlitlilaquiatl*.[13]

Inic cempoalli omome capitulo: intechpa tlatoa in suchiqualnamacaque ioã in tlaqualnamacaque

SUCHIQUALPAN TLACATL:

in suchiqualnamacac, suchiquale, suchiqualmama, tlaôtlatocti, tlacemanqui quauhtoca, quaoaquia, suchiqualtequi, tlatequi, pixca, suchiqualchioa.

quinamaca ooatl, in elotl, in xilotl, in elotamalli in elotlaxcalli, in nenepanolli, in tlecoiotl, in eloixcalli, in tzopelic, tlaxcalli, tamalli, in uilocpalli, in tochizquitl, in quececatlaxcalli, in tlatepacholli in necutlaquequeçalli, necuizquitl, necuizquipinolli, in necutlatzoionilli. in aiooachtli, chien necpan tlatzoionilli, in aiotlaxcalli, tamalli, in xilotamalli, xilotlaxcalli, in nochtlaxcalli, nochtamalli, aiôtli, aiopaoaxtli, aiotlatlapantli, aiotepçolli, aiôtemalli, chaiotli, camotli, xicama, quauhcamotli, tlalcamotli, tolcimatl, cacomitl, cacapxon, matzatli, tzapotl, atzapotl, totolcuitlatzapotl, tliltzapotl, quauhtzapotl, eheiotzapotl, etzapotl, tetlapotl, maçaxocotl, chichiltic, coztic, atoiaxocotl, tlâcolxocotl, xalxocotl, texocotl, capoli, elocapoli, tlaolcapoli: quinamaca nochtli, coznochtli, tlapalnochtli, iztac nochtli tlatocnochtli, anochtli, tlanexi, tzaponochtli, tzooalnochtli, camastle, xoconochtli, azcanochtli, xaltotomatl, atlitlilatl, atlitlilaquiatl

---

1. Corresponding Spanish text: *"las tortillas de masa mezclada con mjel, que son como guantes."* See also *Florentine Codex*, Book X, fol. 51r.

2. *Chayotli: Sechium edule* Sw. (Hernández, *op. cit.*, I, p. 167).

3. *Xicama: Pachyrhizus angulatus* Rich. (*ibid.*, II, 523).

4. "Earth sweet potatoes"; unident.

5. "Reed roots" (Sahagún, Garibay ed., IV, p. 359).

6. *Cacomitl: Tigridia pavonia* Ker. (Hernández, *op. cit.*, p. 657).

7. Unident. edible root (Sahagún, Garibay ed., IV, p. 325).

8. *Quauhtzapotl, eheiotzapotl, etzapotl:* cf. *Florentine Codex*, Book XI, fol. 121v. Various kinds of *tzapotl* are identified in Hernández, *op. cit.*, I, pp. 267sqq. (*Lucuma, Annona, Diospyros, Achras, Ternstroennia* genera.)

9. Unident.

10. Unident.; *tlaçolxocotl?*

11. *Texocotl: Crataegus mexicana* Moc. et Ses. (Santamaría, *Diccionario de Americanismos*, III, p. 150).

12. Unident.; cf. *Florentine Codex*, Book XI, fol. 139v.

13. Unident.

THE FISH SELLER[14] fishes with a net. [He is] a man of the water, of the river banks. He fishes; he catches with nets, with snares; he fishes with a fishhook; he uses a weir, a spear; he waits for freshets;[15] he catches [the fish] in his hands.

He sells shrimp, fish, large fish, shellfish, turtles, gourd fish, sea turtles, eagle fish, spotted fish, *axolotl* fish, eel, cayman, large white fish, black fish, white fish, small white fish from awaited freshets, tiny fish, toasted fish wrapped in maize husks, fish wrapped in maize husks and cooked in an olla, those roasted in leaves, large-bellied fish, small thick fish, *axolotl*,[16] shrimp, tadpoles. He sells fresh fish; wet, recently caught ones; dried fish. He sells fish eggs, fish egg tamales, fish roe; water fly[17] eggs, tortillas of water fly eggs; tortillas, tamales of water fly eggs, balls of water fly eggs; water flies, tamales of water flies, [water flies] made into a paste; worm tamales, [another kind of] water fly tamales [and] water fly tortillas; water worms, worm excrement, "worm flowers." [18]

XOQUIIACANAMACAC, tlatlama, atlacatl, atenoa, tlatlama, tlamatlauia, tlatzonuia, tlapipiloa tlaacacuexuia, tlacoiolacauia, achia, tlamâmapachoa,

quinamaca chacali, michin, tlacamichi, teccizmichi, aiomichi, xicalmichi, chimalmichi, quauhxouili, ocelomichi, axolomichi, coamichi, acuetzpali, xouili, iaiauhqui, amilotl, iztac michi, achialli, michçaquan, michpictli, michtlapictli, izoac tlaxquitl, cuitlapetotl, topôtli, axolotl, chacali, atepocatl: quinamaca hauicmichi paltic iancuic michoacqui: quinamaca michpili, michpiltamalli, michpiltetei, aoauhtli, aoauhtlaxcalli, aoauhtamalli, aoauhtetl, axaxaiacatl, axaxaiacatamalli, tlapitzinilli, ocuiltamalli, amoiotamalli, amoiotlaxcalli, ocuiliztac, ocuillaçolli, ocuilsuchitl

THE MEAT SELLER

The meat seller [is] an owner, a possessor of meat —a meat owner, an animal owner. He hunts; he pursues game. Or he is a meat dealer. He keeps [animals] — raises them.

He sells turkeys, turkey meat, venison, rabbit meat, hare, duck, crane, goose, mallard; bird meat, roast birds, quail meat, eagle meat; meat of wild beasts, of opossum; the meat of Castilian [animals] — chickens, cattle, pigs,[19] sheep, goats, etc. He sells the meat fresh, uncooked; jerked meat, oven-cooked, baked, dried meat; roasted, cooked [meat], cooked in an olla.

The bad meat seller sells spoiled meat — sour, moldy, evil-smelling, bruised, discolored, mashed, mushy, revolting. He claims dog meat to be edible.

THE WOOD SELLER [is] a woodsman,[20] a forester, a forest owner; an axe owner, a feller of trees, a wood-

NACANAMACAC:

in nacamacac, axcaoa, naque nacaoa iolcaoa, tlatlama, anqui, anoço nacananauhqui, tlanemitia, tlaoapaoa,

quinamaca totoli, totolnacatl, maçanacatl, tochnacatl, cîtli, canauhtli, tocuilcoiotl, tlalalacatl, concanauhtli, totonacatl, totoizquitl, çolnacatl, quauhnacatl, tequannacatl, tlaquatl, tlaquatzin, castillannacatl, totoli, quanaca, quaquaue pitzotl, coiametl, ichcanacatl, quaquauhtentzonnacatl, etª. quinamaca in aûic nanacatl, in iancuic, in nacatlatepioatzalli, tlatentli, tlatemalli, nacatlaoatzalli, tlatleoatzalli, icucic tlapaoaxtli.

In tlaueliloc nacanamacac: quinamaca in nacapalan, xococ, poxcauhqui, hiiac, eeztentli, tlaxôxouiltecalli, tlaeztemalli, tlanacaatoltilli, tlaellelaxitilli, quiqualo tlapiquia in itzcuinnacatl.

QUAUHNANAMACA, quauhtlãcatl, quauhtencatl, quauhtenoâ tepuze, quauhtlaçani, quauhtequini, tla-

---

14. Cf. corresponding Spanish text: *"El que vende pescado."* Nahuatl text: stench-seller.

15. Cf. corresponding Spanish text.

16. *Axolotl: Amblystoma tigrinum* Cope; *Proteus mexicanus* L.; *Sideron humboldti* Dum.; *S. mexicanum* Baird (Santamaría, *op. cit.,* I, p. 70 — *ajolote*).

17. *Axayacatl:* hemipterous water insect (Santamaría, *Diccionario de mejicanismos,* p. 100); not precisely ident. Their eggs are *auauhtli.*

18. Problematical. Corresponding Spanish text apparently includes all these worms in *"vnos gusanos blancos que son buenos para aues o paxaros."*

19. Although naming native animals in Book XI, fol. 11r, of the *Florentine Codex,* Sahagún states: *"Algunos llamã coiametl al puerco de castilla por la semejanza que tiene, con este llaman tambien peçotli al puerco de castilla."*

20. Read *quauhtlacatl.*

cutter, a user of the axe. He cuts with an axe; he fells trees — cuts them, tops them, strips them, splits them, stacks them.

The CARPENTER sells cedar, fir, pine, cypress. He sells large beams, small beams, wooden pillars, roofing, lintels, wooden columns, boards, planks, thin strips for hoops, thick boards. He sells new, rotten, broken, hardened [wood].

The WOODCUTTER sells oak, pine, alder,[21] madroña; wood which produces colored flames — good burning wood; logs, toppings, kindling wood; bark — green, dry, [or] fresh. He sells dart shafts, dried maguey leaves, dried maize stalks, sun flower [stalks].[22]

tepuzuiani, tlatepuzuia, quauhtlaça tlatequi, tlatzontequi, tlatzaiana, tlaxeloa tlauelteca.

IN QUAUHXINQUI: quinamaca in tlatzcan, in oiametl, in ocutl, in aueuetl, quinamaca in uepantli, quaoacatl, quauhtectli, quammimilli calquauitl, tlaquetzalli, quauhtemimilli, oapalli, tlapechoapalli, oapalçoiatl, oapaltilaoac: quinamaca in iancuic in quappallan, in nanaltic, in quauhtioa.

IN QUAQUAUINI: quinamaca in teuquauitl, in aoatl, in ocoquauitl, ili, tomazquitl, in nêcalizquauitl, in tlatlapâtli, in mimiliuhqui tlatzontectli, in tlamapuztectli, in tlaxipeoalli, in xoxouhqui in quaoatzalli, in auic: quinamaca in tlacoquauitl, in meçotl, in aoaquauitl, in chimalacatl

---

21. *Ilin*: ash, in *Florentine Codex*, Book XI, fol. 112*v*.

22. For making shields. *Chimalacatl* is identified as *Verbesina crocata* (Cav.) Less. (?) or *Helianthus annuus* L. (Hernández, *op. cit.*, I, pp. 99–100).

Twenty-third Chapter, which telleth of the olla makers, the clay workers, and the makers of large baskets [and] of small baskets.

THE CLAY WORKER, a dealer in clay objects, sells ollas, cooking ollas, water jars, large pitchers, jars for water, glazed pottery basins, earthen basins, large braziers, candle holders; bowls — wooden bowls, polished ones, reddish ones, offering bowls, merchants' bowls, white ones, black bowls; ladles; combs; sauce bowls — incised, polished: sauce bowls which have been polished; frying sauce bowls, frying bowls.

He sells well-fired [bowls], hard-fired ones, [those which] sound cracked; the fire-cracked, the poorly fired, imperfect, poorly made, porous, spongy, incompletely fired, inferior. [They are] reddened, treated with resin, treated with yellow coloring.

THE GRIDDLE MAKER [is] one who moistens clay, kneads it, tempers it with [soft pieces of] reed,[1] makes it into a soft paste. He moistens [the clay], tempers it with [soft pieces of] reed, kneads it. He makes griddles; he beats [the clay], flattens it, polishes it, smooths it; he applies a slip. He places [the unfired pieces] in the oven; he feeds the fire, makes the oven smoke, cools the oven.

He sells hard-fired [griddles] which ring, [which are] well tempered, [as well as those which are] poorly fired, smudged, blackened, discolored, poorly made, inferior, sounding as if cracked — cracked in firing.

THE SELLER OF LARGE BASKETS

The seller of large baskets is a maker of large baskets. He concerns himself with reeds. He soaks the reeds in water, softens them, beats them with a stone. He arranges them, provides the rim, fastens it with a cord.[2] He makes the bottom of reeds.

He sells large baskets; his specialty is palm leaf.[3] [He sells] baskets made of spiny plants, baskets with serrated edges, large baskets, cylindrical baskets, tortilla baskets, baskets for hot things, food baskets; reed baskets, shallow baskets . . . ; of tightly twisted weave, firm; loosely woven, crude, round, distended, fat — really unpresentable.

Inic cempoalli omei capitulo: intechpa tlatoa, in conchiuhque in çoquichiuhque; ioan in chiquiuhchiuhque, in tanachiuhq̄.

ÇOQUICHIUHQUI, çoquinanauhqui: quinamaca comitl, paoazcomitl, acomitl, tzotzocolli, apilolli, cuecueio, apaztli, tlalapaztli, apantlecaxitl, tlauiltetl, caxitl, quauhcaxitl, petzcaxitl, tlauhcaxitl, tlamamanalcaxitl, puchtecaiocaxitl, ticeoac, tlilcaxitl, xomatli, motziquâtli, mulcaxitl, ixtecqui, petzmulcaxitl, mulcaxpetztli, tlemolcaxitl, tlatetzonilcaxitl:

quinamaca uel icucic, tletlemicqui, nanalca, tlemotzinqui, aicucic, aommacic, cacamactic, çonectic, çaçamactli, camaoac, çaçana, tlatlauilli, tlaoçalli, tlaçacatlaxcaluilli.

IN COMALNAMACAC, çoquipaloani, tlaxaqualoani, tlatolcapouiani, tlatzacutiliani, tlalciaoa, tlatolcapouia, tlaxaqualoa, comalchioa, tlatzotzona, tlaixtlaça, tlapetzoa, tlacalania tlaquili, tlatexcaltema, tlatlemina, tlapocheoa, texcalceuia,

quinamaca tletlemicqui, tzitzilictic, chicaoac, aicucic, pocheoac, puchectic, çaçamactic, cacamac, çaçanaca, nanalca tlemotzinqui.

CHIQUIUHNAMACAC:

in chiquiuhnamacac, ca chiquiuhchiuhqui, acatl quimauiltia, tlaaciaoa, tlacamaoa, tlatetzotzona, tlauipana, tlatentia, tlamecauia, tlatzinacauia:

quinamaca in chiquiuitl, in tonalçoiatic, chiquiuhnetzolli, tentzitziquiliuhqui, chiquiuhtopilli, chiquinmimilli, tlaxcalchiquiuitl, totoncachiquiuitl, tlaqualchiquiuitl, acachiquiuitl, chiquippechtli, chiquiuhpepelli, tetzictic, chicaoac, uixaltic, xoxoquiui, totolontic, xixicuintic, xixicuinpol, çan nimā acan tlacanezqui.

---

1. Corresponding Spanish text: *"moja muy bien la tierra, y la soba, y mezclala, con el floxel de las espadañas."*

2. *Ibid.: "echa vn cordonzillo de nequen y vna caña partida por medio al rededor en el hondon por de fuera."*

3. *Acad. Hist. MS: yn itonal çoyatic.*

THE SELLER OF SMALL BASKETS sells small round baskets, straight ones, cylindrical ones; small palm leaf baskets; small reed, leather, wooden baskets; woven reed coffers. He sells work of closely-woven sort; of tight, very tight weave.

THE SELLER OF SALT

The seller of salt is a salt producer or a salt retailer. The salt producer gathers [salty] earth, hills it up, soaks it, wets it, distils, makes brine, makes ollas for salt, cooks it.

The salt retailer displays salt. He sets out on the road, travels with it, goes from market to market, makes use of markets, sells salt. He sells salt balls, salt bars, salt ollas — thick, clean, full-bodied; like white chalk; of good taste, savory; tasting of lime, bitter . . . , tasteless, insipid, salt, salty, very salty, briny. He sells thin bars of salt, sandy [salt]. He sells grains of salt — good, very white.

IN TANANAMACAC: quinamaca in tanaiaoalli, tanamelactli, tanamimilli, çoiatanatl, acatanatli, eoatanatli, quauhtanatli, petlacalli, quinamaca tlatepitzchioalli, tlapacholli, tlateteppacholli

IZTANAMACAC:

in iztanamacac, ca iztachiuhqui, anoço iztanecuilo: in iztachiuhqui, tlalcui, tlaololoa, tlaciaoa tlaapachoa, tlâxitza, iztaiochioa iztaconchioa, tlaxca.

In iztanecuilo iztamana, tlaotlatoctia, tlanenemitia, tianquiztôtoca, tlatianquiçoa, iztanamaca: quinamaca iztaiaoalli, iztaxopilli, iztacomitl, tilaoac chipaoac, nacatic, chimaltiçatic, uelic, auiiac, nexcococ, chichic, itztonquauitl, acecec, acecepatic, poec, poeltic, poelpatic, popoiec, quinamaca iztacanactli, xallo, quinamaca iztaxalli, qualli, aztapiltic.

Twenty-fourth Chapter, which telleth of the turkey sellers, of those who sell eggs, and of those who sell various medicines.

THE EGG SELLER [is] an owner of turkeys, a breeder of fowl, a raiser [of fowl]. He sells turkey eggs, duck eggs, quail eggs — the good ones. [These are made into] tortillas, boiled in an olla, made into a broth. He who mocks the people sells rotten eggs — turkey excrement, duck eggs, crow eggs, turkey buzzard eggs, vulture eggs.

THE TURKEY SELLER [is] an owner of turkeys — a raiser, a breeder [of turkeys], a livestock owner, a buyer and seller, a breeder of turkeys. He raises turkeys, he sells Mexican turkeys, birds of Castile — those with wattles;[1] fat, fleshy, corpulent, of [good] breast and thigh; tender. [He sells] turkey pullets, turkey cocks. [The evil turkey seller] sells old turkey hens — poorly cooked turkeys, like rubber, tough, hard; sick turkeys; snuffling turkeys, with colds; dying turkeys; spoiled [ones].

THE OBSIDIAN SELLER

The obsidian seller is one who, [with] a staff with a crosspiece,[2] forces off [blades; he is] one who forces off [blades], who forces off obsidian blades. He forces off obsidian blades, he breaks off flakes. He sells obsidian, obsidian razors, blades, single-edged knives, double-edged knives, unworked obsidian, scraping stones, V-shaped [pieces]. He sells white obsidian, clear blue obsidian,[3] yellow obsidian, tawny obsidian,[4] obsidian chips.

THE MEDICINE SELLER, THE MAN ON THE REED MAT

The medicine seller is a knower of herbs, a knower of roots, a physician. He sells all things, medicines, herbs, wood, stones, milk, alum — [the herbs] *iztauhiatl*,[5] *tlaquacuitlapilli*,[6] *cuicuitlapile*,[7] *çaçalicpatli*,[8] *tla-*

Inic cempoalli, onnaui capitulo intechpa tlatoa in totolnamacaque in totoltetl quinamaca ioan in nepapan pâtli quinamaca

TOTOLTENAMACAC, totole, totolnemitiani, tlaoapani, quinamaca in totoltetl, canauhtetl, çoltetl, qualli iectli totoltetlaxcalli, tlaapaoaxtli, tlamololli. In teca mocaiaoa, quinamaca totoltepalan, totolin iiauh patostetl, cacalotetl, tzopilotetl, cozcaquauhtetl.

TOTOLNAMACAC: totole, tlaoapaoani, tlanemitiani, iolcaoa tlanecuiloa, totolnemitiani, totoloapaoa: in quinamaca, mexico totoli, castilla totoli, quanaca, tomaoac, nacaio, nanatztic, elmetze, celtic, ichpuchtotoli, uexolotl, quinamaca ilamatotoli, totollalichtli, iuhquin olli, quauacqui, quappitztic, totolcocoxq̄ totoliacaquiquintli, tzompiliui, totolmicqui, cuitlapalanqui

ITZNAMACAC:

in itznamacac ca itzcolotli, ezcolotli, tlauipeoani, tlauipeuhqui, itzuipeuhqui, itzuipeoa, tlapaneoa: quinamaca itztli, neximalitztli, tlapaneoalli, teputzmimiltic, ome iten, itztetl, tlachictetl, tlaquamantli, quinamaca iztac itztli, toltecaitztli, coztic itztli, itzcuinitztli, itztapalcatl.

PANAMACAC: PETLAPANTLACATL:

in panamacac, ca xiuiximatini, tlaneloaiomatini, ticitl ixquich quinamaca in pâtli, in xiuitl, in quauitl, in tetl, in memeiallotl, tececec, iztauhiatl, tlaquacuitlapilli, cuicuitlapile, çaçalicpatli, tlatlauhcapâtli, puz-

---

1. *Acad. Hist. MS* adds *quauhtotoli*.

2. Corresponding Spanish text: *vn instrumento de palo, estribando con los pies, y con las manos.*" Cf. Molina, *op. cit., colotli.*

3. Cf. *Florentine Codex*, Book XI, fol. 208*v*.

4. *Loc. cit.*

5. *Artemisia mexicana* Willd. (Emmart, *op. cit.*, p. 248).

6. Opossum tail [tree? plant?]; cf. *infra*, chap. xxviii, § 4, n. 11.

7. *Cuicuitlapile*: described (unident.) in Hernández, *op. cit.*, III, p. 721; called *Cuicuitlapilli Glandularia* in Nardo Antonio Reccho: *Rervm Medicarvm Novae Hispaniae Thesavrus sev Plantarvm Animalivm Mexicanorvm ex Francisci Hernandez* (Rome: Vitalis Mascardi, 1651), p. 248. Cf. also *Florentine Codex*, Book XI, fol. 139*v*. According to August Freiherr von Gall, "Medizinische Bücher (tici-amatl) der alten Azteken aus der ersten Zeit der Conquista," *Quellen und Studien zur Geschichte der Naturwissenschaften und der Medizin*, VII, 4–5 (1940), p. 110, it is perhaps *Valerianoides* sp.

8. *Çaçalic patli: Laserpitium peucedanoides* L.? — *Levisticum officinale* Koch.? — *Bidens* sp.? (Hernández, *op. cit.*, III, pp. 782, 835).

tlauhcapatli,[9] *puztequizpatli,*[10] *çaçalic,*[11] *iztac patli,*[12] *aatepocatic,*[13] *aoatzitzi,*[14] *tlalcacaoatl,*[15] *chichipilli,*[16] *tzonpopoto,*[17] *cicimatic.*[18] He sells all laid out on a reed mat. He sells things cooked in ollas — cooked beans.[19]

THE REED MAT SELLER, the reed mat weaver possesses reeds; he possesses palm leaves. He weaves reed mats; he makes a beginning, lays out [the reeds], arranges them, selects the best ones. He sells smooth reed mats,[20] red reed mats, painted reed mats, varicolored ones; palm leaf mats, small deep baskets, small deep baskets of palm leaves; reed mats — reed mats,[21] mats of triangular reeds,[22] mats of thick reeds, mats of bruised reeds, mats of frayed reeds, selected mats. He sells mat cords, round mats, narrow mats, radiating mats, varicolored ones; seats with backs; shiny [mats], sleeping mats,[23] small seats, pillows, seats — varicolored ones. [The evil mat seller sells] rotten, bruised, frayed ones.

THE SELLER OF STOUT CANE CARRYING BASKETS [is] a weaver of stout cane baskets, an owner of stout cane baskets, a possessor of stout cane baskets, a buyer and seller of stout cane carrying baskets. He weaves stout cane baskets, splits [the canes], arranges them, establishes the rims. He sells round stout cane baskets, square stout cane baskets, baskets made of slats — with legs, provided with lids, having lids.

THE DISPLAYER OF NECKLACES, the arranger of necklaces, the dealer in necklaces is a seller of necklaces — various kinds of necklaces. He sells necklaces of [worked] obsidian, of rock crystal, of amethyst, of

tequizpatli, çaçalic, iztac pâtli, aatepocatic, aoatzitzi, tlalcacaoatl, chichipilli, tzōpopoto cicimatic, quinamaca in ixquich petlapā onoc, quinamaca in tlapaoaxtli in epaoaxtic

PETLANAMACAC, petlachiuhqui, tole, çoiaoa, petlachioa, tlapeoaltia, tlatema, tlauipana, tlatzonana: quinamaca alaoacapetlatl, ezpetlatl, petlatlacuilolli, cuicuiliuhqui, çoiapetlatl, tonpiiatli, çoiatompiatli, tolpetlatl, toliaman, nacaze, tolcuexçolli, tolpapatztli, tolxaqualli, tlatzonantli, quinamaca petlamecatl, petlaiaoalli, petlapitzaoac, petlamoiaoac, cuicuiliuhqui: tepotzoicpalli, petlanqui, netlaxoni, tzinicpalli tzonicpalli, icpalli cuicuiliuhqui, petlapalan, petlapuxcauhqui, petlaxaxaqualli.

OTLACHIQUIUHNAMACAC, otlachiquiuhchiuhqui: otlachiquiue otlachiquioa, otlachiquiuhnecuilo, otlachiquiuhchioa, tlatzaiana, tlauipana tlatenuimoloa, quinamaca otlachiquiuhmimilli, otlachiquippatlachtli, quauhchiquiuitl, icxe, tzaccaio, tzacqui.

COZCATETECPANQUI, cozcauiuipanqui, cozcapantlacatl, ca coznamacac, nepapan cozcatl quinamaca, in itzcozcatl, in teuilotl, tlapalteuilotl, in apoconalli, in tezcapoctli, in tlapitzalli, in acatic, in ololtic, in ilacatztic,

9. *Tlatlauhcapatli: Geranium carolinianum* L. in Martínez, *op. cit.,* p. 210.

10. *Puztequizpatli — poztecpatli?* Unident. Reccho, *op. cit.,* describes one kind as *"folia habens parua, serrata, Origano similia, binaq; . . . flores purpurascentes ex albo"* (p. 146); another, *"folia habens Ocymi penè figura, & nonnihil vndulata, ex viridi purpurascentia. caules purpureos, tenues, ac volubiles flores in postremis ramis"* — known also as *omimeztli* (p. 277); and a third, *"folia Mali Persicae similia ferens, bina per singulos caulis nodos ordine disposita, inferne coccinea . . . flores quinque constantes folijs rubescentibus eadem forma"* (p. 291). Cf. also Hernández, *op. cit.,* III, p. 961.

11. *Çaçalic: Bidens* sp.? — *Mentzelia* sp.? (*ibid.,* pp. 780, 785; several kinds are described). The term is *çacacili* in the *Acad. Hist. MS — Lithospermum* sp. (?), in Hernández, *op. cit.,* pp. 825–826 (*zacazilin*).

12. *Iztac patli: Psoralea pentaphylla* L. (Martínez, *op. cit.,* pp. 77*sqq.*).

13. *Aatepocatic:* perhaps *Anona aquamosa,* according to von Gall, *op. cit.,* p. 224.

14. *Aoatzitzi — ahoatzitzin:* small oak (Hernández, *op. cit.,* I, p. 48).

15. *Tlalcacauatl: Arachis hypogaea* Linn. (Hernández, *op. cit.,* III, pp. 915–20).

16. *Chichipilli — chichipiltic?* Unident.; desc. in Reccho, *op. cit.,* p. 367: *"Rami rubent. Flores verò vt in Vicia ex caeruleo rubescunt. Et vt planta integra praesefert, ex leguminoso genere est."*

17. *Tzonpopoto — tzonpopoton: Conyza filaginoides* Hieron.? (Hernández, *op. cit.,* I, p. 137).

18. *Canavalia villosa* Benth. (*ibid.,* p. 204).

19. *Epaxayotic* (skunk excretion) in *Acad. Hist. MS.*

20. Cf. Anderson and Dibble, *op. cit.,* Book VIII, p. 31.

21. Cf. Sahagún (Garibay ed.), III, p. 328.

22. *Loc. cit.*

23. *Netlaxivani* in *Acad. Hist. MS.*

amber,[24] of black mirror-stone, of cast gold — cylindrical,[25] round,[26] twisted; necklaces of Castile [which] resemble emeralds,[27] rock crystal — white, yellow, herb green, green — green, herb green, ruddy, black, sky blue, azure, blue, rose colored, cochineal, verdigris color, brown.

THE MIRROR-STONE SELLER, the mirror-stone maker [is] a lapidary, a polisher. He abrades; he uses abrasive sand; he cuts; he carves; he uses a glue of bat excrement, polishes with a fine cane, makes it shiny. He sells mirror-stones — round, circular; pierced on both sides,[28] [which] can be seen through; two-faced, single-faced, concave; good mirror-stones, white mirror-stones, black mirror-stones.

THE NEEDLE SELLER, the copper caster [is] one who pours [molten] copper, who makes bells, who melts [copper]. He polishes, abrades, casts copper. He makes bells,[29] needles, awls;[30] he pours [molten] copper. He sells needles, awls, punches, copper crossbow bolts, bells, wrist-band bells. He sells axes, claws, adzes, fish hooks, chisels.

THE RUBBER SELLER, a possessor of rubber, a possessor of rubber trees, a collector of rubber, collects rubber, sells rubber — balls of rubber, wide masses of rubber, thin masses; rubber to play the ball game, bouncing, noisy, noise-making.

THE BROOM SELLER, the besom seller [is] a possessor of brooms, a possessor of besoms, a possessor of brooms for sweeping. [He is] a gatherer [of straw], one who reaps with a sickle. He gathers [straw] for brooms, he gathers [straw] for besoms. He sells besoms, he sells brooms; he sells long ones, stiff ones, stubby ones, white ones.

THE GLUE[31] SELLER, the digger of glue plant [roots] digs glue plant [roots], trims glue plant [roots], beats them with a stone, pulverizes them. He sells glue plant [roots] uncooked — pulverized, ground. [The evil glue seller sells glue][32] coarsely ground, with pulverized maize stalks, with ground grains of maize, with ground beans.

castillan cozcatl, momatlalitznenequi, moteuilonenequi, iztac, coztic, quiltic, xoxocti, xoxouhqui, quiltic, tlatlauhqui, tliltic, texotic, matlaltic, mouitic, tlaztaleoaltic, nochpaltic, quilpaltic, camiltic.

TEZCANAMACAC, tezcachiuhqui, tlatecqui, tlapetlauhqui tlachiqui, tlatexaluia, tlatequi, tlacuicui, tlatzinacancuitlauia, quetlaquetzalôtlauia, tlaiottouia: quinamaca in tezcatl, in iaoaliuhqui, in iaoaltic necoc xapo, nalquizqui, necoc tlachia, centlapallachia acaltezcatl, qualli tezcatl, iztac tezcatl, tezcapuctli.

VITZMALLONAMACAC, tepuzpitzqui, tepuztecac, coiolchiuhqui, tlaatiliani, tlapetlaoa, tlâchiqui, tepuzpitza, colchioa, uitzmallochioa, coiolmichioa: tepuzteca quinamaca in uitzmallotl, coiolomitl, tepuzomitl, tepuztlachichtli, coiolli, coioltecuecuextli quinamaca tlaxeloloni, mactepuztli, matepuztli, acatepuztli, quaooani.

OLNAMACAC, ole, olquaûe, olcuicuini, olcuicui: quinamaca olli teololtic, olpatlachtli, olpitzaoac ollamaloni, tzicuictic, capanqui tlacapanilli.

POPONAMACAC, izquiznamacac popooa, izquize, ochpaoaçe, tlapini, tlaotlapaloazuiani, popopi, izquizpi, izquiznamaca, poponamaca, quinamaca uiiac, chicaoac, tetepontic, teteztic.

TZACUNAMACAC, tzacutatacani: tzacutataca, tzacuxima, tzacutetzotzona, tzacupinoloa, quinamaca tzacuxoxouhqui, tzacupinolli, cuechtic, papaiaxtic ooaquauhtexio, tlaoltexo, etexio

---

24. Read *apoçonalli*.

25. Corresponding Spanish text: *"como cañutillos."*

26. *Ibid.: "como bodoqujllos."*

27. *Acad. Hist. MS* adds *moquetzalitznênequi, moximmatlalitznênequi.*

28. Cf., however, Spanish text *"espejos de dos hazes, pulidos de ambas partes."* Molina, *op. cit.*, Spanish-Nahuatl section (*Espejo de dos hazes. necoc xapo tezcatl*).

29. *Acad. Hist. MS: coyolchiva.*

30. *Ibid.: coyolomichiva.*

31. *Tzacutli: Bletia campanulata; Epidendron pastoris* Ll. & Lex. (Santamaría, *Diccionario de Americanismos*, III, p. 224).

32. Cf. corresponding Spanish text.

THE PINE RESIN SELLER [is] a woodsman, a collector of pine resin. He collects pine resin, he sells pine resin. He sells uncooked pine resin; cooked pine resin, boiled in an olla; pine resin mixed with lampblack; the resin of [other] trees.

THE SELLER OF LIQUIDAMBAR [is] a possessor of pine resin — a possessor of pine resin trees, of good, pure pine resin. [The evil seller] sells that [which appears] genuine; he deceives people by [mixing] pine resin with ground beans [or] ground maize grains.

THE SMOKING TUBE SELLER, the tobacco [tube] seller, is one who provides a covering [for the tobacco tube] — a maker of reed smoking tubes, a cutter of reeds. He strips them, he removes the outer surface; he prepares charcoal, he grinds charcoal. He covers [the reeds with moist charcoal dust]; he paints them, he colors them, he gilds them. He sells the tobacco [tubes] destined for fondling in the hand — long, of an arm's span, [covered with] a thickness of clay,[33] [with] a thickness of charcoal [dust], whitened with chalk, gilded, painted, painted with a hidden design,[34] mottled, painted with flowers; [he sells] tobacco tubes in the form of a blow gun, [painted with] fish, eagles, etc. There are made market tobacco [tubes], tobacco [tubes] of little value; they flake off, they crumble. [There are] shredded tobacco, chopped tobacco, scented tobacco, cigars, tobacco tubes. The tobacco burns. [The smoking tubes] are filled with tobacco, the inside is filled, crammed, the opening is closed, the end is closed. [The seller] prepares tobacco, rubs it in his hands, mixes it well with flowers, with *uei nacaztli*,[35] with bitumen, with *uacalxochitl*,[36] with *tlilxochitl*,[37] with *mecaxochitl*,[38] with mushrooms, with *poyomatli*,[39] with "obsidian tobacco."[40]

BITUMEN [is] black, very black, black; [it is] that which flakes, crumbles, breaks up. It comes from the ocean, from the sea; it is produced within the ocean. When it comes forth, [it is] according to the time count. The waves cast it forth. It comes forth, it

OCUTZONAMACAC, quauhtlacatl, ocotzocuicuini, ocutzocuicui ocutzonamaca: quinamaca xoxouhqui ocutzotl, tlacuxitl, ocutzotl, tlapaoaxtli, tlilocutzotl, quauhocotzotl.

SUCHIOCUTZONAMACAC, ocutzooa, ocutzoquaue, iectli, qualli, ocutzotl, quinamaca, ioltica, ic teca mocaiaoa, etexio, tlaoltexio ocutzotl.

ACAQUAUHNAMACAC, iienamacac, ca tlapepecho, acaquauhchiuhqui, acatecqui, tlatoxoma, tlaoaçoma, tecullalia, teculteci, tlapepechoa, tlacuiloa, tlatlapalaquia, tlateucuitlaauia, quinamaca in iietl, itonal tlamatoctli, uiiac, ce ciiacatl, coquitilaoac, tecultilaoac, uel tiçaio, teucuitlaaio, tlacuilolli, ichtaca tlacuilollo puxcauhqui, suchitlacuilollo, tlacaloaziietl, michi, quauhtli etc muchioa tianquizietl ça çan ie iietl, papaiaca, cacaiaca, pilietl pipilietl, suchietl, poquietl, acaiietl, iietlatia, iietema, tlaiollotia, tlacacatztza, tlaeltzaqua, tlaquatzaqua, iietlachioa, ca tlamatiloa, uel quinamictia, suchio vei nacazio, chapupuio, oâcalsuchio, tlilsuchio, mecasuchio, nanacaio, poiomaio, itziieio.

IN CHAPUPUTLI, tliltic, tlilpâtic, caputztic, cacaiacani, papaiacani, paianini, teuapan, ilhuicaapan vitz, teuatl, iitic in muchioa, çã tlapoalpan, in oalquiça, acueiotl quioallaça, çan metztlapoalpan, in oalquiça, in oaluetzi, inic oalquiça iuhquin petlatl patlaoac tila-

---

33. Read çoquitilaoac.

34. Corresponding Spanish text: *"Otros ay, que tienẽ pintura encubierta, que no se vee sino quando se van gastando con el fuego."*

35. *Cymbopetalum penduliflorum*; cf. *supra*, chap. xxi, nn. 5, 6.

36. Emmart, *op. cit.*, p. 234 — *Xanthosoma* sp.; Santamaría, *op. cit.*, II, p. 102 — *Phyllodendron affine* Hemsl.

37. *Vanilla planifolia*; cf. *supra*, chap. xxi, n. 3.

38. *Piper amalago*; cf. *ibid.*, n. 4.

39. Hernández, *op. cit.*, II, p. 337 — unident. fern or narcotic root; corresponding Spanish text — *"rosa."*

40. *Ibid.*: *"una yerua"* (unident.).

drops out according to the phase of the moon.[41] When it comes forth, [it is] like a mat, wide, thick. Those of the seashore, those of the coast lands gather it there. They gather it, they pick it up from the sand.

The bitumen [is] fragrant, of pleasing scent; its scent, its odor [is] precious. When it is exposed to the fire, when it is cast in the fire, its scent spreads over the whole land.

Bitumen is used for two [purposes]. The first [purpose] for which it is used is to be mixed with pulverized tobacco, so that the pulverized tobacco may be made pleasing. The pleasing scent of the tobacco with bitumen spreads over the whole land. As its second use, it is used by women; they chew the bitumen. And what they chew [is] named chicle. They do not chew it alone; they provide it with *axin*.[42] They mix it with *axin*. It cannot be chewed alone; it crumbles. And in this manner it is improved: *axin* is provided, *axin* is mixed in, so that it is softened, smoothed.

And the chewing of chicle [is] the preference, the privilege of the little girls, the small girls, the young women. Also the mature women, the unmarried women use it; and all the women who [are] unmarried chew chicle in public.

One's wife also chews chicle,[43] but not in public. Also the widowed and the old women do not, in public. But the bad women, those called harlots, [show] no fine feelings; quite publicly they go about chewing chicle along the roads, in the market place, clacking like castanets. Other women who constantly chew chicle in public achieve the attributes of evil women.

For this reason the women chew chicle: because thereby they cause their saliva to flow and thereby the mouths are scented; the mouth is given a pleasing taste. With it they dispel the bad odor of their mouths, or the bad smell of their teeth. Thus they chew chicle in order not to be detested. The men also chew chicle to cause their saliva to flow and to clean the teeth, but this very secretly — never in public.

The chewing of chicle [is] the real privilege of the addicts termed "effeminates." [It is] as if it were

oac, oncan quicui in atẽoaq̃, in anaoaca, ilhuicaaxalpan in quicui in quipepena

In chapuputli, hauiac, uelic, hiiac, tlaçotli in iiaca in iuelica, in tletl quitta, in tleco motlaça centlalli momana in iiauiiaca.

In chapuputli: ontlamantli inic monequi. Inic centlamantli ic monequi: iietlalli moneloa ic mauialia in iietlalli centlalli momana in iiauiaca iietl chapupuio. Inic ontlamantli imonecca: cioa intech monequi quiquaqua in chapuputli. Auh inin quiquaqua itoca tzictli, amo çan iuhqui in quiquaqua, caxuia, axin quineloa, in çan iuhqui amo uel moquaqua, çan papaiaca, auh inic qualtia maxuia, axin moneneloa, ic atia, ic iamania.

Auh in inpaniti tzicquaqualiztli in innemac, iehoantin in ichpopuchtotonti, in ichpuchtepitoton, in cioapipiltotonti: no iehoantin intech monequi in ie uel cioa in ie uel ichpopuchti: ioan muchin in cioa, in ichpopuchti mixmana in tzicquaqua.

In tecioaoan no tzicquaqua no tzicquaqua iece amo mixmana: no iehoanti in cacaoalti, ioan ilamatque tzicquaqua, amo mixmana. Auh in cioa tlaueliloque in mitoa auiianime, atle innemamachiliz, uel mixmana: injc mantinemi in tzicquaqua, in utlica in tianquizco motzictlatlatza: in oc cequintin cioâ in teixpã tzitzicquaqua cioatlauelilocaiotl câci.

Inic tzicquaqua cioa ipãpa ic quiquixtia in imiztlac, ioan ic mocamaauiialia, mocamauelilia, ic quipoloa in incamaxoquiaca in anoço intlaniiaca ipampa in tzicquaqua inic amo ihiialozque. In oq̃chtin no tzicquaqua: inic quiquixtia imiztlac ioan ic motlanpaca: auh inin cenca ichtaca, çan niman amo mixmana.

In cocoxque in intoca chimouhque: uel innemac, in tzicquaqualiztli, iuhquinma imaxca, iuhquinma

---

41. *Ibid.:* "*conforme al creciente de la luna.*"

42. *Coccus axin:* "axi, axin or aje, an oily yellowish substance which is produced by a scale insect of the same name upon the branches of *Jatropha curcas, Spondias,* and other trees" — Paul C. Standley: "Trees and Shrubs of Mexico," *Contributions from the United States National Herbarium* (Washington: Government Printing Office, 1923), Vol. 23, Pt. 3, p. 641.

43. Repetition of *no tzicquaqua* appears in the Nahuatl text.

their privilege, their birthright. And the men who publicly chew chicle achieve the status of sodomites; they equal the effeminates.

The bitumen is mixed with copal, with liquidambar. With these there is incensing, there is perfuming.

THE AXIN [is] yellow, very yellow, quite yellow, pulverized, soft, viscid, hot. This *axin* [is] an insect. Thus is it engendered: it settles on the tree named *axquauitl*.[44] A little insect like a fly settles on it; then it eats the leaves of the *axquauitl*. It lays its eggs on it; there they hatch in countless numbers. When they have enlarged, have become well rounded, then the inhabitants shake them off. They then are boiled in an olla. When they are cooked, they break open their shells. Something just like wool, like flour, comes out. Then they wrap it in maize husks.

The essence of *axin* [is] hot; they say [it is] like fire. The traveler anoints himself with it in order that the cold will not oppress him exceedingly. Where the sickness named the gout occurs, wherever it is, [*axin*] is spread on. It soothes [the gout]. In order that frost will not injure the lips, an *axin* unguent is applied; it is spread on the lips. It is said, *axin* is applied to the lips. This is not used alone as a cure for gout; it is mixed with the herb called *colotzitzicaztli*.[45] In order for this *axin* to serve as an unguent, to be used as an unguent, lampblack is added; thus one does not go on constantly applying an unguent.

This *axin* [is] a remedy for diarrhea. When someone cannot stop his diarrhea, when he has diarrhea just like water, *axin* is boiled. And when it has cooled, when [it is] tepid, it is given as an enema to one who has diarrhea. It is thus cured; his diarrhea is thus stopped.

THE MOUNTAIN CHICLE, or wild chicle, is just like [ordinary] chicle. It is also chewed. As it is chewed, [it is] like beeswax. It does not sicken one; it does not give one a headache. [It is] very pleasing and sweet. But the [other] chicle, when it is chewed, tires one's head; it gives one a headache. The mountain chicle is an herb; [the substance] is extracted from its root.

intonal. Auh in aquin teixpā tzicquaqua in toquichti cuitoiutl câci, chimouhcaiutl quineuiuilia

In chapuputli, copalli, suchiocutzotl moneloa, ic tlapupuchhuilo, ic tlaauililo.

IN AXIN coztic, cozpâtic cozpiltic, cuechtic, iamanqui, atic, totonqui. Inin axin ioioli inic moxinachoa, itech motlalia in itoca axquauitl: in itech omotlali ioioliton iuhquin çaioli, niman quiqua in ixiuhio axquauitl itech motetia vncan tlacati, in amo çan tlapoalli. In iquac oueueixque uel totolonaui: nimā quitzetzeloa in chaneque, nimā quimapaoaci, in oicucique, quinpitzinia, uel iuhquin tomiol in quiça, iuhquin testli, niman ic izoatica quiquimiloa.

In axin: in ihiio totonqui, quitoa iuhquī tletl: in nenenqui ic moça, inic amo cenca quiuitequi in cecec. In canin onoc: in canin câ in cocoliztli, in itoca cooaciztli, vncā onmoteca quiiamania: inic amo quiuitequiz cetl in texipalli, ic momateloa tetenio ommoteca mitoa netenaxuilo. Inin amo çan mixcauia inic mopâtia cooaciuiztli: moneloa in quilhuia colotzitzicaztli. Inin axin inic neoçalo inic matilolo motlilhuia inic amo cemicac tzotlantinemiz

Inin axin ipâio in apitzalli: in aquin aoc uel motzaqua in iapitzal in ça iuhqui atl quinoquia, moquaqualatza in axin. Auh in iquac oceuh: in iquac ça iamanqui, itlanipa momaca in mapitza ic pati, ic motzaqua in iapitzal.

IN TEPETZICTLI tecanaltzictli, anoço tacanaltzictli: ca çan no iuhqui tzictli, ca no moquaqua: iuhquinma xicocuitlatl, inic moquaqua: amo tecoco amo quicocoa in tetzontecon, cenca tepac, ioā tzopelic. Auh in tzictli inic moquaqua: ca tetzontecon quaquauhtilia, quicocoa in tetzontecon. In tepetzictli: ca xiuitl ineloaio itech quicui

---

44. Lit., *axin* tree — *Jatropha curcas, Spondias* sp. etc. (Standley, *loc. cit.*, citing Urbina, *Naturaleza* 7:363–365, 1902).
45. *Urera* sp.? (Emmart, *op. cit.*, p. 297); *Jatropha* sp.? (Hernández, *op. cit.*, II, p. 385).

Twenty-fifth Chapter, which telleth of the candle sellers, and the bag sellers, and those who sell sashes.

THE CANDLE SELLER, a candle maker, prepares beeswax — blanches, washes, boils, purifies, melts, cooks, prepares, bathes it. He forms it into a roll, makes it like a stone column, provides a center for it . . . , makes it cylindrical like a wooden roller,[1] places a wick.

He sells candles; he sells white, yellow, black ones . . . ; [candles] overlaid with wax, thick-wicked; very smooth, slender; stubby, lumpy, uneven.

THE BAG SELLER

The bag seller is a seller of bags for gold. [He is] a cutter. He sews; he rubs in dough; he provides cords, loosely braided leather thongs, loosely braided cotton thongs. [He makes bags] small and narrow within, roomy, of enlarged top, small, narrow and short, short and narrow — small bags, little bags.

THE SASH SELLER, the belt seller [is] a cutter of cloth, a cutter of narrow strips. He cuts straight [strips of cloth]; he provides them with loops, with metal fasteners. He sells broad, narrow, sufficiently broad and thick, yellow, white, black, [and] red[2] [sashes].

THE SHOE SELLER, the maker of Castilian shoes, provides soles; cuts them; stitches sandals. He stitches, sews, stitches firmly. He sells narrow [shoes], the privilege of wise men.

THE PEDDLER [is] a retailer; a retailer of diverse objects: one who procures things in wholesale lots, who peddles them. He sells metal, paper, scissors, knives, needles, cloth, lengths of cloth, bands of cloth, bracelets. All [these] he stores — as many as he can.

THE BLUE DYE SELLER dyes one. [She is] a seller of black clay [which] dyes one — a gatherer of clay. She carries clay on her back[3] [to] dye one, [to] dye objects. She mixes it with *uixachin*[4] [leaves,] with

Inic cempoalli ommacuilli capitulo: intechpa tlatoa, in candelanamacaque, ioan in xiquipilnamacaque, ioan in necuitlalpiloni quinamaca

CANDELANAMACAC, candelachiuhqui, xicocuitlachioa, tlaztalia, tlapaca, tlapaoaci, tlachipaoa, tlaatilia tlatzoionia tlateteca, tlaaltia, tlamimiloa, tlatemimiloa tlaiollotia, tlatlaoiotia, tlaquammimiloazuia, tlacpaiotia:

candelanamaca quinamaca iztac coztic, tliltic tlatlaoiotilli, tlaixauilli, tlacpaiotomaoalli, tetzcaltic, piaztic, tetecuitztic, xixipuchtic, côcomotztic.

XIQUIPILNAMACAC,

bulsanamacac: ca teucuitlaxiquipilnamacac, tlatecqui tlatzoma, tlatexiotia, tlamecaiotia, cuetlaxpoxatli, tilmapoxatli, coiaoac hite, ontlaaqui, tlaquaxixiqui, tepiton titichtontli titichpil, chitictontli, chiticpil.

NELPILONAMACAC, talabartenamacac: tlapitzaoacatequini, tlapitzaoacasutlani, tlamelaoacatlaxotla, tlauicollotia, tlatepuziotia: quinamaca patlaoac, pitzaoac, ipan qualli, patlaoacatilaoac, coztic, iztac, tliltic, tliltlactic

ÇAPATOSNAMACAC, castillan cacçoc: tlacacoapalhuia, tlatequi, cacço, tlaçô, tlatzoma, tlatepitzço, quinamaca pitzaoac, mîmati itonal, tetonal.

TLACÔCOALNAMACAC: tlacemãqui, tlacecemanqui, tlacẽcuini tlacôcoani, quinamaca tepuztli, amatl, tixeras, cuchillos, uitzmallotl, paños lienços, tlatentli, macuestli, muchi quipie, in quexquich ueliti.

SIUHQUILNAMACAC, tepa, palnamacac, tepâ: çoquicuini, coquimama, tepâ, tlapa, tlauixachiotia, tlaquauhtepuziotia: quinamaca in palli, çan mulhui çoquitl, uixachio, quauhtepuzio.

---

1. *Acad. Hist. MS* inserts *tlaixauia* — overlays (wax).

2. *Ibid.*: *tlatlactic*.

3. Read *çoquimama*.

4. *Acacia farnesiana* (L.) Willd. (Standley, *op. cit.*, Pt. 2, p. 378).

quauhtepoztli[5] [bark]. She sells black clay, ordinary clay, with *uixachin* [leaves], with *quauhtepoztli* [bark].

THE FEATHER SELLER [is] a bird owner. She raises birds; she plucks them. She plucks feathers; she treats them with chalk. She plucks feathers from the back and the breast; she peels downy feathers. She spins split ones. She spins feathers — spins them into an even thread, trims them. She spins them loosely, she spins firmly; she uses the spindle, turns them loosely about the spindle, turns them firmly about the spindle.

She sells soft, spun [feathers]; long, even thread — trimmed,[6] loose, loosely woven; white feathers, tail feathers, chick feathers, back and breast feathers, darkened ones, brown[7] ones; goose feathers, domestic duck feathers, Peru duck feathers, wild duck feathers,[8] turkey feathers — black, white, yellow, bright red, tawny, carmine colored.

THE HERB SELLER[9] is a producer of herbs, a field worker, a plucker of herbs. She plucks greens; she produces herbs. She sells *eloquilitl*,[10] *moçoquilitl*,[11] *tzitziquilitl*,[12] *tepicquilitl*,[13] *matzalquilitl*,[14] *tzayanalquilitl*,[15] *auexocaquilitl*,[16] *chilquilitl*,[17] amaranth greens, amaranth heads, several varieties of sorrel,[18] *ayauhtonan*,[19] *tacanalquilitl*,[20] watercress,[21] *popoyauhquilitl*,[22] *atziuequilitl*,[23] *calauauhquilitl*,[23] a species of purslane.[24]

HIHUJNAMACAC: totooa, totonemitia, tlauiuitla, totouiuitla, tlatiçauia, alapachuiuitla, tlachcaio mumutzoa, tlamaxactzaoa, hihuitzaoa, tlatemimiloa, tlatatacaloa, tlapuxaoatzaoa, tlatetziltzaoa, tlamalacaania, tlaxaxalmalacauia, tlaquauhtemalacauia,

quinamaca molõqui tlatzaoalli, temimiltic, tatatictic, poxâtic, poxaoac, poxactic, iztac, hihuitl, tzinhihuitl, pilihuitl, alapachtli, catzaoac, camilhuiltic, tlalalacahihuitl, patoshihuitl, pelonhihuitl, canacacauhhihuitl, totolîhuitl, tliltic, iztac, coztic, chichiltic quappachtic, nochpalli.

QUILNAMAC: ca quilchiuhqui cuenchiuhqui, quîquilpic, quîquilpi, quilchioa, quinamaca eloquilitl, moçuquilitl, tzitziquilitl, tepicquilitl, mâtzalquilitl, tzaianalquilitl, auexocaquilitl, chilquilitl, oauhquilitl, oauhquiltzontli, xoxocoioli, xoxocoiolpapatla, xoxocoioluiuilan, quauhxoxocoioli, miccaxoxoioli, xoxocoiolcuecuepo aiauhtona, tacanalquilitl, mexixi, popoiauhquilitl, atziuequilitl, calaoauhquilitl, itzmiquilitl

---

5. Cf. *Florentine Codex*, Book XI, fol. 113v. Siméon, *op. cit.*, describes it as the bark of a tree mixed with black clay and *uixachin* leaves; von Gall, *op. cit.*, pp. 217*sqq.*, believes it may be *teposan*, a *Budleia* sp., possibly *sessiliflora*.

6. *Acad. Hist. MS: tatacaltic*.

7. *Ibid.: camiltic*.

8. *Ibid.: canavivitl*.

9. Read *Quilnamacac*.

10. *Bidens pilosa* L. Cf. Anderson and Dibble, *op. cit.*, VIII (Kings and Lords), p. 38, n. 17.

11. *Eupatorium deltoideum* Jacq. (*ibid.*, n. 18).

12. *Erigeron pusillus* Nutt. ("little greens") — Sahagún (Garibay ed.), IV, p. 366.

13. *Mesembryanthemum blandum* L. — Bernardino de Sahagún: *Historia general de las cosas de Nueva España* (México: Editorial Pedro Robredo, 1938; hereafter referred to as Sahagún, Robredo ed.), III, p. 338.

14. Unident.; possibly *matzatli* (*Ananas sativus*)? — Santamaría, *op. cit.*, II, p. 260.

15. Water greens (Anderson and Dibble, *op. cit.*, p. 38).

16. Same as *achochoquilitl* (*loc. cit.*)? Or *Salix* sp.? — Santamaría, *op. cit.*, I, p. 65.

17. *Eriogonum* sp.? (Hernández, *op. cit.*, II, p. 421).

18. Various *Oxalis* sp. Cf. Anderson and Dibble, *loc. cit.* and p. 68; Standley, *op. cit.*, Pt. 3, p. 517; Sahagún (Robredo ed.), III, p. 339; Sahagún (Garibay ed.), IV, pp. 350, 370. — *Miccaxoxoioli*: read *miccaxoxocoiolli*.

19. *Cuphea jorullensis* H. B. K. (Hernández, *op. cit.*, I, p. 55); *Porophyllum coloratum* D. C. — Sahagún (Robredo ed.), *loc. cit.*

20. Unident.

21. Emmart, *op. cit.*, p. 239.

22. *Raphanus raphanistrum* Linn. (Hernández, *op. cit.*, I, p. 241).

23. Unident.

24. Anderson and Dibble, *op. cit.*, p. 68.

Twenty-sixth Chapter, which telleth of the atole sellers, and the sellers of prepared chocolate, and the sellers of saltpeter.

THE ATOLE SELLER sells hot atole; thick, white atole; atole of maize cooked in lime; atole of raw ground maize; bean atole, toasted maize atole, fruit atole, chili atole, black atole; tortilla atole, boiled chili atole; atole treated with lime, atole with honey.

She sells cold atole, pinole, wrinkled *chía*, amaranth pinole. The good [is] smooth, thick; the bad [is] overflowing, clotted. It has things on top: chili on top, honey on top.

THE SELLER OF FINE CHOCOLATE

The seller of fine chocolate [is] one who grinds, who provides people with drink, with repasts. She grinds cacao [beans]; she crushes, breaks, pulverizes them. She chooses, selects,[1] separates them. She drenches, soaks, steeps them. She adds water sparingly, conservatively; aerates it, filters it, strains it, pours it back and forth, aerates it; she makes it form a head, makes it foam; she removes the head, makes it thicken, makes it dry, pours water in, stirs water into it.

She sells good, superior, potable [chocolate]: the privilege, the drink of nobles, of rulers — finely ground, soft, foamy, reddish, bitter; [with] chili water, with flowers, with *uei nacaztli*, with *teonacaztli*,[2] with vanilla, with *mecaxochitl*,[3] with wild bee honey, with powdered aromatic flowers. [Inferior chocolate has] maize flour and water; lime water; [it is] pale; the [froth] bubbles burst. [It is chocolate] with water added — Chontal water . . . [fit for] water flies.

THE SELLER OF SALTPETER [is] a guide to places where there is saltpeter, one who heaps up saltpeter. He sells saltpeter [which is] white; with potsherds; yellow; [as fine] as soil; viscous; [he sells] red saltpeter.

Inic cempoalli onchiquacen capitulo: intechpa tlatoa in atulnamacaque, ioan in cacaoatlaquetzalnamacaque ioan in tequisquinamacaque

ATOLNAMACAC: quinamaca atolli totonqui, quauhnexatolli, nextamalatolli, iolatolli, etlatolli, izquiatolli, xocoatolli, chilatolli, tlilatolli, tlaxcalatolli, chilpoçonalli, tenexatolli, nequatolli:

quinamaca itztic atolli, pinolli chientzotzol, michipinolli, qualli tetzcaltic, tlatztic, amo qualli, ixmemeia, papachca, pane, chilpane, necupane.

TLAQUETZALNAMACAC,

atlaquetzalnamacac, tecini, teatlitiani, teihiiocuitiani, cacaoateci, tlaxamania, tlapaiana, tlacuechoa tlatzontequi, tlacentlaca, tlacenquixtia, aciaoa, tlaciaoa, tlaapachoa, tlaamauhtia, tlaaiçauia, tlaacana, tlatzetzeloa, tlaatzetzeloazuia, aquetza, tlaacana, tlatzotzontlalia, tlapopoçonallalia, tlatzotzoncui, tlatetzaoacaquetza, tlatetzaoacaacana, tlaaquechia, tlaatecuinia

quinamaca qualli iectli, ioani, tetonal tecpilatl, tlâtôcaatl, cuechtic, iamanqui, tlatzotzõcuitl, tlatlauhqui, chichic, chilatl, suchio, uei nacazio, teunacazio, tlilsuchio, mecasuchio quauhnecuio, suchaio, texatl, nextamalatl, iztalectic, xixittomoni, tlaaquechilli, quauhchontalatl, quaoatl achiquilichtli.

TEQUIXQUINAMACAC, tequixquipan tlaiacanqui, tequixquiololoani, quinamaca tequixquitl iztac tatapalcatic coztic, tlaltic alaoac, tlapaltequixquitl

---

1. Read *tlacentlaça*, as in *Acad. Hist. MS.*

2. Cf. *supra*, chap. xxi, nn. 5, 6; probably *Cymbopetalum penduliflorum* and *Chiranthrodendron pentadactylon*, respectively.

3. *Piper amalago*; cf. *ibid.*, n. 4.

THE CHALK SELLER [is] one who masses [chalk] with his hand[4] — who masses it with his hand. He masses it with his hand; he cooks it.[5] The chalk [which] he sells [is] soft, spongy, fluffy; limestone.

THE PROCURESS is one who procures. She is of a house [of ill fame]. Gentle of words, [she is] a corrupter, an inducer. She induces, seduces with words, incites others. Adroit of language, skilled of speech, she is a fraud. She acts as a procuress. She receives guests. She secures recompense, payment from others. She robs one — she constantly robs one.

THE PROSTITUTE, the woman who sells herself, who repeatedly sells herself, [is] a harlot, destitute, besotted, drunk, gaudy, vain, filthy; a perverted woman. She ornaments herself well, places herself at the market, adorns herself at the market place; she adorns herself; she is pompous.

She sells her body, her flesh, her heritage, her possession, her vulva — an evil woman, proud, very proud. [She is] a little girl, a small girl, then a pleasing little one, a pleasing young woman, a maiden, a wretched maiden; an old woman, a wretched old woman, a little old woman, a corrupt old woman. Restless on the water, living on the water, she is flighty; she travels along the road — travels shamefully along the road; she walks as if a part of the market place; she walks painted in the market place. She walks back and forth many times along the road; she walks circling, constantly. She nowhere finds lodging. She settles anywhere, she sleeps anywhere, she [wakes at] dawn anywhere. In any manner whatsoever night [and] day overtake her.

THE SELLER OF FINE TOBACCO sells fine tobacco, . . . , small tobacco.[6] He rubs it between his hands. He who finds fine tobacco chews it. And some prefer wormwood to tobacco. Fine tobacco affects one; it makes one drunk, it aids one's digestion, it dispels one's fatigue.

TIÇANAMACAC: tlamatzoani, tlamamatzo, tlamamatzoa, tl tlaxca tiçatl quinamaca, poxaoac, poxactic, popoxactic, tetiçatl.

TETZINNAMACAC: ca tetlanochili, tecalloti, camasuchitl, tetlacuepili, tecôconauiani, tecoconauia, tetensuchitzotzona, teiollapana, camatoli, tentoltecatl tentlama, tetlanochilia tecacallotia tetlacuepilia teca motlaxtlauia, teichtequi, tehihichtequi

MONAMACAC: motzinnamacac, motzîtzinnamacac, auiiani, iellelacic, tlaoanqui, xocomicqui, topalpol, xacampol, tlailpol, suchicioatl, moiêiecquetza, motiamicquetza, motiamicchichioa, mîmihimati, moquêquecimmati,

quinamaca in itlalnacaio, in inacaio, in iiôcauh, in iaxca, in ineneuh, cioatlaueliloc, cioacuecuel, cuecuetolcioatl, ichpuchpil, ichpuchtontli, quin uelicaton, uelica cioatl, ichpuchtli, ichpuchpol: ilama, ilamapol, ilanton, auililama, anenqui apan, apannemini, atzintlaltechpachiui, ŷtli, quitotocatinemi, vtli quimamatilitinemi, tianquiztli quiuiuiltectinemi, tianquiztli quîcuilotinemi, vtli quicuecuelpachotinemi, moiaoatinemi, cêmântinemi, acan chanitta, ça can uetzi, ça can cuchi, ça can tlatui, ça quê uetzi in iooalli, in cemilhuitl.

PICIENAMACAC: quinamaca picietl, xicôiietl, tlalietl, quimaxaqualoa: in aca quitta picietl, quiqua. Auh cequintin iztauhiatl in quipiciepoa: in picietl tetech quiz, teiuinti, tetlatemouili, teciauizpôpolo.

4. *Acad. Hist. MS: tlamâmatzoani.*
5. The separate *tl* is an error in the *Florentine Codex.*
6. *Erigeron Scaposus* DC. (Hernández, *op. cit.,* I, p. 248).

Twenty-seventh Chapter, which telleth of the intestines, and of all the internal organs, and of all the external organs, [and] of the joints pertaining to men and pertaining to women.[1]

First paragraph, which telleth[2] of the body, of the skin of men and of women.

Inic cempoalli on chicome capitulo: intechpa tlatoa in cuitlaxculli, ioan in ixquich tehitic onoc, ioan in ixquich pani onoc, uiuilteccaiutl, in totech câ, in toquichti, ioan in cioa intech câ.

Inic ce parrapho: itechpa tlaton, in tonacaio, in teaoaio in toquichti, ioan in cioa.

Skin	Eoatl,	rough	chachaquachtic,
our skin	teoaio,	wet	paltic,
our outer skin	topaneoaio,	tender	camaoac,
white	iztac,	moist	cuechaoac,
ruddy[3]	tlatlactli,	harsh	quappitztic,
chili-red	chichiltic,	harsh	quappitzauhqui,
very chili-red	chichilpâtic,	thick	tilaoac,
very ruddy	tlatlacpâtic,	thick	tilactic,
swarthy	iaiactic	very thick	tilacpâtic,
swarthy	iaiauhqui,	very thick[6]	quauhtilac
dirty-colored	catzaoac,	wrinkled	xolochtic,
black	cacatzactic,	very wrinkled	xoxolochtic,
black	cacatzactli,	having long hairs	pilinqui,
black	tliltic,	pale	pinectic,
rubber-colored	oltic,	pale	pineoac,
chalky[4]	teceoac,	good	qualli,
ashen	nextic,	clean	chipaoac,
warm	iamanqui,	it becomes pale	pineoa,
hot	totonqui,	it has long hairs	pilini,
cold	itztic,	it becomes wrinkled with age	xolochaui,
cold	cecec,		
very cold	itzcaltic,	it becomes very wrinkled here and there	xoxolochaui,
very cold	itzcapatic,		
cold	cecec,	it becomes warm	iamania,
very cold	cecepatic,	it becomes smooth	tetzcaliui,
very cold[5]	cecepalalâtic,	it becomes thick	tlatztia,
rough	oapaoac,	it becomes fat	nanatziui,
rough	oapactic,	it becomes stretched[7]	motiticana,
rough	tequaqua,	it droops	chapani,
rough	teçontic,	it hangs	mopiloa,

1. Chapter xxvii is a catalogue of the human body as it was known to the Nahua. Hence it is presented here (as in the *Florentine Codex* and the *Academia de la Historia MS*) as a list of parts and attributes, and our translated text departs from its accustomed style. For this part, Sahagún provided no Spanish version whatever; instead, he discussed *los officios, y abilidades, vicios y virtudes, que despues [del tiempo de su infidelidad] aca an aqujrido.*

Information on Nahua ideas of anatomy comes mostly through the sixteenth-century vocabularies at our disposition. These were compiled by Spaniards trained according to Medieval traditions. Knowledge of anatomy was limited and inaccurate. In addition, what the Aztecs saw or looked for can often only be guessed. Hence, many questions which arise in chap. xxvii cannot be satisfactorily answered.

See especially Rafael Martín del Campo's excellent study, "La anatomía entre los mexica" (*Revista de la Sociedad Mexicana de Historia Natural*, XVII, Nos. 1–4 [1956], pp. 145–167); also von Gall's translation of Chapter xxvii and other parts of Book X, "Medizinische Bücher (tici-amatl) der alten Azteken aus der ersten Zeit der Conquista" (already cited), not all of whose definitions, however, we have accepted. Note is taken of important variances in translation.

2. Read *tlatoa.*

3. *Acad. Hist. MS: tlactlactli.*

4. *Ibid.: ticevac.*

5. *Ibid.: cecepalalâctic.*

6. *Ibid.: ãuhtilactic.*

7. *Ibid.: motltivana. motitivana.*

it becomes ruddy	tlatlauia,	it becomes pale	iztaleoa,
it becomes chili-red	chichiliui,	it improves	qualtia,
it whitens	iztaia,	it becomes clean	chipaoa,
it becomes green	xoxouia	it becomes tender	celia.

Skin of the head	**Quaeoatl,**	tough	tlalichtic,
skin of the face	ixeoatl,	loose	atic,
skin of our back	tocuitlapaneoaio,	rubbery	oltic,
skin of the abdomen	itieoatl,	lean	pipinqui,
skin of the hip	quezeoatl,	extended	tilinqui,
skin of the thigh	metzeoatl,	much extended	titilinqui,
skin of the knee	tlanquaeoatl,	thin[8]	canaoac,
skin of the calf of the leg	cotzeoatl,	it becomes tough	tlalichaui,
skin of the sole of the foot	xocpaleoatl,	it becomes rough	teçonaui,
skin of our buttocks	totzintamaleoaio,	it extends	tîtilini,
skin of our neck	toquecheoaio,	it becomes black[9]	tileoa,
skin of our hand	maieoaio,	it becomes [brown][10]	canaliui,
foreskin	xipineoatl,	it becomes filthy	tecuitlaiui,
thick	tilaᴖac	it becomes blotched	cuitlacochiui.
enveloping	peiotic,		

Flesh	**Nacatl,**	chili-red	chichiltic,
fleshiness	nacaiutl,	bloody	ezio,
clay	çoquiotl,	fatty	suchio,
earth[11]	tlallotl,	fatty[13]	puchquio,
our clay	toçoquio,	greasy	chiaoacaio,
foundation	pepechillotl,	having serous fluids	chiauizaio,
our foundation	topepechillo,	having pus	temallo,
that which is our foundation	topepechiuhca,	thick[14]	tilaoacaio
flesh of the head	quanacatl,	extensive[15]	ecapac,
flesh of the face	ixnacatl,	flabby	tzotzoltic
flesh of the lips	tennacatl,	tissue-like[16]	ciciotic,
flesh of the neck	quechnacatl,	tubular	cocotic,
flesh of the chest	elnacatl,	blue-green	quilpaltic,
flesh of our hip	toqueznacaio,	green[17]	xoxocti,
flesh of the thigh	metznacatl,	blotched	cuitlacochtic,
flesh of the knee	tlanquanacatl,	blue	texôtic,
flesh of our knee	totlanquanacaio,	moist	paltic,
flesh of the calf of the leg	cotznacatl,	dry	oacqui,
flesh of the ankle	quequeiolnacatl,	festered	palanqui,
flesh of the sole of the foot	xocpalnacatl,	gangrenous	xoxouhqui,
flesh of the navel	xicnacatl,	full of blood	eztenqui,
flesh of one's navel[12]	texicnacaio,	greasy	chiaoac,
flesh of the palm of the hand	macpalnacatl,	firm	tetzaoac,
		swollen	pozactic,
		oily	chiactic,
flesh of the toe	xopilnacatl,	it grows	mozcaltia
flesh of the finger	mapilnacatl,	it develops	mooapaoa,

---

8. *Ibid.*: *tilavac* follows *canavac*.

9. *Ibid.*: *tlileva*.

10. Read *camilivi*, as in *ibid*.

11. *Ibid.*: *totlallo* follows *tlallotl*.

12. The *Acad. Hist. MS* does not include *xicnacatl* nor *texicnacaio*, but has, in place, *tocxinacayo* (flesh of our foot).

13. See n. 29, *infra*.

14. *Acad. Hist. MS*: *tilavac*.

15. *Ibid.*: *vêcapa*.

16. *Ibid*: *ciciotqui*.

17. *Ibid.*: *xoxoctic*.

it evolves	motoma,	it becomes damaged	itlacaui,
it grows big	ueiia,	it sickens	cocoia,
it enlarges	tomaoa,	it becomes sick	cocolizcui
it becomes grease-stained	chiaoa,	it becomes tired	ciiaui,
it becomes chili-red	chichiliui,	it is ripped	tzaiani,
it becomes pale	iztaleoa,	it is cut	motequi
it becomes blue-green	quilpaltia,	it is pierced	coioni,
it becomes firm	tetzaoa,	it is split	xeliui,
it becomes tender	celia,	it stretches	motitioana,
it becomes lean	oaqui,	it becomes loose	atia,
it becomes very lean	quauhoaqui,	it is resilient	oltia,
it bursts open	pitzini,	it becomes hot	totonia,
it heals	pati,	it becomes glowing hot	totontlapetztia,
it becomes fat	nanatziui,	it becomes cold	ceceia,
it swells	poçaoa,	it becomes cold	itztia.
it festers	palani,		

Thickness[18]	**Tilaoacaiutl,**	it droops	chapani,
the various thicknesses	titilaoacaiutl,	it is alive	ioiolca,
our thickness	totilaoaca,	it is alive	iôiolca
our various thicknesses	totitilaoaca,	it is living	ioiolcatica,
extensive	uecapā	it trembles	uiuiioni,
thick	tilacpol,	it quivers	papatlaca,
thick	tilactic,	it trembles	uiuiioca,
flabby	tzotzoltic,	it shakes	comotziui,
pale	iztaleoac,	it stinks	xoquiui,
blood-flecked	ezcuicuiltic,	it shrinks	patziui,
very bloody	eêzio,	it is depressed	caxiui,
bloody	ezio	it shrinks	patzaoa.
it becomes soft	atoliui,		

Flabbiness[19]	**Tzotzollotl,**	flabbiness of our neck[20]	toquechquechtzotzol
flabbiness	tzôtzollotl,	flabbiness of the stomach	hititzotzolli,
flabbiness	tzotzoliuhcaiutl,	greasy	chiaoacaio,
flabbiness	tzôtzoliuhcaiutl,	fatty	suchio,
flabby	tzotzollo,	heavy	etic,
our flabbiness	totzôtzoliuhca,	wet	çoquitic
flabbiness of our chest	teltzotzol,	moist	paltic
flabbiness of our lips	totentzotzol,	it becomes grease-stained	chiaoa.

Fat	**Suchiotl,**	warmed[22]	tlaiamanilli,
our fat	tusuchio,	it heats	tlatotonilia,
oily	chiactic	it stains things with grease	tlachiaoa,
yellow	coztic,	it brings about development	tlatzmolinaltia,
fatty	suchitic,	it brings about a filling out	tlacelialtia,
very yellow[21]	cozpatic,	it fattens	tlananatzoa,
very yellow	cozpiltic,	it fattens one	tenanatzoa,
warm	iamanqui,	it makes one big	teueilia,
hot	totonqui,	it enlarges one[23]	tetâtaanoa,

---

18. von Gall, *op. cit.*, pp. 122 & *passim: Arterien.*

19. Charles E. Dibble: "Nahuatl Names for Body Parts," *Estudios de Cultura Náhuatl* (México: Universidad Nacional Autónoma de México, Instituto de Historia, Seminario de Cultura Náhuatl, I [1959], pp. 27–29). In von Gall, *op. cit.*, p. 123, *tzotzollotl* is translated as *Venen.*

20. *Acad. Hist. MS: toquechtzotzol.*

21. *Ibid.: cozpâtic.*

22. *Ibid.: tlayamanilia.*

23. In the *Florentine Codex, tenanatzonoa* appears to have been corrected to correspond to the *Acad. Hist. MS* text (*tetâtalanoa*).

it makes one large	tetatalaiuiltia,	it dissolves	pati
it distends one's navel[24]	texicuitoltilia,	it liquefies	atia.
Fat[25]	Ceceiotl,	squeezable	patzcallo,
our fat	toceceio,	compressible	patzconi,
white	iztac,	greasy[26]	chiaoac,
soft	iamaztic,	very oily	chiacpâtic,
very soft	iamazpatic	it stains with grease	chiaoa,
of fine texture	cuechtic,	it stains things with grease	tlachiaoa.
liquid	aio		
Our grease	Tochiaoaca,	white	iztac
liquefied	atic	very white	iztacpâtic,
soft[27]	iamanqui,	it stains things with grease	tlachiaoa.
Tissue[28]	Ciciotcaiutl,	stringy	mecatic
our tissue	tociciotca,	fibrous	ihichio,
our breast tissue	telciciotca,	tissue-like	ciciiotic,
white	iztac,	it becomes white	iztaia.
very white	iztacpatic,		
Fat[29]	Puchquiiutl,	enveloping	peiotic,
our fat	topuchquio,	fluid	atic,
white	iztac,	it becomes fluid	atia,
very white	iztacpâtic,	it becomes white	iztaia,
papery	amatic,	it dissolves	pati.

24. *Acad. Hist. MS: texicuitoltilia.* The Florentine Codex appears to correspond.

25. *Ceyotl:* marrow; see also Martín del Campo, *op. cit.*, p. 158: *médula ósea;* von Gall, *op. cit.*, p. 124: *Netzfett.*

26. *Loc. cit.: feist.*

27. *Iamanqui:* alternative meanings are possible; the context appears to govern precise meaning.

28. von Gall, *loc. cit.: Nerven.*

29. *Ibid.,* p. 125: *Lymphgefässe.* Book XI, cap. ix (fol. 215r), of the *Florentine Codex* refers to *apopoçoqujllotl, vel qujtoznequj apochqujotl, iuhqujnma ipochqujotl atl;* cap. x (fol. 216v) mentions that *nocheztli . . . chamava mopochqujotia. . . . mopochqujoqujmjloa;* whence it may be inferred that some sort of fatty substance was recognized.

SECOND PARAGRAPH, which telleth of the head and all which pertaineth to it.

INIC OME PARRAPHO: itechpa tlatoa in tzontecomatl, ioan in ixquich itech ca.

Head	Tzontecomatl,	it becomes bumpy	xixipuchaui,
our head	totzontecõ;	it softens	patziui,
(that is to say, the celestial part)	(quitoznequi, ilhuicatl)	it is toe-like	xopiliui,
		it becomes mano-like	metlapiliui,
our head	toqua	it becomes partly soft	chicopatziui,
our upper extremity	tocpac	it becomes concave[2]	oacaliui,
little	tepito,	it becomes covered with hair	tzoniooa,
minute	piciltic,	hair forms	tzonquiça.
tiny	piciltontli,	We shake our heads	Titotzonteconuiuixoa,
big	uei,	we lift our heads [in pride]	titoquatlaça,
like a jar[1]	tecontic,	we shave ourselves	titoxima,
round	ololtic,	we cut our hair	titoquateçonoa,
broad	patlachtic,	we shake our heads [in disapproval]	titoquacuecuechoa,
toe-like	xopiltic,	we repeatedly shake our heads [in disapproval]	titoquâquacuecuechoa,
concave	oacaltic,	we rest [our heads]	titocpaltia,
mano-shaped	metlapiltic	we bind our heads	titoquailpia:
cylindrical	mimiltic,	I hit him on the head[3]	nicquitequi,
soft	patztic,	I break his head	nicquatlapana,
movable	comotztic,	I split his head	nicquatzaiana,
bumpy	xixipuchtic,	I kick his head	nicquatelicça
bowl-like	caxtic,	I make his head ring	nicquatlatzinia,
bowl-like	caxiuhqui,	I brain him	nicquatetexoa,
hairy	tzonio,	I hit his head with my fist	nicquatepinia,
smooth	xipetztic,	I bash his head	nicquatepitzinia,
it grows hair	tzonixoa,	I smash his head	nicquapitzinia,
it grows big	ueia,	I pierce his head	nicquacoionia,
it grows	mozcaltia,	it becomes smooth	xipetziui.
it becomes round	ololiui,		
it broadens	patlachiui,		
it becomes movable	comotzaui,		
Celestial part	Ilhuicatl	with mouth	camae,
that is to say, our head	quitoznequi, totzontecon,	that which venerates	tlamauiztiliani,
the rememberer	tlalnamiquini,	humble	mocnomatini,
the knower	tlamatini,	it remembers	tlalnamiqui,
achievement	tlancaiutl,	it knows	tlamati
conclusion	tzonquizcaiutl,	it is prudent	mimati,
honor	mauiziotl,	it venerates	tlamauiztilia,
venerable	mauiztioani,	it is humble	mocnomati,
with eyes	ixe,	it humbles itself	mopechteca,
with ears	nacaze,	it corrupts itself	hitlacaui,
with nose	iaque,	it becomes bad	tlaueliloti.
Hair	Tzontli:	brown	camiltic,
it is black	ca tliltic,	yellow	coztic,
like charcoal	tetecoltic,	chili-red	chichiltic,
like charcoal	teconaltic,	ruddy[6]	tlatlactle,
dark blue[4]	mouitic,	white	iztac,
green[5]	xoxoctic,	twisted	cototztic,

---

1. *Acad. Hist. MS: tencontic.*
2. Alternatively, "paralyzed" (Molina, *op. cit.*); or "impotent" (Rémi Siméon, *op. cit.*).
3. Read *nicquavitequi*, as in the *Acad. Hist. MS.*
4. Standley: *op. cit.*, Pt. 5, pp. 1345–1346.
5. *Acad. Hist. MS: xoxoxoctic.*
6. *Ibid.: tlatlactic.*

curly	colochtic,	it becomes ruddy	tlatlauia,
curly	cocolochtic,	it whitens	iztaia,
wavy	cocoltic,	it becomes lousy	ateniooa,
coarse	chamaoac,	it becomes full of nits	acelloa,
bent	tlateputztic,	it becomes wormeaten	ocuilqualo,
thick	tomaoac,	it whitens	tetezaui,
fine	pitzaoac,	it becomes curly	colochaui,
like corn silk	xilotzontic,	it becomes wavy	cocoltia,
long	ueiac,	it becomes tousled	pâçoliui,
stubby	tetepontic,	it is made tousled	pâçoltia,
white	teteztic,	it becomes mussed	neliui,
cropped	teçontic,	it lies flat	piaciui,
cropped	teçonauhqui,	it is straight	melaoa
sparse	caciltic,	it falls out	motepeoa:
sparse[7]	cacaiactic,	it rots	palani,
sparse	caiaoac,	it decays	quaqualo,
heavy	tilaoac,	it breaks	puztequi,
matted	pepechtic,	it shrivels	matzoliui,
lousy	atenio,	I shave it	nicxima,
full of nits	acillo,	I cut it	nictequi,
full of nits	acello,	I break it	nicpuztequi,
wormy	ocuillo,	I tear it	nictzaiana,
it forms	ixoa,	I comb it	nictziquaoazuia,
it becomes pointed	iacaomiti,	I part it	nicxeloazuia,
it lengthens	mana,	I smooth it with water	nicapetla,
it grows	mozcalia,	I twist it	nicmalina,
it grows long	ueiaquia,	I put it in order	nicuipana,
it becomes black	tliliui,	I make a headdress	nictzoncalchioa,
it becomes yellow	coçauia,	I make it into a braid	nictzõoazchioa
it becomes chili-red	chichiliui,	I dye it	nicpa.

Crown of the head	**Tocuezco:**	without fuzz[9]	atômio,
the middle of the head	quanepantlatli,	hairless[10]	atzoio,
the middle of our head	toquanepantla,	it becomes round	teuilacachiui,
the roundness of the head[8]	quateuilachiuhcaiutl,	it becomes smooth	xipetziui,
round	iaoaltic	it becomes bare	tlatziui,
round	teuilacachtic,	it is made bare	tlatlatztic muchioa.
clean	chipaoac,		

Nape of the neck[11]	**Cuexcochtli:**	hairy	tzõio,
the nape of our neck	tocuexcoch,	grooved	acaliuhqui,
possessing an eminence	tiltic,	it becomes grooved	acaliui,
possessing an eminence	teltic,	hair appears	tzonixoa.
possessing an eminence	tiliuhqui,		

Occiput[12]	**Cuexcochtetl:**	I make it crack	nictlatzinia,
our occiput	tocuexcochteuh,	I crack him on his occiput	niccuexcochtlatzinia,
pointed	uitztic,	I make his occiput crack	niccuexcochcapania,
possessing an eminence	tiltic,	with it I press down	ic nitlacça,
hard	tepitztic,	with it I rest	ic nonoc,
firm	tlaquaoac,	I put it on his head	niquicpaltia.

---

7. *Ibid.: cayactic.*

8. *Ibid.: quatevilacachiuhcayotl.*

9. *Ibid.: ǎoomio*, or possibly *ǎtomio.*

10. Read *atzonyo.*

11. Molina, *op. cit.: colodrillo.* Martín del Campo, *op. cit.*, p. 151: *región occipital;* von Gall, *op. cit.*, p. 129: *Hinterhaupt.*

12. Molina, *op. cit.: cogote* or *nuca;* von Gall, *loc. cit.: Nacken.*

Bald pate[18]	**Quaxipetztli:**	very bare	tlatlatztic,
smooth	xipetztic,	estimable	mauiztic,
soft	iamãqui,	marvelous[14]	mauizço,
very soft	iaiamaztic,	it shows old age[15]	tlaueuenextia,
clear	naltic,	it becomes shiny	petziui,
very clear	nanaltic,	it glistens	pepetziui,
bare	tlatztic,	it becomes shiny	conaliui.

Forehead	**Ixquatl:**	wrinkled[16]	xoxolochtic,
our forehead	tixqua,	radiant	tonameio,
possessing an eminence	tiltic,	it reveals beauty	tlaqualnextia,
bumpy	xixipuchtic,	it makes one illustrious	tetleiotia,
very bumpy	xixipuchauhqui,	it glorifies one	temauiziotia,
bulbous	tolontic,	it makes one appear wise	teixtlamatcanextia,
bare	tlatztic,	it makes one radiant	tetonameiotia,
smooth	xipetztic,	it makes radiant	tlatonameiotia.
smooth	xipetziuhqui,		

Forehead wrinkles	**Ixquaxolochtli:**	like a ladder	mamatlatic,
our forehead wrinkles[17]	tixquaxolochauhca,	it becomes wrinkled	xolochaui,
very wrinkled[18]	xoxochtic,	with age	
very furrowed	âacaltic,	it becomes furrowed	acaliui,
very furrowed	âacaliuhqui,	it becomes like a ladder	mamatlatia.

Eyelid[19]	**Ixquatolli,**	with hair	tzontica
cylindrical	mimiltic,	with a dark cast	tlilpoiaoac,
cylindrical[20]	mîlmiltic,	hair forms	tzonixoa,
cylindrical	mimiliuhqui,	it shows anger	tlaqualancanextia,
hairy	tzonio,	it blinks	quatoliui,
with eyebrow	ixquamollo	it becomes smooth	xipetziui.

Eyebrow	**Ixquamolli:**	it forms	ixoa,
hair	tzontli,	dark	poiaoac,
fuzz	tomitl,	thick	tilaoac,
black	tliltic,	sparse	caciltic,
yellow	coztic,	coarse[21]	chamaoac,
ruddy	tlatlactic,	it reveals beauty	tlaqualnextia,
fuzzy	tomitic,	it is resplendent	tlatlacanextia,
pointed at the end	iacaomitic,	it gives a black outline	q̃tlilania,
pointed at the end	iacauitztic,	it gives a dark cast[22] to the	quitlilpoiaoa, in xaiacatl, in
small	tepiton,	face, the forehead, the eye	ixquatl, in ixtelolôtli.

Orbit	**Ixcallocantli:**	round	iaoaliuhqui,
our orbit	tixcallocan	it becomes hollowed	comoliui,
hollowed	comoltic,	it fills [with tears]	temi,
round	iaoaltic,	it exudes [tears]	panuetzi.

---

13. Martín del Campo, *op. cit.*, p. 151: *calva frontal.*

14. *Acad. Hist. MS: mavizyo.*

15. *Ibid.: tlavevênextiani.*

16. *Ibid.: xolochtic* precedes *xoxolochtic.*

17. *Ibid.: tixquaxochiuhca.*

18. *Ibid.: xoxolochtic.*

19. Martín del Campo, *loc. cit.: arco ciliar; ibid.,* p. 166: *párpado del ojo,* citing Molina, *op. cit.*

20. *Acad. Hist. MS: mîmiltic.*

21. *Ibid.: tlaqualnextiani, qualnexovani* follow *chamaoac.*

22. *Ibid.: quitlilpoyava.*

Hollow of our eye	Tixcomol,	deep down	uecatla, tlani,
hollows of our eyes	tixtecocomol,	it becomes deep	uecatlaniui,
our eye sockets[23]	tixtecocoio,	they are sunken	coioni.
hollowed	comoltic,		
Interior of the eyelid[24]	Ixquempalli,	that which sparkles	pepeiocani,
the covering of the eye	ixquimiliuhcaiotl,	that which comes together	mopiquini,
thin	canaoac,	they join	mopiqui,
paper-like	amatic,	they meet	monamiqui,
wet	paltic	they sparkle	pepeioca,
it blankets	tlatlapachoa,	with them the eyes are made to shine[25]	ic neixpepetzalo.
it covers	tlaquentia,		
edges of eyelids	ixtentli,		
Lachrymal gland[26]	Ixtencuilchilli,	it expels, it pours out the tears	quioallaça, quioaltopeoa, in ixcuitlatl.
chili-red	chichiltic,		
Our eyelashes	Tocochia:	ruddy	tlatlauic,
hair	tzontli,	like a fan	êcaceoaztic,
black	tliltic,	with them there is winking[27]	ic neixcueionilo,
chili-red	chichiltic,		
yellow	coztic,	with them the eyes are made to shine	ic neixpepeiotzalo.
ruddy	tlatlactic,		

---

23. *Ibid.: tixtecocoyoc.*
24. von Gall, *op. cit.,* p. 131: *Bindehaut* (conjunctiva tunica).
25. *Acad. Hist. MS: neixpepetztzalo.*
26. von Gall, *op. cit.,* p. 133: *Lidwärzchen.*
27. *Acad. Hist.* MS adds *yc neixcuecueyonilo.*

Third paragraph

THIRD PARAGRAPH, which telleth of the eye and all which pertaineth to it, and of the nose and all which pertaineth to it.

INIC EI PARRAPHO: itechpa tlatoa in ixtelolotli, ioan in ixquich itech poui ioan itechpa in toiac, ioan in ixquich itech ca.

Eye	Ixtelolotli:
mirror	tezcatl,
delicate[1]	chonequiztli,
soft	iamanqui,
round[2]	tolonlontic,
mano-shaped	metlapiltic,
pestle-shaped	texolotic,
white	iztac,
yellow	coztic,
bright red	xuxutla,
transparent	teuilotic,
black	tliltic,
clouded	popoiutl,
bowl-like	caxtic,
blotched	patzactic,
it moves	molinia
it rolls	mocuechinia,
it wanders	auic iauh,
it closes	motzaqua,
it opens	tlapoui,
with it there is seeing	ic tlachialo,
there is seeing to the side	nacaztlachialo,
with it there is looking up	ic âco tlachialo,
with it there is looking down	ic tlalchi tlachialo,
it recognizes people	teiximati,
it recognizes things	tlaiximati,
it sees	quitta,

Whites of our eyes	Toztacauh
flesh	nacatl,
full of nerves	tlaloaio,

Our iris	Totliliuhca:
black	tliltic,
transparent	teuilotic,

Pupil of our eye	Tixtotouh:
our animated [organ]	toioiolcauh,
pupil of our eye	tixteouh,
transparent	atic,
delicate	chonequiztli,
very delicate[5]	chonequizpâtic,
our complete master	tocentecuio,
torch[6]	ocuitl,
light	tlauilli,
brilliance	tlanextli,
mirror	tezcatl.

it illuminates one	tetlauilia,
it enlightens one	tetlanextilia,
it leads one	teiacana,
it guides one	teuica,
it sustains one	tenemitia,
it becomes ailing	cocoia,
it decays	palani,
it becomes clouded	popoioti,
it becomes bowl-like	caxiui,
it reduces	patzaoa,
it roughens	tepetlati,
it becomes covered	tlatlapachiui,
it swells	poçaoa,
it bursts open	cueponi,
a calcareous substance emerges	tenextequiça,
it becomes flesh-covered	nacaquimiliui,
it becomes filled with flesh	nacapachiui,
it becomes discolored	xoxouia,
it becomes yellow	côcoçauia,
it sleeps[3]	cochi,
by means of it there is sleep	ic cochioa
it is relaxed	iamania,
it moves restlessly	auic motlaça
water runs	atotoco,
with it there is looking here and there	ic auic tlachialo.

they become yellow	cocoçauia,
they have a calcareous excretion[4]	nextamalcuitlatoa.

ashen	têtenextic,
round	iaoaltic,
clear	atic.

our mirror	totezcauh,
instrument for seeing	tlachialoni,
[that by which] all live	nemoani,
precious[7]	tlaçotla
the esteemed	mauiztlaçotli,
guardian of honor	mauizpialoni,
it illuminates	tlauia,
it illuminates one	tetlauilia,
it enlightens one	tetlanextilia,
it leads	tlaiacana.

---

1. *Ibid.: chineq'ztli.*
2. *Ibid.: tolontic.*
3. *Ibid.: yc avic tlachialo* follows *cochi.*
4. *Ibid.: nextamalcuitlatia.*
5. *Ibid.: chinequizpâtic.*
6. *Ibid.: ocutl.*
7. *Ibid.: tlaçôtli.*

Nose	Iacatl:	smoke hole	tlecalli,
our nose	toiac,	smoke hole	tlecalco,
our sense of smell	totlânecuia,	the smoke hole of our body	itlecallo, in tonacaio,
cylindrical	mimiltic,	it smells	tlânecui,
cylindrical	mimiliuhqui,	it is wiped	mitzomia,
harpoon-like	chichiquiltic,	it has hairs[8]	tzôtzoniotica,
pointed	uitztic,	with it there is smelling	ic tlâneco,
flattened	pachtic,	there one's nose is wiped	vncan nêtzomilo,
thick	tomaoac,	it has a cold	tzompiliui,
thin	pitzaoac,	it sneezes	acuchoa,
provided with a hole	coionqui,	it sneezes[9]	acuxo,
provided with holes	cocoionqui	it inhales	tlaihiioana.
provided with holes	côcoioctic,		
Length of the nose	Iacaquauhiutl:	bowl-like	caxtic,
curved	teputzûtic,	cylindrical[10]	mimiliuhtic,
cylindrical	temimiltic,	it extends far up	uecapaniuhtoc,
flattened	pachtic,	it extends like a harpoon	chichiquiliuhtoc.
Thin part of our nose	Toiacapitzaoaca:	a little thin	pitzaton,
like a small harpoon	chichiquiltontli,	thin	canaoac,
Nostrils[11]	Iatomolli	possessing an eminence	tiliuhqui,
our nostrils	toiacatomol,	round	ololtic,
possessing an eminence[12]	tiltic,	it has eminences	tomoliui.
Nose-tip[13]	Iacâtzulli,	resilient	oltic,
our nose-tip	toiacatzol,	firm	tlaquaoac,
our nose-tip	in toiacâtzol,	it grows	mozcaltia,
pointed	uitztic,	it becomes pointed	uitzaui,
soft	iamanqui,	it becomes tough	sucuichaui,
wide	patlachtic,	it becomes tough	tlalichaui,
V-shaped	quamanqui,	it becomes resilient	oltia,
The nose-hair of living persons[14]	In iolqui: iiacatzon,	it becomes firm	tlaquaoa,
tough	tlalichtic,	a rubbery [substance] exudes	olquiça.
Our nose	Toiacac:	[capable of] snorting	quiquintic,
with smoke hole	tlecallo,	our breathing place	toneihiiotiaia,
distended	coiaoac,	our source of life[15]	tonenca, toiolca,
each distended	cocoiaoac,	the place of entrance and egress of air	êhecatl, icalaquia, iquiçaia,
like a passage-way	quiquiztic,	there, there is smelling	vncan tlanêco.
like a passage-way for blowing	pitzquiquiztic,		
Our septum[16]	Toiacelica:	soft	iamanqui,
tender	celic,	broad and thick	patlachtilaoac,

---

8. *Ibid.: tzotzontjca.*

9. *Ibid: acuxoa; acuchoa* is omitted.

10. *Ibid.: mimiliuhtoc.*

11. Martín del Campo, *op. cit.*, p. 162: *ala de la nariz* (alae), citing Molina, *op. cit.* (bexa). Cf. also Rémi Siméon, *op. cit.: yacatomololiuhcayotl;* also Molina, *op. cit.* — *Acad. Hist. MS: yacatomolli.*

12. *Ibid.: tliltic* (black).

13. Currently in use as "nose" in Milpa Alta. — *C. E. Dibble.* In von Gall, *op. cit.*, p. 137: *Nasenschleim.*

14. *Acad. Hist. MS: yyacâtzol.*

15. *Ibid.: tonêya.*

16. Martín del Campo, *op. cit.*, p. 162: *tabique nasal* (septum).

it partitions	tlaeltzaqua,	moist	paltic,
it partitions our nose	queltzaqua in toiac,	hair emerges	tzonquiça
it divides it	quixeloa,	it has hair	tzoniooa.
it has mucus	iacacuitlaiooa,		

Our nostril chamber[17]	Toiacacomoliuhca:	bowl-like	caxiuhqui,
grooved places of our nose[18]	toiacaacaliuhia,	it becomes grooved	acaliui,
grooved	acaltic,	it becomes bowl-like	caxiui,
bowl-like	caxtic	it forms a hollow	comoliui.

---

17. von Gall, *op. cit.*, p. 138: *Nasenhöhle* (nasal cavity).
18. *Acad. Hist. MS: toyaacaliuhya comoltic.*

Palate[1]	Camatapalli:	blotched	cuitlacuchtic,
chili-red	chichiltic,	it becomes chili-red	chichiliui,
chili-red	chîchiltic,	chili-red	chîchiltic,
ruddy	tlatlactic,	colored like ripened fruit	xaoallo,
brown	camiltic,	ruddy	tlatlauillo,
brown in color	tlapalcamiltic,	brown[2]	camillo,
full of water	atenqui,	rose-colored	tlapalpoiaoallo.
viscous	tecuitlatic,		
Malar region	Ixtilli,	lump-like	tôpoliuhqui,
our malar region	tixtil,	it forms an eminence	tiliui,
our malar region	tixteliuhca,	it forms a lump	tôpoliui,
lump-like[3]	tôpoltic,	it becomes firm	tlaquaoa.
Cheek	Camatetl,	fleshy	nacatepul,
our cheek	tocamateuh,	soft	patztic,
distended	poçaoac,	very soft	papatztic,
distended	poçactic,	it softens	patziui,
thick	tilaoac,	it breaks	pitzini,
thick	tilactic,	it thickens	tilaoa,
round	ololtic,	it swells	çoneoa.
Cheek	Cantli:	round	ololtic.
our cheek	tocan:		
Lower Jawbone	Camachalli.	it crackles	nanatzca,
bone	omitl,	it resounds	caquizti.
that which crackles	nanatzini,		
Grooved part of the lower jaw[4]	Camachalacaliuhcantli:	grooved	acaltic,
		grooved	acaliuhqui,
grooved part of our lower jaw	tocamachalacaliuhca,	concave	oacaltic,
		it becomes hollow[5]	cacaliui.
flesh	nacatl		
Concave part of the lower jaw[6]	Camachaloacaliuhiantli:	jawbone	camachalli,
		hollowed	oacaltic,
concave part of our lower jaw	tocamachaloacal,	hollowed	oacaliuhqui,
		thin	oaqui,
concave part of our lower jaw	tocamachaloacaliuhia,	it becomes sparsely fleshed	nacaio, totochaui,
of sparse flesh	nacaio, totochtic,	it becomes hollowed	oacaliui.
Lip	Tentli:	chili-red colored	chileoatic,
our lip	tote,	pale	iztaleoac,
soft	iamanqui,	swarthy	iaiactic,
chili-red	chichiltic,	swarthy	iaiauhqui,
ruddy	tlatlactic,	thick	tilaoac,

1. von Gall, *op. cit.*, p. 138: *Der harte Gaumen.*

2. *Acad. Hist. MS:* camilolo.

3. Read *tapaltic* (cf. *tapaliui*).

4. von Gall, *op. cit.*, p. 139: *Kinnbacken.*

5. Read *oacaliui.*

6. von Gall, *loc. cit.: Kaumuskeln* (?).

like a reed leaf	acazoatic,	it blows	tlalpitza,
thin	canaoac,	it blows a trumpet	tlapitza,
it becomes thin	canaoa,	it blows the fire	tlepitza
thick	tilaoac,	I beat him on the lips	nictentzôtzona,
it becomes pale	iztaleoa,	I strike him on the lips	nictenuitequi,
it becomes chili-red	chichiliui,	I silence him	nictêtzaqua,
it quivers	papatlaca	I put unguent on his lips	itenco nicalaoa,
it trembles	uiuiiioca,	I paint his lips[7]	itenco nicchioa,
it controls the word, the breath	quimati in tlatolli, in ihiutl,	I spread it on him	nicteca.

Mouth	**Camatl:**	there it is filled	vncan mocontema,
our mouth	tocama,	there [is the place where food is] left	vncan caoani,
hole	coionqui,		
like a passage way	quiquiztic,	there, [there is] sound, discourse	vncan caquizti, in ihiiutl, in tlatolli,
wide	coiaoac,		
place for eating	tlaqualoia,	it eats[8]	tlaqua,
our place for eating	totlaquaia,	it bites	tlacampaxoa,
place for receiving	tlaceliloia,	it talks	tlâtoa,
there it is closed	vncã motzaqua	it sings	cuica.
there is placed the food in order to eat [it], in order to chew [it]	vncan motlalia in tlaqualli, inic moqua, inic mocuechoa,		

Palate[9]	**Copactli:**	varied in color	tecuicuiltic,
the palate	in copactli,	hollowed	comoltic,
chili-red	chichiltic,	soft	iamanqui,
dark	iaiactic,	our place of tasting	totlauelmatia,
swarthy	iaiauhqui,	it tastes	tlauelmati.

Gum	**Quetolli:**	it holds	tlatzitzquia,
chili-red	chichiltic,	it grips	tlapachoa,
dark	iaiactic,	it grips the teeth	quipachoa in tlantli.
holder	tlatzitzquiani,		

Tongue	**Nenepilli,**	soft on one side	centlapal, iamanqui,
that which moves	moliniani,	rough on one side[10]	centlapal tençontic,
that which is agitated	mocuecuetzoani,	it controls discourse	quimati, quichioa in iiutl, in tlatolli,
agitated	cuecuetztic,		
thick and wide	patlachtilaoac,	it sputters	motlatzinia,
of pointed tip	iacauitztic,	it crackles	cacalaca,
tapered	quauitztic,	it ejects saliva[11]	chichitlatopeoa.

Fraenum of the tongue[12]	**Cueianenepilli:**	moist	paltic
our tongue fraenum	tocueianenepil,	pink	tlaztlaleoaltic,
soft	iamanqui,	dark	iaiactic,
soft	iamaztic,	it becomes soft	iamania.

Tip of our tongue	**Tonenepiliacauitzauhca:**	thin and long	pitzaoac,
the end of our tongue	tonenepilqua,	that which moistens	tlapaloloni,
pointed	vitztic,	it moistens	tlapaloa.
pointed	vitzauhqui,		

---

7. *Acad. Hist. MS: nichiva;* read *ni-ichiua.*

8. *Ibid.: nêmatcatlaqua* follows *tlaqua.*

9. von Gall, *op. cit.,* p. 141: *Der weiche Gaumen.*

10. *Acad. Hist. MS: teçõtic.*

11. *Ibid.: chicha. tlatopeva.*

12. *Ibid.: Cuecueyanenepilli.*

Wide part of our tongue[13]	Tonenepilpatlaoaca	thick	tilaoac,
it thickens[14]	tlatilaoa,	it thickens	tilaoa.
Thick part of our tongue[15]	Tonenepiltilaoa:	fleshy	nacatepol.
thick	tilactic		
Root of our tongue	Tonenepilitzintla:	it becomes rough	chachaquachiui,
soft	iamanqui	it becomes rough	teçonaui,
moist	paltic,	it is being moist	paltitica,
rough	chachaquachtic,	it is moist	palti,
rough	teçontic,	it is being moist	paltixtica.
Our smoke hole	Totlecallo:	bored	coionqui,
place of entrance and egress	toiacacpa,	passing through	nalquizqui,
of air from our nose	ehecatl icalaquia, iquiçaia,	there is a hole	coionticac,
our place for breathing	toneihiiotiaia	there is a passage	nalquizticac.
Our uvula[16]	Totozcatequacuil:	it becomes inflamed	mopitza,
divided	maxaltic,	it sounds	naoati,
cylindrical	mimiltic,	it tastes	tlauelmati.
Voice[17]	Tozquitl:	that which becomes hoarse	çaçauini,
our voice	totozqui,	that which is hoarse	çaçaoani,
the blower	pitzaloni,	it is cleared	moiectia,
the sounder	naoatini,	the voice is cleared	motozcaiectia,
there we speak	vncan titlatoa,	it has a cold	tlatlaci,
our speaking place	totlatoaia	it roars	quaqualaca,
it barks	oaoaciui,	it groans	cotaloa,
it is hoarse	çaçaoaca,	it sputters	iztlacmeia.
Esophagus[18]	Cocotl:	it swallows	tlatoloa,
gullet	tlatolhoaztli,	it forces [down]	tlatopeoa,
the swallower	tlatololoni,	it swallows things smoothly	tlapetztoloa.
there[19] the food is slipped	vncān mopetzcoa		
down[20]	in tlaqualli,		
Vocal cords[21]	Camaxitecuilli:	moist	paltic,
our vocal cords	tocamaxitecuil,	they are bared	xipeoa,
thick	tilaoac,	they swell	tomoni,
narrow	tzotzoltic,	they become soft	iamania.
soft	iamāqui		

---

13. von Gall, *op. cit.*, p. 142: *Unser Zungenrücken.*

14. *Acad. Hist. MS: tlatilavaya.*

15. von Gall, *loc. cit.*: *Der untere Teil unserer Zunge* (?). — The term is *tonenepiltilavaca* in the *Acad. Hist. MS.*

16. Martín del Campo, *op. cit.*, p. 161: also *toyoyolca.*

17. von Gall, *op. cit.*, p. 143: *Kehle.*

18. Martín del Campo, *op. cit.*, p. 162: *tráquea.* There is confusion in this among various terms as defined in vocabularies. See *ibid.*, p. 149.

19. So written (*vncān*) in the *Florentine Codex.*

20. *Acad. Hist. MS: tlaqualiztli.*

21. von Gall, *op. cit.*, p. 144: *Kehlkopfdeckel.*

FIFTH PARAGRAPH, which telleth of the teeth, and the molars, and the eyeteeth.

INIC MACUILLI PARRAPHO: itechpa tlatoa in tlantli ioã tlancochtli, ioan tocooatlan.

Tooth	tlantli:	decayed	quaquâ,
the tooth is a bone	in tlantli, ca omitl,	decayed	ocuilquaquâ,
white	iztac,	rotten	palanqui,
white	ticeoac,	smutty[1]	puxcauhqui,
white	ticectic,	blotched	cuitlacochtic,
yellow	coztic,	dirty	cuitlaio,
yellow	coçauhqui,	dirty	tlãcuitlaio,
like ripe maize	pixquic,	scummy	texio,
maize-dough-colored	nextamaltic,	with thick scum	textilaoac,
very white	iztacpatic,	of decayed root	tzinquaquâ,
like a seashell	tecciztic,	long and thin at the root	tzinpitzaoac,
darkened	tlamiaoallo,	it bites things	tlaquetzoma,
black	tliltic,	it cuts things	tlatlancotona,
varicolored	cuicuiltic,	it chews things	tlatetequi,
stained with cochineal	nochezio,	it pulverizes things	tlatetexoa,
stained	tlapallo.	it grinds things	tlateci,
long	ueiac,	it grinds	teci,
small	tepito,	it turns yellow	coçauia,
minute	piciltic,	it is decayed	quaqualo
long and thin	pitzaoac,	it becomes blotched	cuitlacochiui,
thick	tomaoac,	it becomes dark	tlamiiaoalloa,
round	ololtic,	it is treated with dry color	tlapaloatzalloa,
round	teololtic,	it rots	palani,
round	temalacatic,	it breaks	tlapani,
like a spindle whorl	malacachtic,	it wiggles	uixaliui,
pointed	uitztic,	it moves	olini,
each one pointed	uiuitztic,	it falls	uetzi,
wide	patlachtic,	I pick my teeth	ninotlancuicui,
comb-like	tziquatic,	I clean my teeth	ninotlaniectia,
comb-like	tziquaoaztic,	I wash my teeth	ninotlampaca,
wiggling	uixaltic,	I darken my teeth	ninotlamiaoa,
wiggling	uixaliuhqui	I break my teeth	nitlancotoni.
broken	tlapanqui,		

Molar	Tlancochtli:	masher	tlacuecholoni,
round like a ball	tatapaioltic,	it breaks things up	tlapaiana,
round like a spindle whorl	malacachtic,	it mashes things	tlacuechoa,
round like a spindle whorl	malacatic,	it is replaced[2]	mopapaltilia,
round like a spindle whorl	malacachiuhqui,	they meet	monanamiqui,
chattering	tetecuitztic,	it resounds	calani,
chattering	têtecuitztic,	it erupts	ixoa,
grinding-stone	memetlatl,	it grows	mozcaltia,
grinder	tlatexoni,	it develops	mooapaoa,
pulverizer	tlapapaiaxoloni,	it lengthens	mana
pulverizer	tlapaianaloni,	it grows larger	veia.

Canine	Coatlantli:	it erupts	ixoa,
our canine	tocooatlan,	it becomes cylindrical	mimiliui,
cylindrical	mimiltic,	it becomes pointed at the end	iacauitzaui.
of pointed end	iacauitztic,		
it pierces things	tlatzoponia,		

---

1. *Acad. Hist. MS: puxpauhq̃.*
2. *Ibid.: mopapatilia.*

Front tooth[3]	Tlanixquatl:	whistler	tlanquiquixoni,
our front tooth	totlanizqua,	whistler	tlanquiquixoani,
wide	patlachtic,	means of pronouncing	tlatenquixtiloni,
wide	patlachiuhqui,	words	
hard	tepuztic,	pronouncer of words	tlatenquixtiani,
edged	tene,	it whistles	tlanquiquici,
sharp-edged	tenitztic,	I whistle through teeth	nitlanquiquici,
biter	tlaquetzomaloni,	I cut something with	nitlatlancotona,
grinder	tlatetexoloni,	my tooth	
it bites	tlaquetzoma,	I grind something	nitlatetexoa,
it grinds	tlatetexoa,	I pronounce something	nitlatenquixtia,
it reduces things to	tlatlâpacilhuia,	I bare my teeth	nitlancuitzoa.
small bits			

---

3. von Gall, *op. cit.*, p. 146: *Zahnoberfläche.*

Soft part of the lips | Totexipaliamanca:
chili-red | chichiltic,
dark | iaiactic,
it is soft | iamania,

Lip | Texipalli:
wide | patlaoac,
thick | tilaoac,
it widens | patlaoa,

Mustache | Tatlia:
hair | tzontli,
black | tliltic,
yellow | coztic,

Chin | Tenchalli:
our long [under] lip | totenuiiaca,
our mano-like lip | totēmetlapil
stubby | tetepontic,

Beard | Tentzontli:
pointed at end | iacaomitic,
sharp at end | iacauitztic,
sharp at end | iacauitzauhqui,
long | ueiac,
stubby | tetepontic,
white | teteztic,
white | teteçauhqui,
straight | melaoac,
twisted | cototztic,
twisted | cocototztic,
curly | colochtic,
black | tliltic,

Hair of cheeks | Camatzontli:
thin | canaoac,
thick | tilaoac,
it is no longer disliked | aoc mauilmati,
sparse | caciltic,
sparse | caiaztic,

Hair of nostrils | Iacatzontli:
thick in each [nostril] | tôtomaoac,
coarse | chamaoac,

Hair of face | Ixtzontli:
it spreads thickly | potzauhtimani,
it spreads thickly | tilaoatimani,

Breath | Ihiiotl:
that is to say, face[1] | q. n. xacacatl,
honored | mauizio,

---

it becomes chili-red | chichiliui,
it becomes dark | iaiauia,
it becomes dark | iaiactia.

it becomes thin | canaoa,
it thickens | tilaoa,
they break open | tzaiani,
it stretches | motitioana.

ruddy | tlatlauic,
white | iztac,
it whitens | iztaia.

V-shaped | quamanqui,
hair emerges | tzonquiça,
hair forms | tzonixoa,
hair thickens | tzõiooa.

chili-red | chichiltic,
ruddy | tlatlauhqui,
it whitens | iztaia,
it becomes curly | colochaui,
it becomes twisted | cototzaui,
it becomes tangled | pâçoliui,
beard is shaved | motentzonxima,
beard is pulled out | motentzonuiuitla,
beard is plucked out | motentzompî
beard is cropped | motentzommomotzoa,
he who has a beard — | tentzone, aoc mauilmati,
    no longer is his beard | in itentzon.
    disliked

it forms | ixoa,
it is sparse | caiaoa,
it is thick | tilaoa,
it spreads thick | potzauhtimani,
it is dark | tlaiooatimani.

pointed at end | iacaomitic,
stubby | tetepontic,
pointed at end | iacaomitic.

it makes one estimable | teixmauhti,
it gives one esteem | tlaixmauhtia.

famed | tleio,
stern[2] | ihiio,
afflicted | cococ,

---

1. *Acad. Hist. MS: xayacatl.*
2. Cf. Sahagún: *"Memoriales con Escolios,"* p. 213.

courteous	tecpiltic,	it has honor	mauiziooa,
good	qualli,	one is honored	momauiziotia,
beautiful	qualnezqui,	it disgraces	auilquiça,
it emanates splendor	mihiiotia,	it becomes calm	ceui.
one is made famous	motleiotia,		

Face	**Xaiacatl:**	it frightens one	temauhti,
clean	chipaoac,	it sickens one	tetlaelti,
dirty	catzaoac,	it offends one	teiolitlaco,
dark	iaiauic,	it improves	qualtia,
dark	iaiauhqui,	it becomes pure	iectia,
blackish	tlilectic,	it becomes white	iztaia,
black[3]	oatzaoac,	it becomes chili-red	chichiliui,
black	tliltic,	it becomes ruddy	tlatlauia,
sweaty	tzocuitlatic,	it refreshes	celia,
good	qualli,	it has honor	mauiziooa,
fair	iectli,	one is esteemed	mauizti,
marvelous	mauiztic,	it emanates splendor	mihiiotia,
precious	tlaçotli,	it is made famous	motleiotia,
necessary	neconi,	it is honored	momauiziotia,
needed	eleuiloni,	it angers others	tequalania,
desirable	nequiztli,	it offends	tlaiôlitlacoa,
constantly desirable[4]	nenequiztli, nenequiztli,	it oppresses	tlatequipachoa,
it becomes angry	qualani,	it sickens	tlatlaêltia.

Face	**Ixtli:**	kind face	ixicnoio,
that is to say, face[5]	q. n. xaiacatl,	beloved face	ixiicnotzin,
it becomes pale	iztaleoa,	sad-faced	ixcococ,
it becomes green	xoxouia,	face is inflamed with anger	mixtleiotia,
it becomes yellowish	camaoa,	face has honor	ixmauiziooa,
it becomes dropsical	atemi,	face festers	ixpalani,
it is covered by a viscous substance	tecuitlaiui,	face blackens	ixtliliui,
		face burns	ixtlatla,
it becomes blotched	cuitlacochiui,	face is skinned	ixipeui,
our face	tix,	face is damaged	ixitlacaui,
in our face	tixco,	he strikes the face	quixuitequi,
famous	tleio,	he spits on the face	quixchicha,
honored	mauizio,	he hits the face with his fist	quixtepinia,
kind	icnoio,	he tells him his faults to his face	quixcomaca,
afflicted	cococ,		
valiant	ixtleio,	he slaps the face	quixtlatzinia,
honored face	ixmauizio,	he kicks the face	quixtilicça.

Face	**Ixtli:**	it falls in his eye[6]	ixtlauetzi,
that is to say, eye	q. n. ixtelolotli,	dust enters his eye	ixco calaqui, in teuhtli,
in our eye	tixco,	it is white in his eye[7]	ixco ca iztac.

I open my eye	**Nixtlapoui,**	that is to say, I uncover my eye	q. n. nixtomi,
or I uncover my eye	anoço nixtomi		
I open my eye	Nixtlapoui,	I am wise[8]	nixtlamati.

---

3. *Acad. Hist. MS: câcatzactic.*

4. The term is repeated in the *Florentine Codex*. In the *Acad. Hist. MS*, the repeated term usually varies because of the circumflex — *nênequiztli.*

5. Cf. Rémi Siméon, *op. cit.*, for some distinctions in meaning.

6. *Ibid.: Ixtli — uetztiuh; oixco uetz.* In the *Acad. Hist. MS, iixco* is consistently written.

7. *Ibid.: ma tlapoui ȳ amix ȳ amoyollo* follows *iztac.*

8. *Ibid.: nixmauhtia* follows *nixtlamati.*

Temple	Canaoacantli:	thin-haired	tzoncaiaoac,
our temple	tocanaoacan,	it is hollowed	comoliui,
hollowed	comoltic,	there are separate depressions	cocomoliui,
sparse-fleshed	nacatotochtic,		
sparse-haired	tzõcaiactic,	hair forms	tzonixoa.
Ear	Nacaztli,	it hears things	tlacaqui,
provided with a hole	coionqui,	with it things are heard	ic tlacaco,
smoke hole	tlecallotl,	it twitters	hicaoaca,
round	iaoaltic,	it crackles	tetecuica,
wide	patlanqui,	it is stopped up	motzaqua,
wide	patlaoac,	ear aches	nacazqualo.
disc-shaped	teuilacachtic,		
Ear cartilage	Nacazquauhiotl:	it becomes firm	tetzaoa,
our ear cartilage	tonacazquauhio,	it becomes tough	oapaoa,
like cartilage	omicelic,	it is strong	chicaoatiuh.
Our ear lobe[9]	Tonacazcelica:	it is suspended	pilcatica,
tender	celtic,	it hangs	pilcac.
little piece of flesh	nacatontli,		
Helix[10]	Nacazteuilacachiuhcaiutl:	cylindrical	mimiltic,
disc-shaped	teuilacachtic,	it is round	iaoaliuhtimani,
round	iaiaoaltic,	it is cylindrical	mimiliuhtimani.
round	iaiaoaliuhqui,		
Spoon-shaped part of our ear	Tonacazcopichauhca:	it becomes spoon-shaped	copichaui,
		it becomes creased	cuelpachiui,
spoon-shaped	copichauhqui,	it uncreases[11]	çoui,
creased	cuelpachiuhq,	it is uncreased	moçooa.
Width of our ear[12]	Tonacazpatlaoaca:	it widens	patlaoa,
wide	patlaoac,	it lengthens	uiaquia.
wide	patlactic,		
Our ear-droplet (tragus)	Tonacazchipinca:	our ear-stopper	tonacaztzacca,
a little pointed	uitztontli,	it is pointed[13]	uitzauhtica,
a little pointed	uitzpil,	it stops it up	tlatzaqua.
In our ear	Tonacazco:	as is said, Do I not hear you from my hearing place?	in iuh mitoa, cuix notlacaquiampa, nimitzcaquiz?
bored	coionqui,	it is bored	coioni
smoke hole	tlecallotl,	it is closed[15]	motzaqua,
there things are heard	vncan tlacaco,	he is hard of understanding	nacaztepetlati,
place of hearing[14]	tlacacoia,	ear aches	nacazqualo.
our hearing place	totlacaquia,		

---

9. von Gall, *op. cit.*, p. 153. *Die Knorpelmasse unseres Ohres.*

10. *Loc. cit.: Ohrläppchen.*

11. Rémi Siméon, *op. cit.: çoa, çoua.*

12. von Gall, *loc. cit.: Unsere Ohrmuschel.*

13. *Acad. Hist. MS: vitzavi* follows *uitzauhtica.*

14. *Ibid.: tlacoya.*

15. *Ibid.: nacaztepetlatia* follows *motzaqua.*

SEVENTH PARAGRAPH, which telleth of the cervix and all which pertaineth to it.

INIC CHICOME PARRAPHO itechpa tlatoa in quechtepolli, ioan in ixquich itech ca.

Neck — Quechtli:
our neck — toquech,
thick — tomaoac
bony — omio
fleshy — nacaio,
full of nerves — tlalhoaio,
strong — chicaoac,
long — ueiac,
small — tepiton,

tiny — tepitic,
dwarf-like — tzapatic,
fat — nanatztic,
neck becomes fat — quechnanatziui,
neck becomes thick — quechtomaoa,
neck becomes fleshy[1] — quechnacaiui,
neck becomes fleshy — quechnacati,
small neck — quechtepi,
dwarf neck — quechtzapa.

Cervical vertebrae[2] — Quechquauhiutl:
our cervical vertebrae — toquechquauhio,
bone — omitl,
strong — chicaoac,
jointed — çacaliuhqui,

jointed like a cane — ihixe,
crackling — tetecuitztic,
they are strong — chicaoa,
they crackle — tetecuitzaui.

Cervix[3] — Quechtepolli:
pointed — uitztic,
bumpy — xixippuchtic,
it becomes bumpy — xixipochaui,

it is pointed — uitzauhticac,
neck's blunt-part is the same as cervix[4] — Quechtetepontli idem est quechtepolli.

Neck bones are the same as cervical bones — Quechomitl: idem est quechquauhiotl.

Our neck region — Toquechtla:
it is soft — tlaiamania,
it thickens[5] — tlamatomaoa,

it becomes small — tlatepitonauhia,
it lengthens — tlaueiaquia.

Our occipital region[6] — Tocuechcochtla:
it becomes hairy — tlatzoniooa,

it becomes smooth[7] — tlaxixipetziui.

Tube [windpipe][8] — Cocotl:
our [windpipe] — tococouh,
thick — tomaoac,
thin and long — pitzaoac,

long — ueiac,
small — tepiton,
it blows — mopitza
it speaks — naoati.

Gullet — Tlatolhoaztli:
our gullet — totlatolhoaz,
swallower — tlatoloani,

that which forces down — tlatopeoani,
it swallows — tlatoloa,
it swallows things smoothly — tlapetztoloa.

Adam's apple, or our Adam's apple, (alternative), or Adam's apple (alternative) — Cocoxittontli: anoço tococopuztecca, anoço cocochittolli,
broken — puztecqui,

sharp — vitztic,
it moves — molinia,
it moves down — temo,
it moves up — tleco,
it swallows things — tlatoloa.

---

1. *Ibid.: quechnânacaivi.*
2. According to Rémi Siméon, *op. cit.,* clavicle.
3. Martín del Campo, *op. cit.,* p. 152: *cuello;* von Gall, *op. cit.,* p. 155: *Dreher.*
4. *Acad. Hist. MS* adds *et quechquauhyotl.*
5. *Ibid.: tlatomavaya.*
6. Martín del Campo, *loc. cit.: nuca (cuexcochtetl — cuexcochtli).* In the *Acad. Hist. MS,* the term appears as *tocuexcochtla.*
7. *Ibid.: tlachipava* is added.
8. Martín del Campo, *op. cit.,* p. 162: *tráquea.* Cf. *supra,* § 4, n. 18.

114

EIGHTH PARAGRAPH, which telleth of the shoulder, and the forearm, and the fingers.

INIC CHICUEI PARRAPHO: itechpa tlatoa in aculli ioã in matzotzopaztli, ioan in mapilli.

Hand [arm] — Maitl:
our hand — toma,
long — ueiac,
very long — uitlatztic,
small — tepiton,
diminutive — tzapa,
it is said, long-hand — mitoa maueiac,
long hands — mauiuiiac
it grasps a handful — mauiuitla,
hand diminishes — matzapa,
hand extends — maçoa,

Shoulder blade — Aculchimalli:
strong — chicaoac,
hard — tepitztic,
firm — oapaoac,

Shoulder — Aculli:
defender — netzacuililoni,
resister — nemapatlaloni,
the shield — mochimaltiani,
with it there is defense — ic netzacuililo,
there is help — nepaleuilo
fleshy — nacaio
very fleshy — nacatepul

Elbow — Molicpitl:
our elbow — tomolicpi,
pointed — uitztic,
pointed at end — iacauitztic
wrinkled — xolochtic,
smooth — petztic,
our place of pushing — totlacçaia,

Forearm[1] — Matzotzopaztli:
long and thick — patlachtilaoac,
flaring toward top — quatomaoac,
tapering toward bottom — tzimpitzaoac,
wide — patlachtic,

Thick part of our forearm[2] — Tomatzotzopaztomaoaca,
fleshy — nacaio,
fat — nanatztic,

Slender part of our forearm[3] — Tomatzotzopazpitzaoaia,
sparsely fleshed — nacaio, totochtic,

Curved inner part of arm[4] — Macochtli:
soft — iamanqui,
loving — tlaçoio,

it casts — maiaui,
it works — tlatequipanoa,
it touches — tlamatoca,
it grasps — tlatzitzquia,
it embraces things — tlanaoatequi,
it embraces one — tenaoatequi,
it embraces something — tlamalcochoa,
it embraces something — tlamacochoa,
it embraces one — temacochoa,
it causes one to embrace — temacochuia,
it carries armloads — tlanapaloa.

it carries things upon the shoulder — tlaquechpanoa,
here we support things — vncan titlaquechpanoa.

fleshy — nacaio,
hard — oaqui,
very hard — quauhoaqui,
it becomes thin — pitzaoa,
it breaks — puztequi,
it helps one — tepaleuia,
it defends one — tetzauilia.

our place of support — tonetlaquechiaia,
with it one is struck [as] with a stone — ic teteuilo,
with it one is shoved — ic tetopeoalo,
it elbows one — temolicpiuia,
it shoves one — temolicpitopeoa.

broad — oapaltic,
with it there is fighting — ic necaltilo,
with it there is resistance — ic nemapatlalo,
it helps one — tepaleuia,
it defends one — tetzacuilia.

it becomes fleshy — nacaiooa,
it becomes fat — nanatziui,
it thickens — tomaoa.

thin — pitzaoac,
it becomes sparsely fleshed — nacaio, totochaui,
it becomes thin — pitzaoa.

it pertains to humanity — tlacaiotl itech ca,
it denotes love of others — tetlaçotlaliztli quinezcaiotia,
it manifests desire — tlanequiliztli quinextia,

---

1. *Acad. Hist. MS: matzopaztli.*
2. *Ibid.: tomatzopaztomavaca.*
3. *Ibid.: tomatzopazpitzavaya.*
4. von Gall, *op. cit.*, p. 158: *Umhalsen.*

it loves one	tetlaçotla,	it embraces one	temacochoa.
it brings about embracing one	temacochuia,		

Wrist bones[5] — Quequeiolli:
our wrist bones	tomaquequeiol:	numbness	cecepoctli,
round	ololtic,	they show to advantage	tlaqualnextia,
hard	tepitztic,	it sets off our hand, the arm	quitlacanextia in toma, in maitl.
hardness	tlaquatl,		

Wrist — Maquechtlantli:
our joint	toçaliuhia	our breaking place	tonepuztequia,
loose	atic,	our doubling place	tonecuelpachoaia,
weak	cuecuetlaxtic,	it becomes wrinkled[6]	xolachaui,
it becomes tired	cuecuetlaxiui,	it becomes smooth	petziui.

Hand [palm][7] — Macpalli:
thick	tilaoac,	ruddy	tlatlactic,
of fleshy surface	ixnacaio,	reddish	tlatlauhqui,
of bony back	teputzomio,	brown	camiltic,
furrowed	aapaio,	brownish	camiliuhqui,
grooved	aacaliuhqui,	one fills the hand	tlamatema,
grooved	aacaltic,	it grasps	tlamotzoloa,
clean	chipaoac,	it seizes	tlatzitzquia,
pale	iztaleoac,	it touches	tlamatoca.

Back of the hand — Macpalteputztli:
bony	omio,	serving as a shield	mochimaltiani,
strong	chicaoac,	it forms a shield	mochimaltia.

Surface of the palm of the hand — Macpalixtli,
fleshy	nacaio,	clapping instrument	tlatlatziniloni,
thick-fleshed	nacatilaoac,	clapper	tlatziniloni,
		one fills the hand	tlamatema.

Middle of the palm of the hand — Macpaliollotli,
hollowed	comoltic,	hollowed	comoliuhqui,
		it becomes hollowed	comoliui.

Joint of the palm of the hand — Macpaluiuilteccaiutl:
fold of the palm of our hand	tomacpalxoxotca,	grooved part of our hand	tomacpalacaliuhca,
		it becomes grooved	acaliui,
		it comes together	mopiqui.

Fleshy part of the palm of the hand — Macpalnacatl:
especially that named the flesh of the palm surface of our hand	oc cenca iehoatl itoca in tomacpalix, inacaio,	it thickens	tilaoa,
		it swells	poçaoa.

Thickness of the palm of our hand — Tomacpaltilaoaca:
at our wrist	tomaquechtlanpa,	the flesh of the palm surface of our hand	tomacpalixnacaio.

---

5. See *quequeyolli, infra,* § 10.

6. *Acad. Hist. MS: xolochaui.*

7. Martín del Campo, *op. cit.,* p. 153: *La cara palmar;* von Gall, *loc. cit. Handfläche.*

Finger — Mapilli:
long — uiac,
small — tepito,
thick — tomaoac,
thin — pitzaoac,
diminutive — tzapatic,
it seizes things — tlatzitzquia
it seizes things firmly — tlateteuhtzitzquia
it accomplishes things[8] — tlatecoa,
it does things — tlaay,
it works at things — tlatequipanoa,
it is capable of all — ixquich iueli
doer of all — moch aini,
it can do all — muchi uel quichioa,
instrument for doing — in chioaloni,
instrument for working — in tequipanoloni.

Finger nail — Iztitl:
it is bone — ca omitl,
hard — tetzaoac,
firm — oapaoac,
strong — chicaoac,
smooth — tetzcaltic,
depressed — patzaoac,
it scratches — tlatataca,
with it there is scratching — ic netataco,
with it there is clawing — ic nemomotzolo.

Thumb — Vei mapilli:
our thumb — toueimapil,
thick — tomaoac,
small — tepito,
it seizes things firmly — tlateteuhtzitzĝa
it seizes things strongly — tlachicaoacatzitzquia,
it envelopes all — tlacemilpia.

Finger — Mapilli:
pointer — tlamapilhuiani
indicator — tetlaittitiani,
with it, it is pointed at — ic tlamapiluilo,
with it, it is indicated — ic tetlaittitilo,
I point at it — nicmapiluia.

Long finger — Mapilli: uiac,
thick — tomaoac,
middle finger — tlanepantla mapilli.

Following finger — Oallatoquilia mapilli,
soft — iamanqui,
toucher — tematocani.

Little finger — Mapilxocoiotl:
small — tepito,
thin — pitzato,
a little thin — pitzactontli,
ear-borer — nenacazmamamalioani,
with it the ear is bored — ic nenacazmamalioa.

All the surface of the fingers — Cemixtli mapilli:
all the surface of the fingers — mapilcemixtli,
all the surface of our fingers — tomapilcemix,
jointed — çaliuhqui,
jointed — çaçaliuhqui.

Between the fingers — Tomapiltzala:
it becomes narrowed — tlatzoliui,
it becomes narrowed — tlatzoliuhca,
place of widening — tlapatlaoaia,
it is triangular — chiquinalca,
they are like mud tortillas — xantlaxcalteuhca,
it becomes narrow — tzoliui,
it widens — patlaoa,
it comes together — mopiqui.

Middle of our hand — Tomatzala:
place of opening — tlaçouhia,
open between our thumb — çouhq̃ itzalan in toueimapil
and the index finger — ioan in tlamapilhuiloni, mapilli.

Armpit — Ciacatl:
hollowed — comoltic,
warm — iamanqui,
hairy — tzonio,
firm — picqui,
it becomes hollowed — comoliui,
it comes together — mopiqui,
hair forms — tzonixoa.

Armpit hair — Ciacatzontli:
sparse — caciltic,
coarse — chamaoac,
pointed — iaque,
of pointed end — iacauitztic,
tapering — iacapitzaoac,
it forms — ixoa,
it becomes coarse — chamaoa,
it grows — mozcaltia,
it grows long — ueiaquia.

---

8. Apparently *tlatecoa* in the *Florentine Codex* and in the *Acad. Hist. MS*; possibly *tlayecoa* or *tlateca* may have been intended.

Ninth paragraph, which telleth of the torso and all which pertaineth to it.

Inic chicunaui parrapho: itechpa tlatoa in totlac, ioã in ixquich itech ca.

Torso[1]

	Tlactli:
our torso	totlac,
the torso	in tlactli,
thick	tomaoac,
thin	pitzaoac,
curved	cultic,
thin	cuillotic
long	veiac,
round	ololtic,
dwarfed	tzapatic,
lean	côcolôtic,
hard-fleshed	nacatetic,
quite fleshy	nacatepol,
quite fleshy in parts	nanacapol,
quite large	ueipol,
corpulent	cuitlatolpol,
of reed-like navel	xitoltic,
distended navel	xicuitolpol,
quite big	talapol,
very big	tâtalapol,
very big	tatalatic,
large and long	talapiaztic,
thin	cicicuiltic,
rib-shaped[2]	omicicuiltecuicuiltic,
reed-like	acatic,

Collar bone

	Omicozcatl:
our collar bone	tomicozqui,
cylindrical	mimiltic,
cylindrical	mimiliuhqui,

Chest

	Elpantli:
our chest	telpan,
that which broadens	tlapatlaoa,
that which thickens	tlatilaoa,
fleshy[4]	nacaio, nacaio,
of thick flesh	nacatilaoac,
of thin flesh	nacacanaoac,

Breast[5]

	Chichioallic
woman's breast	cioachichioalli,
man's breast	oquichchichioalli,
old collapsed breast[6]	quauhtzotzocatl,
characteristics of child's breast	ineixcauil in conechichioalli,
undeveloped	tzotzocatic,
girl's breast	in cioapilchichioalli,
budding	tomoltic,

shaped like a bell	cacalachtic,
thick-skinned	eoaio, tilaoac,
soft-skinned	eoaioxococ,
lean	quappitztic,
like a sliver of pine	ocutic,
he carries things all in one piece	tlacennapaloa,
it thickens	tomaoa,
it lengthens	ueia,
it becomes round	toloniui,
it fattens	nanatziui,
it accumulates fat	moceceiotia,
it becomes tender	celia,
it becomes corpulent	cuitlatoliui,
it is made corpulent	cuitlatoltia,
it becomes distended of navel	xicuitoliui,
it hardens	oaqui,
it becomes thin	pitzaoa,
it becomes very hard	quauhoaqui,
it becomes thin	cîcicuiliui,
it becomes rib-shaped[3]	omicicuiltecuicuiliui,
it becomes dry	topopochaui,
it becomes pale	ticeoa.

uneven	chicouiac,
it becomes cylindrical	mimiliui,
thick	tomaoac.

of sparse flesh	nacatotochtic,
it broadens	patlaoa,
it thickens	tilaoa,
it expands	uecapaniui,
it fattens	nanatziui,
it becomes hollowed	comoliui,
it becomes grooved	acaliui.

maiden's breast	ichpuchchichioalli,
like fruit	xocotic,
like hard fruit	xocotetic,
resilient	iôiollo.
pregnant womans breast	Otztli ichichioal:
of darkened tips	iacatlileoac,
hard	têtepitztic,
milk flows	mêmeia,
it hangs	piloa,

---

1. Martín del Campo, *op. cit.*, p. 152: *tórax*.

2. *Acad. Hist. MS: omĭcicuiltecuiltic.*

3. *Ibid.: omĭciltecuicuilivi.*

4. The term *nacaio* is repeated in the *Florentine Codex*.

5. *Acad. Hist. MS: chichivalli;* literally, nipples.

6. *Ibid.:* following *quauhtzotzocatl,* the phrasing appears to be *oquichchichivalli yneixcavil. in cunechichivalli. . . .*

her breast [is] very long	ichichioal, uiuiiac,	nourishes	tlaoapaoa,
like tump lines	memecapaltic,	it nourishes one	teoapaoa,
woman of long breasts	chichioalmecapalli,	it nourishes man	tlacaoapaoa,
soft	atoltic.	it is milked	mopatzca,
The much collapsed breast	In quauhtzotzocatl,	it is sucked	mochichi,
collapsed	tzotzocatic.	it suckles	quichichi.
The woman's breast	In cioachichioalli,		

Chest muscle[7] | **Elmetztli:** | with tissues | ciciotqui,
thickness of our chest muscle[8] | telmetztilaoaca, | it thickens | tilaoa,
 | | it fattens | nanatziui,
fat | suchio, | it enlarges | veia.

Flabbiness of the chest[9] | **Eltzotzolli:** | suety | ceceio,
flesh of our chest | telnacaio, | it becomes fat | suchiooa,
thick | tilaoac, | it becomes suety | ceceiooa,
greasy | chiaoacaio, | it stains | chiaoa.
fat | suchio,

Sternal groove[10] | **Elacaliuhiantli:** | blunted[11] | tetecuintic,
grooved | acaltic, | sparse-fleshed | nacaiototochtic,
grooved | acaliuhqui, | it becomes grooved | acaliui.

Hollow part of chest[12] | **Elcomoliuhiantli:** | it becomes hollowed | comoliui,
hollowed | comoltic, | it becomes bowl-shaped | caxiui.
bowl-shaped | caxtic,

Thorax | **Chiquiuhiotl:** | bony | omio,
our thorax | tochiquiuhio, | strictly of bone | motquitica omitl.

Chest | **Elchiquiuitl:** | like an olla | xoxoquiuhqui,
our chest | telchiquiuh, | it becomes like an olla | xoxoquiui,
strong | chicaoac, | it becomes like an olla | xoquiui.
broad | oapaoac,

Rib | **Omicicuilli:** | each one curved | nônoltic,
thick | tomaoac, | bowed | tlauitoltic,
thin | pitzaoac, | they are curved | noliui,
curved | noltic, | they are bowed | tlauitoliui.

Sternum[13] | **Eltepicicitli:** | jointed | çaçaliuhqui,
our sternum | teltepicici, | it crackles | tetecuitzaui.
crackling | tetecuitztic,

Xiphoid[14] | **Eltototl:** | wide | patlachtic,
lower end of our sternum | teltotouh, | wide | patlachiuhqui,
of cartilage | omicelic, | it is hanging | pilcatica,
pointed | vitztic, | it widens | patlachiui.
of pointed end | iacauitztic,

---

7. von Gall, *op. cit.*, p. 166: *Busen.*

8. *Acad. Hist. MS: telmetztilavacayo.*

9. Rémi Siméon, *op. cit.: Graisse dure qui vient dans les mamelles de certains animaux; jabot, double gorge;* von Gall, *loc. cit.: Männliche Brust.*

10. *Ibid.*, p. 167: *Brusteinschnitt des Mannes.*

11. *Acad. Hist. MS: tetecuitic.*

12. von Gall, *loc. cit.: Brusteinschnitt der Frau.*

13. *Loc. cit.: Die echten Rippen.*

14. *Ibid.*, p. 168: *Falsche Rippen.*

End of rib[15]	Omicicuiliacatl:	each one soft	cecelic,
soft	celic,	it softens	celia.
Our flank[16]	Tococoioia:	it becomes very soft	papatziui.
very soft	papatztic,		
Side	Iomotlantli:	our resting place	tonoia
our side	toiomotla,	it becomes fleshy	nacaioa,
fleshy	nacaio,	it becomes bony	omiooa,
bony	omio,	it becomes broad	patlachiui.
wide	patlachtic,		
Back	Teputztli:	it curves	coliui,
our back	toteputz,	it protrudes	quiça,
curved	coltic,	it becomes humped	teputzoiui.
humped	teputzotic,		
Our thoracic curve	Toteputzcoliuhca:	it curves	coliui
possessing an eminence	tiltic,	bowl-shaped[17]	tlacaxiuh.
it possesses an eminence	tiliui,		
Back	Cuitlapantli:	it becomes wide	patlaoa,
our back	tocuitlapa,	it becomes thin	pitzaoa,
broad	patlaoac,	it becomes grooved	acaliui,
long	ueiac,	it crackles	comotzaui,
strong	chicaoac,	it crackles	côcomotzaui,
of thick flesh	nacatilaoac,	it becomes thick	tilaoa,
with folds	tzotzoltic,	it becomes folded	tzotzoliui,
with folds	tzôtzoltic,	it becomes thick-fleshed	nacaiotilaoa.
Waist[18]	Cuitlacaxiuhiantli:	it becomes thin	tlapitzaoa,
our waist	tocuitlacaxiuhia,	it is bowl-shaped	caxiuhtimani.
Our waist	Topitzaoaia,	thin	tacapitztic,
place where our waist	totacapitzauhia,	it becomes thin	tacapitzaui,
[is] thin	pitzaoac,	it becomes thin	pitzaoa.
Our lumbar curve[19]	Tocuitlaxilotca:	tender	celic,
thick	tomaoac,	it thickens	tomaoa,
thin	pitzaoac,	it becomes thin	pitzaoa.
long	uiac		
Our loins[20]	Tomimiliuhca:	cylindrical	mimiliuhqui,
cylindrical	mimiltic,	they become cylindrical	mimiliui.
Our lungs[21]	Tomimiaoaio:	it has a pain in the side	quâquauhti,
our wind	têcauh,	the pain in the side returns	quaquauhtiliztli,
that which receives a pain	quaq̄uhtini,		mocuepa.
in the side			

---

15. *Loc. cit.: Brustbein*.

16. *Acad. Hist. MS: tocoyoya*.

17. Not found in the *Acad. Hist. MS.*

18. von Gall, *op. cit.*, p. 169: *Achselhöhle*.

19. *Ibid.*, p. 170: *Unsere Mannes-Hüften*.

20. *Loc. cit.: Unsere Weibes-Hüften*.

21. Rémi Siméon, *op. cit.: mimiauatl* (honeycomb). See Martín del Campo, *op. cit.*, p. 153 (*ijada*); cf. also *tomjmjiaoaio* below, § 12; von Gall, *loc. cit.: Unsere Weichen*.

Grooved part of our back[22]	Tocuitlapanacaliuhca:	sparse-fleshed	nacaiototochtic,
grooved	acaltic	it becomes grooved	acaliui,
grooved	acaliuhqui,	flesh thins	nacaiocanaoa.
of thin flesh	nacaiocanaoac,		
Spine	Cuitlatetepontli:	it crackles	tetecuitzaui,
strong	chicaoac	it breaks	puztequi,
jointed like a cane	ihixe,	they are separated [23]	momcaoa,
jointed	çaçaliuhqui,	crackling	natzini.
crackling	tetecuitztic,		
Our hip	Tocuitlaxaiac:	sparse-fleshed	nacaiototochtic,
wide	patlaoac,	they widen	patlaoa.
thin-fleshed	nacaiocanaoac,		
Abdomen[24]	Ititl,	swollen	poçactic,
abdomen	itetl,	soft	patztic,
our abdomen	titi,	very soft	papatztic,
our abdomen	tote,	like an olla	xoxoquiuhqui,
it is thin	ca pitztic,	it becomes like an olla	xoxoquiui,
it is thin[25]	ca pitzauhqua	it becomes very soft	papatziui
large	uei,	abdomen swells	itipoçaoa,
round	ololtic,	abdomen drags	îtiuilani,
dragging	uilanqui,	abdomen breaks	ititlapaniui,
dragging	uilaxtic,	abdomen drags	itiuilaxtia.
Lower part of abdomen[26]	Xiccueiotl:	cylindrical	mimiltic,
thick	tomaoac,	it becomes cylindrical	mimiliui,
thin	pitzaoac,	it thickens	tomaoa.
Navel	Xictli:	it protrudes	quiça
hollowed	comoltic,	it becomes like a little fish[27]	tôpoliui,
possessing an eminence	tiltic,	it becomes like a mano	metlapiliui
like a little fish[27]	topoltic,	it becomes bowl-like	caxiui,
like a mano	metlapiltic,	it becomes hollowed	comoliui.
protruding	quizqui,		
Navel hole	Xicatlacomolli:	it enlarges	coiaoa,
enlarged	coiaoac,	it deepens	uecatlaniui.
deep	vecatla,		
Navel's roundness	Xicteuilacachiuhiantli:	it becomes round like a top	pepeliui,
round	iaoaltic,	it becomes round	teuilacachiui,
round	teuilacachtic,	it becomes deep	uecatlaniui,
deep	uecatlan,	it becomes round	iaoaliui.
like a round top	pepeltic,		
Abdomen[28]	Xillantli:	I break	ninopuztequi,
our place which doubles	tonecuelpachoaia	I have a pain in the abdomen	noxillã mococoa.
our place which breaks	tonepuztequia,		
I double myself	ninocuelpachoa,		

22. *Loc. cit.: Unsere Taille* (?).
23. *Acad. Hist. MS: momacava.*
24. *Martín del Campo, op. cit.,* p. 152: *hipogastrio . . . "barriga o vientre"* (citing Molina, *op. cit.*).
25. *Acad. Hist. MS: pitzauhqui.*
26. *Ibid.: xicueyotl.*
27. Read *tapaltic, tapaliui.*
28. See n. 24, *supra.*

Hip depression[29]	**Queztli:**	bowl-like	caxtic,
our hip depression	toquez,	sparse-fleshed	nacaio, totochauhqui,
hollowed	comoltic,	it becomes hollowed	comoliui.
Hip[30]	**Quappantli:**	strong	chicaoac,
our hip	toquappa,	like a harpoon	chichiquiltic,
our hip	toquauhpa,	it becomes like a harpoon	chichiquiliui.
like a jar handle	connacaztic,		
End of hip bone[31]	**Quappaiacatl:**	tender	celic,
end of our hip bone	toquappaiac,	it becomes tender	celia.
Buttocks[32]	**Tzintli:**	fleshy	nacaio,
our buttocks	totzin	they become fleshy	nacaiooa,
bony	omio,	they become bony	omiiooa.
Buttocks	**Tzintamalli:**	it is thin	ca pitztic,
fleshy	nacaio	fat	natztic,
round	ololtic	fat	nanatztic,
ball-like	tapaioltic,	wrinkled	xolochtic,
thick	tilaoac,	much wrinkled	xoxolochtic,
resilient	oltic,	it becomes wrinkled	xolochaui,
tough	tlalichtic,	it becomes much wrinkled	xoxolochaui,
tough	tlalichauhqui,	it becomes smooth	petziui,
soft	patztic,	it becomes soft	patziui,
very soft	papatztic,	it becomes very soft	papatziui.
of heavy flesh	nacatetic,		
Coccyx[33]	**Tzinchocholli:**	our pressing place	totlacçaia,
bone	omitl,	with it I press	ic nitlacça
strong	chicaoac,		
Ischial tuberosity	**Tzintepitztli:**	our sitting place	tonetlaliaia,
our ischial tuberosity	totzintepitz,	on it we are	ipan ticate,
hard	tepitztic,	with it we are pressing	ic titlacçaticate.
strong	chicaoac,		
Anus	**Tzincamactli:**	it becomes deep	uecatlaniui,
deep	uecatla	it becomes round like a top	pepeliui
round like a top	pepeltic,		
Anal crevice[34]	**Tzinatlauhtlitl:**	it contracts	tlatzoliui,
our anal crevice	totzinatlauhio,	it contracts	tzoliui,
it expands	tlapatlaoa,	it becomes narrow	pitzaoa,
it narrows	tlapitzaoa,	it expands	patlaoa.
Anus	**Tzoiotl:**	it smokes	pocheoa,
bored	coionqui,	it opens	tlapoui
smoky	pochectic,	it passes excrement	moxixa,
smoky	pocheoac,	it passes excrement	cuitlaioa.
it is bored	coioni,		

---

29. von Gall, *op. cit.,* p. 173: *Schenkelbeuge.*

30. *Loc. cit.: Steg.*

31. *Loc. cit.: Damm.*

32. Martín del Campo, *op. cit.,* p. 162: *ano* (citing Molina, *op. cit.*). This definition does not fit the present context.

33. von Gall, *op. cit.,* p. 174: *Steiss.*

34. *Acad. Hist. MS: tzinatlayotl.*

Lip of anus	**Tzoiotentli:**	gripping	motzoliuhqui,
gripping	motzultic,	it grips	motzoliui.
Anus[35]	**Cuilchilli:**	soft [36]	iamaztic,
cylindrical	mimiltic,	it becomes chili-red	chichiliui,
chili-red	chichiltic,	it becomes tender	celia
tender	celic,	it has hemorrhoids	cuilchilquiça.
Edge of anus	**Cuilchiltentli:**		
thick	tilaoac.		
Crotch	**Maxactli:**	it becomes forked	maxaliui,
his crotch	imaxac	forked place	tlamaxaliuhia
our crotch	tomaxac,	whence is said, crossroads	vnde dr. ŷmaxac
forked	maxaltic,	tree crotch	quanmaxac.
Clamping place [of thigh][37]	**Nepiciantli:**	constricted	tacapitztic,
		it narrows	tlatzoliui,
our clamping place	tonepicia,	it clamps	mopiqui,
grooved	acaltic,	it breaks open[38]	motzaia.
Groin	**Quexilli:**	full	tetenqui,
our groin	toquexil,	full of flesh	nacatemi,
broad	patlaoac,	it slaps	cacalachiui,
thin	pitzaoac,	it broadens	patlaoa.
Penis[39]	**Tepolli:**	it deflowers	tlaxapotla,
	xipintli, tototl,	it deflowers one	texapotla,
	xolo, tlamacazqui,	it has sexual relations	tlacui,
	quatlaxcon, tocincul,	with it sexual relations are had	ic tlacuioa,
the penis	in tepolli,		
thin	pitzaoac,	with it there are sexual relations with one	ic tecuicuioa,
thick	tomaoac,		
long	ueiac,	with it one is begotten	ic tlacachioalo,
stubby	tetepontic,	it is skinned	xipeoa,
instrument for sexual relations	tlacuioani,	[its] head ejects liquid	quatoxaoa,
		it urinates	maxixa,
instrument for begetting	tlacachioaloni,	it ejects	tlaxaxaoatza.
Prepuce	**Xipineoatl:**	it becomes soft	iamania,
thin	canaoac,	it becomes thin	canaoa.
soft	iamãqui,		
Glans penis[40]	**Xipintzontecomatl:**	very soft [41]	iamazpâtic,
round	ololtic	titilating	quêquele
roundness of the head of our penis	toxipin iquaololauhca,	ticklish	quêquelmicqui.

---

35. von Gall, *op. cit.*, p. 175: *Mastdarm*.

36. *Acad. Hist. MS: yamazpâtic*.

37. Cf. *tonepicia, infra,* § 13. Martín del Campo, *op. cit.*, p. 159: *genericamente, las coyunturas del cuerpo* (citing Molina, *op. cit.*); *hueco poplíteo*, p. 154.

38. *Acad. Hist. MS: motzayana*.

39. Suggested meanings of varient terms: *xipintli*, flayed member; *tototl*, bird (cf. Martín del Campo, *op. cit.*, p. 163); *xolo*, servant boy; *tlamacazqui*, priest or one who makes offerings; *quatlaxcon* (from *quauhtlaça?*), possibly inferring frequent sexual relations; *tocincul* (from *tzincouia?*), possibly inferring sexual relations with a prostitute. The context of passages which follow suggests that *tepolli* (penis) and *xipintli* (prepuce) were used interchangeably.

40. Martín del Campo, *op. cit.*, p. 164: *prepucio*.

41. von Gall, *op. cit.*, p. 177: *ganz glatt*.

Opening at the head of the penis[42]	Texipinquacoioncaiutl:	small hole small outlet [43]	coioctontli, quiquiztontli, quiquiz-tontli,
opening at head of our penis split like an outlet like an outlet	toxipinquacoionca, tzaianqui quiquiztic, quiquiçauhqui,	there, with the hole, with the split, with the outlet, there is urination	vncan oalneaxixalo, coiontica, tzaiantica, quiquiçauhtica.
Soft part of head of penis delicate[44] it becomes soft	Xipinquaiamancaiotl: chonequiztli, iamania,	it is bare it is exposed	xoleoa, chipeliui.
Round neck of penis[45] cylindrical	Xipinquechtemalacatl: mimiltic,	tender it becomes round	celic, temalacaiui.
Vulva[46] her vulva[46] it has two lips vulva[46] hot eminence	Tepilli: nenetl, cocoxqui, icocoxcauh, ome iten, cioapilli, totonqui, tlatilli	her eminence adobe[-like] her adobe possessing an eminence possessing an eminence it forms an eminence	itlatil, xaxantli, ixaxan, tiltic, tlatiltic, tiliui.
Labia soft	Tepiltentli: iamanqui,	they open they split	motlapoa, motzaiana.
Labia[47] thick thin	Tepiltexipalli: tilaoac, canaoac,	lips come together mouth comes together they split	motenpiqui, mocamapiqui, motzaiana.
Labia thick-fleshed soft	Tepilcamaxitecuilli, nacatilaoac, iamanqui,	they swell they swell outwards	potzaui, oalpotzaui.
Her vagina[48] long and narrow constricted place	Yatlauhiacac: tlapitzaoac, tlatzoliuhia,	it constricts it comes together	tzoliui, mopiqui.
Hymen her hymen	Chittolli: ichittol.		
Clitoris pointed	Çacapilli: vitztic,	wide it broadens	patlachtic, patlachiui.
End of clitoris end of her clitoris	Çacapilquatl: içacapilqua,	pointed it is pointed	uitztic, uitzaui.
Her looking place her place of joy it gives joy	Iittaloia, ipaquia, paqui	intercourse is had intercourse is had	moiecoa, iecolo.

---

42. Cf. *tepulcamapiccatl* (*meato urinario*) in Martín del Campo, *loc. cit.*

43. The term *quiquiztontli* is repeated in the *Florentine Codex*.

44. *Acad. Hist. MS: chinequiztli.*

45. von Gall, *op. cit.*, p. 178: *Hoden.*

46. Suggested meanings for terms used alternatively with *tepilli: nenetl*, doll or idol; *cocoxqui*, sick member; *icocoxcauh*, her sick member; *cioapilli*, lady.

47. Martín del Campo, *loc. cit.: labios majores.*

48. von Gall, *op. cit.*, p. 180: *Eingang in die Scheide.*

INIC MATLACTLI PARRAPHO: itechpa in tocxi ioan ixquich itech poui.

Leg	Icxitl:	thin-legged	xopipitzac,
bony	omio,	thin-legged	xopitzac,
fleshy	nacaio,	thick-legged	xotomaoac,
long	ueiac	foot becomes like a melon cactus	xoteuconaui,
each one long	ueueiac,	leg becomes thick	xotomaoa,
very long	uitlatztic,	leg becomes slender	xopitzaoa,
like a cord	mecatic,	leg becomes long	xouiaquia,
twisted	nenecuiltic,	leg becomes very long	xouitlatziui,
whence is said, lame	vnde dr̄ Xonênecuil	leg becomes very long	xouiuitlatziui,
long-legged	xoueiac,	leg becomes very long	icxiueiaquia.
cord-like legs	xomemeca,		
of cord-like legs	xomecatic,		
Hip depression[1]	Quezcomoliuhiantli:	it becomes bowl-like	caxiui,
hollowed	comoltic	it becomes hollowed	comoliui.
bowl-like	caxtic,		
Thigh	Mêtztli:	it becomes slender	pitzaoa,
our thigh	tometz,	it grows	mozcaltia,
the length of the thigh	quezquauhiotl,	it lengthens	uiaquia,
the length of our thigh	toquezquauhio,	it extends	mana,
the length of our thigh	tometzquauhio,	one locks legs with another	temetzuia,
flaring at the top	quatomaoac,	with it there is the locking of legs with another	ic temetzuilo,
narrowing at the bottom	tzimpitzaoac,		
like a hilled plant [2]	tlalquimiltic,	I put his leg in	nicmetzaquia,
whence is said, the thigh [is] an old hilled plant	vnde dr̄. metztlatlalqui-milpol,	I strike his leg	nicmetzuitequi,
it thickens	tomaoa,	I break his leg	nicmetzpuztequi,
		he tears his leg	quimetztzaiana.
Thick part of our thigh	Tometztomaoaia:	it is made flabby	tzotzoltia,
thick-fleshed	nacaio, tilaoac,	it becomes thin	oaqui,
flabby[3]	tzotzoltic,	it becomes slender	pitzaoa.
it becomes flabby	tzotzoliui,		
Slender part of our thigh	Tometzpitzaoaia:		
it becomes slender	pitzaoa.		
Part above our knee[4]	Totlanquaticpac:	it becomes smooth	petziui.
it becomes wrinkled	xolochaui,		
Knee	Tlanquaitl:	that which straightens	melaoaloni
hard	tepitztic,	it becomes round	ololiui,
round	ololtic,	I bend [the knee]	ninocototzoa,
constrictor	mocototzoani,	I straighten myself	ninomelaoa.
that which constricts	cototzoloni,		
Our kneecap[5]	Tontlanquaiacac.		

---

1. *Ibid.*, p. 181: *Gelenkkapsel des Oberschenkels.*
2. Cf. Molina, *op. cit.*: *tlalquimiloa.*
3. Depending upon the context, *tzotzoltic* appears to admit variant meanings.
4. von Gall, *op. cit.*, p. 183: *Haut an unserem Knie.*
5. *Acad. Hist. MS: Totlanquayacac.* The same MS then adds: *Tocotzco. tonepicya. tocototzauhya. mopiqui. momelava.*

Shank[6]	**Tlanitztli:**	small shank	tlanitztepiton,
bony	omio,	curved shank	tlanitzcocol,
fleshy[7]	nacacaio,	wide shank	tlanitzpatlach,
long	ueiac,	it becomes wide	patlachiui,
small	tepito,	it becomes twisted	noliui,
diminutive	tzapa.	it becomes slender	pitzaoa,
cylindrical	mimiltic,	it lengthens	ueiaquia,
twisted	noltic,	shank becomes slender	tlanitzpitzaoa,
twisted	noliuhqui,	shank becomes thick	tlanitztomaoa,
long-shank	tlanitzuiac,	shank becomes curved	tlanitzcôcoliui
of diminutive shank	tlanitztzapa,	shank becomes wide	tlanitzpatlachiui.
Calf of leg	**Cotztetl:**	sparse	totochtic,
calf of our leg	tocotzteuh,	quivering	uiioctic,
round	ololtic,	it quivers	uiioni,
very fleshy	nacatepol.	it becomes round	ololiui.
Calf of leg	**Cotztli:**	**Above our calf**[8]	**Tocotzteiacac.**
(*cotztli*) is the same as	idem est cotztetl.		
calf (*cotztetl*)			
Point of our calf	**Tocotzteiacac:**	it bulges	peiaoa.
place which bulges	tlapeiaoaca,		
Slender part of our leg	**Toxopitzaoaca:**	shank becomes slender[9]	tlanitzpitzaoa,
slender part of our shank	totlanitzpitzaoaca,	slender place	tlapitzaoaia.
Ankle	**Xoquechtlantli:**	pliable	caxanqui,
our ankle	toxoquechtla	mover	moliniani,
loose	atic,	it moves	molinia.
Ankle bone[10]	**Quequeiolli:**	it becomes round	ololiui,
ankle bone of our leg	tocxiquequeiol,	it becomes round	ololaui,
round	ololtic,	it becomes hard	tepitzaui,
hard	tepitztic,	it protrudes	xixipuchaui.
protruding	xixipuchtic,		
Foot[11]	**Xocpalli:**	it breaks clods of earth[12]	papaxiui,
foot	icxitl,	it breaks	tzatzaiani,
bony	omio,	we break with the foot	tixotzaiani,
fleshy	nacaio,	our doubled foot	toxocueloa,
wide and thick	patlachtilaoac,	our lame foot	toxonecuiloa,
we raise it	tiquiiaoa,	we run a thorn into the foot	titixili,
with it we kick	ic titlatelicça	one who walks quietly	xoquenmachnênemini,
with it, it is walked	ic nênemoa,	he travels quietly	xoxoquenmachnenemi.
walker	nênemoani,		
Heel	**Quequetzolli:**	callused	chacaioltic,
a ball of the foot	quequetzilli,	tough	tlalichtic,
rubbery	oltic,	firm	chicaoac,

---

6. Martín del Campo, *op. cit.*, p. 159: *tibia*.

7. *Acad. Hist. MS: nacayo.*

8. Read *tocotzicpac*, as in *ibid.*

9. *Ibid.: tlapitzava.*

10. Cf. *supra*, Paragraph 8.

11. Martín del Campo, *op. cit.*, p. 155: *cara plantar;* cf. also von Gall, *op. cit.*, p. 185. *Xocpalli* and *icxitl* appear to be alternative terms.

12 . *Acad. Hist. MS: papayaxivi.*

chili-red	chichiltic,	like a tomato	xitomatic.
smooth	petztic		
Our arch	**Toxocpalpitzaoaca:**	constricted	tacapitzauhqui,
constricted	tacapitztic,	it becomes constricted	tacapitzaui.
Instep	**Xocpalteputztli:**	it possesses an eminence	tiliui,
our instep	toxocpalteputz,	it bulges	peiaoa.
possessing an eminence	tiltic,		
bulging	peiaoac,		
Toe	**Xopilli:**	thick	tomaoac,
it has joints like a cane	ihixe,	small	tepiton,
each breaks	popuztequi,	it grasps something	tlamotzoloa,
it has nails	izte	it seizes something	tlatzitzquia,
[there are] five	macuil	it kicks something	tlatelicça.
long[13]	piac,		
Big toe	**Vei xopilli:**	small	tepiton,
thick	tomaoac,	it is thick	tomaoa,
round like a ball	tolontic,	nails extends	iztiquiça.
Instrument for sandal-	**Necactiloni:**	it is looped to toes	xopilli intech tlauicollotilo,
wearing		it seizes something	tlatzitzquia.
instrument for sandal loop	necacuicollotiloni,		
Following toes	**Oallatoquilia xopilli:**		
Little toe	**Xopilxocoiotl:**	thin and small	pitzato,
small	tepito,	it comes last	tetzacuia,
diminutive	tzapato,	it is last	tetzacuticac,
diminutive	tzapatic,	it is last of all	tecentzacuia.
Nail	**Iztetl:**	it shows things to	tlaqualnextia.
nail	iztitl,	advantage	
shower of things to	tlaqualnextiani,		
advantage			
Sole of the foot	**Xocpalixtli:**	it is scratched	michiqui,
callosity	caccolli,	it thins	canaoa,
our callosity	tocaccol,	it is torn	tzaiani,
skin of sole of foot	xocpaleoatl,	. . .	peti,
skin of sole of our foot	toxocpaleoaio,	it is anointed	motematiloa,
thick	tilaoac,	a thorn is run in [foot]	mîxili,
tough	pipinqui,	it is pierced	motzoponia,
tough	tlalichtic,	I scrape my foot [14]	ninocxichiqui.
tough	tlalichauhqui		
Our kicking places	**Totlatelicçaia,**		
the surface of our heel [15]	toquequetzolix.		

---

13. *Ibid.: viac.*

14. Following *ninocxichiqui*, the *Acad. Hist.* MS has the following: *Totlacçaya, tliltic. nitlacça. nitlatelicça.* For *totlacçaya* and *totlatelicçaia*, von Gall, *op. cit.*, pp. 187, 188, has *Worauf wir treten.*

15. Following *toquequetzolix*, the *Acad. Hist.* MS adds *nitlatelicça.*

ELEVENTH PARAGRAPH, which telleth of all the bones on which the flesh resteth.

INIC MATLACTLI OCE PARRAPHO itechpa tlatoa in ixquich tomio, tonacaio inic onoc.

Skull	Quaxicalli:
hollow in the interior	hiticoionqui,
like an olla	contic,
like a jar	tecontic,
round	ololtic,
round	ololiuhqui,
soft	patztic,
wide	patlachtic,
partly soft	chicopatztic,
toe-like	xopiltic,
pointed	uitztic,
concave	oacaltic,
bowl-like	caxtic,

Occiput	Crexcochtetl:
pointed	uitztic,
possessing an eminence	tiltic,

Our face bones[1]	Tixomio:
our frontal bone	tixquaxical,
our cheek	tixteliuhca,
our jaw	tocamachal,

Cervical bones[3]	Quechtetepontli:
cervix[4]	quechtepolli.
cervical vertebrae	quechquauhiotl,
our thorax	Tochiquiuhio.
collar bone	Omicozcatl,
our shoulder blade	Tâculchimal
point of our shoulder blade	Tâculuiuitzauhca.
length of our shoulder[5] [blade]	Tâculquauhio:
shoulder	aculli.
elbow	Molicpitl.
point of elbow	Molicpiacatl,
point of our elbow	tomolicpiac.
forearm[6]	Mâtzopaztli, matzotzopaztli.
wrist bone	Quequeiolli
our wrist bone[7]	tomaquequeiol,
our wrist bone	Toquequeiol.
finger	Mapilli:
our finger bone	tomapilomio.
our thorax	Tochiquiuhio.

hollowed	comoltic,
it is hollow inside	îticoioni,
it becomes round	ololiui,
it is soft	patziui,
it broadens	patlachiui,
it becomes toe-like	xopiliui,
it becomes concave	oacaliui,
it becomes like a round stone	teololiui,
it becomes like a mano	metlapiliui,
it becomes like a digging stick	uitzoquiui.

it possesses an eminence	tiliui,
it becomes pointed	uitzaui,
one rests one's head	mocpaltia.

our chin	totenchal,
it creaks	nanatzca,
instrument which creaks[2]	natzini.

chest	Elchiquivitl.
sternum	Eltepicicitli.
lower end of sternum	Eltototl.
rib	Omjcicujlli.
end of rib[8]	Omjcicujliacatl.
spine	Cujtlatetepontli
spine ridges	Cujtlateputzchichiqujlli
pelvis	tzinquauhcaxitl,
our pelvis	totzinquauhcax.
coccyx[9]	tzinchocholli.
head of femur[10]	queztepolli.
rounded part of our femur	Toqueçololiuhca.
end of head of our femur	Toqueztepoliac.
rump bone[11]	tzintepitztli.
hip bone	Quezquauhiotl.
pubic bone[12]	Tepilquaxicalli.
kneecap[13]	Tlanquaxicalli.
shank	Tlaniztli,
shank bone[14]	tlanitzquauhiotl
our toe bone	Toxopilomjo,
toe[15]	xopilli.

1. von Gall, *op. cit.*, p. 188: *Unser Scheitelbein.*
2. *Acad. Hist. MS: nanatzini.*
3. von Gall, *op. cit.*, p. 189: *Atlas.*
4. *Loc. cit.: Dreher.*
5. *Acad. Hist. MS: tâculquayo.*
6. von Gall, *loc. cit.: Speiche* for *mâtzopaztli; Elle* for *matzotzopaztli.*
7. *Acad. Hist. MS: toxoquequeyol* follows *tomaquequeiol.*
8. von Gall, *loc. cit.: Brustbein.*
9. *Loc. cit.: Kreuzbein.*
10. However, cf. Martín del Campo, *op. cit.*, p. 159: *cadera.*
11. von Gall, *op. cit.*, p. 190: *Schwanzbein.*
12. *Loc. cit.: Weibliches Becken.*
13. Martín del Campo, *op. cit.*, p. 158: *cabeza ósea;* see also p. 160.
14. *Acad. Hist. MS: tlanitzquauhyo.*
15. After *xopilli,* the *Acad. Hist.* MS adds *nacatl tlani onoc tlapachiuhqui.*

TWELFTH PARAGRAPH, which telleth of the organs which are within.

JNIC MATLACTLI OMOME PARRAPHO, ytechpa tlatoa, in toujujltecca in tlattic onoc.

Brain	Quatextli,
brains	quatetextli,
white	iztac,
fine-textured	cuechtic
fine-textured	cuechiuhquj,
moist	axtic,
very fine-textured	cuechpatic,
very white	iztacpatic,
cold	itztic,
Thickness	Tilaoacaiutl:
our thickness	totilaoaca,
it is everywhere	noujan ca,
in our face	tixco,
at our neck	toquechtla,
on our shoulder	taculpa,
on the calf of our leg	tocotzco,
on our chest	telpa,
Fat	Xochiotl:
our fat	toxochio,
it is on our chest	telpā ca,
yellow	coztic,
very yellow	cozpiltic,
very yellow	cozpatic,
Fat[2]	Ceceiotl:
our fat	toceceo,
white	iztac,
greasy	chiaoac,
heavy	hetic,
very heavy	cujtlaxocotl,
it makes one lazy	tetlatziujti,
Greasiness	Chiaoacaiutl,
just like fat, suet	çan no iuhquj in xochiotl, in ceceiotl,
Flabbiness	Tzotzoliuhcaiutl:
tender	ceceltic,
thick	tilaoac,
greasy	chiaoac,
Flabbiness of our neck	Toquechtzotzol:
flabbiness of our lip	totentzol,
flabbiness of our breast	teltzotzol,
flabbiness of our abdomen	tititzotzol,
flabbiness of the calf of our leg	tocotztzotzol,
Tissue[3]	Ciciotcaiutl:
our tissue	ticiciotca,
white	iztac

very cold	itzcaltic,
rememberer	tlalnamjconj,
knower	tlamachonj,
it causes others to know	tetlamachitia,
it causes others to remember	tetlalnamjctia,
it is said, crazy-headed [1]	mjtoa quauhtlaueliloc,
mad	iollotlaueliloc,
of turned head	ixmalacachiuhquj.
on our thigh	tometzpa,
on our abdomen	titipa,
thick flesh	nacatl tilaoac,
it is thick	tilaoa,
it swells up	poçaoa,
it enlarges	tlaveilia,
it enlarges one	teueylia.
soft	iamanquj,
hot	totonquj,
it softens	tlaiamanjlia,
it heats	tlatotonilia
it makes tender	tlaceliltia,
it causes filling out	tlatzmolinaltia.
it makes one heavy	teetili,
it improves one	tequaltilia,
it freshens one	teceliltia,
it fills one out	teitzmolinaltia,
it increases one in size	tetoma,
it enlarges one	teveilia.
it stains things with grease	tlachiaoa.
it becomes tender	cecelia,
it becomes greasy	chiaoa,
it stains things with grease	tlachiaoa.
it makes it heavy	tlaetilia
it keeps the body erect	tlâciqujltia,
it becomes flabby	tzotzoliuj.
cord-like	memecatic,
it becomes white	iztaia,
it becomes cord-like	memecatia.

---

1. *Ibid.*: *quatlaveliloc.*
2. Martín del Campo, *op. cit.*, p. 156: *tejido adiposo.*
3. *Ibid.*, p. 160: *musculatura pectoral de las aves.*

. . . [4]	Thocotca:	chili-red	chichiltic,
. . .	thoocotca,	it is straight	melaoa,
straight	melaoac,	it is rough	oapaoa,
rough	oapaoac,	it becomes chili-red	chichiliuj.
Fat [5]	Puchqujotl:	transparent	atic,
our fat	topochqujo,	one is fattened	mopochqujotia,
white	iztac,	fat dissolves	puchqujotlamj.
Small of our back [6]	Tocujtlaxilotca:	it becomes long	viaquja,
cylindrical	mjmjltic,	it becomes cylindrical	mjmjlivj.
straight	melaoac,		
Our loins [7]	Tomjmjliuhca:	then all the names [of parts] wherever we [are] cylindrical	njman ie muchi ytoca, yn noujan tomjmjliuhca.
especially that which accompanies the backbone	oc cenca iehoatl in tocujtlatetepon qujtocaticac:		
Our lung [8]	Tomjmjiaoaio:	whence it is said, he has a stitch in his side [9]	vnde dicitur, ymjmjiaoaio moquetza:
our breath	têcauh,	it pants	hicica,
it sickens	cocolizcuj,	it has a pain in its side	quaquauhti.
that which pants	icicanj,		
panting animates it	yciquiztli qujiolitia,		
Testis [10]	Cujtlapanaatetl:	it brings pleasure	paquj,
	cujtlapanaaiecotli,, ioiomoctli, pactli, chiquiztli, tochiquiz,	it is dented under pressure	mopatzcomoloa,
		it is treated with pacxantzin [11]	mopacxanoa,
bringer of pleasure	paqujni,	it brings pleasure	chitepaquj,
pleasurable	pacoanj,	one feels its rubbing	conmati yn jchiquiz.
Semen	Omjcetl:	fine-textured	cuechtic,
seed	xinachtli,	hot	totonquj,
seed of man	tlacaxinachtli,	warm	iamanquj,
our moisture	taio,	it benefits woman	qujqualtilia in cioatl,
our manliness	toqujchio,	it opens her	qujtoma,
nobility	eztli, tlapalli,	it fattens her	qujnanatzoa,
essence of lineage	oxiotl, ocutzoiotl,	it makes her bloom	qujceltilia,
solicitude	nemociujlli,	it impregnates her [12]	cotztili
white	iztac,	it gives her a big abdomen	qujcujtlapiciooa.
transparent	atic,		
Heart [13]	Joiollotli:	that by which there is existence	nemoanj,
our heart	toiollo,	life	ioliliztli,
round	ololtic,	it makes one live	teiolitia,
hot	totonquj,		

---

4. von Gall, *op. cit.*, p. 193: *Unsere Luftröhre* (to+cocouh).

5. *Loc. cit.*: *Lymphgefässe.*

6. *Loc. cit.*: *Unsere Speiseröhre.*

7. *Loc. cit.*: *Unsere Milz* (?).

8. *Mimiauatl*=honeycomb (Rémi Siméon, *op. cit.*). Cf. Martín del Campo, *op. cit.*, p. 153: *tomiauayocan=ijada*; cf. also *supra*, § 9.

9. *Acad. Hist. MS*: *moquequetza*; cf. Molina, *op. cit.*

10. Martín del Campo, *op. cit.*, p. 163: *riñones*. This meaning appears not to fit the context.

11. Reccho: *op. cit.*, p. 222: "*PACXANTZIN, quam alij* Tenextlacotl, *seu virgam calcis vocant. . . . lus decocti radicum medetur satietati, debilem ventriculum roborat, pectus calefacit. . . . folia tusa, permixtaq;* Chichiantic, & Tlatlaolton *aequis portionibus, ac contuso loco admota, quidquid humoris ad eum defluxit, siccant, atque discutiunt. . . .*" The paragraph is headed, "*De PACXANTZIN, seu planta subsidente.*"

12. *Acad. Hist. MS*: *cotztia.*

13. *Ibid.*: *Yollôtli.*

it sustains one	tenemjtia,	I am troubled	njiolpoliuj,
it lives	ioli,	I faint	njiolmjquj,
it beats	tecujnj,	my heart is delighted	njiolpaquj,
it jumps	chôcholoa,	I know in my heart	noiollo qujmati:
it beats repeatedly	motlâtlamotla:	heart disease	iollomjmjquj,
I feel in my heart	noiollo conmati,	the heart rules all	qujcemjtquj yn iollotli.

Liver	**Eltapachtli:**		
wide and thick[14]	pachtilaoac,	it has an edge	tene,
		chili-red	chichiltic.

Saliva[15]	**Chichitl:**		
our saliva	tochîchi.		

Bile	**Chichicatl:**		
our bile	tochichicauh,	our anger	totlauelcuja,
thick[16]	mimjltic,	it arouses one to anger	tequalanalti,
greenish	xoxoctic,	it swells one with anger	tepoçoni,
blue	texotic,	whence it is said, has my	vnde dicitur, cujx
		bile not [arisen]	anjchichicaoa.

Our stomach[17]	**Totlatlaliaia:**	rough[18]	tlalictli,
	totlatlalil, totlatlalilteco,	strong	chicaoac,
	cujtlatecomatl,	it fills	temj,
enlarged	coiaoac,	it is filled	temjtilo,
restricted	tzoltic	it stretches	cacatzca,
irregular	chachaquachtic,	it extends	titilinj.

Intestine[19]	**Cujtlaxculli:** coatl,	long	viac,
thick	tomaoac,	it breaks	tzaianj,
thin	pitzaoac,	it is harmed	itlacauj.

Womb	**Conexiqujpilli:**	it forms one	tetetzaoa,
enlarged	coiaoac,	it forms	tlatetzaoa,
restricted	tzoltic,	it carries one	teitquj,
hot	totonquj,	it carries	tlatquj.

Uterus[20]	**Cioatl,**	it becomes pregnant	cocoia,
her uterus	ycioaio:	her womb sickens her	ycioaio in qujcocoa,
soft	iamanquj,	her womb is sick	ycioaio mococoa.
subject to pregnancy	cocoianj,		

Testis[21]	**Joiomoctli:**	it stirs	iomonj,
delight	paqujztli,	it swoons with lascivious-	iôionmjquj,
rubbing [against body][22]	chiqujztli,	ness	
it brings delight	paquj,	it rubs	onchiquj,
it moves lasciviously	moioma,	one feels its rubbing	cõmati, yn jchicqujz.
both move lasciviously	moiôioma,		

Bladder	**Axixtecomatl:**	tough	tlalichtic,
our bladder	taxixteco,	provided with nerves	tlaloatic,

---

14. *Ibid.: patlachtilavac.*

15. Martín del Campo, *op. cit.*, p. 162: *pulmones*; von Gall, *op. cit.*, p. 197: *Bauchspeicheldrüse.*

16. Cf. Rémi Siméon, *op. cit.* (*mimiltic*=*rond, gros, épais*).

17. Alternatives: *totlatlalil*, our repository; *totlatlalilteco*, our storage vessel (cf. Rémi Siméon, *op. cit.*: *tlalia, tlatlalilli, tlatlaliloyan*); *cujtlateco-matl*, abdominal vessel.

18. *Acad. Hist. MS: tlalichtli.*

19. Alternative term: *coatl*, serpent.

20. von Gall, *op. cit.*, p. 198: *Hymen.*

21. Cf. n. 11, *supra*; von Gall, *loc. cit.: Scheide.*

22. *Acad. Hist. MS: chicquiztli.*

it fills	temj,	it has sand	xalloa,
it becomes calm	cactiuetzi,	it fills with sand	xaltemj,
it breaks	tzaiani,	it fills with fine [sand]	textemj.

Urethra[23] — Cocôtli:

our urethra	tococôio,	one's urethra is intermit- tently obstructed	meltecujnja,
tube	piaztli,	it fills with fine-textured material	textemj,
our tube	topiazio,	[when] the tube is vertical, the urethra [is] good	vel icac in piaztli, qualli, in cocôtli,
reed	acatl,	[when] the reed is vertical, one urinates	vel icac yn acatl, maxixa,
our reed	tacaio,	there, there is urination	vncn oalneaxixalo,
long	veiac,	it passes water	tlanoquja.
wide	coiaoac,		
like a passage way	qujquiztic,		
thin	pitzaoac,		
one's urethra is obstructed	meltzaqua,		

Blood — Eztli,

our blood	teezio,	it wets the flesh; it moistens it like clay	qujpaltilia, qujçoqujtilia in nacatl,
red	tlapalli,	it refreshes it [25]	qujceltilia,
our redness	totlapallo,	it reaches the surface	oalpavetzi,
our liquid	taio,	it covers one [as] with earth	tetlatlalhuja,
our freshness	tocelica,		
our growth	totzmolinca,	it makes things chili-red	tlachichiloa,
our life [is] blood	tonenca in eztli,	it makes things ruddy	tlatlatlactilia,
it is chili-red [24]	ca chichiltic,	it strengthens one	techicaoa,
that which gives one life	nemoanj,	it strengthens one greatly	techîchicaoa,
our life	toiolca,	one is strengthened	mochicaoa,
it becomes chili-red	chichiliuj,	one is greatly strengthened	mochichicaoa.
it moistens	tlacuechaoa,		

Perspiration[26] — Jtonalli:

our perspiration	titonal,	of fetid smell	xoqujac,
liquid	atic,	it exudes	meia,
hot	totonquj,	it flows	totoca.

Serous fluid[27] — Chiaviçatl:

liquid	atic,	very fetid	xoqujalpâtic,
rotten	palãquj,	it rots	palantiuh,
fetid [28]	xoqujiatic,	it stinks	yiaxtiuh,
		it corrupts	ytlacatiuh.

Bloody pus — Eztemalli:

mingled with blood	ezcujcujltic,	rotten	palanquj,
thick	tetzaoac,	it rots	palanj,
liquid	atic,	it stinks	ŷiaia.

Pus — Temalli, timalli:

stinking	hiiac,	it stinks	îiaia.

Pus — Temalcujtlatl,

very thick	tetzacpatic,	like doughy excrement	nextamalcujtlatic,
like *atole*	atoltic,	smelling of excrement	cujtlâiac,
		smelling of death	mjqujciiac,

---

23. Cf. Martín del Campo, *op. cit.*, p. 163.
24. After *chichiltic*, the *Acad. Hist.* MS inserts *xoq̃ac. atic. tetzavac. chiavizatic.*
25. *Ibid.: quiceliltia.*
26. von Gall, *op. cit.*, p. 200: *Gesundes Blut.*
27. *Loc. cit.: Verdorbenes Blut.*
28. *Acad. Hist. MS: xoq'yaltic.*

smelling much of death	mjqujciialtic,	evil-smelling thing	îiatatl,
wounding the head	tetzonujtec,	it stinks	potonj,
it smells like a corpse	vel mjcoanj ynic yiac,	it stinks of death	mjqujzîiaia.

Blood vessel	**Ezcocotli:**	thick	tomaoac,
our reed	tacaio,	each one thick	tôtomaoac,
our reeds	taâcaio,	one is bled	mitzmjna,
stream	atoiatl,	it is bled	itzminalo,
hollow	coionquj,	[blood] falls drop by drop	xaxaoaca,
hollow within	îticoionquj,	tube stands out	mopiazquetza.
tube-like	piaztic,		

Nerve	**Tlaloatl:**	all the nerves [are] what we are bound together with	iehoatl in ie muchi tlaloatl, in toôlpica.
thin nerves	tlaloapitzaoac,		
thin nerves	tlaloapitzactli:		

Bundle of nerve fibers[29]	**Omitlaloatl:**	firm	oapaoac,
nerve	tlaloatl,	firm	oapactic,
strong	chicaoac,	very firm	oapacpâtic.

---

29. von Gall, *op. cit.*, p. 202: *Rückenmark*.

THIRTEENTH PARAGRAPH, which telleth of the rest of the very small organs which pertain to the body.

JNIC MATLACTLI OMEY PARRAPHO, itechpa tlatoa, yn oc cequj tepitoton touiuilteca: in tonacaio itech ca.

Our breaking our breakings those by which we break [in] various places;	Topoztecca: topôpoztecca iehoatl inic tipopoztecque:	everywhere indicated	noujian tlateneoa.
Our breaking our breakings	Topoztecca, topopoztecca,	these indicate where we break	iehoatl qujteneoa yn vncan tipopuztecque.
Our joint our joints	Toujltecca, toujujltecca:	those with which, one says, we join	iehoatl qujtoa, ynjc tiujujltecque.
Our joint our joints	Toujltecca: toûiuiltecca,	where we join	yn vncan tiûjujltecque.
Our joint our joints	Toçaliuhca: toçaçaliuhca,	that by which ends of our bones, of our flesh, are joined	iehoatl ynjc moquanamictia, tomjio, tonacaio.
Our joint our joints	Toçaliuhca: toçaçaliuhca,	our joints where we join	toçaçaliuhia, yn vncã tiçaçaliuhque.
Our [cane-like] joint[1] our [cane-like] joints	Tixio: tiixio,	that by which we are jointed [like canes][2]	iehoatl injc tiixoque.
Our jointedness our jointednesses	Tixioca, tiixoca,	the places where we are jointed[2]	yn vncan tiixoque
Our place of bending our places of bending	Tonecuelpachoaia, tonecûecuelpachoaia:	that by which we bend	iehoatl ynjc ticuelpachiuhque
Our bending[3] our places of bending	Tonecuelpachoa, tonecûecuelpachoaia,	the place where we bend	yn vncan titocuelpachoa.
Our folding place[4] our folding places	Tocototzauhca, tocôcototzauhca:	that by which we fold ourselves	iehoatl inic titocototzoa.
Our folding our folding our folded place	Tocototzauhca, tocôcototzauhca, tocototzauhia,	our folded places place where we fold ourselves[5]	tococototzauhia, yn vncan titocototzoa.
Our clamping place[6] our clamping places	Tonepicia, tonênepicia:	place where we clamp	yn vncan titopiquj.
Our tube[7] our tubes	Tacaio, taâcaio:	that which we use as a tube	iehoatl ynjc tacaioque.
Place of our tube[7] places of our tubes	Tacaiôca: taâcaioca,	places which we use as tubes	yn vncan taâcaioque.

1. *Ibid.*, p. 203: *Unser Glattes.*
2. *Acad. Hist. MS: tiixyoque.*
3. *Ibid.: tonecuelpachoayá.*
4. von Gall, *op. cit.*, p. 204: *Unsere Steifheit.*
5. *Acad. Hist. MS: titocôcototzoa.*
6. Cf. § 9, *supra* (*Nepiciantli*); von Gall, *loc. cit.*: *Wo selbst wir gelenkig sind.*
7. Cf. § 12, *supra, Cocótli,* etc.

Our tube[7] our tubes	Tococoio, tocôcocoio:	that which we use as a tube	iehoatl ynjc ticocoioque.
Place of our tube places of our tubes	Tococoioca: tocococoioca:	places which we use as tubes[8]	yn vncan ticocoionque.
Our tube[9] our tubes	Topiazio: topipîazio:	that which we use as a tube	iehoatl ynjc tipiazioque.
Place of our tube[9] our tubes	Topiazioca, topîpiazioca:	places which we use as tubes	in vncan tipipiazioque.
Our cartilage[10] our cartilages our cartilages[11]	Tocelica: toceceli, tocecelica:	that bone, flesh, [which is] tender, very tender, very tender	iehoatl in omjtl in nacatl, celic, cecelic, ceceltic.
Our cartilage our cartilages[12]	Tocelica: tocecelica,	places where we are cartilaginous	yn vncã ticecelique.
Our thickness our various thicknesses	Totilaoaca, totîtilaoaca:	the thick flesh	in nacatl tilaoac.
Our thickness our various thicknesses	Totilaoa, totitilaoaca:	places where we thicken[13]	y vncan tititilaoaque.
Our pressing place our pressing places	Totlacçaia, totlatlacçaia:	that with which we press; our leg, our foot, our elbow	iehoatl ynjc titlacça in tocxi, in toxocpal, in tomolicpi.
Our pressing place our pressing places	Totlacçaia: totlatlacçaia,	[that] wherewith we press, and the place where we press	ynic titlacça: yoan yn vncã titlacça.
Our moving places[14] our helping places	Tomaiauja, tonepaleujaia:	these [are] our arms, our legs, our eyes	iehoatl in toma in tocxi, in tixtelolo.
Our moving places our helping places	Tomaiauja, tonepaleujaia:	places where we help ourselves	yn vncan titopaleuja.
Our extensions[15] places where we are useful to ourselves: on our face, on our mouth, on our arm, on our leg	Totlatecoaca: yn vncan titopaleuja, in tixco, in tocamac, in tomac, in tocxic.		
Our sense of feeling[16] our senses place where we feel place where we tremble	Tonematia, tonênêmatia: in vncan titimati, yn vncan titolinja,	places where we tremble when we move ourselves[17]	yn vncan titoholinja in titocuechinja.

---

8. *Acad. Hist. MS:* ticocoyoque.
9. Cf. n. 7, *supra.*
10. Martín del Campo, *op. cit.,* p. 160: *cecelicayotl — los tendones.*
11. *Acad. Hist. MS:* tocĉcelica.
12. *Ibid.:* tocecelicá tocĉcelicá.
13. *Ibid.:* the section reads: *totilavá. totĭtilacá in ūcan titilavaque. titĭtilauaque.*
14. von Gall, *op. cit.,* p. 206: *Womit wir auf den Boden werfen.*
15. *Loc. cit.: Wo wir unterstützen.*
16. *Ibid.,* p. 207: *Woselbst wir klug sind.*
17. *Acad. Hist. MS* inserts here *tacaliuhca. taâcaliuhca. yehoatl inic taâcaltique.*

Our grooving our groovings our grooved place	Tacaliuhca: taâcaliuhca, tacaliuhia,	our grooved places places where we are grooved	taâcaliuhia, yn vncan taâcaliuhque.
Our glistening[18] our glistenings	Tocûecueio: tocûecuecueio,	everywhere we glisten	ynjc novia ticuecueioque.
Our glistening place our glistening places	Tocuecueiôca, tocûecuecueioca:	where we glisten	yn vncan ticuecueioque.
Our wrinkling our wrinklings[19]	Toxolochauhca, toxoxochauhca:	the wrinkled flesh	yn nacatl xolochtic.
Our wrinkling our wrinklings	Toxolochauhca, toxoxolochauhca:	place where we are wrinkled	yn vncan tixolochauhque.
Our gripping place our gripping places the gripping place of our face	Tomotzoliuhca, tomomotzoliuhca, in tixmotzoliuhca,	the anal sphincter, etc.	in tzinmotzoliuhcaiotl, et.a
Our gripping place our gripping places	Tomotzoliuhca, tomômotzoliuhca,	our gripping places[20]	tomômotzoliuhcaioca.
Our flabbiness our flabbinesses[21]	Totzoliuhca, totzotzoliuhca.		
Our flabbiness our flabbinesses	Totzoliuhcá, totzotzolicá:	place where we are flabby	yn vncan titzoliuhque.
Our pores our pores[22]	Toqujqujçauhca: toqujqujçauhca:	whereby we have pores	ynjc tiqujqujztique.
Our pores our pores place where our body has pores	Toqujqujztica, toqujqujçauhca: yn vncan qujqujztic tonacaio,	place where our perspira- tion issues	yn vncan titonalqujça.
Smoke hole smoke holes our smoke hole our smoke holes our mouth our nose	Tlecallotl, tlêtlecalotl, totlecallo, totlêtlecallo, yn tocama, yn toiac,	our throat those of our front those of our back our places with smoke holes	in totozcac, yn tîxpampa, in tocujtlapãpa, totlêtlecaloca.
Width of our shank[23] our wide shank	Totlanjtzpachiuhca, totlanitzpatlach.		
Width of our shank wide place of our shank	Totlanjtzpatlachiuhca, totlanitzpatlachiuhia:	place where the shank [is] very wide	yn vncan papatlachtic tlanitztli.
Twist of the calf of our leg twists of the calves of our legs	Tocotznoliuhca, tocotznônoliuhca.		

---

18. von Gall, *loc. cit.*: *Unsere juckenden Teile.*
19. *Acad. Hist. MS: toxôxolochauhca.*
20. *Ibid.*: *in ûcan* ends this section.
21. *Ibid.*: *totzôtzolica.*
22. The cedilla is omitted in the *Florentine Codex.*
23. *Acad. Hist. MS: totlanitzpatlachiuhca.*

Twist of the calf of our leg	Tocotznoliuhca,	place where [calf is]	in vncan noltic.
twists of the calves of our legs	tocotznonoliuhca:	twisted	
Our curving	Tocoliuhca:		
our curvings	tocôcoliuhca.		
Our curving	Tocoliuhca,		
our curvings	tocôcoliuhcá		
Arch of our back[24]	Toteputzcoliuhca.	curve of our neck	Toquechcoliuhcá.
arch of our back	Toteputzcoliuhcá.	lumpiness of the buttocks	Tzintôpoli.
curve of our neck	Toquechcoliuhca.	our lumpy buttocks	Totzintopol.
Hair	Tzontli.	hair about navel	xictzontli.
our hair	Totzon.	hair of buttocks	tzintzontli
our hairiness	Totzonio.	hair of buttocks	tzintamaltzontli
our hairiness in various places	totzôtzonio.	pubic hair[25]	ymaxtli.
		hair of face	ixtzontli.
hair of the hand	matzontli	hair of cheeks	camatzontli.
hair of the thigh	Metztzontli.	hair of ear	nacaztzontli.
hair of the calf of the leg	Cotztzontli	eyebrow	ixquamolli.
hair of the finger	mapiltzontli.	our eyelashes	Tocochia.
hair of the toe	xopiltzontli	mustache	Tatlia.
hair of the foot	xocpaltzontli	hair of throat	Cocotzontli.
armpit hair	Ciacatzontli.	fuzz	Tomjtl.
hair of chin	Tentzontli	our fuzz in various places[26]	tototomjo.
hair of groin	quexiltzontli.		
Knuckle[27]	Cecepoctli.	our cartilaginous places	tocecelica
like tender bone	Omjcelic	sensitive	quêquelli.
Mole[28]	tlâciuiztli:	hair	tzontli,
the mole	in tlâciuiztli,	ruddy	tlatlactic,
black	tliltic,	ruddy	tlatlauhquj,
white	iztac,	white	iztac.
chili-red	chichiltic,		
Skin blemish[29]	Tochiciuiztli,		
of blemished skin	Tochiciuhquj.		
Albino	Tlacaztalli.		
Short-fingered	Mapiltzatzapa.		
short-toed	Xopiltzatzapal.		
Near us	Totloc.	near our ear	tonacaztlan.
by us	tonaoac.	near our foot	tocxitlan.
to our left	topochco.	next to our foot	tocxititlan.
at our throat [30]	totozcac.	near our arm	tomatlan, tomatlá.
at our head	toquatla.	near our neck	toquechtla.
on our head	tocpac.	near our wrist	tomaquechtlan.
before us	tixtlan.	near our ankle	toxoquechtlan.

---

24. *Ibid.: toteputzcoliuh.*
25. Cf. Martín del Campo, *op. cit.*, p. 157. In the *Acad. Hist. MS,* tentzontli follows ymaxtli.
26. *Ibid.: totomio.*
27. Cf. Martín del Campo, *op. cit.*, p. 159; von Gall, *op. cit.*, p. 211: *eingeschlafen.*
28. Martín del Campo, *op. cit.*, p. 155.
29. von Gall, *loc. cit.: Hasenscharte;* von Gall's discussion is convincing.
30. *Acad. Hist. MS: totzcac.*

FOURTEENTH PARAGRAPH, which telleth of the rottenness, the filth, which issueth from the body.[1]

JNIC MATLACTLI ONNAUJ PARRAPHO, itechpa tlatoa, yn ipalanca, yn itlahello, yn itech qujça in tonacaio.

Our interior	Titic	corrupted matter from vulva	Tepiltemalli,
interior of the vessel	Comjc.	corrupted watery matter from vulva	tepiltemalatl.
excrement	Cujtlatl.		
human excrement	tlacacujtlatl.	humor	tzonqualactli,
fluid intestinal evacuation	apitzalli	rectal humor	tzintzōqualactli.
flux	tlahelli, tlahilli.	vulvar humor	Tepiltzonqualactli.
bloody flux	eztlahelli, eztlahilli.	oily secretion of vulva	Tepiloxitl, tepiloxiotl.
purulent flux	iztac tlahelli, iztac tlahilli.	resin-like secretion of vulva	Tepilocotzotl, tepiloco-tzoiotl.
corncob-shaped excrement	Cujtlaolotl.		
dry excrement	Cujtlaoaqujztli.	blood of vulva	Tepileztli.
hardened excrement	Cujtlatexcaloaquiztli.	vulva rag	tepiltzotzomatl.
purulent excrement	Cujtlatetemalli, cujtlati-timalli.	Perspiration	Tzotl: tzoiotl,
		our perspiration	totzoio,
mouldy excrement	Cujtlapoxcaujliztli.	perspiration	tzocujtlatl.
rheum of the eye	Yxcujtlatl.	perspiration of face	Ixtzocujtlatl,
wax of ears	nacazcujtlatl.	heavy perspiration of face	ixtzocujcujtlatl
nasal mucus	iacacujtlatl: iacatolli.	perspiration of body	tlactzocujtlatl,
mucus of the throat	Tozcaiacacujtlatl	perspiration of arm	matzocujtlatl,
dirt about the lips	Tencujtlatl, tencujcujtlatl.	heavy perspiration of arm	matzocujcujtlatl.
tooth filth left in the teeth	Tlancujtlatl, tlancujcujtlatl	perspiration of foot	Xocujtlatl,
coated tongue	Nenepiltextli,	much perspiration of foot	xocujcujtlatl.
coating covering the tongue	nenepiltexqujmiliuhcaiotl	perspiration of groin	quexiltzocujtlatl.
dirt of buttocks	Tzincujtlatl, tzincuj-cujtlatl.	perspiration of vulva	Tepiltzocujtlatl
		moisture from vulva	Tepiltenqualactli
smegma	Tepolquatextli, tepolqua-tetextli.	moisture from buttocks	Tzinqualactli,
		moisture from penis	tepoltenqualactli.
scurf of prepuce	Xipinquaxoneoatl.	small bit of filth about the groin	Quexilqujmichcujtlatl,
corrupted watery matter from penis[2]	tepoltemalacatl.		
coating of vulva	Tepiltetextli, tepiltetex-cujtlatl.	small bits of filth about the groin	quexilqujqujmjchcujtlatl
Urine	axixtli,	yellowness of urine[3]	axixcoçavializtli
urine with pus	temalaxixtli	gall stones	axixcocolli.
bloody urine	ezaxixtli		
Saliva	chichitl	nasal mucus	netzomjlli
throat mucus	tozcaiacacujtlatl	coughing	tlatlaçiztli
Phlegm	Alaoac	livid phlegm	xoxoctic alaoac
white phlegm	yztac alaoac	purulent phlegm	temalalaoac.
yellow phlegm	coztic alaoac.		

---

1. The *Acad. Hist. MS* precedes the list with *ycacatzavaca ȳ tonacayo*.
2. *Ibid.: tepoltemalatl*.
3. Also jaundice, according to Rémi Siméon, *op. cit.* (for which yellowness of urine is a symptom).

Twenty-eighth Chapter, which telleth of the ailments of the body and of medicines suitable to use for their cure.[1]

First paragraph, which telleth of the ailments of the head, the eyes, the ears, the nose, and the teeth.

Splitting of the hair[2]

Its cure is the trimming off, the cutting,[3] of the hair; then the head is washed with urine. Then [an ointment] of the root named *nanacace*[4] is spread on, but the *nanacace* is washed off with urine. And if the hair is not trimmed off, it is washed with urine; the hair is [combed] down with [an ointment of] *axin*[5] mixed with lampblack [and] with [pulverized] avocado pits. Then is applied the black clay used for color, with sufficient [powdered bark of] *quauhtepuztli*[6] [and] of *uixachin*.[7]

Dandruff

The hair trimmed, there is washing of the head with urine. Then *coyoxochitl*[8] or *yiamolli*[9] leaves are applied to cure it. Or there is washing of the hair

Injc cempoalli onchicuej capitulo: itechpa tlatoa, in icocolizio in tonacaio, ioan in patli in jnanamjc in jpatica mochioa.

Inic ce parrapho: itechpa tlatoa, in jcocolizio in tzontecomatl, in ixtelolotli, in tonacaz, in toiac, ioan in totlan.

Tzonocujlqualiztli:

ipaio neximaliztli, neconaloliztli: niman axixtica mamovia, njman ic mamovia tlaneloatl itoca nanacace: çan ie in axixtli ic mopaca in nanacace: auh in amo moxima axixtica mamovia tlilaxi ic mopiloa in tzontli, aoacaiolloio: çatepan motlalia in çoquitl, in palli, vel quauhtepuzio, vel vixachio.

Quatequjxqujiciviliztli:

neximaliztli, axixtica neamovilo: njman onmotlalia, in coioxochitl, anoço iiamoli yxiuhio ic mopa, anoço iztauhiatl tlillo, aoacatl tlillo, ic neamovilo aoa-

---

1. Nahuatl plant names in chap. xxviii are retained, although in previously translated Books of the Codex they have, when possible, been identified by a common English or a botanical term. Often these are satisfactory. Just as often, however, they may be better accepted as tentative, partly because botanical equivalents for Nahuatl plant names are sometimes unavailable, partly because there is some confusion in a number of identifications. Cf., for example, n. 59 of § 1, this chapter; or the alternatives possible for *chilpanxochitl* in Hernández's *Historia de las Plantas de Nueva España* (already cited), III, pp. 739, 830. See also von Gall's comments (*op. cit.*, pp. 88–89) on the translation of chap. xxviii.

We are grateful for suggestions on the materials in this chapter made to us by Dr. George S. Diumenti, Bountiful, Utah, and the late Dr. Aaron Margulis, Santa Fe, New Mexico.

2. *Färberflechte*, according to von Gall, *op. cit.*, p. 217.

3. Read *necotonaloliztli*.

4. Nanacace: "*planta angulossa, y con esquinas. . . . la rayz es amarga y . . . pica tantico*" — Francisco Ximenez: *Quatro Libros de la Naturaleza y virtudes medicinales de las Plantas y Animales de la Nueva España* (N. León, ed.; Morelia: José R. Bravo, 1888), p. 167. According to Reccho, *op. cit.*, p. 205, "*herba est, folia vitis ferè vinifera ferens, sed aliquantuum oblonga, & in purpureum colorem vergentia. caulem vnicum, purpureumque. flores iuxta acumen luteos, squamosis, oblongisq; contectos calycibus. radicem verò crassam, & breuem in Ponticarum Nucum quandam similitudinem, velut diuisam, fibratam, obrutamq; languine. . . . curetque, aliunde vacuata caussa, febres, aut rigoribus pulsis. Aiunt etiam Indi Medici, crudam sudorem euocare, aliumq; ciere, coctam verò mederi dyarrhoeis, atque dysentericis. . . . vim adstringendi, idem huic herba cocta euenire putandum est.*"
von Gall, *op. cit.*, p. 217, thinks it may be *Malpigiaccee Byrsonima cotonifolia*.

5. *Coccus axin*; cf. *supra*, chap. xxiv, n. 42.

6. Corresponding Spanish text: "*vna corteza, del palo que en la lengua mexicana se dize, quauhtepuztli, que es como alcornoque, saluo que es pesado.*" Cf. also *supra*, chap. xxv, n. 5.

7. *Acacia farnesiana*; cf. *ibid.*, n. 4.

8. Unidentified, though described in Hernández, *op. cit.*, III, pp. 795sqq. Santamaría, in *Diccionario General de Americanismos*, I, p. 410, considers *coyosúchil* a variant of *coyolsúchil* (*Bomarea hirtela* Herb.); see also III, p. 379; Hernández, *op. cit.*, II, pp. 503sqq.; von Gall, *op. cit.*, p. 218 (also *Tecoma pentaphylla*).

9. *Yiamolli*: cf. *Florentine Codex*, Book XI, fol. 133v. *Phytolacca octandra* Linn., etc. (Hernández, *op. cit.*, I, p. 277). Although the corresponding Spanish text reads *amolli*, a distinction between the two is made in chap. vii of Book XI.

[with] wormwood[10] [powdered] with lampblack, [or powdered] avocado pits with lampblack, [or] avocado pits with *axin* [and] the black clay used for color, with sufficient [powdered bark of] *quauhtepuztli* [and] of *uixachin,* and *chipili,*[11] [and] *itzcuinpatli.*[12]

Head scabies, tinea

The hair is trimmed off — cut smooth. The head is washed with urine. With a very thick layer of [powdered] avocado pits it is cured. One applies water in which resinous pine wood is steeped, with [powdered] cotton seed;[13] [or] hot wormwood. With these it is cured.

Head abscesses

Lime with small tobacco[14] is spread on in quantity; with this they may abate. If this should fail, [the abscess] is cut in the form of a cross; the pus comes out; it exudes. Then it is washed with urine.[15] A turpentine ointment is applied as a poultice; later a poultice[16] is made with pine resin.[17]

Headache

Its cure is to inhale an herb named *ecuxo,*[18] or to inhale [green] small tobacco. The head is to be well covered, well wrapped, and the exposing to incense [may follow]. And if it becomes worse, an herb named *çoçoyatic,*[19] which is dried and pulverized, is to be inhaled. If [the ache] should increase, [the pulverized herb] is applied in drops in the nose. If it has worsened, if the nose [treatment] no longer helps, the use of an obsidian point, of incising,[20] of bleeding there [on the head] is necessary.

Broken skull, skull wound

If the skull is only wounded, it is washed with urine. [Cooked] maguey leaf sap is applied. And

caiollotli axio palli vel quauhtepuzio, vel vixachio, ioan chipili, itzcujnpatli.

Quatotomoctli: chaquachtli,

moxima, maiochiquj, axixtica mamovia, aoacaiollotli cenca tilaoac ic mopa, oxiatl ichcaichio qujtlalia, totonquj iztauhiatl ic mopa.

Quaxocociviztli:

tenextli picieio onmopalteuhteca, ic iloti, in aueli motequj mopapalotequj oalqujça, oalvetzi in palanquj: njman axixtica mopaca ca oxitl ic mopotonja in çatepan ocotzotica in mopotonja.

Tzonteconcocolli

ipaio mjnecuj xivitl itoca ecuxo, anoço picietl mjnecuj, vel moquaqujmjloz, vel moquailpiz: ioan nepopochviliztli: auh intla tlanavi mocoxonjz in jtoca çoçoiatic onmjnecujz, in totoca onmochichipinjz in toiacac in otitlanauhque aocmo qujmati in toiac ic monequj neitzaoaviliztli nepa xotlaliztli, neitzmjnaliztli.

Quaxicalpetiliztli, quaxicaltzaianjliztli,

in çan tzaianj quaxicalli axixtica mopaca, meolli onmotlalia: auh in ie ixpalanj chipili onmotlalia totol-

10. *Artemisia mexicana* Willd.; cf. *supra,* chap. xxiv, n. 5.

11. *Crotalaria* sp.; see Hernández, *op. cit.,* III, p. 801; Santamaría, *op. cit.,* I, p. 513.

12. *Senecio canicida, Schoenocaulon officinale* Gray, or *Veratrum officinale* (Emmart, *op. cit.,* p. 251).

13. *Gossypium mexicanum* Tod. (*ibid.,* pp. 213, 233).

14. *Nicotiana rustica* L. (*ibid.,* p. 259); Hernández, *op. cit.,* I, p. 245, (*tabaco pequeño*).

15. *Acad. Hist. MS* omits *ca.*

16. Corresponding Spanish text: "*vna bilma de ocotzote, o de oxite, con su pluma.*"

17. The translation of *ocotzotl* is problematic; two different materials are mentioned, both resinous and both with medicinal properties. For *ocotzotl,* Molina, *op. cit.,* gives *resina de pino o trementina.* According to Standley, *op. cit.,* Pt. 2, p. 317, it is a resin or balsam of the *Liquidambar styraciflua* L.; speaking of *Pinus teocote* Schlecht. & Cham. Linnaea, he states (p. 56): "The tree produces turpentine ('ocotzol,' 'trementina de pino,' 'trementina de ocote') which is used in medicine as a balsamic stimulant, and for other purposes for which turpentine is generally employed." Sahagún consistently translates *ocotzotl* as pine resin and *xochiocotzotl* as liquidambar.

18. In the *Acad. Hist. MS, ecuxo* is crossed out and replaced by *ecuchoton,* which Emmart, *op. cit.,* p. 227, calls "sneeze-plant." See also Molina, *op. cit.,* under *estornudar.*

19. *Veratrum sabadilla, V. frigidum,* or *Stenanthium frigidum* (Schlecht. et Cham.) Kunth.; or of the genus *Zygadenus* or *Schoenocaulon* (Hernández, *op. cit.* III, pp. 855sqq.); as a sneeze-medicine, it is probably of the genus *Veratrum.*

20. Read *xoxotlaliztli.*

if it is festered on the surface, [powdered] *chipili* leaves with [the white of] an egg are applied, or a few *toloa*[21] leaves with [the white of] an egg. If [the skull] is broken, [the break] is joined with a bone awl; it is covered with maguey sap, or a grated green maguey leaf is applied.

Infected ear

Its cure is to apply drops of tepid *coyoxochitl* sap with chili in the ear thrice daily; also the same by night. These bring out either phlegm or pus. And the scrapings of seashells[22] with salt in tepid [water] are applied in drops in the ear.

Ear ulcers[23]

A few drops of liquid rubber are placed inside [the ear].

Ear ulcers[24]

[Pulverized] *coyoxochitl* [leaves] mixed with a pine resin are applied on the outside as a poultice, and, mixed with *axin,* pressed in the openings [of the ulcers]. And they are continually washed with urine. And [the herb] *cicimatic*[25] with [the white of] an egg is applied; [or] all the medicines for infections[26] — *chichi[patli]*,[27] *chipili,* avocado pits.

Infected ears[28]

These cause the face or the temples to swell. [Powdered] *cococxiuitl*[29] with *axin* and lampblack is laid on.

Swelling [of the face]

Its cure is to eat a fried chameleon; then the ailment which is within will go away. And all the purgatives are its cure,[30] especially the root named *ololtic.*[31] And when this is drunk, [the ailment] is cast out from the mouth and from below. And if the

teio, anoço achiton toloa ixiuhio totolteio, intla onpeti omjtica motlamanjlia, meoltica motzaqua, anoço mexoxouhquj mjchiquj onmotlatlalia.

Nacazqualiztli:

ipaio coioxochitl, chillo iamanquj ōmochipinia in tonacazco expa cemjlhujtl. no ivi in iooaltica, qujqujxtia in aço alaoac, in aço temalli, ioan cuechtli mjchiquj iztaio, iamanquj in mochipinia tonacazco.

Nacazpalanjliztli:

in achi tlatic ollachipinjlli onmoteca

Nacazpalanjliztli:

çan panj coioxochitl ocotzoio ic mopotonja: ioan tlaaxneloltica mopepechoa, ioan axixtica mopactinemj, ioan ōmotlalia totolteio cîcimatic: ic mochi in ixqujch palancapatli in chichic in chipili, aoacaiollotli.

Nacazqualiztli:

qujpoçaoa in toxaiac, anoço tocanaoaca onmoteca cococxivitl tlilaxio.

Cacamaoaliztli:

ipaio qujquaz tlatetzoionjlli in tapaiaxi qujn oqujz in jitic ca cocolli, ioan ie mochi ipaio in tlanoqujlonj oc cenca iehoatl in tlanelhoatl in jtoca ôololtic, in jquac mj, y, tocamacpa noqujvi: ioan totlanipa auh in ie mâmana, cocoxqui iolatolli conj anoço totolaiotl

---

21. *Toloa: Datura* sp. (Emmart, *op. cit.,* p. 253).

22. According to Ignacio Ancona H. and Rafael Martín del Campo, in "Malacología Precortesiana" (*Memoria* del Congreso Científico Mexicano, México, 1953), VII, p. 14, *cuechtli* is a *Gastropoda;* "Seguramente son especies del género Oliva."

23. Corresponding Spanish text: *"las llagas, que estan dentro de los oydos."*

24. *Ibid.: "las llagas, que estan fuera de los oydos."*

25. *Canavalia villosa* Benth.; cf. *supra,* chap. xxiv, n. 18.

26. Santamaría, *op. cit.,* II, p. 376: *Solidago mexicana, S. montana, S. vetulina; Senecio vulneraria, S. pauciflorus* HBK; *Grindelia glutinosa,* and others; used in lotions for wounds.

27. Probably *chichicpatli (Guayacum arboreum);* cf. Sahagún (Garibay ed.), IV, p. 333; see also Ximenez, *op. cit.,* p. 10.

28. Corresponding Spanish text: *"las hinchazones del rostro que proceden del dolor de los oydos ᵹ en indio se dize nacazqualiztli."*

29. Cited in Emmart, *op. cit.,* p. 256 (stinging herb). Cf., however, corresponding Spanish text—*"cualquier yerua, que quema."* Von Gall, *op. cit.,* p. 222, thinks it is *Papaveracee Bocconia arborea* or *frutescens,* a local anesthetic.

30. Here the *Acad. Hist. MS,* while essentially in agreement with the *Florentine Codex* text, enters a revision which, following *ipaio,* reads: *motlanoquiliz, achtopa yehoatl quiz ỹ ohloltic tlanoquiloni.*

31. In Reccho, *op. cit.,* p. 184, called also *ayotic;* cf. also Hernández, *op. cit.,* I, pp. 161sqq., where it is identified as perhaps *Euphorbia campestris.*

patient is of unsettled stomach, he drinks an *atole* of raw, ground maize, or turkey broth. Twice — thrice — he yet purges the ailment.[32] Thereafter he eats [a large fried lizard,[33] or a roast lizard.[34] With this he will be cured.]

And to make [the patient] well, they proceed to make him drink water [in which wood of the] so-called *tlatlauhqui*[35] tree is boiled; and [they use] its heart, not its bark.

oc oppa expa qujoalnoquja in cocolli, çatepan tlaqua: [acaltetepon tlatletzoyonili anoço cuetzpalin tlatleoatzalli, ic patiz.]

Auh injc qujqualchioa catlitinemj quauitl itoca tlatlauhquj mopaoaçi: auh ie in jiollo amo no ie in jxipeoallo.

Face wheals,[36] face blotches[37]

For face wheals,[38] the traces of which appear internally from hemorrhoids, pustules, or inflammation somewhere, perhaps in the groin,[39] one is to drink raw [the sap of the herb] called *tletlemaitl*.[40] And when he finally drinks it four times, then, on bathing in the sweat bath, he will throw off the ailment. When [the blotches] have come to the surface, one is to apply *yichcayo*[41] herb [powdered].[42]

Ixiâiapaleoaliztli, ixiicuxiliztli,

ixiâiapaleoaliztli, inezca itic manj xochiciviztli, nanaoatl, aço cana tlapalanj, anoço quexilivi: conjz çan xoxouhquj in jtoca tletlemaitl: auh in iequē nappa conj, njman ipan motemaz qujoalpantlaçaz in cocoliztli, in onpanvetz onmotlaliliz in xivitl yichcaio.

Face blisters

A blotched face, [or] the face wheals of a woman recently delivered, are cured in this manner: One is to drink [an infusion of] assorted cooked [herbs]: *tlatlauhcapatli*,[43] *tlacoçaçalic*,[44] *coztomatl*,[45] *atepocapatli*,[46] *aatepocatic*,[47] *tochtetepo*,[48] *tlamacazqui ipa-*

Ixaatemj:

ixiicuci, ixiaiapaleoa in omocaxanj, injc pati tlanechicolli, qujz tlatzoionjlli, tlatlauhcapatli, tlacoçaçalic, coztomatl, atepocapatli, aatepocatic, tochtetepo, tlamacazquj ipapa, aoatoto, quachtlacaloaztli, cujcujtlapile, quappatli, tlalpatli, nantzin, mjzqujtlaxipe-

32. Following *cocolli*, instead of *çatepan tlaqua* the *Acad. Hist. MS* revision reads: *auh çatepā quiquaz acaltetepon tlatletzoyonili anoço cuetzpalin tlatleoatzalli, ic patiz.* The addition has been inserted in our text in brackets.

33. "*Lagarto*" (*Heloderma horridum*) — Santamaría, *op. cit.*, I, p. 29.

34. "*Lagartija*" (*Saurius* sp.) — Sahagún (Garibay ed.), IV, p. 331.

35. *Tlatlauhqui*(*quauitl*), *le bois rouge et très dur, paraît être l'acajou* — Seler: *Gesammelte Abhandlungen*, II, p. 653. See also Dibble and Anderson, *op. cit.*, Book IX, p. 91.

36. Molina, *op. cit.: cardenales.*

37. *Ibid.: manzilla.*

38. In the *Acad. Hist. MS*, the first three words are crossed out; *Ixtotomonaliztli tēchichipeliuiliztli, yacaxaxaquachiuiliztli* are substituted.

39. Corresponding Spanish text: "*La enfermedad del paño del rostro, o manchas, que suelen proceder de la enfermedad, de las almorranas, o de las bvuas, o de alguna llaga interior, o del mal de las ingles*" — probably the early effects of syphilis. See Seler's translation and discussion of this section, "Ueber den Ursprung der Syphilis," *op. cit.*, II, pp. 96–99.

40. Corresponding Spanish text: "*moliendose, y rebolujendose, el çumo con agua, y beujendose.*" — *Tletlemaitl: Plumbago* sp.? (Sahagún, Garibay ed., IV, p. 365); *Euphorbia* sp.? (von Gall., *op. cit.*, pp. 108–109).

41. Probably the *ychcacalotic* or *tlapanquipatli* mentioned by Hernández, *op. cit.*, III, p. 808 (unident.); von Gall, *op. cit.*, pp. 97–98, 223, discusses medicinal properties of *ichcatl* (*Gossypium* sp.).

42. In the *Acad. Hist. MS*, *yichcaio* is crossed out and *cococaton tlacoxomilli* inserted: dried, powdered *cococaton* — *Stellaria nemorum* Linn. or *S. media* (Hernández, *op. cit.*, II, p. 624; see also III, p. 1059).

43. *Geranium carolinianum* L.; cf. *supra*, chap. xxiv, n. 9.

44. *Tlacoçaçalic: Bidens* sp.? (Hernández, *op. cit.*, III, pp. 780, 786, 793). See also Santamaría, *op. cit.*, III, p. 319 — *zazaltacopacle, Stevia salicifolia* Cav., *Mentzelia hispida* Willd.

45. *Coztomatl*, yellow tomato: *Physalis coztomatl* Moc. et Sessé ex Dunal (Hernández, *op. cit.*, III, p. 702).

46. *Atepocapatli: Zexmenia aurea* Benth. & Hook., or *Z. pringlei*, in *ibid.*, I, p. 155.

47. *Aatepocatic*: perhaps *Anona squamosa*; cf. *supra*, chap. xxiv, n. 13.

48. *Tochtetepo*: "*pata de conejo*" (unident.) suggested in Sahagún (Garibay ed.), IV, p. 358; in Book XI (see Vol. III, p. 293), it is so described: "*tiene las hojas menudas como las del árbol del Perú, (y) . . . las raíces blancas; y si alguno la come o bebe luego muere, porque le hace pedazos las tripas. . . . Así se dice de los hechiceros.*"

pa,[49] aoatoto,[50] quachtlacaloaztli,[51] cuicuitlapile,[52] quappatli,[53] tlalpatli,[54] nantzin,[55] mizquitlaxipeoalli,[56] tzatzayanalquiltic.[57] One takes a hot bath therein. Then one is also anointed with still other assorted [herbs].

Roughness of the face

As its cure, the face is washed with hot urine; then the face is smeared with [powdered] yellow chili. When the chili falls off, the face is once again washed with urine, or with wormwood [sap]. And the face is always washed with hot *azpan*[58] [sap]. And one is to drink [the sap] of the herb named *tlatlauhqui*.[59] The ailment which is within he will expel in the urine. His urine [will be] red, or [have] pus or kidney stones. And one is to be purged. One will not drink wine [or] maguey wine; one will not eat spoiled, fat [food]. One is to go on drinking only cold water.

Eye pains

When they begin to be considerable, the eyes are to be encircled with [powdered] *iztecauhtic mixitl*[60] [or] perhaps settled maguey wine, or cherry-leaf [sap], or *chicalotl*[61] [sap]; or mesquite gum is applied in drops in the eyes; and, after a few days, drops of *tonalchichicaquilitl*[62] or *tlachinoltetzmitl*[63] [sap]. One is purged and is to drink a little [of an infusion of] *xoxouhcapatli*.[64] And the head is patted with this [liquid], and one is bled with an obsidian blade.

oalli, tzatzaianalqujltic: ipan motema, niman ic moça in oc no nepapan tlanechicolli.

Ixchachaquachiviztli:

ipaio totonquj axixtli ic nexamjloz: njman chilcoztli ic nexaoaloz, oc ceppa axixtica nexamjloz in ooaluetz chilli, anoço iztauhiatica: ioan mochipa ic mjxamjtinemjz in azpan totonquj, ioan conjz xivitl itoca tlatlauhquj, caxixaz in jtic ca cuculti, chichiltic, anoço temalli, anoço xallo in jaxix: ioan netlanoqujliloz, amo qujz in vino, in octli, amo qujquaz in xoqujiac, in chiaoa çan itztic atl in qujtinemjz.

Ixcocoliztli:

in qujn peoa cenca iztecauhtic mjxitl ic mjxteiaiaoaloz, anoço vctli otlaqualcauh iixco onmochichipinjz, anoço capulxiujtl, anoço chicalotl imemeiallo, anoço mjzqujtl iiacacelica: auh in ie iquezquilvioc, tonalchichicaquilitl onmochipinja, anoço tlachinoltetzmjtl imemeiallo, motlanoquiliz, ioan achi conjz in xoxouhcapatli ioan ic moquatzotzonaz, ioan mjtzmjnaz.

---

49. *Tlamacazqui ipapa*: possibly *Lycopodium dichotomum* Jacq. (Hernández, *op. cit.*, III, p. 1034).

50. Cf. *aguaton* in Santamaría, *op. cit.*, I, p. 61; Hernández, *op. cit.*, I, p. 46: *Pernettia ciliata* Schlecht & Cham.

51. *Quachtlacaloaztli*: *Mentzelia hispida* Willd.? (*ibid.*, III, p. 955).

52. *Cuicuitlapile*: unident.; possibly *Valerianoides* sp. Cf. *supra*, chap. xxiv, n. 7.

53. According to von Gall, *loc. cit.*, equivalent of *tepopotl* — *Baccharis* sp.

54. *Tlalpatli*: cited in Emmart, *op. cit.*, pp. 226, 301; she considers it the same as *tlapatl* (*Datura* sp.). Likewise von Gall, *loc. cit.*

55. *Nantzin*: *Byrsonima crassifolia* (L.) DC (Martínez, *op. cit.*, p. 185). See also Standley, *op. cit.*, Pt. 3, p. 564.

56. *Mizquitlaxipeoalli*: bark of the mesquite, *Prosopis juliflora* (Swartz) — Standley, *op. cit.*, Pt. 2, p. 351.

57. *Tzatzaianalquiltic*: *Deanea tuberosa* Coult et N. (Hernández, *op. cit.*, II, p. 603).

58. Unident. in *ibid.*, I, p. 199; described as *"hierba de dos codos de altura, con raíces a manera de fibras, hojas como de almendro aserradas y un poco menores, y tallos delgados en cuyas últimas ramillas brotan flores blancas que antes de abrir son parecidas a la semilla de coriandro. . . . cura las lepras, las tiñas, los empeines y los barros así como otras afecciones sucias de la piel."*

59. Possibly the same as *tlatlauhcapatli* (*Geranium carolinianum* L.; see n. 43 of this chapter). In Reccho, *op. cit.*, p. 427, however, there is Hernández's brief description of *tlatlauhqui*: *"Radix rotunda; caulis scandit: folia tria Phaseoli modo sed longiora. Flores Fabae."* There are likewise a *tlatlauhqui patli* (*ibid.*, p. 428): *"Calyx Ecchio similis radijs quinque constans rubris, quid flauum inexplicatum continentibus."* There are likewise a *tlatlauhcapatli alsinifolia* (*ibid.*, p. 166); another, *species . . . Geranij* (p. 294); a third (p. 428): *"Radix Minij colore: flos in summo ruber: folia Ocymi non serrata, nec bino ordine è directo sibi opposita."* A fourth (p. 264) is also called *atehuapatli* or *ahoatepatli* — *Achimines coccinea* Pers. in Hernández, *op. cit.*, I, pp. 65–67.

60. Unident., described as a seed among *ciertas hierbas que emborrachan* in Book XI, chap., vii (Sahagún, Garibay ed., III, p. 292); Diego Muñoz Camargo, in *Historia de Tlaxcala* (México: Ateneo Nac. de Ciencias, 1947), p. 146, writes of the *grano que llaman* Mixitl. In the *Acad. Hist. MS*, *cenca iztecauhtic mixitl* is crossed out; on the margin is inserted *matlalitztic*, which may, according to Martínez, *op. cit.*, p. 303*sqq.*, be *Commelina pallida* Willd., *C. tuberosa* L., *C. erecta*, or of the genus *Tradescantia*.

61. *Chicalotl*: *Argemone mexicana* or *A. ochroleuca* Sweet.; cf. *supra*, chap. xviii, n. 8.

62. *Tonalchichicaquilitl*: *Oenothera lacinata* Hill is suggested in Sahagún (Garibay ed.), IV, p. 359.

63. *Tlachinoltetzmitl*: *Kohleria deppeana* or *Croton draco* Schw. are suggested in *ibid.*, p. 362. See also Standley, *op. cit.*, Pt. 3, p. 615.

64. According to Sahagún (Garibay ed.), IV, p. 370, green medicine of various ingredients; in III, p. 315, *xoxouhcapatli* is the same as *quauhxoxouhqui*, which Martínez (*op. cit.*, p. 507) thinks may be *Datura* sp., and von Gall, *op. cit.*, p. 111, perhaps *Caesalpina crispa*.

Worms in the eyes, which live in the edges of the eyelids; or crab lice in the eyelids; cataracts. [The eyelids] are rubbed with *cocoztic*[65] root. And by night [the sap] is applied as drops during sleep. And [the interior of] the eyelids is rubbed with *malinalli.*[66] Woman's milk or settled white maguey wine are applied in drops, or *acaoxitl*[67] [ointment] is spread on the eyelid edges. And one is to proceed to drink a medicine named *iztac quauitl,*[68] which grows in the hot lands. One is to be bled — bled with an obsidian blade; one is to be purged.

Fleshy growth over the eyes

As its cure,[69] the growth over the eye is raised up with a maguey thorn; it is cut. The eyeball is [rubbed] around with drops of woman's milk mixed with [juice] of *chichicaquilitl,*[70] or drops [from an infusion of] *iiztaquiltic*[71] are applied. These destroy the flesh[y growth].

Squint eyes, blindness, blindness from cataracts, sun-blindness, blinded vision. [For] their alleviation, no more is one to expose himself much in the sun, the cold, the wind.

Opacity

One's eyes become white. The medicine, [an herb] named *azcatzontecomatl,*[72] is applied as drops [in the eyes]. And drops from the root of *tlalayotli*[73] applied [in the eyes] cure it; they alleviate it. And one is bled with an obsidian blade.

Films over the eyes

Drops of lizard excrement with lampblack are applied, and [drops of] copper rust[74] with tomato.

Catarrh

As its cure, green herbs named *yecuxoton* and named *icuexo* are taken, inhaled; or small tobacco is

In ocujli teixco: teixtenco nemj, anoço ixtamaçoliciviztli, ixchichiticaviliztli, ic mochichiquj in tlaneloatl côcoztic: auh in ioaltica onmochipinjz ipan cochiz, ioan mochichiquj malinaltica in tixten, chichioalaiotl, anoço iztac vctli otlaqualcauh onmochipinja, anoço acaoxitl onmalaoa in tixtenco: ioan qujtinemjz in patli itoca iztac quavitl tonaian mochioa, moçoz, mjtzmjnaz, motlanoqujliz.

Ixnacapachiviztli:

ipaio vitztica macomana in tixpeioio, motequj, moiaoaloa, in tixtelolo, chichicaqujllo, chichioalaiotl onmochipinja, anoço iiztaqujltic ineloaio onmochipinja qujpalanaltia in nacatl.

Ixcuepoctli: ixpopoiotiliztli ixtezcaîciviztli, ixtotoliciviztli, ixmjmjquiliztli, ixpopoiotlachializtli ipaleviloca aocmo cenca mjxnamjqujz in tonalli in cecec in ehecatl.

Ixaiauhpachiviztli:

iztac onmotlalia in tixco, in patli itoca azcatzontecomatl onmochichipinja: auh qujpâtla qujtlacevilia in tlalaiotli ineloaio onmochipinja, ioan mjtzmjna.

Ixcitlaliciviztli:

onmochichipinja tlillo cuetzpalcujtlatl, ioan tomaio matlali.

Tzonpiliviztli:

ipaio motlatia anoço xoxouhquj in xivitl in jtoca iecuxoton: ioan itoca icuexo onmjnecuj, anoço picietl

---

65. *Côcoztic: Thalictrum hernandezii* Tauch. (Martínez, *op. cit.,* p. 87). After *côcoztic,* the *Acad. Hist. MS* inserts *Auh mociaoa ỹ ça ye no yehoatl côcoztic tlanelhoatl ça ye yn iteuilotca ỹ yoaltica.*

66. *Malinalli;* a similar treatment is described by Emmart (*op. cit.,* p. 222), who suggests use of an herb of the genus *Elymus;* von Gall, *op. cit.,* p. 227, suggests a *Baccharis* sp. Corresponding Spanish text: *"cierta yerua aspera llamada çacamalinalli."*

67. Sahagún (Garibay ed.), IV, p. 319: cane oil (kind unspecified).

68. *Iztac quauitl*: Emmart (*op. cit.,* p. 274) suggests the *Mimosaceae,* or the *Caesalpiniaceae* family.

69. In the *Acad. Hist. MS,* the entire section following *ipayo* is crossed out and the following is substituted on the margin: *Mitzminaz. auh ye ỹ moçoz toquichtlalhoayo anoço tixtlalhoayo auh çatepan onmochichipiniz ỹ cocoztic tlanelhoatl vt Supra.*

70. *Chichicaquilitl: Carraja mexicana* or *Sonchus siliatus* (Sahagún, Garibay ed., IV, p. 333); *Mimulus glabratus* H. B. K. (Hernández, *op. cit.,* II, p. 568).

71. *Iiztaquiltic*: perhaps identical with *iztac quilitl.*

72. *Azcatzontecomatl*: unident. — lit., "ant-head."

73. *Tlallaiotli: Asclepias linaria* or *Gonolobus erianthus* DC., in Sahagún (Garibay ed.), IV, p. 362. See also Standley, *op. cit.,* Pt. 5, pp. 1168, 1185, 1192.

74. Corresponding Spanish text: *"el cardonillo."*

inhaled; and the gullet is massaged, and there is vomiting. And one is not to drink cold things; only tepid [or] hot things is one to drink [and] eat. And one is to take care not to come upon, not to encounter, the cold. Also one is not to expose himself to the sun.

Snuffles, which affect little children — little babies. Morning dew is dropped into their nostrils, and [drops of] woman's milk, and *cimatl*[75] sap. And the inside of their mouths is massaged with tomato juice or with salt.

The stopped nostrils [of children]. The nose is anointed with salve of pine resin. And likewise the cure for snuffles alleviates.

Dryness of the nostrils

Its remedy, its cure, is also that for roughness of the face. And if slight, if moderate,[76] if the ailment does not worsen,[77] [the nostrils] are washed with urine. The face is washed; they wash out their nostrils with a hot [infusion] of *azpan.* And salted liquid rubber is applied as drops [in the nostrils]. And the nostrils are washed with a hot [infusion of] wormwood. Then deer fat is placed in them.

Scabs of the nostrils

The face is washed with [an infusion of] *iztac patli* to which *chichipiltic* and wormwood are added. And one is to drink a little yellow tomato juice. And also one is to wash the nostrils with yellow tomato juice, and with it one is to wash his lips or his teeth. Or else bee honey, or thickened maguey syrup, or *axin,* is spread in the nostrils.

Hoarseness

Many times the throat is massaged with liquid rubber. And bee honey is to be drunk, and many times through the nose, bee honey or thickened maguey syrup will drop [into the throat].

Wounding of the nose[78]

The severing of the nose is thus helped: one's nose, which has been cut off, is replaced, sutured with hair. It is bathed with salted bee honey.

onmjnecuj: ioan nepâpacholo in totozcac, ioan neçotlalo: auh amo mjz in itztic, çan ie in iamanquj in totonquj in mjz, in moquaz: ioan nemalviloz amo mottaz amo mjxnamjqujz in itztic: amo no tonalli motlamjz.

Iacaçoçolonjliztli: in jpan mochioa pipiltotonti coconetotonti, iooalaoachtli iniacac onmochipinja, ioan chichioalaiotl, ioan cimatl ipatzcallo, ioan tomatica anoço iztatica mopapachoa in jncamac.

Iacacimaiciviztli: moiacapotonja ocutzotica, ioan çan no ie ic pati in jpaio iacaçoçolonjliztli.

Iacachachaquachiviliztli:

no ie inamjc in jpaio ixchachaquachiviztli: auh in çan ipan, in can veli in amo totoca, axixtica mopaca, totonquj azpan ic mjxamja ic qujpaca injac, ioan iztaio ollachipinjlli onmotlalia, ioan totonquj iztauhiatl ic mopaca: niman onmoteca maçacetl.

Iacacocopeviliztli:

iztac patli ic mjxamja, qujnamjquj chichipiltic, ioan iztauhiatl: auh achi conjz in coztomatl, auh ioan ic moiacapacaz in coztomatl, ioan ic qujpacaz in jtexipal, anoço in jtlan, anoço quauhnecutli, anoço tetzaoac necutli, anoço axi onmalaoa in toiacac.

Içaoaqujliztli:

mjecpa nepapacholoz intotozca oltica, ioan onmoltequjz in quauhnecutli, ioan mjecpa toiacacpa onvetziz in quauhnecutli, anoço in tetzaoac necutli.

Iacaqujqujnaviliztli:

iacacotociotl ic palevilo onmotlalia iniac in otecoc onmjtzoma tzontica quauhnecutli iztaio ic onmaltia.

75. *Cimatl: Phaseolus coccineus* Linn. or *Canavalia villosa* Benth. (Hernández, *op. cit.,* I, pp. 201–203); *Desmodium amplifolium* (Sahagún, *op. cit.,* p. 327).

76. *Acad. Hist. MS:* çan.

77. *Ibid.:* tototoca.

78. Corresponding Spanish text: *"La cortadura, y herida de las narizes."*

The cutting off of the nose, the loss of the nose, is helped by forming a nose of something [else].[79]

Laceration of a lip

While still fresh, it is sewed with hair. Salted maguey sap is applied. And if the scar or the lip cut persist, it is cut or burned along the sides of the lip laceration.[80] Then the lip is joined; it is sutured with hair. Salted maguey sap is applied.

Lip sores

When just the sun, or the wind, or the cold have affected one, bee honey or [maguey] syrup are put on; or drops of liquid rubber are spread on. But for the ailment of sore lips which comes from within, which comes to the surface of the lips, which is called an infection, one is to apply or put on [powdered] *tlatlauhcapatli* [root]. And one is to clean the teeth with this [*tlatlauhcapatli* and] with salt, and go on drinking this medicine.

Swollen gums

The gums are pierced, pricked; then salt is put on and the inside of the mouth is massaged.

Tooth infection

As its cure, pine resin mixed with ground *conyayaoal*[81] worms is placed as a poultice over the surface. And one presses a heated chili upon the tooth, and one presses salt upon the tooth. And the gums are pricked, and [the herb] *tlalcacauatl*[82] is applied on the tooth. If nothing reduces [the infection], the tooth is extracted; salt is inserted [in the cavity].

Tooth infection; swollen gums

In order that this should not befall one, in order that the teeth should not become infected, one should eat [and] drink things not very hot; only tepid. And if [something] hot is eaten, one should not immediately eat [something] cold; one should not immediately drink cold water. First the teeth are to cool off. And then the eaten food is to be picked from the teeth; they are to be cleaned, brushed. Especially is

Iacacotoctiliztli, iacaquatiliztli ic palevilo itla moiacatia.

Netentzaianaliztli:

in oc iancujxtica mjtzoma tzontica, meolli iztaio onmotlalia: auh injc vecaoa tenquatli, anoço netentzaianaliztli, in nenecoc itêtitzaianquj moxoxotla, anoço motletzoionja: niman motennamjctia, tzontica mjtzoma, meolli, iztaio onmotlalia, anoço metl tlachictli.

Tenchipeliviztli:

in çan tonalli, anoço ehecatl, anoço cecec itech oqujz, quauhnecutli, anoço necutli, onmoteca, onmalaoa, anoço ollachipinjlli: auh in coculli, tenchipeliviztli, in titic vitz in totenxipalco oalpauetzi, in mjtoa palanjliztli, tlatlauhcapatli contlaliz, anoço contemaz, ioan ic motlampacaz injn iztaio, ioan qujtinemjz injn patli.

Tlanatonaviztli:

motzoponja, motzotzopotza in toquetol: njman iztatl onmotema, ioan nepapacholo in tocamac.

Tlanqualiztli:

in jpaio mocotzoneloa in coniaiaoal, panj ic mopotonja: auh in tlanj qujtlanpachoa totonquj chilli, ioan iztatl contlanpachoa, ioan motzotzopotza in toquetol, ioan tlalcacaoatl onmotlalia in totlanco, in atle qujmopachivia moqujxtia in totlan, iztatl onmaquja.

Tlanqualiztli: tlanatonaviztli,

injc amo tepan mochioaz, injc amo cocoiaz in totlan, amo totontlapetztic in moquaz in mjz, ça iamanquj: auh intla omoqua totonquj, amo iciuhca moquaz iitztic, amo iciuhca mjz in itztic atl, oc ceviz in totlan: ioan njman netlancujcujoaz in ontlaqualoc, netlaniectiloz, netlanpopoaloz: oc cenca ie in nacatl, atle mocaoaz in totlanco, ca tetlan nacatzitzitzalti, ca qujtlatia qujccuixitia, qujpalanaltia in totlan.

---

79. *Ibid.*: "*las pondras postizas de otra cosa.*"

80. *Acad. Hist. MS*: *y tetentzayanqui.*

81. Cf. *Florentine Codex*, Book XI, fol. 7*v*. In Reccho, *op. cit.*, p. 320, Hernández's version of it and its medicinal use reads: "*Vermis est genus praedurum Coyayahoal, ab alij Tzinehuilin, & ab alijs Ichcaton nuncupatum, supernè fuluum, pedibus autem ex albo purpurascentibus, numerosisque, quorum gratia fortassis posset in scolopendriae differentias referri. Arefactus hic, tritus, & ex aqua resolutus, illitusque maxillis bis quibusuis singulis diebus, dolores dentium sedat.*" Corrseponding Spanish text: "*el gusano Reboltõ*" — vine worm.

82. *Tlalcacauatl: Arachis hypogaea;* cf. *supra*, chap. xxiv, n. 15.

146

no meat to be left in the teeth, for small particles of meat in the teeth consume them; they cause the teeth to soften, to decay.

Scum on the teeth; tartar on the teeth

The teeth are to be washed with cold water; polished with a cloth; rubbed with [powdered] charcoal; cleaned, made attractive, with salt. The teeth are to be washed with *tlatlauhcapatli* root mixed with salt [and] chili. And some will place — will put — the dissolved medicine on the teeth; with this medicine the teeth are rubbed; with it the mouth is washed; and the teeth are to be darkened with chili, with salt, with cochineal. And the teeth are to be darkened with *tliltic tlamiaualli*[83] herbs; however, these blacken the teeth. Or one will proceed washing [them] with urine, or *chichicquauitl* is to be placed on the teeth; or one is to go on washing [them] with wormwood. And many times the teeth are washed with [an infusion of the bark of] the *quauhtepuztli*. And the [powdered bark] is placed on the teeth; and the scum is to be scraped. And the calcareous material from the food, the scum, is to be scraped with metal, chipped off with metal. Then alum, or cochineal, salt, [and] chili are to be put on.

Abscess of the tongue

The swelling is to be pierced, lanced. Blood or pus will come out. And a salted thread is inserted where it is pierced. And one is to drink [an infusion of] the so-called *iztac quauitl* wood. This will expel the infection. One will urinate bloody, yellow urine, or kidney stones, or purulent urine.

Swelling of the tongue

It is washed with that which is acid. Or the tongue is bled on the under surface with an obsidian blade.

Tongue blisters, of one who, it is said, lives with a hot mouth. Alum is dissolved in the mouth. And the mouth is to be washed with acid water;[84] and the mouth is to be washed with [juice] of the sweet tomato.[85]

Protruding tongue, dripping tongue. They are to massage it with liquid rubber.

Tlancujtlatiliztli: tlantexqujmiliviztli,

motlanpacaz itztic atl ica, tilmatica mopopoaz, tecoltica mochichiqujz, iztatica motlaniectiz, momavizmatiz in totlan, iztaio, chillo, ic motlanpacaz in tlatlauhcapatli, auh cequj contecaz contetemaz in jtlanco, in oçiiaoac patli ic motlanchichiqujz, ic mocamapacaz injn patli, ioan chillo, iztaio, nocheztli ic motlamjaoaz, ioan tliltic tlamjaoalli ic motlamjaoaz: iece injn qujtliloa in totlan anoço axixtica mopactinemjz, anoço chichic quavitl totlanco onmotemaz, anoço iztauhiatica mopactinemjz: auh mjecpa ic mopacaz in totlan in quauhtepuztli, ioan vnmotlaliz in totlanco, ioan mooaoanaz in tlancujtlatl: auh in otexcalqujz tlaqualli, in tlancujtlatl tepuztica mooaoanaz, tepuztica mochichitonjz: niman tlalxocotl onmotemaz, anoço nocheztli poec, chillo.

Nenepillaxoaliztli:

moçoz, motzopinjz in poçaoa, oalqujçaz in eztli, anoço temalli: auh in vncan omoçoc, icpatl iztaio onmaqujz: auh catliz in jtoca iztac quavitl, qujqujxtiz in coculli, in caxixaz ezatic, coztic, anoço xallo, anoço timalatl.

Nenepiltapaioliviliztli:

ic mopacaz in tlein xococ, anoço mitzmjnaz in tonenepil teputzco.

Nenepilchacaioliviliztli: in mjtoa, totonqui tocamac nemj, tlalxocotl mocamapatlaz, ioan xocoatica necamapacoz, ioan ic necamapacoz in mjltomatl tzopelic.

Nenepilqujçaliztli: nenenepilatlaliztli, olli ic qujpachozque.

---

83. *Tliltic tlamiaualli:* "Espiga negra. Medicina hecha de varias plantas" (Sahagún, Garibay ed., IV, p. 365).

84. Hernández, *op. cit.,* III, p. 878: "*Suelen también preparar con agua y maíz molido y hecho masa, dejándolos juntos durante la noche, el xocoatl o agua agria.*" Cf. also Sahagún, *op. cit.,* IV, p. 369: "*Agua de fruta. En especial, la de cacao, un tanto avinagrado . . .*"

85. *Miltomatl:* Physalis philadelphica Lam. (Hernández, *op. cit.,* III, p. 702).

This begins when [children] already large still nurse. It is necessary that small children be quickly weaned, quickly given food.

An injury to the tongue; biting of the tongue; laceration of the tongue. Its treatment is to cook chili [with] salt, which is to be spread on. Then bee honey or thickened maguey syrup is to be spread on.

Nenepilchampochiviztli: *tentzitzipitlatoliztli,*

ic peoa in ie quauhtic noma chichi: ic monequi iciuhca caoaltilozque, in inchichioal pipiltotonti, iciuhca macozque in tlaqualli.

Nenenepilqualtiliztli: nenenepilqualiztli, nenepiltzaianaliztli, ipaio chillo motzoionjz in iztatl vnmotetecaz çatepã quauhnecutli, anoço tetzaoac necutli vnmotetecaz.

SECOND PARAGRAPH, which telleth of the ailments, and their cures, of the neck and throat.

Swelling of the throat[1]

Its cure is massage — vomiting. And [the herb] named *cococxiuitl,* with lampblack, is placed on the throat. And water of the *aacaxilotic*[2] [herb is drunk].

Stiff neck, benumbed neck

[One is cured] with hot water or in a sweat bath. [The neck] is pressed. If it worsens, a poultice of assorted [herbs] is applied; *tecomaxochitl,*[3] *coyoxochitl, quimichpatli,*[4] *tzitzicaztli,*[5] *iietl, xoxouhqui.*[6] All are remedies where numbness, stiffness spread.[7]

Cyst

When it occurs on the throat, it is incised; the small core is removed. Then small tobacco [and powdered] tobacco, [mixed] with lime [and] salt, are placed hot in [the incision]. And if it becomes festered, a maguey leaf is cut up; dried, powdered, it is packed [in the incision] or used as a poultice.

Abscesses on the neck

They are washed with urine. A poultice of assorted [powdered herbs] is applied: very hot pine [resin] and *chichic quauitl*[8] and wormwood, and soot, and *yapaxiuitl*[9] root, and a little salt, cherry leaves, and *itzcuinpatli.* And a considerable amount of salt is placed in the pustules.

Coughing

As its cure, there is to be vomiting, there is to be massaging of the throat. One is to drink [an infusion of] *tlacopopotl*[10] root, [or] lime water mixed with chili, [or] the water of cooked wormwood; [or] one is to drink [an infusion of] the root [of an herb]

INIC VME PARRAPHO: itechpa tlatoa, in jcocolizio, ioan in jpaio in toquechtepul, ioan in tococouh.

Quechpuçaoaliztli:

ipaio nepapacholiztli, neçotlaliztli, ioan tlillo onmotecaz in toquechtlan, in jtoca cococxivitl, ioan iiauhpoviz âacaxilotic.

Quechnenetiliztli: quechcoaciviztli

atotonjltica, anoço temazcalco mopachoz, in totoca ic mopotonja in tlanechicolli, tecomaxo coioxochitl qujmjchpatli, tzitzicaztli iietl xoxouhquj, ie mochi inamjc y, in canjn moteca coaciviztli, oapaoaliztli.

Coatetl:

in tequechtlan motlalia, moxotla, moqujxtia in textotonti: njman piçietl, iietl tenexio, iztaio totonquj vnmaquja. Auh in ie ixpalanj, motetequj in metl mooatza, mocoxonja, vnmotemilia, anoço ic mopotonia

Quechpalanjliztli:

axixtica mopaca, ic mopotonja in tlanechicolli, in ocotl cenca tzomonqui, ioan chichic quavitl, ioan iztauhiatl, ioan calcuechtli, ioan iapaxivitl ineloaio, ioan achi iztatl, capulxivitl, ioan itzcujnpatli: auh in jnanaoac iztatl vnmopalteuhtecaz.

Tlatlaciztli:

in jpaio, neçotlaloz, nepapacholoz in totozcac, vnmjz tlacopoputl in jneloaio iaio, ioan tenexatl chillo, ioan tlatzoionjlli iztauhiatl: ioan vnmjz tlaneloatl, itoca pîpitzaoac: in conetontli ça centlacotl in conjz, in vei tlacatl nauhtlacotl in conjz, iamanqui atl ypan

---

1. Corresponding Spanish text: "*paperas*" — hence also possibly goiter or mumps. See Molina, *op. cit.*; von Gall, *op. cit.*, p. 239.

2. *Aacaxilotic: Plantago mexicana* Link, *Maranta arundinacea* L., *Alpinia* sp., or *Canna indica* L. (Hernández, *op. cit.*, I, pp. 105–106); *Maisblüte* (von Gall, *loc. cit.*).

3. The *Acad. Hist.* MS reads *tecomaxochitl coyoxochitl. — Tecomaxochitl: Maximiliana vitifolia* (Willd.), in Standley, *op. cit.*, Pt. 3, p. 836. Hernández, *op. cit.*, II, pp. 442–444, suggests *Datura arborea* L., *D. candida, Amphitecna macrophylla* Miers, the genus *Bignoniácea,* or *Solandra grandiflora;* Sahagún (Garibay ed.), IV, p. 353, *Swartia guttata* St.

4. *Quimichpatli: Buddleia sessiliflora* or *Sebadilla officinarum;* cf. *supra*, chap. xxi, n. 9.

5. *Tzitzicaztli: Jatropha urens* L. (Standlay, *op. cit.*, Pt. 3, p. 636).

6. *Xoxouhqui:* presumably *xoxouhcapatli,* unident.; Martínez, *op. cit.*, pp. 509–511, thinks it may be *Ipomoea* sp. See also *Florentine Codex,* Book XI, fol. 142r. Possibly it may be read *iietl xoxouhqui,* green tobacco [leaves].

7. *Acad. Hist.* MS: *vapaviztli.*

8. *Chichic quauitl: Cornus urbiniana* Rose or *Garrya laurifolia* Hartw. (Hernández, *op. cit.*, II, pp. 569–570); *Coutarea latifolia* Moc. (Sahagún, *op. cit.*, IV, p. 333).

9. *Yapaxiuitl:* perhaps *Amaranthus* sp. (*ibid.*, p. 371).

10. *Tlacopopotl: Arundinella hispida* (*ibid.*, p. 361).

named *pipitzauac*.[11] [Of these,] small children are to drink only one-fourth pint; grown men are to drink one pint. One is to drink it[12] in warm water or in maguey wine. Either [the mucus] will be vomited up or one will pass it through.

If one just passes it through, his mouth is rubbed with salted tomato,[13] or [the infusion of an herb] named *yiztaquiltic* is to be drunk. A small child is to drink [what is absorbed by] two, [or] three, saturated cotton wads. And the mother from whom the child will take [his milk], from whom he will nurse, is to drink some. And grown persons are to drink a dose in warm water or in maguey wine. One will pass the mucus through or vomit it up. Twice, thrice it is to be drunk. And also one's throat is to be massaged. Then one is to drink boiled chili-water. And his food [is to be] turkey hen, rabbit, quail, dove, deer; and he is to eat toasted tortillas. And no more is he to drink much water. He is to drink the water of the *chipili* herb, [or infusions of] *coatli*,[14] or a little wine, or a little maguey wine. He is to be without food. And he is to drink boiled chili-water, [or] atole with yellow chili and honey. He will not drink cold water. He will abstain from chocolate, fruit, yellow maguey wine. He will avoid the cold, the chill; he will cover himself well. Also the sweat bath will help him. There in the sweat bath he will inhale the hot air.

in qujz, anoço vctli ipan, aço mjçotlaz, anoço qujtemoviz:

intla ça qujtemovi, iioma atica mopapachoz in jcamac iztaio, anoço iehoatl vnmjz, in jtoca iiztaqujltic, in conetontli vnpopulli, epupulli in conjz: auh cequj conjz in tenan itechpa canaz in piltzintli qujchichiz. Auh in vei tlacatl centetl in qujz, iamanquj atl ipan anoço vctli ipan qujtemoviz in tlatlaciztli, anoço qujoaliçotlaz quen oppa, expa in mjz, auh oc no mopapachoz in jtozcac: njman conjz chilpoçonalli, auh in jtlaqual totoli, tochi, çoli, vilotl, maçatl, ioan totopuchtli qujquaz: auh aocmo cenca atl qujz, atliz, in jiauh chipili, coatli, aço achi vino, aço achi vctli, ie in amo tlaquale: ioan quiz in chilpoçonalli, in chilnequatolli, amo quiz in itztic atl, in cacaoatl qujcaoaz, in xuchiqualli, in avctli, amo qujttaz in itztic, in cecec, vel motlaquentiz: no qujpaleviz in temazcalli, in vncan temazcalco, qujhiioanaz in totonquj ihiiotl.

---

11. *Pipitzaoac: Perezia adnata* A. Gray (Martínez, *op. cit.*, p. 216).

12. *Acad. Hist. MS: quiz* is crossed out and *ymiz* inserted.

13. For *iioma atica*, read *tomatica;* see *ibid.*

14. *Coatli: Eysenhardtia polystachya* (Ortega) Sarg. (Standley, *op. cit.*, Pt. 2, p. 443).

Chest ailments, or cough, or [shortness of breath from] running

The remedy [consists of the herbs] named *chichicpatli* [and] the *chichicquauitl* of Uexotzinco. They are ground; they are cooked. One drinks [an infusion thereof] tepid, or in maguey wine. One is to drink it two [or] three times. Or one is to drink [the water in which] is cooked the so-called *ezpatli*,[1] boiling it with chili [and] squash seeds; one is to drink it tepid. Especially is one to take the trouble not to eat in a hurry. Those who run, the messengers, drink it as they go on the road.

The nursing woman who no longer produces milk

She is to drink [an infusion of] *tzayanalquiltic* root, which is to be pulverized with a stone. Then one is to wash her breasts with saltpeter. Or [she is to drink the infusion] many times when she comes from the sweat bath. But when the milk comes, when it comes anew, it will still give the child diarrhea. Hence it is necessary that the little child shall drink two doses [of the infusion], which will purge him. [The nursing woman] is not to eat avocados. And she is also to drink [an infusion of] *tzilacayo ayotl*,[2] which is to be boiled in an olla; or she is to drink it in maguey wine, [or] in an infusion of *cuetlaxxochitl*.[3] She is to take a hot bath in it. Or, also, she is to eat roasted the penis of a dog. Or she is to eat *izcauitli*[4] [worms]; she goes on consuming the water therefrom. Or she is to drink [an infusion of] *toonchichi*[5] root in maguey wine; she is to take a hot bath in it. She is to drink only four fingers of it.

Breast tumor

Herbs named *ixyayaual*[6] and *eloquiltic*[7] are cut, [ground up, and] mixed together. These bring it to a

In telchiquiuh mococoa: aço tlatlaciztli, anoço netlalolli:

in jnamjc itoca vexotzincaiotl chichicpatli, chichicquavitl, moteci, motzoionja, iamanquj conj, anoço vctli ipan, oppa, expa in conjz, anoço iehoatl qujz in jtoca ezpatli, motzoionja, chillo, aiooachio, ipan quaqualaca, iamanquj conjz, oc cenca qujhiiooviz, amo iciuhca tlaquaz in motlaloa, in motitlanj, qujtiuj in vtlica.

In aocmo meia chichioa:

conjz, motetzotzonaz in tlaneloatl in tzaianalqujltic, njman tequjxqujtica qujpacaz in jchichioal, aço temazcalco, mjecpa in qujz: auh in oalmeiaz, in iancujcan meiaz, oc capitzaltiz in piltontli: ic monequj vnpopulli conjtiz in piltontli qujcujtlaxcoliectiz, amo qujquaz in aoacatl: ioan no conjz in tzilacaio aiotl, poçonjz, anoço conjz, iehoatl conjz vctli ipan cuetlaxxuchitl, ipan motemaz: auh anoço iehoatl qujquaz in itzcujntepulli, motleoatzaz, anoço iehoatl qujquaz in izcavitli, qujltectinemjz in jaio, anoço iehoatl conjz, in toonchichi ineloaio, vctli ipan, ipan motemaz, çan nâmapilli in conjz.

Chichioallaxoaliztli:

vnmotequjlia in xiujtl itoca ixiaiaoal, ioan eeloqujltic moneloa, qujcuxitia, anoço qujlochtia: auh intla

---

1. Corresponding Spanish text: *"hecho de diuersas yeruas."*

2. *Tzilacaio aiotl (tzilacayotli): Cucurbita ficifolia* Bouché (Hernández, *op. cit.*, I, p. 158).

3. *Cuetlaxxochitl: Euphorbia pulcherrima* Willd. (Standley, *op. cit.*, Pt. 3, p. 600).

4. *Izcauitli*: unident.; water-worm described in *Florentine Codex*, Book XI, fol. 69r, as *pitzaoac, pitzactontli, necoc iacavitztic, tlatlauhqui: ioioli* — thin, thin and small, pointed at both ends, reddish insect.

5. *Toonchichi* (read *totōchichi*; see *Acad. Hist. MS*): *Solanum nigrum* (Hernández, *op. cit.*, III, p. 710).

6. *Ixiaiaoal*: *"parece sin duda especie de nepata ó de calamita, hasta aora no conocida"* (Ximenez, *op. cit.*, p. 182). — *"Radix magna per transuersum repens fibris scatens cineratij, cū caulibus quamplurimis, coloris: folia bina, ex quorum exortu ramuli exeunt foliati . . . cordis figura & serrata non leuiter. Maiora instar Cochleariae concaua sunt, subtus diluti supra saturi viroris"* (Reccho, *op. cit.*, p. 448).

7. *Eloquiltic*: in *ibid.*, p. 210, *xotlilitzi* and *tlatlancuaye* are alternatives. The latter may be a *Piper* sp. or *Peperomia* sp.; or, more likely, *Iresine calea* St. (Emmart, *op. cit.*, pp. 241, 282; Martínez, *op. cit.*, p. 277).

head or dissolve it. And if they bring it to a head, it is to be lanced. And if only a core is formed, it is lanced. And the herbs mentioned are to be placed where it has been lanced, as well as when the infected surface reddens. Or pulverized *chichicaquilitl* [and] pine resin are to be mixed, to be placed — to be put on — as a poultice. And one drinks the water [from the herbs] named *yamancapatli*,[8] [or] *tetetzmitic*.[9]

If the chest, the back, the ribs, the rib cage hurt, if she aches in all parts of her body, she is anointed with a collection of divers herbs: *tlalquequetzal*,[10] *tonalxiuitl*,[11] *atzitzicaztli*,[12] *atzomiatl*. They are ground; they are mixed with lampblack [and] *axin* in order to be applied as an ointment. But first she is to bathe in hot wormwood [water].

And if her body itches, she takes a hot bath. And when she has taken a hot bath, she is to drink [an infusion of] assorted [herbs], named *tememetla*,[13] *tececec, texiotl*,[14] *tlachinoltetzmitl*. They are to be steeped in water or in acid water. When she has drunk it, the ailment will pass out in the urine.

Jigger fleas [which] always settle on the back

The remedy is not to bathe in the beginning. Some effect a cure in this wise: if there is an opening, [powdered] *toloa* leaves and pine resin, mixed, are applied; a poultice of the *toloa* is placed on top. And when the flesh [swelling] has gone down, [powdered] *iztac patli* is put on to heal the sore. But if [the poultice] does not bring [the swelling] down, it is cut in the form of a cross. That which has not burst forth — the parasite, which is like a fly egg[15] — then comes out; it is extracted.

Then green tobacco, [the kind] named *itzyetl* or *xicoyietl,* is gathered; lampblack [and] hot lime are added; [this mixture] is applied in drops. And then [the back] is poulticed with pine resin. Also it is bathed in the *xicoyietl* [juice mixed] with lampblack; the [tobacco] named *tlalyietl* is added. Or perhaps a nopal [leaf] is cut in a circle; it is to be fitted, being tied on. Then pine resin is placed where a hole is

qujcuxiti moçoz, auh intla çan motetlalia moço: auh in onmoçoc, vnmotlaliz in omjto xivitl: auh in ie ixpalanj, paltic, anoço coxonquj onmotlaliz, onmotemaz, moneloz in chichicaqujlitl, ocutzotl ic mopotonjz: auh in jauhpoujz, itoca iamancapatli, têtetzmjtic.

In mococoa telchiqujuh: tocujtlapa, tomjcicujl, tochiqujuhio, in noviian tlatlaxvizti in jnacaio: ic moça in tlanechicolli, in nepapan xivitl, tlalquequetzal, tonalxivitl, atzitzicaztli, atzomjatl, moteçi tlilli moneloa, axio, quezqujpa injc moçaz: auh achtopa ic maltiz totonquj iztauhiatl,

auh in ie cuêcuetzoca in jnacaio, motema: auh in jquac omoten, qujz in tlanechicolli, in jtoca tememetla, tececec, ioan texiotl, tlachinoltetzmjtl atica, anoço xocoatica mociaoaz: in oqujc, caxixaz in coculli.

Qualocatl: çan mochipa tocujtlapan in motlalia,

inamjc amo maltiz in opeuh. In cequjntin ic qujpatia vnmotema: in vncan coionquj in toloa iiatlapal, ioan moneloa ocotzotl, pani ic mopotonja in tuloa: auh in oonactiuetz tonacaio, vnmotema iztac patli ic oalnacatemj: auh in aqujmopachivia mopapalotequj: njman vnmaiavi, qujoalqujxtia in aiamo tlapanj, in tlaquanj, iuhqujn aoauhtetl:

njman vnmotlalilia in xoxouhquj iietl, in jtoca itzietl, anoço xicoiietl, tlillo, totonquj etenexio vnmochapanja: auh njman mopotonja ocotzotica, no ic maltia in xicoiietl tlillo, qujnamjquj in itoca tlaliietl: auh anoço moiaoaliuhcatequj in nopalli, onmaqujz in tompiliuhtica: njman oxitl vnmoteca in vncan coionquj, mematl ie in amo tlapactli: njman motlatia in oxitl, mototonja, njman tzotzopoca, oppa, expa in motlalia, ix-

---

8. *Iamancapatli*: *Asclepias verticillata* L. (Hernández, *op. cit.*, III, p. 924). Emmart (*op. cit.*, p. 289) suggests a species of *Manihot* (*Euphorbiaceae*).

9. *Têtetzmitic*: *Sedum dendroideum* Moc. et Sess. (Martínez, *op. cit.*, p. 455; Emmart, *op. cit.*, p. 223).

10. *Tlalquequetzal*: *Achillea millefolium* L. (*ibid.*, p. 244).

11. *Tonalxiuitl*: *Stevia salicifolia* Car. or *Veronica americana* Swed. (Sahagún, *op. cit.*, IV, p. 359). Hernández, (*op. cit.*, I, pp. 56–62, 63–65) describes five plants so named.

12. *Atzitzicaztli*: *Urera caracasana* (Jacq.) Griseb (Emmart, *op. cit.*, p. 229; see also Standley, *op. cit.*, Pt. 1, p. 219).

13. *Tememetla*: Emmart (*op. cit.*, p. 242) suggests *Echeveria* sp.

14. *Texiotl*: perhaps also *Sedum dendroideum* Moc. & Ses. (*loc. cit.*; Santamaría, *op. cit.*, III, p. 165, *texiote*).

15. *Aoauhtetl*: cf. *ibid.*, I, p. 61.

made in the nopal leaf, there where it is not stopped up. Then the pine resin is set afire; it becomes hot. Then [the sore] burns. Twice, three times it is applied. Up to three [times] is one's flesh burned; one brings this about three [times]. Then it is poulticed with pine resin mixed with *yiauhtli*.

One's food [is] tortillas, toasted tortillas, [and] birds' eggs. One abstains from all chili, from spoiled, greasy [meat]. One's drink [is] cold water. One avoids hot atole, chocolate, maguey wine, wine; that is to say, [he is to drink water] boiled with *coatli*.[16]

The breaking [of bones]

In injuries, whether of the spine, or the ribs, or the leg, etc., [or] whatsoever bone is injured, first that which is broken is pressed, stretched, joined. Then *çacacili*[17] root is cut; a very thick poultice [of the pulverized root] is applied. Wooden splints are pressed on; they are bound about it. And if there is a swelling around [the break], it is pricked with an obsidian blade. Or [pulverized root of] *iztac çaçalic*[18] is spread on; it is spread on with [pulverized] *tememetlatl* root. Some bathe in it, some drink it in maguey wine, [some] take a hot bath in it when there is itching. Or it is applied; [the herb] named *xipetziuh* is applied. Some rub themselves with it, but some drink it mixed with *iztac çaçalic;* they also drink it in wine. And if one is very sick, and his body is much fevered, and the bone is exposed; a very resinous stick is cut; it is inserted within the bone, bound within the incision, covered over with the medicine mentioned.

Swelling from sprains

Its remedy is to proceed spreading on [powdered] charred cobs of maize, those which are striped red, and blotched with red, and tawny-colored; or the *teçonpatli*[19] [herb]. And [the swelling] is pressed many times, whereupon the medicines mentioned are put on.

A constant cough

One constantly coughs up mucus; then pus is expelled; [one goes on spitting it out; then blood clots are expelled in quantity] from the nose.[20]

Its remedy is [an infusion of] *teouaxin* with chili [and] salt; it is to be cooked. One is to drink it many

qujchica iie tlatla inacaio, iie qujmati: njman ocutzotica mopotonja, iiauhtli moneloa:

in jtlaqual, tlaxcalli totopuchtli, totoltetl: **mochi** qujcaoaz in chilli, in xoqujac, in chiaoac: in jauh itztic atl, qujcaoaz in totonquj atolli, cacaoatl, vctli, vino, qujtoz in coatli poçonjz.

Nepuztequjliztli:

in anoço tocujtlatetepon itlacavi, anoço tomjcicujl, anoço tocxi. Etc. in çaço tlein itlacavi omitl. Achtopa mopachoa, motilinia, monamjctia in tlein opoztec: njman vnmotequilia in çacacili ineloaio, cenca tilaoac ipan mopotonja, ipan molpia, moquaquappachoa: auh in jnânaoac intla poçaoa mjtzaoavia, anoço iehoatl vnmotecaz in jztac çaçalic, in jneloaio tememetlatl vnmoteca, cequj ic maltia, cequj conj vctli ipan, ipan motema in jquac ie cuecuetzoca, anoço vnmotlalia itoca xipetziuh vnmotlalia, cequj ic moça, auh cequj conj, moneloa in jztac çaçalic, no vctli ipan. Auh in cenca aveli moxotla in inacaio, panj moquetza in omjtl, moxima cenca tzomonquj ocutl: vnmaquja, in tomjo itic, in tacaiocan ipan molpia, ic mopepechoa in omjto patli.

Matzatzapaliciviztli:

inamjc çintli tzatzapalli, ioan xochicintli, ioan quappachcintli, motlatia, vnmotecatinemj, anoço iehoatl in teçonpatli: auh mjecpa mopachoa çatepã moteca in omjto patli.

Tlatlaztinemj:

amo çan quexquich in alaoac qujtlaça: njman temalli mocuepa qujchicha, cenca iiac,

inamjc in teuaxi, chillo, iztaio, motzoionjz mjecpa in qujz, qujtinemjz: auh moquaqualatza ynin teuoa-

---

16. Cf. § 2, n. 14, *supra;* corresponding Spanish text: "*su beujda sera agua fria, o el agua del guaiacan.*"
17. *Çacacili: Lithospermum* sp. (Hernández, *op. cit.,* III, p. 826).
18. *Iztac çaçalic:* unident.; cf. descriptions, *ibid.,* p. 792; Reccho, *op. cit.,* p. 284.
19. *Teçonpatli:* unident.; described in Emmart, *op. cit.,* p. 214, and Ximenez, *op. cit.,* p. 156.
20. After *mocuepa,* the *Acad. Hist.* MS adds *quichichatinemi nimã eztemalli mocuep y;* see bracketed insertion, in English text.

times; one constantly goes on drinking it. And this *teouaxin* is [also] boiled; one goes on drinking it with neither chili nor salt.[21] Or one is to drink many times [an infusion of] twigs[22] named *iztac chichicquauitl* boiled in maguey wine. One is not to eat immediately; one is to abstain from fruit; one is to abstain from cold things; one is to drink — one is to eat — everything warm; wine, maguey wine, white maguey wine also help. Only one drink [is required].

And its remedy is [an infusion of the wood] named *chichiualquauitl,* [which is] disagreeable to taste. It is not cooked; it is only warmed in the sun, prepared in the morning. One is to drink this medicine all day. And the next day one is still to drink [the water in which] *tlapalezquauitl*[23] is cooked. A little colored saltpeter is dropped in.

The spitting of blood[24]

One is to drink chocolate [with] *tlilxochitl,*[25] *mecaxochitl,*[26] *vei nacaztli;*[27] with liquid rubber, with small chilis — scorched chilis.[28] One is to drink these in water. But if one is to drink it in maguey wine, it is without liquid rubber, without chili. Or one is to drink [an infusion of] *tlapalezquauitl* wood. Or one is to go on drinking the *ezpatli*[29] [medicine].

xi, catlitinemjz amo chillo amo poec, anoço iehoatl tlacotl itoca iztac chichicquavitl, vctli ipan quaqualaca mjecpa conjz, amo njman iciuhca tlaquaz, qujcaoaz in xuchiqualli, qujcaoaz in jtztic, mochi iamãquj in qujz, in qujquaz, no qujpalevia, in vino, in vctli, iztac vctli, çan centlailli,

ioan inamjc itoca chichioalquavitl tetelqujc, amo icuci, çan tonaian iamanja, tlatvic mochioa: cemjlvitl qujz injn patli: auh in jmoztlaioc, oc ie qujz in tlapalezquavitl motzoionja, achiton tlapaltequjxqujtl ipan vnvetzi.

Eztli tiquicchicha:

conjz cacaoatl tlilxuchitl, mecaxuchitl, vei nacaztli, ollo, chiltecpiio, tlatlanchilli, atl ipan in quiz: auh intla vctli ipan qujz amo ollo, çan chillo, anoço iehoatl conjz in tlapalezquavitl, anoço iehoatl in ezpatli catlitinemiz

21. *Acad. Hist. MS: aocmo chillo, aocmo no poec.*

22. Spanish text varies from the Nahuatl: *"cierta rayz que se nombra iztac chichicquavitl."*

23. *Tlapalezquavitl: Jatropha spathulata* or *Eysenhardtia polystachia* (Santamaría, *op. cit.,* III, p. 186 — *tlapalespacle*).

24. *Acad. Hist. MS: Eztli ticchicha.*

25. *Tlilxochitl: Vanilla planifolia;* cf. *supra,* chap. xxi, n. 3.

26. *Mecaxochitl: Piper amalago* L.; cf. *supra,* chap. xxi, n. 4.

27. *Vei nacaztli: Cymbopetalum penduliflorum* (Dunal) Baill.; cf. *supra,* chap. xxi, nn. 5, 6.

28. Read *tlatla chilli* or *tlatlac chilli;* cf. corresponding Spanish text — *chiltecpin, muy tostado.*

29. *Ezpatli:* a number of plants which produce a red sap, called "Dragon's blood." Standley (*op. cit.*) mentions *Pterocarpus draco* L. (Pt. 2, p. 508), *Croton draco* Schlecht. (Pt. 3, p. 615), and various species of the *Jatropha* genus (Pt. 3, pp. 637–639). Corresponding Spanish text: *"se haze de diuresas yeruas, moliendolo y rebolujendolo con el agua."*

FOURTH PARAGRAPH, which telleth of the internal ailments, the ailments of the stomach [and] of the bladder.

Stomach pain

Its remedy is purging. One is to eat pine nuts; two, three of them one is to eat, to roast for himself. [The purging] is stopped by atole of ground maize, or one is to drink yellow tomato [juice] with chili, with gourd seeds, with chocolate, with small tomatoes; or one is to drink [an infusion of] *chichicquauitl* wood, or lime water. And it is necessary to give, as an enema, [the herb] named *xoxocoyoltic,* adding *xococotl* to it. It cleans the stomach, the bowels. It brings out the worms, perhaps the earth-dwelling *tzoncoatl*[1] worm. It expels [the ailment] through the urine. And later one is to drink [an infusion of the herb] named *yamanquipatli*. It will expel, alleviate the ailment. This is a complete cure for the colic, [and] for constipation.

Colic

Flaked whitewash [and] a little saltpeter, with liquid rubber and chili, are worked to the consistency of potter's clay,[2] into a suppository inserted into the rectum. It is expelled from the rectum. It eliminates all one's food which is within.

A flux, a suppurative or bloody flux

Its remedy is *ciuapatli*[3] [leaves] cooked together with lampblack and [the white of] an egg. Four, five times is one to drink it. Or one is to drink chocolate with lime water. The lime which is required is put to soak late in the day. A well-toasted chili is mixed with the chocolate. And one's food is tortillas smelling of ashes, or toasted tortillas.[4] One is not to eat the flesh of cattle, the flesh of swine baked [or] cooked in an olla; turkey, quail, rabbit, eggs which are fried; but only sip heated [broth] with salt.[5]

Strangury

For this will be drunk what is named "yellow urine medicine," [6] the root of [the herb] *amaxtlatl*,[7]

INJC NAVI PARRAPHO: itechpa tlatoa, in jti cocoliztli, in jcocolizio in totlatlaliaia in taxixteco.

Totlatlalia: itlacavi,

inamjc tlanoqujliztli conquaz in quauhtlatlatzin, vntetl, etetl, in conquaz conmoxqujz, ic motzaqua, iolatolli anoço conjz coztomatl, chillo, aiooachio, cacaoaio: miltomaio, anoço conjz chichicquavitl, anoço tenexatl itevilotca: ioan monequj itlampa qujmacazque in jtoca xoxocoioltic, xococotl qujnamjquj, tlapaca in tocujtlapan in ixilla qujnoalquixtia ocujltin, anoço tlalocujli tzoncoatl caxixtlapoa: auh çatepan conjz in jtoca iamanqujpatli, qujoalqujxtiz, qujoalpachoz in coculli, inin icempaio in netextemaliztli, in cujtlaoaqujliztli.

Netextemaliztli:

itlampa momacaz calcuechtli, achiton tequjxqujtl, oltica mopoloa chillo, moololoa vnmotlatlaxilia in jtlampa qujoaltepeoa in jtlaquaqual, in ixqujch yitic ca.

Tláelli: in iztac anoço eztlaelli,

inamjc cioapatli motzoionja, tlillo, ioan mocenneloa totoltetl itevilotca, nappa, macujlpa in conjz, anoço iehoatl qujz in tenexcacaoatl, teutlacpa in mociaoa tenextli ic in jtevilotca monequj, moneloa cacaoatl, vel tlatla chillo: auh in jtlaqual nexaviiac, anoço totopuchtli, amo qujquaz in quaquauhnacatl, in pitzonacatl tlaoatzalli tlacompaoaxtli, totoli, çoli, tochin, totoltetl tlatzoionjlli, anoço çan tlatotonjlli qujltequjz iztaio.

Axixcocoializtli:

iehoatl onmiz, in itoca coztic axixpatli, amaxtla inelhoaio, aço çan atl ipan, aço cacaoatl ipan: aço

---

1. *Tzoncoatl:* "'Serpiente cabello.' Lombriz" (Sahagún, *op. cit.,* IV, p. 366); intestinal worms (von Gall, *op. cit.,* p. 255). *Florentine Codex,* Book XI, fol. 104*sq.*: *in titlaca itzinco oalpotzavi, ocujtli: no tzõcooatl, in chichi itzinco oalpotzavi ocuiltli: no tzoncooatl, in juhquj tlalcuitlaxcolli. In maceoalli itech ca, in jtzinco oalpotzavi iztactotonti, in ocujltoton: iuhquj, in q'n ie peoa nacatl, palanj yiocujllo çan iquac in cochi oalqujça: auh in chichi iquac in momanavia valneci.*

2. Corresponding Spanish text: "*sera bueno curarse con el hollin* [lampblack? *olli*=rubber?] *mezclado con el tequjxqujte, y el ulli, y chile.*"

3. *Cioapatli: Montanoa tomentosa* Cervant. (Standley, *op. cit.,* Pt. 5, p. 1531).

4. *Nexaviiac:* corresponding Spanish text: "*tortillas de granos de mayz, cozidos, no muy lauados.*"

5. *Ibid.:* "*si le diere muy gran deseo, podra sorber el caldo echandole alguna sal.*"

6. *Axixpatli* (unident.) is described in Hernández, *op. cit.,* II, pp. 465, 483; *axixcozahuilizpatli,* a name meaning much the same as *coztic axixpatli,* is identified (p. 465) as *Berberis* sp.

7. *Amaxtlatl (amamaxtla* in *Acad. Hist. MS): Rumex mexicana* Meissn. (Santamaría, *op. cit.,* I, p. 90).

whether only in water, or in chocolate, or in maguey wine with chili [and] gourd seeds, or in very little water.

Dysuria[8]

Either pus is urinated or one urinates blood. One is to drink [an infusion of] *coanenepilli*[9] and of *çayolquauitl*,[10] and of a tree named *tlaquacuitlapilli*,[11] all ground together; one is to drink it in water, or in chocolate, or in maguey wine. But at the very first one is to be given an enema with a [powdered herb] named *cacamotic poxauac*.[12] And also this medicine, *cacamotic*, is for loss of semen. Then one drinks the medicine mentioned, or one is to drink [water in which is soaked] the pith of the *iztac quauitl* [tree], which grows in Coatitlan. Or one is to drink [liquid with powdered] opossum[13] tail — a little of the tail of the female, a little of the male. It is to be drunk in maguey wine. Or one is to go on to drink the root of the *iztac axixpatli*[14] shrub in wine.

Hemorrhoids

Their remedy is to drink [an infusion of] *tletlemaitl;* a hot bath is to be taken in it. And if the hemorrhoids are in the rectum, [an infusion of] *tletlemaitl* is cast in the rectum; but if they appear only on the surface, they are covered with the pulverized [herb].

vctli ipan, chillo, aiooachio, anoço çan achi pactli ipan.

Neaxixtzaqualiztli:

anoço temalli maxixa, anoço eztli caxixa: conjz coanenepilli, ioan çaiolquauitl, ioan quavitl itoca tlaquacujtlapilli mocenteçi, atl ipan qujz, anoço cacaoatl ipan, anoço vctli ipan: auh oc ie achto icujtlapampa iaz, in jtoca cacamotic poxaoac: auh no ixpampa vetzi injn patli in cacamotic: çatepan conj in omjto patli, anoço iehoatl conjz in iztac quavitl yiollo, in coatitlan mochioa, anoço iehoatl conjz in tlaquaton icujtlapil: achi cioatl, achi oqujchtli icujtlapil, in mjz vctli ipan, anoço iztac axixpatli ineloaio tlacotl, vctli ipan in qujtinemjz.

Xochiciviztli:

inamjc tletlemaitl õmjz, ipan netemalo: auh intla icujtlapan icac in xuchitl, icujtlapampa vnmotlatlaça in tletlemaitl: auh intla ça nen opanvetz coxonquj onmopachoa.

8. In Molina, *op. cit.,* both *axixcocoyaliztli* and *neaxixtzaqualiztli* are translated as *estangurria;* von Gall, *op. cit.,* pp. 258*sqq.,* terms the disorder *Blasenkatarrh,* and in consideration of symptoms, speculates on the possibility of *andere Krankheiten. . . . , wie Gonorrhöa o. ä. oder Schwarzwasserfieber.*

9. *Coanenepilli:* probably *Passiflora jorullensis* H. B. K. (Emmart, *op. cit.,* p. 264), or *P. suberosa* Linn. (Hernández, *op. cit.,* II, p. 587).

10. *Çaiolquauitl: Buddleia* sp. (*ibid.,* III, p. 846).

11. *Tlaquacuitlapilli:* opossum-tail tree (unident.). In von Gall, *op. cit.,* p. 259, *quavitl* (tree) is assumed to be an error, since opossum tail was used for urinary difficulties. Cf. Reccho, *op. cit.,* p. 330.

12. *Cacamotic:* of genus *Ipomoea* (Hernández, *op. cit.,* II, p. 527; see also Emmart, *op. cit.,* p. 253).

13. *Tlaquatzin, tlaquatl: Didelphis* sp.; cf. *supra,* chap. xxi, n. 7.

14. *Iztac axixpatli:* "white urine medicine"; cf. n. 6, *supra.*

FIFTH PARAGRAPH, which telleth of other ailments and their remedies, their cures.

Pustules[1]

Their cure is the same [as for hemorrhoids]. One will proceed to drink [an infusion of] *tletlemaitl;* one will take a hot bath in it. One is to cover [the pustules] over with the [powdered herb,] *tlalquequetzal,*[2] or with copper filings.

And there are two kinds of pustules. The name of one kind [is] "filthy pustules," and they gave [the other][3] the name "silk-cotton tree[4] pustules" [or] "small pustules." They are very painful, very paralyzing. They cause twisting of the hands [and] the feet, because the ailment penetrates completely. And when they erupt, one drinks [an atole of] fish-amaranth seeds. And one is to drink [an infusion of] *quauhtlepatli;*[5] four times, five times [a day] one is to drink it. One is to take a bath in it. And if one's hands [and] one's feet become twisted, one is to drink a purgative, the root [of an herb] named *tlatlapanaltic,* which is like *caxtlatlapan.*[6] And later one is bled with an obsidian blade.

And this same cure is for the "filthy pustules."

Skin sores[7]

When they are small, [the core] is removed with a pine resin,[8] and squashed black beetles[9] are spread thereon, and a poultice is formed. And later *tlalamatl*[10] [root] is applied; pine resin is applied. Or one is to apply [ground] *atlepatli*[11] [leaves]. And when one takes a hot bath, one is to bathe in [an infusion of] *itzcuinpatli* [leaves]; it lowers the temperature of the body.

The remedy for the "divine sickness"[12]

When it begins, then the eyebrows fall out and one suffers much hunger. One takes a hot bath three [or]

INJC MACUJLLI PARRAPHO: itechpa tlatoa, in oc cequj cocoliztli, ioan in jnanamjc in jpaio.

Nanaoatl:

çan no ie ipaio, qujtinemjz in tletlemaitl, ipã motemaz, compapachoz in tlalquequetzal, anoço iehoatl in tepuztlalli.

Auh ca ontlamantli in nanaoatl: inic centlamantli itoca, tlacaçolnanaoatl, ioan quitocaiotia puchonanaoatl: in tecpilnanaoatl cenca tecoco, cenca coacivizio, qujteteputzoquixtia in toma, in tocxi, tecocototzo: ipampa çã mocententica in coculli: auh injc oalpavetzi, michioauhtli conj: auh conjz in quauhtlepatli, quen nappa, macujlpa in qujz, ipan motentiaz. Auh in jquac ie teteputzo qujça ima, iicxi, conjz tlanoqujlonj, itoca tlatlapanaltic ineloaio, iuhqujn caxtlatlapan, auh çatepan mjtzmjna:

auh inin çan no ie ipaio in tlacaçolnanaoatl.

Xixiotl:

in qujn tepiton ocutzotica mocuilia, ioan vncan onmoteca, onmopitzinja in tlalxicuapilli, auh mopotonja: auh çatepan onmotlalia in tlalamatl mocotzovia, anoço onmotlaliz in atlepatli: auh in jquac motema, ic maltiz in itzcujnpatli, qujiamanja in jnacaio.

Teucocuiliztli inamjc

in qujn peoa, iie motepeoa in ixquamol: ioan cenca teucivi, motema expa, nappa: auh iquac oalqujça te-

1. Seler considers this ailment symptomatic of syphilis. See *supra,* § 1, n. 39.
2. *Tlalquequetzal: Polypodium lanceolatum* L. (Hernández, *op. cit.,* II, p. 338); *Achillea millefolium* (Santamaría, *op. cit.,* III, p. 185).
3. *Tlacaçolnanauatl — buuas grandes y pestilenciales; tecpilnanaoatl — buuas pequeñas* (Molina, *op. cit.*). Corresponding Spanish text: *"las vnas son muy suzias, que se dizen tlacaçolnanaoatl, y las otras son de menos pesadübre, que se llamã tecpilnanaoatl, o por otro nombre puchonanaoatl."* In *Acad. Hist. MS,* this passage reads: *auh ca õtlamãtli ỹ nanavatl. inic. i. ytoca tlacaçolnanavatl. ynic õtlamãtli tecpilnanavatl yoã quitocaiotia pochũnanavatl. ỹ tecpilnanavatl cẽca tecoco. . . .*
4. *Pochotl: Ceiba pentandra* (L.), in Standley, *op. cit.,* Pt. 3, p. 791.
5. *Quauhtlepatli: Euphorbia calyculata* H. B. K., *Croton calyculata,* or *Lippia geminata* H. B. K. (Hernández, *op. cit.,* I, pp. 182–186).
6. *Caxtlatlapan:* a species of *Ipomoea,* or *Convolvulus jalapa* (*ibid.,* III, pp. 844, 864).
7. Corresponding Spanish text: *"la enfermedad de los empeines."*
8. *Ibid.: "quando no son muy grãdes, sera necesario hazer vn pegote de ocotzote, pegandolo muchas vezes, para que salga la raiz."*
9. *Ibid.: "cireto animalejo nõbrado carraleja"* — Spanish blistering beetle?
10. *Tlalamatl: Gonolobus parviflorus,* or *Desmodium urbiculare;* cf. Sahagún (Garibay ed.), IV, p. 362.
11. *Atlepatli: Ranunculus stoloniferus* Hemsl. (?). (Hernández, *op. cit.,* I, p. 177).
12. See Seler, *op. cit.,* II, pp. 100–103, "Nachrichten über den Assatz in alten Mexikanischen Quellen." Corresponding Spanish text: *"la lepra."*

four times. When one emerges from the sweat bath, one washes in an assortment of herbs:[13] *iyauhtli, cococxiuitl,* roots of *çacamolli,* roots and leaves of *tecpatli.*[14] And one drinks a little [of the infusion of] *tecpatli.* And if, [after] four [or] five times, it does not help one, they leave him in the forest, [or] on the plains.

Diarrhea

Whether a child, whether a grown person, one is to drink the [water in which is] cooked [the herb] named *tzipipatli.* Three [or] four times one is to drink it. And the mother of the child from whom it takes its milk, should also drink it. And grown people are to drink an atole of wrinkled *chía,* [with] toasted *chía* tortillas, [and] with chili added on top. But the child is to drink [the atole] without [chili] on top, or he is to drink [an infusion of] the bark [of a tree] named *iztac quauitl,* which grows, which is produced, here in Coatitlan, cooked in chocolate. This [medicine] is also a remedy for a [bloody] flux. And if nothing else can stop the diarrhea, perhaps a measure of *axin* is boiled; it is given as an enema. If they may be able to drink it, some will drink it, but if one cannot drink it, he is to drink the surface scum of hen broth. This [is] also a remedy for a [bloody] flux.

Tumors: they are cut.[15]

Knee swelling

Perhaps it is lanced. When the humor comes out, a poultice of [powdered] *toloa* foliage is placed on top. [This helps] a little.

Leg swelling

It is pricked with an obsidian point. A poultice of [powdered] *coatl xoxouhqui*[16] [seeds] mixed with pine resin is applied.

Humors of the feet[17]

mazcalco ic maltia in tlanechicolli, in xivitl iiauhtli, cococxiujtl, çacamolli ineloaio, tecpatli ineloaio, ioan ixiuhio, ioan achi conj, in tecpatli: auh in ie nappa macujlpa, aqujtlacamati, concaoa quauhtla, ixtlaoaca.

Apitzalli:

aço piltontli, aço vei tlacatl: conjz in jtoca tzipipatli, tlatzoionjlli, expa, nappa in qujz: auh in piltontli inantzin, no conjz, itechpa canaz in ichichioalaioio: auh in vei tlacatl in qujz atolli, chientzotzolli, chientlaxcaltotopuchtli, quinamjquj chilpani: auh in piltontli conjz amo pane, anoço ieohatl conjz, in jtoca iztac quavitl ixipeoallo: njcan mochioa coatitlan, mochioa cacaoatl ipan tzoionj, no inamjc in in tlaêlli. Auh intla çan njman aoc tle vel qujtzaqua, in apitzalli, aço cemolotl vnmoquaqualatza in axi, itlampa momaca, intla uel qujz, cequj conjz: auh intlaca oc vel quj, iehoatl conjz in totolaiotl, in ixiotl: inin no inamjc in tlailli.

Xoxalli: motequj.

Tlanquaalaviztli:

anoço motzopinja, in oalqujça tzonqualactli, pani ic mopotonja, toloa ixiuhio, çan ipan qualli.

Icxicocolli:

mjtzaoavia, ic mopotonja, in coatl xoxouhquj, mocotzovia

Xotevconaviztli.

---

13. Corresponding Spanish text: *"saliendo de los baños, sera tambien bueno, vntarse con las yeruas, e rayzes de suso nombradas molidas."*

14. *Tecpatli* (or *tecpaolotl*): unident.; described in *Florentine Codex,* Book XI, fol. 133*v.* See also Ximenes, *op. cit.,* p. 155; Emmart, *op. cit.,* p. 246; Santamaría, *op. cit.,* III, p. 156 (*tepacle*).

15. The *Acad. Hist. MS* notes marginally, instead of *motequi: çā no yuh pati in yuh pati coatetl no moxotla auh çā no yuhqui textli oalmoquixtia* — it is cured as a cyst is cured; it is also incised. In the same way the core is forced out.

16. *Coatl xoxouhqui:* desc. in *Florentine Codex,* Book XI, fol. 129*v* — *Ay vna ierva que se llama coatl xoxouhquj, y crian vna semilla que se llama ololiuhquj, o coatl xoxouhqui.* The identification of *ololiuhqui* is doubtful. *Datura ceratocaula, Ipomoea sadaefolia* Choisy, and *Rivea corymbosa* have been suggested. See Martínez, *op. cit.,* pp. 508*sqq.*

17. Cf. *infra,* "Humors of the feet" — "Xoteuconaviliztli." In the *Acad. Hist. MS,* a marginal addition reads: *ypayo totonqui axixtli yc mopaca auh yn omopac nimā ōmotetemilia y̆ coxōqui tlatlauhcapatli y̆ vncā cocoyōtica auh y̆ ye nappa anoço ye macuilpa ōmotema y̆ patli y̆ omoteneuh nimā oc ceppa axixtica mopaca: auh yn omopac nimā ye yc mopotonia ocutzotica moneloa yn çan ye no yehoatl patli omoteneuh çā yccē yc oalnacatemi yc pati* — [as] its cure they are washed in hot urine, and, when washed, then covered with ground *tlatlauhcapatli* [*Geranium carolinianum*] there where they are split open. And four or five times they are bathed with the medicine mentioned. Then once more they are washed in urine. And when washed, then they are poulticed with pine resin mixed with the same medicine mentioned. Later by these means the flesh grows back and is cured.

The treatment just related appears to fit *xoteteçonauiliztli* (splits, cracks in the feet) rather than *xoteconauiztli.* Corresponding Spanish text: *"Los humores de los pies."*

Benumbed feet

If [the feet] go to sleep, if there is no improvement, wormwood is cooked;[18] [the feet] are rubbed with it, washed with it, several times. Or [the herb] named *tlatlanquayexiuitl*,[19] which grows in Tepoztlan, is cooked; with it one's legs are washed. Or they are anointed with *axin* [mixed with powdered] *tzitzicaztli*.[20]

Urinary obstruction

Perchance our semen injures us, perchance indigestion or large lumps of foreign matter[21] — whatever stops our urine, our excrement — injure us. [An infusion of] the roots of [the herbs] named *cococpatli* [and] *tzontecomaxochitl*,[22] which grow in Quauhtepec, and where it is desert, is given as an enema. And the liquid of [these roots], perhaps two syringes of it, is put in one's member. It is also the remedy when a child falls down, when he ruptures an intestine. Also it is the remedy when the child has a fatal cough. The child is to drink one finger of the liquid. [These roots] are also a remedy for one who has a cold; the roots are chewed, the saliva swallowed.[23] And he who goes about constantly coughing is to drink [an infusion of] one long [root][24] in maguey wine. And when one has a headache, drops [of the sap] are put in the nose:[25] this alleviates the head[ache] very much; it brings out much mucus and sometimes brings out pus, clotted with blood. And to him whom this medicine no longer cures, it is an indication that this is the end, that the patient is confined to bed to no avail.

Fever

One drinks [an infusion of the root of] *chichipilli*, [with] alum [and] acid water. First one is purged;

Xomjmjqujliztli:

in cepoa, in aocmo mjmati, motzoionja in iztauhiatl, ic motzôtzona, ic mopaca quezqujpa, anoço iehoatl motzoionja, ic mopaca in iicxi, in jtoca tlatlanquaiexivitl tepuztlan mochioa, anoço axtica moçaz, tzitzicazio.

Neaxixtzaqualiztli:

aço toquichio techpoloa, aço cujtlapalanjliztli, aço tocujtlatetemallo in techpoloa, in tlein qujtetzaqua, in taxix, in tonemanavil, tlacopuztecquj vnuetzi in tocujtlapampa, in jtoca cococpatli, tzontecomaxuchitl ineloaio quauhtepec, ioan in campa ixtlaoacan in mochioa: auh in jtevilotca, aço vme tepuztli gerinca vnvetzi in tixpampa: no inamjc in piltontli melvitequj, in mocujtlaxcoltzaiana, no inamjc, in mjmjquj tlatlaçi piltontli, cemmapilli ixpampa conjz: no inamjc in tlatlaciztli, vnmoquaquaqua, mototoloa in toztlac. Auh in aqujn totolcatinemj, cemolotl in conjz, vctli ipan: auh in totzontecon mococoa, vnmochichipinja in toiacac: cenca conmati in totzontecon, cenca qujqujxtia in alaoac, in quenman qujqujxtia timalli, ezoacquj: auh in aqujn aocmo qujmati, inin patli, inezca ca ie ixqujch, ca çan nen monoltitoc, in cocuxquj.

Motlevia:

conj chichipili inelhoaio, chichicaqujlitl, tececec, xocoatl: achto motlanoqujlia, çatepan qujtoc, in qua-

18. The *Acad. Hist.* MS adds: *mochi mocêneloa ÿ tepopotl ytzin anoço picietl.*

19. *Tlatlanquaiexiuitl: Iresine calea* (Ibáñez) Standl. (Standley, *op. cit.*, Pt. 1, p. 259; see also Emmart, *op. cit.*, p. 241).

20. *Acad. Hist.* MS: in place of *tzitzicaio,* a marginal correction reads: *colotzitzicayo auh ÿtlacamo quimopachiuia mitzminaz.*

21. *Ibid.*: for *cujtlapalanjliztli, aço tocujtlatetemallo,* a correction substitutes *tlaoaquiliztli ÿ anoço tlahelli quitlaztinemi.*

22. *Tzontecomaxochitl: Caliandra anomala* (Sahagún, *op. cit.,* IV, p. 366).

23. *Acad. Hist.* MS marginal correction replacing the passage beginning with *tlacopuztecqui,* which is crossed out: *conjz ÿ vey nacaztli tlilxochitl mecaxochitl yoã quezquitetl cacaoatl aço matlactetl anoço vel cêpoaltetl yn ioã ypã conjz yoã achito tlaquatzin auh ÿtlacamo quimopachiuia yc monequi yxpampa momacaz gerincatica yn iteuilotca tlacoxochitl. Melhuitequi yn anoço mocuitlaxcultzayana piltontli yehoatl ic pati ÿ toçan cuitlaxcolli yoã aço [?] quen cêpoaltetl tlaolli ypã moteci yn iuhqui ytexio mochioa quitinemi yc pati. Mimiqui tlatlaçiztli ypayo yztac pipitzaoac mixnamiquj tomatl yehoatl yn ca itic [?] mopatzca yehoatl conj aço quê ôpopolli anoço epopolli ceppa yoatzinco auh ceppa ye teotlac —* he will drink [an infusion of] *uey nacaztli, tlilxochitl, mecaxochitl [Cymbopetalum penduliflorum, Vanilla planifolia, Piper amalago]* and a few cacao [beans] — perhaps ten, perhaps indeed twenty — and also in it he will drink as well a little [powdered] opossum [tail]; but if he is not cured by this, it is necessary to inject in his member liquid of *tlacoxochitl [Bouvardia termifolia]* with a syringe. If a child falls down or ruptures an intestine, he is cured by [powdered?] mole's intestine with perhaps as many as ten maize grains ground up with it like flour; he proceeds to drink it [in water]; he is cured by it. The cure for a fatal cough [is an infusion of] white *pipitzauac [Perezia adnata]* together with the soft interior of tomato. This he drinks — perhaps [what is absorbed by] two or three cotton wads — once in early morning and once at evening.

24. *Ibid.*, marginal insertion: *yehoatl cococpatli* — unident.; cf. Hernández, *op. cit.,* II, pp. 618-619; von Gall, *op. cit.,* p. 272, thinks it may be *cococxiuitl (Bocconia frutescens),* as does Garibay in Sahagún, *op. cit.,* IV, p. 328.

25. *Acad. Hist.* MS, marginal insertion: *ÿ çã ye no yehoatl cococpatli.*

then [an infusion from] the edible root of the sand tomato is drunk, adding to it the root of *tacanalquilitl*.[26] The grown people drink [an infusion of] two sand tomato roots; small children drink [an infusion of] four.[27] And five kernels of maize are mixed in this. And when there is fever, one is to drink [an infusion of the root of] *aitztoli*[28] in acid water.

Humors of the feet[29]

Their remedy is *uei patli*,[30] [an herb] which grows in Tepepulco. It is ground; it is spread on abundantly. And it is the cure for swelling of the groin.

Festering; or burns, cuts

Their remedy is [the tree] named *chichicquauitl*, which grows in Tepepan. It is ground; it is applied; or pulverized it is put on mixed with [the white of] an egg.

lonj xaltotomatl ineloaio, qujnamjquj, in tacanalqujlitl ineloaio, in cemolotl ineloaio xaltomatl, vmentin quj in veveintin. In pipiltotonti navintin quj. Auh injn moneloa: macujltetl tlaolli, ioan conjz in motlevia, aitztoli, in xocoatl ipan.

Xoteuconaviliztli:

inamjc vei patli, tepepulco mochioa, moteçi, vnmopalteuhteca, ioan ipaio in quexiliviztli.

Palanjliztli: anoço nexotlaliztli, netequjliztli,

inamjc in jtoca, chichicquavitl tepepan in mochioa: moteci vnmotlalia, anoço mocoxonja, vnmotema, totoltetl moneloa.

---

26. *Tacanalquilitl:* unident.; described in *Florentine Codex*, Book XI, fol. 135v.

27. Corresponding Spanish text: *"los grandes pueden beuer della, como cantidad, de vn quartillo, y los muchachos como cantidad de medio quartillo."*

28. *Aitztoli:* probably of genus *Cyperus* (Sahagún, *op. cit.*, IV, p. 320); described in *Florentine Codex*, Book XI, fol. 162v.

29. *Acad. Hist. MS*, in a marginal correction, prescribes substantially the same treatment for *quexilihuiliztli* (swelling of the groin), instead of for *xoteuconaviliztli*.

30. *Uei patli:* unident.; desc. in *Florentine Codex*, Book XI, fol. 161v.

SIXTH PARAGRAPH, which telleth of the medicines to cure one when wounded, or to set broken bones.

If someone breaks a leg, it is cured in this way. *Acocotli*[1] root is added to nopal root, [and] they are ground. They are placed there where the leg is broken. And when they are placed on, then [the leg] is wrapped with a cloth bandage. And on four sides splints are pressed, tightly bound, tied with cords. And when it has been tied with cords, then the blood comes out[2] where it is swollen. There between the great toe [and the second toe], there where the vessels join, it is bled in order that it may not worsen, [not] become festered. And after twenty days it is untied. When it has been untied, then a poultice of liquidambar, to which a powdered maguey [root][3] and lime have been added, is applied. And when the poultice[4] has been applied, then when his leg [is] strong, when it becomes whole, a hot bath is taken.

If someone has dislocated his leg or his arm, first his leg or his arm is pressed; [then] it is stretched. And then the medicine called *cococpatli*[5] with lampblack is applied. Either two or three or four times it is applied to effect a cure. And if it is seen that it becomes worse, that it is inflamed, then it is quickly bled there where the leg is wrenched or the arm dislocated, in order that it will not swell, [not] become inflamed.

If one has wrenched his neck, first his neck is massaged, relaxed, straightened there where it is wrenched. When it has been stretched, then one quickly drinks [an infusion of] the cooling *coaxiuitl*[6] [herb]. Twice or three times one drinks it. It distributes, circulates, the blood in order not to damage his heart. And later one is to be bled with an obsidian blade there where it is wrenched, perhaps on the left side, so that it will not swell. And one is bled on a vessel of the head.

If someone has a head wound, first the blood is quickly washed away with hot urine. And when it has been washed, then hot maguey sap is squeezed

INJC CHIQUACEN PARRAPHO: itechpa tlatoa, in patli, injc pati in açaca oqujvitecque, in anoce opuztec omjtl, injc monanamjctia.

Intla aca mocxipoztequj: iehoatl ic pati, in acocotli ineloaio, monamjctia, in jneloaio nopalli moteci, vncã vnmotema, in vncan omocxipuztec: auh in vnmotecac, çatepan liençotica moqujmjloa. Auh nauhcampa, in moquappachoa, moteteujlpia, momecaicuja: auh in vmomecaicujx, çatepan qujca in eztli, in oitlacauh: vncan in toveixopil itzalan, in vncan nepanjvi ezcocotli, vncan in moçoz, injc amo tlanaviz, palanjz: auh cempoalilvitica in motoma: in omoton, catepan ocutzotica mopotonja, monamjctia in metl, mocoxonja, ioan tenextli: auh in omototonj, çatepan motema: iquac in ie chicaoac, in ie qujvelmati, iicxi.

Intla aca omocxicuetlanj: in anoço omomacuetlanj, acachto mopachoa, moteteoanjlia in iicxi, in anoço ima: auh çatepan vnmotequjlia in patli, in moteneoa cococpatli, tlillo, aço vppa, anoço expa, anoço vel nappa in motequjlia, ic pati: auh intla motta, in tlanavi, in motleiotia: njman iciuhca moço, vncan, in canjn omocxinatzinj, in anoce vncan omomacuetlanj, injc amo poçaoaz palanjz.

Intla aca omoquechnatzinj: achto mopapachoa, moiamanjlia, motitioana in jquech, in vncan omoquechnatzinj, in jquac omotititz noviian: njman içiuhca qujtiuetzi itztic, in coaxivitl, aço vppa, anoço expa in conj, qujmoiaoa, qujtemovia in eztli, injc amo qujtlacoz iiollo: auh çatepan mjtzmjnaz, vncan in campa ie: oitlacauh, in aço iiopuchcopa, injc amo poçaoaz: auh iehoatl ipan moçoz in totzontecon iezcocoio.

Intla aca oquacoionjloc: achtopa mopaqujlitiuetziz in eztli, ica totonquj axixtli, auh in omopaqujli, niman vncan vnmopatzca in meolli, totonquj: auh in

1. *Acocotli: Arracacia atopurpurea* Benth. & Hook.; *"una especie de* Ligusticum *de la familia de las* Umbelíferas"; *Dahlia variabilis* Desf.; or *Euphorbia hypreicifolia* Linn. (Hernández, *op. cit.,* I, pp. 25–29); *Lagenaria vulgaris* var. or *Pentacripta purpurea* Cav. (Santamaría, *op. cit.,* I, p. 35). See also Emmart, *op. cit.,* p. 305.

2. Corresponding Spanish text: *"la sangrança."* — *Qujca:* read *qujça.*

3. Cf. *ibid.* — *Catepan:* read *çatepan.*

4. *Tomototoni:* read *omopotoni,* as in *Acad. Hist. MS.*

5. *Cococpatli:* perhaps *Bocconia frutescens* (cf. § 5, n. 24, *supra*).

6. *Coaxiuitl: Lythrum alatum* Pursh. (Hernández, *op. cit.,* II, p. 601). — Corresponding Spanish text: *"la yerua, que es muy fria, que se llama coaxivitl."*

161

thereon. When it has been squeezed out on the place where the head is wounded, then once again maguey sap, to which are added [the herb] called *matlalxiuitl*[7] and lampblack with salt stirred in, is placed on it. And when [this] has been placed on, then it is quickly wrapped in order that the air will not enter there, and so it heals. And if one's flesh is inflamed, [this medicine] is placed on two or three times. But if one's flesh is not inflamed, this medicine which has been mentioned is placed on only once and for all. And when it quickly heals over, then a poultice is finally applied.

When they stab someone or strike him with metal or with a club, he is cured in the same manner as mentioned.

If someone is struck with a lash or a stick, when his flesh swells, or his flesh is much covered by welts, then *poçaualizpatli*[8] is smeared on just once. And when one is cured, then he is introduced into the sweat bath. And there one drinks [an infusion of the root of] *iztac patli, chichipiltic,* and a little chili, [or one drinks it] in white maguey wine to cure, to circulate, the blood.

If someone falls, striking himself, if perhaps he falls crashing or falls striking his chest, he should quickly drink hot urine and quickly ingest four ground, uncooked lizards, drinking them in the urine. And lampblack is mixed with this. And afterwards he drinks [an infusion of] a collection of herbs which [are] very acid: *mecoatl*[9] and *macoçauhqui,*[10] and then *tlapalezquauitl* and *yichcatic.*[11] And blood is drawn; the heart vessel is bled in order that a major ailment may not occur later; perhaps he might grow thin; his stomach might swell; he might spit blood or just go about coughing.

And as medicine for constant coughing, or when one spits blood, he drinks [an infusion of the root of] *coçauicpatli,*[12] which is to be well boiled. But he

vnmopatzcac, in vncan oquacoionjloc: njman oc ceppa onmotequjlia in meolli, monamjctia, in moteneoa matlalxivitl, tlilli moneloa, ioan iztatl: auh in vnmotequjli, njman iciuhca moqujmjloa, injc amo vncan calaqujz ehecatl, auh ic oalnacatemj: auh intla aca tleio inacaio, vppa, anoço expa vnmotequjlia: auh in amo tleio inacaio, çan ceppa in moteca, inin patli vnmoteneuh, çan iccen: auh in ie nexeoativitz, njman ic mopotonja ça iccen.

In aca quĵxili: anoço qujvitequj tepuztica, anoço quauhtica: çan ie no ie ic pati, in vnmoteneuh.

Intla aca ovitecoc mecatica: anoço tlacotica, in poçaoa inacaio, in anoço vel ipaleoa inacaio: njman ic môça, in poçaoalizpatli, çan ceppa: auh in opatic, njman ic calaquj, in temazcalco, auh vmpa conj in jztac patli, in chichipiltic, ioan achiton chilli, iztac vctli ipan, ic pati, ic moiaoa in eztli.

Intla aca motlaujtequj: in aço mocoxonjtiuetzi, in anoço melhujtectiuetzi: iciuhca conjtiuetziz axixtli totonquj, ioan motemôtiuetzi navintin cuecuetzpaltin, moxoxouhcateçi ipan conj in axixtli: auh inin tlilli moneloa, auh çatepan conj, in tlanechicolli in cenca chichic, iehoatl in mecoatl, ioan macoçauhquj: auh niman ieehoatl in tlapalezquavitl, ioan yichcatic, auh qujçaz in eztli, iehoatl in moçoz, in toiollo imecaio, inic amo çatepan vei cocoliztli mocuepaz, aço quâoaqujz, itipoçaoaz, eztli qujchichaz, in anoço çan tlatlaztinemjz:

auh injc pati in totolcatinemj, in anoço eztli qujchicha: conjz in coçavicpatli, moquaqualatzaz, auh ça iamanquj in conj, aço vppa, expa in quj: auh intlaca

7. *Matlalxiuitl: matlalxochitl?* (*Comelina* sp. — Emmart, *op. cit.,* p. 220); cf. also Sahagún, *op. cit.,* IV, p. 341. Reccho, *op. cit.,* p. 385 (*matlalxiuitl*) — "Truncus videtur parum spinosus & viridis; ramuli Lentisco sunt similes, nouenis binorum foliorum oppositorum constantes ordinibus: vltimum tamen solum vni ferè adnatū, folia etiā adhaerent latitudine quadam vt in Lentisco: Vascula sunt coloris carnei; flosculi caerulei coloris qualis in Gentianis conspicitur."

8. *Poçaualizpatli:* composed of various herbs (Sahagún, *op. cit.,* IV, p. 349). A plant so named is found in Reccho, *op. cit.,* p. 398 — "Vesicula Lychnidi similis, florem continet flauum quatuor foliorum." In von Gall, *op. cit.,* p. 278, the current term pozual is tentatively suggested (*Croton cortesianus*).

9. *Mecoatl:* maguey root (*mecual*) or maguey bud or shoot (*mecuate*) — Santamaría, *op. cit.,* II, p. 266.

10. *Macoçauhqui:* unident.

11. *Yichcatic: ichcayo?* — cf. § 1, n. 41, *supra.*

12. *Coçauicpatli:* unident. — *Cozahuico?* (*Achras zapota* — Standley, *op. cit.,* Pt. 4, p. 1120); *cosahuico?* (*Sideroxylon capiri* — *ibid.,* p. 1123). *Coçauhcapatli* is described in Reccho, *op. cit.,* p. 372 — "Radix Napi castanea, vt & rami: fructus strias habet quatuor, colore ex viridi in castaneum tendente."

drinks it only tepid; he drinks two or three times. And if this does not cure, if his stomach swells, if in spite of it he grows thin, then at once he is to drink a purgative, and is to be given an enema to be cured.

The above was examined [by] the Mexican physicians whose names follow:[13]

Juan Pérez, of San Pablo

Pedro Pérez, of San Juan

Pedro Hernández, of San Juan

José Hernández, of San Juan

Miguel Garciá, of San Sebastián

Francisco de la Cruz, [of] Xiuitonco

Baltasar Juárez, of San Sebastián

Antonio Martínez, of San Juan

vel pati, intla ie itipoçaoa, intlanoce ic quâoaquj: njman iciuhca conjz in tlanoqujlonj, ioan icujtlapampa momacaz ic patiz.

Lo sobredicho fue examjnado: los medicos mexicanos, cuyos nombres se siguen.

Ioan perez, de sanct Pablo.

Pedro perez, de sanct Joan.

Pedro hernandez, de san Joan.

Joseph hernandez, de san Ioan.

Miguel garcia, de san Sebastian.

fran.co de la Cruz, xivitonco.

Balthasar Juarez, de san Sebastian.

Antonjo martinez, de san Ioan.

---

13. *Acad. Hist. MS.: Yehoantin hin yn oquicxitocaque yn hin ticiamatl mochintī mexica.*

Twenty-ninth Chapter, which telleth of the various kinds of people, the people who dwelt everywhere here in the land; those who arrived, who came to settle, who came to cause the cities to be founded.

IN THIS PARAGRAPH, here, the Tolteca[1] are mentioned, the first who settled here in the land; who [were] like the inhabitants of Babylon, wise, learned, experienced.

First, those named the Tolteca, so-called: these first came to live here in the land, called land of the Mexica, land of the Chichimeca. And for several four-hundreds of years they dwelt in the vicinity of Tollantzinco. Since they really lived there, they left many of their traces which they had fashioned. In that area they made what was their temple; its name was "house of beams." Today it stands; it exists, considering that it is indestructible; for it is of rock, of stone.

Then there they went — they went to live, to dwell on the banks of a river at Xicocotitlan, now called Tula. Because verily they there resided together, they there dwelt, so also many are their traces which they produced. And they left behind that which today is there, which is to be seen, which they did not finish — the so-called serpent column, the round stone pillar made into a serpent. Its head rests on the ground; its tail, its rattles are above. And the Tolteca mountain is to be seen; and the Tolteca pyramids, the mounds, and the surfacing of Tolteca [temples]. And Tolteca potsherds are there to be seen. And Tolteca bowls, Tolteca ollas are taken from the earth. And many times Tolteca jewels — arm bands, esteemed green stones,[2] fine turquoise, emerald-green jade[3] — are taken from the earth.

And these Tolteca were called Chichimeca. There [was] no real word for their name. Their name is taken from — it comes from — their manner of life, their works.[4] The Tolteca were wise. Their works

Injc cempoalli vnchicunavi capitulo: itechpa tlatoa in nepapan tlaca, in novian tlaca, in onoque in njcan tlalli ipan, in ecoque, in tlacapixoco in tlaaltepetilico.

IN JPAN JN PARRAPHO: vncan moteneoa, in tulteca, in achto tlacapixoco, in njcan tlalli ipan: in iuhqujma babylonja tlaca, in mjmatinj in tlamatinjme, in jxtlamatque./.

Inic centlamantli: intoca tolteca, iuh mjtoa: iehoantin achto nemjco, in njcan tlalli ipan in mjtoa mexicatlalpan, in chichimeca tlalpan: auh quezqujtzonxivitl nenque, in vmpa tullantzinco, in ca nelli vmpa nenque: mjec innezca qujtlaliteoaque, in vmpa qujchiuhque in jntevpan catca, in jtoca oapalcalli: in axcan caca ca manj: tel injc avel polivi, ca tetl ca texcalli:

njman vmpa iaque, vmpa nemjto, njman vmpa nenque in atoiatenco, in xicocotitlan: in axcan motocaiotia tulla, in ca nelli vmpa cemonoca, vmpa nenque: ca no mjec in jnnezca, in qujchiuhque: auh in qujcauhteoaque, in axcã ca onoc, ca itto, in amo qujtzonqujxtitiaque, in mjtoa coatlaquetzalli: in temjmjlli coatl mochioa, ytzontecon tlalpan tlacçaticac, icujtlapil, in jcuech in aco ca: auh ca itto in tolteca tepetl, auh ca onoc in tolteca tzaqualli, in tlatilli. auh in tolteca tlaquilli, auh onoc in tolteca tapalcatl itto: auh ano in tlalla in tolteca caxitl, in tolteca comjtl: auh mjecpa ano in tlallan, in tolteca cozcatl, in macuextli in maviztic, in chalchiujtl, in teuxivitl, in quetzalitztli.

Auh injque in tulteca: ca mochichimecaitoa, atle vel cencamatl intoca: çan intech man, intech qujz, in jntoca, in jnnemjliz, in jntlachioal injc tolteca, mjmatinj, mochi qualli, mochi iectli, mochi mjmati, mochi

---

1. To maintain consistency within this chapter, names of populations elsewhere anglicized (Toltec, Chichimec, etc.) are left in the form in which they appear in the Nahuatl text.

2. *Chalchiuitl:* "Common jade of green and white color," according to William F. Foshag: "Mineralogical Studies on Guatemalan Jade," *Smithsonian Miscellaneous Collections*, Vol. 135, No. 5 (Washington: Smithsonian Institution, 1957), p. 8.

3. Cf. *loc. cit.;* also Emmart, *op. cit.,* p. 280.

4. Corresponding Spanish text: "*Estos dichos tultecas todos se nombrauan chichimecas, y no tenjã otro nombre particular, sino el que tomaron de la curiosidad, y primor de las obras que hazian, que se llamarõ tultecas, que es tanto como si dixessemos officiales pulidos, y curiosos, como aora los de flandes.*"

were all good, all perfect, all wonderful, all marvelous; their houses beautiful, tiled in mosaics, smoothed, stuccoed, very marvelous.

Wherefore was it called a Tolteca house? It was built with consummate care, majestically designed; it was the place of worship of their priest, whose name was Quetzalcoatl; it was quite marvelous. It consisted of four [abodes].[5] One was facing east; this was the house of gold. For this reason was it called house of gold: that which served as the stucco was gold plate applied, joined to it.[6] One was facing west, toward the setting sun; this was the house of green stone, the house of fine turquoise. For this reason was it called the house of green stone, the house of fine turquoise: what served as the stucco within the house was an inlay of green stones, of fine turquoise. One was facing south, toward the irrigated lands; this [was] the house of shells or of silver. That which served as the stucco, the interior of the walls, seemed as if made of these shells inlaid. One was facing north, toward the plains, toward the spear house; this [was] the red [house], red because red shells were inlaid in the interior walls, or those [stones] which were precious stones, were red.[7]

And there was the house of feathers. That which served as the stucco within the house was a covering of feathers. It also consisted of four [abodes. One] was facing east. Within the house, applied to the wall surface, was a covering of yellow feathers, such as parrot feathers; and all was yellow, of very yellow feathers. And [one] was facing west, toward what is called the sun's setting-place; it was called the house of precious feathers. For this reason was it called the house of quetzal feathers, the house of blue cotinga feathers: they placed — they pasted — the quetzal feathers, the blue cotinga feathers, to capes or nets [and] then hung them on the wall. Hence was it called house of quetzal feathers. And the house of white plumes was facing south, toward the irrigated lands, and it was called the white house. For this reason was it called the white house: of white feathers was the covering of the house walls, and that which was white was feathers, such as eagle feathers. And [one] was facing north, toward the plains, toward the spear house. Also red was the covering of feathers, such as the red spoonbill, the red arara, etc.

maviztic in jntlachioal, qualli in jncal, tlaxiuhçalolli, tlatlachictli, tlatlaquilli, vel maviztic:

canmach mjto in tulteca calli? vel tlatlamachtlalilli, vellatoltecavilli, in jtlateumatian catca, in jnteupixcauh catca, in jtoca quetzalcoatl, vellamaviçolli catca. Nauhtemanca: centetl tlapcopa itzticaca, injn teucujtlacalli, injc mjtoa teucuitlacalli, in tlaquilli povia: iehoatl in coztic teocujtlatl, tlatemantli, tlaçalolli. Centetl çioatlampa itzticaca: in tonatiuh icalaqujampa, injn chalchiuhcalli, teuxiuhcalli: injc mjtoa chalchiuhcalli, teuxiuhcalli, chalchiujtl, teuxivitl: in tlaçalolli caliticpa, in tlaquilli povi: centetl vitztlampa, amjlpampa itzticaca: injn teccizcalli, anoço iztac teucujtlatl, in tlaquilli povia: in caliticpa tepantli mochiuhtoca, iehoatl in tecciztli tlaçalolli. Centetl mjctlampa, teutlalpampa, tlacochcalcopa itzticaca: injn tlatlauhquj, injc tlatlauhquj: iehoatl in tapachtli, tlaçalolli, in caliticpa tepamjtl, in anoço in tlein tlaçotli tetl, tlatlauhquj.

Ioan vnmanca in ivicalli: ivitica in tlatzontli, calitic, in tlaqujlli povi: no nauhtemanca, in tlapcopa itzticaca, coztiqujvitica, in tlatzontli catca, in calitic icaltechio, in iuhquj toztli, ioan in ie mochi in tlein coztic, in vel icucic hivitl. Auh in çioatlampa itzticaca: in mjtoa tonatiuh icalaqujampa, mjtoaia quetzalcalli: injc mjtoa quetzalcalli, xiuhtotocalli, tilmatitech, anoço matlatitech qujtecaia, qujçaloaia in quetzalli, in xiuhtototl: njman caltech qujçoaia, ic mjtoa quetzalcalli. Auh in vitztlampa in amjlpampa itzticaca: aztatzoncalli, ioan mjtoa aztacalli, injc mjtoa aztacalli, iztac hivitl inic tlatzontli in caltechtli, ioan in tlein ticeoac hivitl: in iuhquj quauhhivitl. Auh in mjctlampa, in teutlalpampa, in tlacochcalcopa itzticaca, no tlatlauhquj in hivitl ic tlatzontli, in iuhquj tlauhquechol cueçali. Etc.

---

5. *Ibid.: "aposentos."*
6. *Ibid.: "en lugar del encalado tenja oro, en planchas, y muy sotilmĕte enclauado."*
7. *Ibid.: "era de pedreria colorada, y jaspes y conchas, muy adornado."*

Very many were the marvelous houses which they made. The house of Quetzalcoatl, which was his place of worship, stood in the water; a large river passed by it; the river which passed by Tula. There stood that which was the bathing place of Quetzalcoatl, called "In the Waters of Green Stones" [Chalchiuapan].[8] Many houses stood within the earth where the Tolteca left many things buried.

And these, the traces of the Tolteca, their pyramids, their mounds, etc., not only appear there at the places called Tula [and] Xicocotitlan, but practically everywhere they rest covered; for their potsherds, their ollas, their pestles, their figurines, their arm bands appear everywhere. Their traces are everywhere, because the Tolteca were dispersed all over.

The Tolteca were skilled; it is said that they were feather workers [who] glued feathers. In ancient times they took charge of the gluing of feathers; and it was really their discovery, for in ancient times they used the shields, the devices, those called *apanecaiotl*, which were their exclusive property. When the wonderful devices were entrusted to them, they prepared, they glued the feathers; they indeed formed works of art; they performed works of skill. In truth, they invented all the wonderful, precious, marvelous things which they made.

And in this way were the Tolteca learned: they knew well, they understood well, that which pertained to herbs, to the nature of their essence; which ones were good, which esteemed, and which of them were just plants, which ones bad, evil, harmful, or really deadly.

They invented the art of medicine. The old men Oxomoco, Cipactonal, Tlaltetecui, Xochicaoaca, were Tolteca. They were the wise men who discovered, who knew of, medicine; who originated the medical art.

So learned were they [that] they were the ones who, for the first time, discovered, found, and, for the first time, used the green stones, fine turquoise, [common] turquoise, then common obsidian, the emerald-green jade — all kinds of wondrous precious stones.

Because of great knowledge [of rocks], if, verily, that which was a precious stone were inside a massive rock, they could find it; and if a wonderful precious stone were somewhere in the earth, they could find it.

Vel mjec in maviztic qujchiuhque calli: ca atlan in jcac ical quetzalcoatl, in jtlatevmatian catca: ypan qujzticac in vei atl, in atoiatl in qujzticac tulla, vnca in jcaca, in jnealtiaian catca Quetzalcoatl: in mjtoa chalchioapan, mjec in tlalla in hicac calli, in vncan tlatlatlatocatiaque, in iehoantin tulteca.

Auh injn: amo çanjo vmpa in neci, in jnnezca tulteca. in jntzaqual, in jntlatil. Etc. in vmpa mjtoa tulla, in xicocotitlan: çan vel novian in quitzacutimanj, ca novian neci: in jntapalcauh, in jncō, in jntexolouh, in jnneneuh, in jncoconeuh, in jnmacuex: novian ca in jnnezca: ipampa ca cenmantoca in iehoantin tulteca.

Mimatia tulteca: mjtoa amanteca catca, hiviçaloque: ca ieppa qujpia, ioan nel iehoantin intlanextil, in hiviçaloliztli: ipampa ieppa qujtitlanj in chimalli, in tlaviztli, in mjtoa, apanecaiotl: ça ie vel iehoan intlatquj, in omotitlanja tlaviztli, in maviztic, qujchioaia, qujçaloaia in hivitl, vel amanteca tlaliaia, vel qujtoltecaujaia: nelli mach in qujiolteuviaia, vel mochi maviztic, tlaçotli, tlamaviçoltic in qujchioaia.

Ioan tlaiximatinj catca: injc iehoantin tulteca, ca uel qujmatia, vel quiximatia, in tlein itech caca xivitl, in quenâamj yhiio, in catle qualli, in catle iectli, in catle tlaçotli: auh catleoatl in çaça ie xivitl, catle in aqualli, in aiectli. in teitlaco, in anoço vel nelli mjcoanj.

Ca iehoatl qujnextique in tiçiotl, ca tulteca catca in veuetque in oxomoco, in çipactonal, in tlaltetecuj, in xochicaoaca, in tlamatinj catca: in qujtztiaque, in qujximattiaque patli, in qujpeoaltitiaque ticiotl.

Injc cenca vellaiximatinj catca: iehoantin iancujcā qujnextique, iancujcan qujttaque: auh iancujcan qujtitlanque in chalchivitl, in teuxivitl, in xivitl: njman tlalitztli. in quetzalitztli, in ie ixquich nepapan tlaçotli tetl in maviztic.

Injc cenca vellaiximatia: intla nel vei tetl iitic ca, in tlein tlaçotli tetl, vel quittaia: auh intla nel tlallan cana ca in tlaçotli, in maviztic tetl, vel qujttaia:

---

8. See also *chalchiuhapan* in Sahagún (Garibay ed.), IV, p. 332.

It is said they found it in this manner: when [it was] still dark, they came forth; they placed themselves somewhere on a high place; they placed themselves facing the sun. And when the sun came up, they took great care to look carefully in all directions, they say, in order to see by means of wet earth where the precious stones were in the ground. And when the sun shone, especially when it appeared, they say, a little smoke, a little mist, arose there where the precious stone was, either in the ground or within a rock. When they saw it, it was as if the rock were smoking.[9]

So is the account, so is their tradition, that they went to find a mine of the rock named turquoise. So the old men went on to say that at Tepotzotlan is a mountain by the name of Xiuhtzone; that there is a mine of turquoise, of fine turquoise. They took it; they removed it therefrom. And they took it there to the river where they washed it; there they cleaned it. Thus is the place called "Where Turquoise Is Washed" [Xippacoia], which has now become the name of a city near Tula. Furthermore, there is accord that they arrived right in Amantlan, in Tula; indeed many of them were scribes, lapidaries, carpenters, stone cutters, masons, feather workers, feather gluers, potters, spinners, weavers. They were very learned. They discovered, they knew of green stones, fine turquoise, common turquoise, the turquoise lands. They went to learn of, to seek out, the mines of silver, gold, copper, tin, mica, lead. They went to learn of all of them. They went to seek all the mines of amber, of rock crystal, of amethyst; they went to marvel at the pearls, the opals.[10] All which now exists was their discovery — the necklaces, the arm bands. Of that which is precious, however, some is forgotten, some lost.

And these Tolteca were very wise; they were thinkers, for they originated the year count, the day count; they established the way in which the night, the day, would work; which day sign was good, favorable; and which was evil, the day sign of wild beasts. All their discoveries formed the book for interpreting dreams.

And so wise were they [that] they understood the stars which were in the heavens; they gave them names and understood their influence. And they understood well the movements of the heavens; their

quilmach injc qujttaia. oc ioac in qujçaia, cana tlacpac in motlaliaia, qujxnamjctimotlaliaia in tonatiuh: auh in jquac ie oalqujça tonatiuh, vel imjx intequjuh, nelli mach in mjxpepetza, qujl inic qujtta, in canjn ca tlallan tlaçotetl, tlacuechaoatica: auh in jquac oalpetzinj tonatiuh, oc cenca iquac in oalmomana, qujl poctontli, aiauhtontli moquetzticac: in vncan ca tlaçotetl, in aço tlallan, in anoço tetl iitic in qujtta, iuhquin popocatica tetl.

Iuh ca tlatlatolli, iuh ca in jnenonotzallo, in tetl in jtoca xivitl, ca qujtztivi in jtepeio, in joztoio: iuh conjtotivi in veuetque, in tepotzotlan ca tepetl in jtoca xiuhtzone, ca itepeio, ca ioztoio in xiuitl, in teuxivitl: vncan qujcuja, vncan qujqujxtiaia: auh vmpa qujtquja in atoiac, in vm compacaia, vmpa conchipaoaia: ic motocaioti xippacoia: in axcan itoca mochiuhtica in altepetl, in jnaoac tulla. çaçan njman ie ic mocemjtoa, vel acique in amantlan, in tulla. vel centzomme, ca tlacujloque, tlatecque, tlaxinque, tetzotzonque, tlaqujlque, amanteca, tlaçaloque, çoqujchiuhque, tzauhque, iqujtque. Vellaiximatinj catca: qujnextique, qujximatque in chalchivitl, in teuxivitl, in çan xivitl, in xiuhtlalli, qujximattivi, qujtztivi in joztoio, in jtepeio, in jztac teucujtlatl, in coztic teucujtlatl, in tepuztli, in amochitl, in metzcujtlatl, in temetztli: mochi qujximattivi, mochi qujtztivi in joztoio, in apoçonalli, in tevilotl, in tlapaltevilotl: mochi qujmaviçotivi in epiollotli, in vitzitziltetl, mochi iehoantin intlaiximach, in axcan nemj cozcatl, macuextli, in tlein tlaçotli: iece oc cequj ilcauh, oc cequj poliuh.

In iehoantin in tulteca: vellamatinj catca, vel moiolnonotzanj catca: ca iehoantin qujpeoaltitiaque, in cexiuhtlapoalli, in tonalpoalli, iehoantin qujtlatlalitiaque in quenjn tlaiaz ceioal, cemjlhujtl, tlê tonalli, catli qualli, catli iectli: auh catli in amo qualli, in mjtoa, tequantonalli: mochi iehoan intlatlalil mochiuh, in temjcamatl:

auh injc tlamatinj catca, qujmjximatia in ilhujcac onoque cicitlalti, qujntocamacaque: auh qujmatia in jmjhiio: auh vel qujmatia in quen iauh in ilhujcatl in quenjn momalacachoa, intech qujttaia in cicitlalti:

9. See the more detailed account in Book XI of the *Florentine Codex*, cap. viii.
10. Cf. Foshag, *op. cit.*, p. 48.

orbits they learned from the stars. And they understood that there were many divisions of the heavens; they said there were twelve divisions. There existed, there dwelt, the true god and his consort. The name of the god of the heavens was Ome tecutli, and the name of his consort, the woman of the heavens, was Ome cihuatl; that is to say, they were lords, they were rulers, over the twelve heavens. It was said that there were we, the common people, created; thence came our souls.[11] When babies were conceived, when they dropped [from heaven], their souls came from there; they entered into their [mother's] wombs. Ome tecutli sent them.

These Tolteca were righteous. They were not deceivers. Their words [were] clear words. They addressed one as "the lord, my elder brother; the lord, my younger brother." They said: "It is true; so is it; it is certain; yes; no."

Their food was that which is now used — maize, grains of maize. It was produced in abundance — green, blue, jade, turquoise [colored maize] with which to make purchases.

Their clothing was — indeed their privilege was — the blue knotted cape;[12] their sandals were painted blue, light blue, sky blue. Also light blue were their sandal thongs.[13]

They were tall; they were larger [than the people today]. Because they were very tall, they ran much and so were named *tlanquacemilhuime*.[14]

They went about using the ground drum, the rattle stick. They were singers; they composed, originated, knew from memory, invented the wonderful songs which they composed.

They were very devout. Only one was their god; they showed all attention to, they called upon, they prayed to one by the name of Quetzalcoatl. The name of one who was their minister, their priest, [was] also Quetzalcoatl. This one was very devout. That which the priest of Quetzalcoatl required of them, they did well. They did not err, for he said to them, he admonished them: "There is only one god; [he is] named Quetzalcoatl. He requireth nothing; you shall offer him, you shall sacrifice before him only serpents, only butterflies." All people obeyed the divine

auh qujmatia, ca mjec tlamantli in ilhujcatl, qujtoaia: ca matlactlanepanolli vmome, vmpa ca, vmpa nemj in nelli teutl: ioan in jnamjc in jlhujcateutl, itoca vmetecutli: auh in jnamic itoca vme cioatl, ilhujcacioatl, qujtoznequj: matlactlomvmepan ilhujcatecuti, tlatocati: mjtoaia vmpa tiiocoelo in timaceoalti, vmpa vitz in totonal: in jquac motlalia, in jquac chipinj piltzintli, vmpa oallauh in jntonal, imjtic calaquj: qujoalioa in vme tecutli.

Injque in tulteca: vel melaoaque catca, amo iztlacatinj catca, in jntlatol naoatlatolli: qujmolhujaia, teutl nachcauh, teutl njccauh: qujtoaia ca nelli ca iuhca, ca neltitica, quemaca, ca amo,

in jntlaqual catca, iehoatl in axcan nemj tonacaiotl, in tlaolli, vel qujmotonaltiaia, in xoxouhquj, in qujltic, chalchivitl, xivitl, injc tlacoaia:

in intlaquen catca, vel itonal catca, ixiuhtlalpilli, in jncac tlaxivicujlolli, xoxoctic, xoxouhquj: çanno xoxouhquj in jncacmecaiouh.

Quaquauhtique catca: oc achi tlacaviaque catca, injc cenca quaquauhtique catca, cenca painaia: ic motocaiotique, tlanquacemjlhujme.

Qujtitlantivi in vevetl, in aiacachtli, cujcanjme catca, qujpiquja, qujçaloaia, qujlnamjquja, qujioltevujaia in cujcatl: maviztic in qujpiquja.

Vellatevmatinj catca, ca ça ce in jnteouh qujcemmatia, in qujnotzaia, in qujtlatlauhtiaia, in jtoca quetzalcoatl, in jntlamacazcauh catca, in jnteupixcauh: çan no itoca quetzalcoatl: auh inin cenca vellateumatinj catca, in tlein qujmjlhujaia in teupixque, in quetzalcoatl, vel qujchioaia, amo qujtlacoaia, ca qujmjlhuj, qujnnonotz: ca ça cen teutl itoca quetzalcoatl, atle qujnequj, çan coatl, çan papalotl in anqujmacazque: in jxpan anqujmjctizque mochi qujchiuhque, in jteunaoatil teupixquj: Auh injc cenca vel qujneltocaia, in inteupixcauh in quetzalcoatl, ioan injc cenca tetlaca-

11. Corresponding Spanish text: "*de alla venja la influēcia y calor con que se engendrauan: los njños o njñas en el viētre de sus madres.*" For *totonal*, Siméon, *op. cit.*, gives *notre âme, notre esprit, l'âme, l'esprit en general*.

12. Read *in xiuhtlalpilli*. Corresponding Spanish text: "*Ropa o māta que tenja alacranes pintados de azul.*"

13. These colors are green to blue-green. Here we follow the corresponding Spanish text.

14. *Ibid.: "que quiere dezir, que corriā ȳ dia entero sin cansarse.*"

command of the priest. And they had very great faith in the priest of Quetzalcoatl and were very obedient, very devout, and very reverent; for all obeyed, all had faith in Quetzalcoatl when he led them from Tula. He caused all to move, to depart, even though they were settled there, even though very marvelous were the temples, the palaces situated at Tula.

And as the Tolteca were spread over all parts and although they were very rich, they departed, they moved; they left their houses, their lands, their cities, their wealth. Since they could not carry all, they buried it. The property of these Tolteca is removed; it is to be seen in places.

And as they had great faith in Quetzalcoatl, they made every effort to remove their women, their children, their sick. The old men, the old women departed; they moved. No one failed to obey; all moved when Topiltzin Quetzalcoatl went to enter into the water at Tlapallan, where he went to disappear.

These Tolteca, as is said, were Nahua; they did not speak a barbarous tongue. However, their language they called Nonoalca. They said as they conversed: "My noble lord; my lord younger brother; my lord elder brother." [15]

They were rich. By reason of their prudence they caused their goods to appear quickly. Thus it is now said of him who quickly gains goods that he is a son of Quetzalcoatl, that he is Quetzalcoatl's son.

And their hair style was cut after the manner of the Nonoalca; they fashioned their hair style like the Nonoalca; they shaved the hair over their foreheads.[16] And these also went by the name of Chichimeca; it is said they were named Tolteca Chichimeca. This is all which is here said as to the nature of those mentioned, who first came to settle here in the land called Mexico.

Still, here a little more needs to be told concerning the Tolteca. All the Nahua, those who speak clearly, not the speakers of a barbarous tongue, are the descendants of the Tolteca, for they are those who remained, those who could no longer migrate; perhaps the old men, perchance the old women, the sick, the recently delivered, those who perhaps for some reason remained of their own will.

THIS PARAGRAPH telleth of the different kinds of Chichimeca who dwelt here in this land.

matinj catca, injc cenca tlatevmatinj, ioan cenca tevimacacjnj catca: ca mochintin qujtlacamatque, mochintin qujneltocaque, in quetzalcoatl: in iquac qujnoalqujxti tulla, mochintin qujmolinj, qujnquetz: macivin vel chan onoca, macivin vellamaviçolli in teucalli, in tecpancalli onoca tulla:

ioan injc novian cenmantoca tulteca, ioan macivi in vel mocujltonotoca, ca moquetzque, ca olinque: qujcauhque in jncal in jntlal, in jmauh, in jntepeuh in jnnecujltonol: ca amo vel mochi qujtqujque, ca qujtocatiaque, ca ano can itto, in jntlatoc, iehoantin tulteca:

auh inic cenca qujneltocaque in quetzalcoatl, ca intlan acque, ca qujmacocque in inçioaoan, in jnpilhoan, in jncocuxcaoan, moquetzque, molinjque, in veventzitzin, in jlamatzitzin: aiac in maca tlatlacama, mochintin olinque, injc ia, inic calac, in atl iitic, in tlapallan, in vmpa polivito: in iehoatzin topiltzin quetzalcoatl.

Injque in tulteca: in iuh mjtoa, ca naoa catca, ca amo popolocaia: iece qujnonoalcaitoaia in jntlatol, qujtoaia injc monotza: nopiltzin teutl, teutl njccauh, teutl nachcauh:

mocujltonoanjme catca, in jpampa innezcaliliz iciuhca quinextiaia in jntlatquj. Ic mjtoa in axcan, in aqujn iciuhca qujnextia tlatqujtl, ca ipiltzin in quetzalcoatl: ca quetzalcoatl ipiltzin.

Auh in jnnexin catca, mononoalcaximaia, qujnonooalcatlaliaia in innexin, qujteteçoaia in jmjxquac. Auh injque in: no qujmotocaiotitivi chichimeca, mjtoa, motocaiotia, tulteca chichimeca. Çan vel ixqujch in njcan vnmjtoa: in jmjuhcatiliz, in mjtoa, achto nemjco: njcan in mjtoa mexicatlalpan.

Oc izca achiton, in no monequj mjtoz, in jntechcopa tulteca. In jxqujchtin naoatlaca: in naoatlatoa, in amo popoloca: ca innecauhcaiooan in tulteca, ca ieoantin in mocacauhtiaque, in aoc vel iaque in at ueuentzitzin, at ilamatzitzin, at cocuxque, at mjxiuhque, in at çaçan noço iniollocopa, motlalique.

INJN PARRAPHO: mjtoa, in quezquj tlamantin chichimeca, in onenque in njcan tlalli ipan.

15. Ibid.: "señor, señor hermano mayor, señor hermano menor."
16. Ibid.: "la manera de se cortar los cabellos era segun su vso polido, que trayan los cabellos desde la media cabeça atras y trayã el celebro atusado como a sobrepeyne."

Those called Chichimeca are of three kinds: the first are the Otomí; the second, those named Tamime; the third, those called Teochichimeca and Çacachichimeca.

The nature, the manner of life, of the Otomí will be told further on.

This name Tamin means "shooter of arrows." And these Tamime were only an offshoot, a branch, of the Teochichimeca, although[17] they were somewhat settled. They made their homes in caves, in gorges; in some places they established small grass huts and small corn fields. And they went mingling with the Mexica, or the Nahua, or the Otomí. There they heard the Nahuatl language, they spoke a little Nahuatl or Otomí, and in a measure they there learned a civilized way of life from them. Also they put on a few rags — tattered capes. Also in places they laid out small maize plots; they sowed them, they harvested them.

They were called Tamime, that is to say, "shooters of arrows," for they went bearing their bows; everywhere they went out hunting, shooting arrows. These were the vassals of some ruler, some nobleman, to whom belonged the land, the city, where they dwelt. Their tribute payments became that which they caught: rabbits, deer, serpents. And these understood very well the power, the essence, of the herbs, of the roots; the healing herbs, the deadly ones, those which dried one up [and] after much time killed one. And also they knew of the so-called *maçacoatl*.[18] They went about carrying their little reed baskets; they went among the houses selling medicinal herbs.

These[19] [were] without their hair cut. The men wore the hair covering them, parted in the middle, hanging long; likewise the women.

The Teochichimeca, that is to say, the real Chichimeca,[20] or extreme Chichimeca, and also those named Çacachichimeca, that is to say, those who lived on the grassy plains, in the forests — these were the ones who lived far away; they lived in the forests, the grassy plains, the deserts, among the crags.[21] These had their homes nowhere. They only went about traveling, wandering; they went about crossing the

In mjtoa chichimeca, etlamantin: injc centlamantin, iehoantin in otomj, injc vntlamantin, iehoantin in jntoca tamjme: injc etlamantin, iehoantin in mjtoa teuchichimeca: ioan mjtoa çacachichimeca.

In otomj inieliz in jnnemjliz njpa mjtoz.

Injn tocaitl tamjn: qujtoznequj tlamjnquj: auh injque in tamjme, çan in cotoncaoa, in vilteccaioan, in teuchichimeca: iece iene achi tlacaçiuhque, oztoc inchanchioa, texcalco, cana achiton qujtlalia inxacalton, ioan achiton inmil: auh qujnoalnelotinemj in mexica tlaca, manoço naoatlaca, in anoço otomj. vncan qujoalcaquj in naoatlatolli, achi naoatlatoa, anoço otontlatoa: ioan vncan tetech qujoalitta, in tlacanemjliziotl. No achitzitzin, tzotzomatzintli, tatapatzintli intech qujtlalia: no achi cana qujtlalia mjltontli, qujtoca, qujpixca.

Injc mjtoa tamjme, in qujtoznequj tlamjnque, çan intlavitol ietinemj: noviian qujztinemj, antinemj, tlamjntinemj. Injque in ca temacooalhoan, ca aca tlatoanj, aca pilli itech povi, in jtlalpan, in jaltepepan onoque: iehoatl intlacalaqujl mochioa, in caçi tochin, maçatl, coatl. Auh injque in, in vel mjec in qujximati, xivitl, tlanelhoatl in jchicaoaliz in jhiio, in patli, in mjcoanj, in quaoaconj, in vecauhtica temjcti: no ioan qujximati, in mjtoa: maçacoatl, intatanatoton ietinemj, in calla oalqujça, in oalpapanamaca:

in jquac in, atle innexin, in oqujchtin motzonquentia, moquaxeloltia motzonviaquilia; no iuhque in cioa.

In teuchichimeca, in qujtoznequj, vel nelli chichimeca, anoço molhuj chichimeca, in joan intoca çacachichimeca, in qujtoznequj, çacatla, quauhtla in nemj: ca iehoantin in vecanemj, in quauhtla, in çacatla, in jxtlaoacan in texcalla nemj: injque in, acan vel inchan, çan qujztinemj, çan otlatocatinemj, çan panotinemj, çaça ie vi in ie vi, in canjn inpan iooatiuh: vncan qujtemoa in oztotl, in texcalli, vncan cochi.

---

17. *Ye nê* in the *Acad. Hist. MS.*

18. *Constrictor constrictor mexicana,* according to Rafael Martín del Campo: "Ensayo de interpretación del Libro Undécimo de la Historia de Sahagún," *Anales del Instituto de Biología,* IX, Nos. 3, 4 (1938), p. 385. Dr. Martín del Campo identifies the three serpents called *maçacoatl* in Book XI.

19. Read *injā y* as in the *Acad. Hist. MS.*

20. Corresponding Spanish text: *"del todo barbaros."*

21. *Ibid.:* "hombres siluestres, eran los que habitauan lexos y apartados del pueblo por campos çabanas mõtes y cueuas."

171

streams; they only went here and there. Where night came upon them, there they sought a cave, a craggy place; there they slept.

These had their leaders, their rulers. That which they caught — were it a wild beast,[22] or bobcat;[23] perchance somewhere they shot an ocelot,[24] a wolf,[25] a mountain lion[26] — they gave its hide and its flesh [to the leader]; and a little additional meat, either rabbit meat or venison. In this way they furnished provisions for the house of the ruler. They presented all to him. Or their tribute became a bow, a long, slender dart — that is to say, an arrow.

The ruler of these had his house, a palace, perhaps a grass house, or only a straw hut or a cave in the cliffs. This ruler had a consort, a wife — only one; he had only one. These Chichimeca had spouses; each one had only one wife. They knew not polygyny. And thus they lived; each couple lived alone, not two couples together. Thus did they seek their sustenance.

So, it was said, there were no adulterers, because they went guarding their women with care. And an adulterer appeared very seldom, almost never. When [one was] discovered, then as many as the ruler governed were summoned, called by a crier. They took the adulterer and the woman before the ruler; he sentenced them. All his vassals assembled together by them somewhere on the desert. Each one shot them with four arrows as long as they still lived.

And the array, the clothing, of the ruler [consisted of] his cape, perhaps of lynx skins, or wild animal skins, or ocelot skins, or wolf, or puma skins, and what was called his squirrel[27] skin head piece, and his circular fan device of yellow parrot feathers.[28] And his wife also had her skin skirt, her skin shift — likewise all the women. [The men] always carried

Injque y, vnca inteiacancauh, vnca intlatocauh, in tlein caci, in aço tequanj, aço ocotochtli, aço cana qujpantilia ocelutl, cujtlachtli, mjztli: conmaca in jeoaio, ioan in jnacaio, ioan oc cequj itla nacatl, aço tochnacatl, aço maçanacatl: iuhqujn ic conjtacatia, in jchan in tlatoanj, mochi conjxpantilia: in anoço intlacalaqujl mochioa, in tlavitolli, in tlacochtli in pitzaoac, in qujtoznequj mjtl.

Injque y, in jntlatocauh: ca vnca ical, in tecpancalli, aço çacacalli, anoço çan xacalli, anoço texcalli oztotl: injn tlatoanj vnca inamjc, vnca içioauh ça ce çan qujxcavia. Injque yn chichimeca: in namjqueque, çan no cecenme in jncioaoa, amo qujximati in tlaomepializtli: auh inic nemj, çan in ceceltin in nemj: amo ovmentin momana, inic qujtemoa in incochca, inneuhca:

iuh mjtoa, amo motlaximanj: ipampa ca çan vel qujnpixtinemj, in jncioaoa: auh cenca çan quenman, cenca çan jca, in neci tetlaxinquj. In onez: njman monotza, motzatzilia, in jxquichtin, in quexqujchtin ce tlatoanj qujnpachoa, iixpan qujvica in tetlaxinquj in tlatoanj: ioan in cioatl qujntlatzontequjlia, in ixqujchtin imaceoalhoan, cana ixtlaoacan inca mocentlalia: mochi tlacatl nananavi ic qujnmjna in mjtl, çan ioioltimani.

Auh in jnechichioal tlatoanj, in jtlaquen, iehoatl in jtilma, aço ocutocheoatl, aço tequaneoatl, aço oceloeoatl, cujtlacheoatl, anoço mjzeoatl: ioan mjtoa itechaloxuchiuh, icoçoiaoalol: auh in jçioauh, no iieoacue, iieoavipil: no iuhque in ie mochintin çioa, mochipa itlavitol ietinemj, acan qujcaoa in nênemj qujtqujtivi, in tlaqua itlan jcac, in cochi itzontlan onoc:

22. *Tequani* ("eater of people") we have consistently translated as "wild beast." Sahagún frequently defines it as *tigre o león.* Eduard Seler, in *Einige Kapitel aus dem Geschichtswerk des Fray Bernardino de Sahagun aus dem Aztekischen übersetzt* (Caecilie Seler-Sachs, Walter Lehmann, Walter Krickeberg, eds.; Stuttgart: Strecker und Schröder, 1927), p. 402, construes it as jaguar. In the Aztec codices, the glyph of *tequani* is an animal of the cat family. Clark, in *Codex Mendoza* (James Cooper Clark, ed. and tr.; London: Waterlow and Sons, 1938), II, p. 120, identifies it as *Felis hernandesii*. See also III, fol. 13v.

23. *Lynx rufus texensis* in Martín del Campo, *op. cit.,* XII, No. 1 (1941), "Los Mamíferos," p. 495. *Lynx rufus texensis* (J. A. Allen) according to Durrant, personal communication.

24. *Felis hernandesii hernandesii*, in Martín del Campo, *op. cit.,* p. 491. *Felis onca hernandesii* (Gray). Jaguar according to Durrant.

25. *Oso mielero; Tamandua, Myrmecopaha, tetradactyla,* in Sahagún (Garibay ed.), IV, p. 331. We have translated as "wolf" after Molina, *op. cit.* The Spanish of the *Florentine Codex,* Book XI, cap. I, fol. 6r, states: *"Este anjmal, por la relaciõ, paresce que es oso: y si no es oso no se a que anjmal se compare de los que conoscemos."*

26. *Felis azteca azteca* in Martín del Campo, *op. cit.,* p. 493. *Felis concalar azteca* (Merriam) according to Durrant.

27. Martín del Campo, *op. cit.,* p. 497: *"Es imposible reconocer alguna especie de ardilla en particular y, por otra parte, el nombre techálotl tiene un valor genérico. Quedan aquí, por tanto, comprendidas diversas especies del género Sciuras."*

28. Corresponding Spanish text: *"ponjanse en la cabeça vna gujrnalda, hecha de vn pelleio de hardilla: de manera, que la cabeça, venja sobre la frente: y la cola, al colodrillo: y vn plumaje a manera de vn auentadorcico redondo de pluma encarnada."*

their bows. They left them nowhere; when they wandered they went carrying them. When they ate, [their bows] stood nearby; when they slept, they rested at their heads. It is said they called them their guardians; they considered them [such]. And their sandals were of yucca or palm [leaves]. And the bed of the ruler — this was of wild animal skins. And his seat and his resting place, the so-called seats with back rests, were all of wild animal skins, most wonderful. Many Chichimeca guarded this ruler.

Also likewise were arrayed all the [Teo] chichimeca, only they took not the wild animal skins, the wild animal seats — they did not belong to them: only small deer skins, small coyote skins, small grey fox skins, grey fox skins,[29] squirrel skins, etc.

Behold, the following were the abilities of these Chichimeca: they were stone cutters: very well did they work[30] the flint, the obsidian. They set it, they placed it as the tip on the reed, which is called the arrow. And also they understood very well about mirrors, for all used mirrors. They always bore them on the small of their backs. And when they went somewhere, as they made their way, following a single leader, in order, in line, there they went looking into the mirror which [the one ahead] went bearing in the middle of his back. And they worked, they abraded the turquoise, the fine turquoise, [for] their necklaces, their ear rings, their pendants.

And they knew the qualities, the essence, of herbs, of roots. The so-called peyote was their discovery. These, when they ate peyote, esteemed it above wine or mushrooms. They assembled together somewhere on the desert; they came together; there they danced, they sang all night, all day. And on the morrow, once more they assembled together. They wept; they wept exceedingly. They said [thus] eyes were washed; thus they cleansed their eyes.

And they were feather gluers, feather workers; for they made, they glued the fan-shaped device of yellow parrot feathers. And they cured skins; they were tanners; for all the clothing of the Chichimeca was of skins, and the skirts of their women were of skins. They tanned the skins; they cut them into thongs.

And when, perhaps, [there was] a little food, they roasted it, broiled it, boiled it. The men did not do the work; only the women, because [the men] protected their eyes exceedingly; they could not endure

qujl itepixcauh in qujtoa, in momati: auh in jcac iehoatl in icçotl, anoço çotoli: auh in jpepech in tlatoanj, iehoatl in tequaneoatl, ioan in icpal, ioan in jnetlaxonjuh, in mjtoa: teputzicpalli, mochi iehoatl in tequaneoatl, vel mavizio: injn tlatoanj mjequjntin in qujpia chichimeca.

No ivi in mochichioa in ie mochintin chichimeca: çan amo qujcuj, amo intech povi in tequaneoatl, in tequanjcpalli: çan maçaieoatzintli, coioieoatzintli, oztoieoatzintli, oztoieoatl, techaloieoatl. Etc.

Izcatquj, in jiolizmatiliz injque y, chichimeca, ca tlatecque, ca cenca vel qujximati in tecpatl, in jtztli, in jiacac qujquetza, qujtlalia in acatl, in mjtoa mjtl: auh ioan cenca vel qujximati in tezcatl, ca mochintin qujtitlanj in tezcatl: mochipa intzintempan qujmana: auh in jquac canapa vi, in vtlatoca, ça ce in teiacana, çan motecpana, ça cenpanti, vmpa vnmotztivi in tezcac in intzintempan mamantiuh: ioan qujxima, qujchiquj in xivitl in teuxitl in jncozquj, in jncuecueioch in jnpipilol:

ioan qujximati in xiujtl, in tlanelhoatl in quenamj, in quen ihiio, iehoantin intlaiximach in mjtoa peiotl: injque, y, in qujqua in peiotl, vctli ipan in qujpoa, in anoço nanacatl, mocentlalia cana ixtlaoacan, monechicoa: vncan mjtotia, cujca ceioal, cemjlhujtl: auh in jmuztlaioc, oc ceppa mocentlalia choca, cenca choca, qujl mjxpaca, ic qujchipaoa in jmjxtelolo:

ioan hiviçaloque, amanteca, ca qujchioa, ca qujçaloa in coçoiaoalolli: ioan cuetlaxoaoanque, tlaiamanjlique: ipampa in jxqujch imeoaquen chichimeca, ioan jmeoacue in incioaoa, ca iehoantin qujiamania, qujoaoana:

auh in aço itla tlaqualli qujxca, qujtleoatza, anoço qujpaoaci: amo iehoan qujtequjpanoa in oqujchtin, can iehoan in cioa: ipampa cenca qujmalhuja in jmjxtelolo, amo qujtitlanj in poctli, qujl qujmjxtlacoa, ca

29. *Urocyon cinereoargenteus* (Martín del Campo, *op. cit.*, p. 495).
30. Read *quixima* as in the *Acad. Hist. MS.*

the smoke.[31] They said that it harmed their eyes, for these Chichimeca saw very far, and they took very careful aim. That at which they loosed an arrow, not twice, not thrice did they shoot it; [but] only once. Even if [the target were] very small, they did not miss it; even if it also were far away, they could hit it with an arrow. They did not miss it, nor did they shoot at it many times.

The following is the food of the Chichimeca: no-pal, tuna, roots of the *cimatl* herb,[32] *tziuactli* cactus,[33] honey, maguey, yucca flowers, yucca sap, maguey sap, bee honey, wild bees, wild honey; and the roots of which they had knowledge, which were in the ground; and all the meats — rabbit, snake, deer, wild animals; and all [things] which flew.

Such was the food of these Chichimeca, that they never sickened much. They became very old; they died only at an advanced age; they went on to be white-haired, white-headed. And if sickness settled upon someone, when after two days — three days — four days — he recovered not, then the Chichimeca assembled together; they slew him. They inserted a bird arrow into his throat, whereof he died. And they likewise slew those who became very old men [or] very old women. As for their killing the sick, the aged, it was said that thus they showed him mercy; it is said [that it was] in order that he would not suffer on earth, and so they would not feel sorry for him. And when they buried him, they paid him great honor; two days, three days, they mourned; there was dancing, there was singing.

Such was their food and so limited their clothing, that they were strong, lean, hard, and very wiry, sinewy, powerful, and they ran much. As they went, as they climbed mountains, it was as if they were carried by the wind, for they were lean — they had no folds of fat — so that nothing impeded them.

These[34] always went taking their women with them, [as] hath been said. And when the woman was already pregnant, her helpmate many times applied heat to her back; he went pouring water on her

cenca veca tlachia injque, y, chichimeca: ioan cenca tlatlamelauhcaittanj, ca in tlein qujmjna, amo oppa, expa, qujtlaxilia çan cen: in manel cenca tepiton, amo qujneoa, in manel noço veca ca, vel qujmjna, amo qujneoa, amo no quezqujpa in qujntlaxilia.

Izcatquj in jntlaqual chichimeca: nupalli, nochtli, cimatl, tlanelhoatl, tzioactli, nequametl, icçoxuchitl, icçonenecutli, menecutli, xiconecutli, pipioli, quauh-necutli: ioan in tlein qujximati tlanelhoatl, in tlallan onoc, ioan in ie ixqujch nacatl, tochin, coatl, maçatl, tequanj: ioan ixqujch in patlantinemj.

Injque in chichimeca: injc iuhquj intlaqual, y, aic cenca mococoa, cenca vecaoa, çan veve mjquj, tzonjz-taztivi, quaiztaztivi: auh intla aca cocoliztli itech motlalia, in ie omjlhujtl, ie eilhujtl, in ie navilhujtl, amo pati: njman mocentlalia in chichimeca, qujmjctia, totomjtl iquechtlan conaqujlia, ic onmjquj: ioan in aqujn ovelveuetic, in ovelilamatic, çan no qujmjctia: injc qujmjctia cocoxquj, manoço veve, qujl ic qujtla-oculia, qujl ipampa in amo motolinjz tlalticpac: ioan injc amo qujntlaocultiz: auh injc qujtoca, cenca quj-maviztilia, omjlhujtl, eilhujtl in mjccaoati, mjtotia, cujca:

injc iuhquj intlaqual y, in joan amo cenca quex-qujch intlaque, vel chicaoaque, vel pipinque, vellalich-tique, ioan cenca ichtique, tlaloatique, ioan tlamol-hoatique, ioan cenca paina injc vi, injc tepetleco, vel iuhqujn ecatoco: ipampa moceceioque, amo tzotzol-tique, injc atle qujmelleltia

injque y, in jnçioaoa omjto: çan mochipa qujnvi-catinemj, auh in jquac ie vtztli in çioatl, mjecpa quj-cujtlapantotonja in jnamjc, concujtlapanatequjtiuh, qujlmach ic qujtema in qujtoa: auh in otlacachiuh,

---

31. *Amo quittitlani* in the *Acad. Hist. MS*. In a marginal gloss, Sahagún changes to *quitlani*. Seler, *op. cit.*, p. 403, construes the phrase as "*nicht vertrügen sie den Rauch.*"

32. See *supra*, chap. xxviii, § 1, n. 75.

33. Unidentified cactus in Sahagún (Garibay de.), IV, p. 366. In Book XI of the *Florentine Codex*, fol. 201r, it is thus described: *Tzioactli itoca, tzivactli in juhquj metontli yoan in jqujioio, chapactontli, mamae, mapipitzaoac, vitzio, qujioio, xiloio: qualonj, paoaxonj: in jxiloio necutic, ixconj: in jqujioio, piaztic, viac, chachaquachtic, tetecujtztic, qujioti, chachaquachivi: mana, motlamjna. In tzivactla tlaovican, ovican* — Tziuactli [is] its name. Tziuactli [is] like a small maguey plant, and its stem [grows] in drop[-like sections]. It has branches, long branches; it has spines, a stem, [and] soft, edible fruit. It is edible; it may be cooked. Its fruit [is] sweet [and] can be cooked. Its stem [is] thin, long, coarse, rustling. It forms a stem; it becomes coarse. It increases in size; it grows. [Places with] many tziuactli [are] of difficult terrain, of dangerous places.

34. The following phrase appears in the *Acad. Hist. MS* after *injque y*, but is crossed out: *in iquac ce quichiva civapiltzintli nimā no ce ytech povi chichimecatlepan.*

back. It was said that he told her that thereby he bathed her. And when she had been delivered, when the child was born, then the Chichimeca [man] kicked this newly delivered woman twice, thrice, in the back. It was said that this stopped the blood. Then they placed their child in a small carrying frame; the woman loaded it on her back. Where night came upon them, there they slept. On the morrow, likewise; [the next day, likewise].[35]

And if their child which was born were a girl, when she became four years old — five years old — then also they gave her to a Chichimeca boy. Then he took her; he always went carrying her.

And if [it were] a boy, when he became one year old, then they gave him a bow; then he went about practising the shooting of arrows. The Chichimeca taught him no play, only the shooting of arrows.

These Chichimeca knew, practised, administered the evil eye, the doing of ill, the blowing of evil. These Chichimeca dispensed with their hair-cut; the hair was merely worn long, parted in the middle; as the men [were], just so [were] the women.

There were also the Nahuachichimeca, those who understood, who also therefore spoke, the Nahuatl language and a barbarous tongue. Also there were the so-called Otonchichimeca. These were called Otonchichimeca because they spoke a barbarous tongue and Otomí. Also there were the Cuextecachichimeca, who were called Cuextecachichimeca because they spoke a barbarous tongue and Cuexteca. These three were peaceful; the way of life which corresponded to them, civilized. They had rulers, they had noblemen; and they were city dwellers, they were clothed, they were clever. There was [food] to eat; they were house dwellers. But also their preoccupations were the arrow [and] the bow.

HERE ARE MENTIONED — are named — those called Nahua. They are the ones who speak the Nahuatl language. They speak a little [like] the Mexica, although not really perfectly, not really pronounced in the same way; they pronounce it somehow.

These thus mentioned called themselves Chichimeca mochanecatoca, that is to say, Tolteca.[36] It is said these caused the Tolteca to disperse when they

in ooallacat piltontli, quen oppa, expa concujtlatelicça injn mjxiuhquj in chichimecatl, qujl ic oallamj in eztli: njman oacaltonco conaquja in jnconeton, conmama in çioatl in canjn impan iooatiuh vncan cochi, moztla ivi:

auh intla cioatl tlacati in inconeto, in ie nauhxiuhtia, in ie macujlxiuhtia: njman noce qujmaca chichimeca telpopil njman cana, mochipa qujvicatinemj:

auh intla oqujchtli, in ie cexiuhtia, njman qujmaca in tlavitolli: njman moieiecotinemj, in tlamjnaliztli: amo tle avilli qujmati in chichimeca, çan ie iehoatl in tlamjnaliztli.

Injque in chichimeca qujmati, qujchioanj, qujmotequjtia, in texoxaliztli, in tetlachiviliztli, in teipitzaliztli. Inique in chichimeca: atle innexin çan motzonviaqujlia, moquaxeloltia, iuhque in oquichtli, iuhque in çioa.

No vncate in naoachichimeca: iehoantin in qujcaquj in no ic tlatoa naoatlatolli, ioan popoloca: no vncate in mjtoa, otonchichimeca, injque y ipampa mjtoa, Otonchichimeca ca popoloca, ioan otontlatoa: no vncate cuextecachichimeca, injc mjtoa cuextecachichimeca ca popoloca ioan cuexteca tlatoa: injn ietlamanjxtin y, tlacaçiuhque intech ca in tlacanemjliztli, tlâtocaoaque, pilloque, auh altepeonoque, motlaquentia, mjmati, vnca qujquani, chanonoque, iece no intequiuh in mjtl in tlavitolli

NICAN MJTOA, moteneoa in aqujque mjtoa naoa. In naoa: iehoantin in naoatlatolli ic tlatoa, in achi mexica tlatoa, in maca nel iuh tlanquj, in maca nel iuh qujzquj, in maço quenjn contlatlalia.

Injque in iuh mjtoa: ca qujmotocaiotia chichimeca, mochanecatoca, qujtoznequj tulteca: qujl iehoantin in qujnchachaiauhteoaque tulteca, in iquac iaque, in

---

35. The *Acad. Hist. MS* adds *moztla ivi.*

36. Cf. Walter Lehmann: *Die Geschichte der Königreiche von Colhuacan und Mexico* (Stuttgart und Berlin: W. Kohlhammer, 1938), p. 62, n. 2: *Leute, die alle aus ihren Häusern vom Winde vertrieben wurden.* Corresponding Spanish text: *"aunque eran naoas: tambien se llamavan chichimecas, y dezian: ser de la generacion de los tultecas, que quedaron quando los demas tultecas salieron de su pueblo, y se despoblaron."*

went away, when Topiltzin Quetzalcoatl entered the water, when he went to settle in the place of the red color, the place of the burning.[37]

These [Nahua] were able; they had lords, nobles, rulers. And the nobles, the lords, the rulers governed the inhabitants of the city; they enlarged, extended, increased their city; they provided song, they set up the ground drum. It is said they enlivened the city; they made it illustrious. There was [food] to eat, provisions. They had drink, food, clothes, necklaces, quetzal feathers, arm bands, homes, houses, gardens, maize bins. They had a god; they addressed him, they prayed to him, they worshipped him as a god. They gave him the name of Night [and] Wind. They were devout: they held vigil, held watch, played the two-toned drum, sat singing, bled themselves, mutilated themselves, inserted maguey spines, blew the trumpet shell, entered into the water. Every twenty-day period they proceeded to observe feast days.

In them were all prudence, industry, and craftmanship. [They were] feather workers, painters, masons, gold workers, metal casters, carpenters, stone cutters, lapidaries, grinders, stone polishers, weavers, spinners; they were adroit in speech, distinctive in food preparation, elegant with capes, with clothes. They had gods; they were devout; they were pray-ers, givers of offerings, offerers of incense. They were brave, able in war, takers of captives, conquerors.

This is all which is here to be told. Still, much is omitted concerning the life of the Nahua, of the Nahua people.

A LITTLE IS MENTIONED HERE of those [who were] the Otomí and of their way of life, their qualities.

The name of the Otomitl comes from, is taken from, the name of him who first became the leader of the Otomí. They say his name was Oton. His children, his descendants, and his subjects were all called Otomí; a single one, Otomitl.

These Otomí had a civilized way of life. The men wore capes, clothed themselves, wore breech clouts, wore sandals. The women wore skirts; they wore shifts. The clothing, the capes, the sandals of the men were of good quality; the skirts, the shifts of the women were of good quality.[38]

jquac atlan calac topiltzin Quetzalcoatl, in ia in motecato in tlapalla in tlatlaia.

Injque in mozcalia tecuioque, pilloque, tlatocaioque: auh pilti, tecuti, tlatocati, tlapachoa, altepeonoque, qujveilia, qujuecapanoa, qujxpatlaoa in imauh, in jntepeuh: cujcamana veuequetza mjtoa, qujxitia in atl, in tepetl, qujcaoanja: vnca qujquanj, motlaiecultianj, aoaque, tlaqualeque, tlaquemeque, cozqueque, quetzaleque, macuexeque, chaneque, caleque, mjleque, cuezcomeque: auh teoaque, quinotzque, qujtlatlauhtique, qujmoteutique in teutl: in qujtocaiotique iooalli ehecatl, tlateumatinj, in ioalli ic qujtlaça tlapia, teponaçoa, cujcatoque, mjço, motetequj, movitztlalia, tlapitza, apan temo. Cecempoaltica in ilhujchiuhtivi,

vel intech ca in jxqujch ixtlamatiliztli, in nematiliztli, ioan in tultecaiutl, amanteca, tlacujloque, tlaqujlque, teucujtlaoaque, tepuzpitzque, tlaxinque, tetzotzonque, tlatecque, tlachiqujnj, tlapetlaoanj, tlaiotovianj, tzauhque, hiqujtque, mjmatque, in jpan tlatolli, mjmati in jpan tlaqualchioaliztli mjmati in tilmatica, in tlaquentica teuoaque, tlateomatinj, tlatlatlauhtianj, tlamananj: tlenamacanj, oqujchtinj, in iaoc mjmatinj, tlamanj, tetopeoanj:

çan cuel ixqujch y, njcan mjtoa, oc mjec in mocaoa, in jnnemjliz in naoa, in naoatlaca.

ACHITON NICAN VNMOTENEOA: in aqujque otomj, ioan in quenamj inieliz, in jnnêmachiliz.

In Otomjtl: in jtoca, itech qujça itech mana in jtoca: in achto inteiacancauh mochiuh in Otomj, qujl itoca catca oton, in jpilhoan in jtech qujzque, ioan in jtlapacholhoan, mochtin motocaiotia otomj, in ça çe Otòmjtl.

Injque y, otomj, intech ca in tlacanemjliztli in oquichti: motlalpilia, motlaquentia, maxtleque caqueque: in cioa cueieque, vipileque: in oqujchti qualli in jntlaquen, in jntilma, in jncac: in cioa qualli in jncue, in jnvipil:

---

37. Lehmann, op. cit., p. 91: ye mòtocayotia yn tlatlayan yn ompa motlatito yn quetzalcoatl — thus is it named place of burning; it is there where Quetzalcoatl went to burn himself.

38. In the Acad. Hist. MS, the following is in the body of the text but has been crossed out: yoã cēca yh ic ome topalti, iuhqui amo mohozcalia in ipã tlaq̄mitl in itechcopa netlalpililli.

There were rulers who governed them; there were nobles, there were lords; there were[39] the so-called stewards; there were leaders; there were priests, the so-called Otomí priests. There was their supreme priest by the name of Tecutlatoa. There was their wise man, whom they called, whom they named, Tlaciuhqui. That is, he performed sorcery for [the god]; he was equal to, he resembled [a god]; he addressed them as if [he were] a god. He addressed the gods; he informed them of that which they desired. The Otomí inquired of [the sorcerer], if it were necessary to go to war, whether perchance they would die in war; they inquired of him whether there would be rain during the year, or whether, perhaps, there would be no [rain]; they inquired [if] famine, if perhaps sickness might come — might spread. They asked many things of the sorcerer. They worshipped [sorcerers] as gods; hence were they very highly esteemed; they were regarded well everywhere.

These Otomí possessed gardens; they possessed maize bins; good [was] their food, good [was] their drink. The name of their god was Iocippa. Very good [was] his temple, which they had erected for him, had dedicated to him — the straw hut of trimmed and smoothed straw called the temple of Oton. All provided themselves with straw huts, grass huts; they did not greatly esteem flat-roofed houses. There in their temples lived the priests, and there the small boys were reared; there they did penance, passed the night, entered the bath; maguey spines were placed; they bled themselves, they cut themselves, they fasted. All night they played the two-toned drum on the top of their temple. It was said they held guard on top. (This they said.)

In this manner were they adorned. The hair of the still small boys was cut short leaving a little hair on the back of the head. They named it *piochtli*. Then lower lips were perforated; lip plugs were provided; ear plugs were provided. And they shaved over the foreheads of the grown men, and on the backs of their heads they left much long hair. Hence were they called *piocheque*.

The lip plugs of the rulers were green stone lip plugs, or sea shell lip plugs, or gold lip plugs. And also the ear plugs of the brave men, the brave warriors, were gold ear plugs or copper ear plugs, or sea shell ear plugs, or mirror stone ear plugs, or turquoise [mosaic] ear plugs. The lip plugs of all the [other]

tlatocati, tepachoa, pilti, tecuti: vncan mjtoa calpixquj, vncan tlaiacanquj, vncate tlamacazque, yn mjtoa otontlamacazque: vnca in jnveiteupixcauh, in jtoca tecutlatoa: vnca in jntlamatinjuh, in qujlhuja in qujtocaiotia tlaciuhquj, qujtoznequj: qujtlaçilhuj, qujnevivili, qujqujxti, anoço iuhquj in teutl qujnnotzaia: no qujnnotzaia in teteu, in tlein qujntlatlanjaia, qujlhujaia, intla monequj iaoqujçazque in otomj, qujlhujaia, in aço iaomjqujzque, qujlhuja in aço vel qujaviz ce xivitl, in acanoçomo, quilhujaia maianaliztli, in aço cocoliztli qujçaqujuh, momanaqujuh: mjec tlamantli in quilhujaia tlaciuhquj, in qujnmoteutiaia: ic cenca vei machoia, novian oalittoia.

Injque, y, otomj, mjleque, cuezcomeque, qualli in jntlaqual, qualli in jmauh: in jnteouh catca itoca Iocipa: vel qualli in jteucal quiquechiliaia, quitonaltiaia, in teteçauhquj xacalli: in motocaiotia otonteucalli, ic mochintin moxacaltiaia, moçacacaltiaia: amo cenca tle ipan qujttaia in tlapancalli, in jnteupan vncan nenca in tlamacazque: ioan vncan oapaoaloia in pipiltotonti, vncan tlamaceoaia, iooalli qujtlaçaia, apan temoia movitztlaliaia, mjçoia, motequja, moçaoaia, ceioal in teponaçoaia, in jcpac inteucal: qujl icpac tlapiaia, (in qujtoaia)

inic mochichioaia: in jnnexin catca in oc pipiltotonti, moquateçonoa, aqujton in cuexcochtlan qujcaoa in tzontli, in qujtocaiotia piochtli: njman motencoionja, monacazcoionja, motentetia, monacochtia: auh in vevei tlaca qujteteçoa in jmjxquac: auh in jncuexcochtlan mjec in qujcaoa tzontli, viac: ic mjtoa piocheque,

in jntenteuh in tlatoque chalchiuhtentetl, anoço tecciztentetl, anoço teocujtlatentetl: no ioan iehoantin in oqujchti, in tiacaoa: in jnnacoch, teocujtlanacochtli, anoço tepuznacochtli, anoço tecciznacochtli, anoço tezcanacochtli, anoço xiuhnacochtli: in ie mochi tlacatl, tevilotl, itztli, anoço tehpuchtli, in jntenteuh:

people were of rock crystal, obsidian, or smoky stone,[40] and their ear plugs were of obsidian or smoky stone, or those known as stalactites, green ones resembling turquoise, or ear plugs made of black beetles, or pottery ear plugs. And furthermore, at last came their ear plugs of dried maize stalks or reed ear plugs.

When the women were still young girls, they cut their hair short; but when [they were] grown, when [they were] young women, the hair covered their shoulders. However, the hair over the forehead was cut. And when one was a mature woman, when perhaps she also [had delivered] her child, the hair was bound about her head. Also they wore ear plugs, and their arms, their breasts, were painted. Their painting was well scratched, well scarified,[41] very green, bluish, very beautiful.

This [was] their food: maize, dried maize ears, beans, chili, salt, tomatoes. Their greatest specialties, or, as I have mentioned it, their great pleasures, [were] fruit tamales, cooked beans, dogs, gophers,[42] deer.

Behold the defects, the faults of the Otomí. They were untrained, stupid. Thus was there scolding, or thus was one scolded; thus was there the scolding of one untrained. It was said: "Now thou art an Otomí. Now thou art a miserable Otomí. O Otomí, how is it that thou understandest not? Art thou perchance an Otomí? Art thou perchance a real Otomí? Not only art thou like an Otomí, thou art a real Otomí,[43] a miserable Otomí, a green-head, a thick-head, a big tuft of hair over the back of the head, an Otomí blockhead, an Otomí...."

With all this one was scolded, one was shamed. It was taken, it stemmed, from the uncouthness of the Otomí.

The Otomí were very covetous, that is, very desirous, greedy. That which was good, they bought all; they longed for all of it even though it was not really necessary.

The Otomí were very gaudy dressers — vain people; that is to say, what there were of capes, of clothing, which were one's special privilege, they took all,

auh in jnnacoch itztli, aço tehpuchtli, anoço iehoatl in mjtoa tenextli, iiacacujtl xoxoctic, moxiuhnenequj, anoço maianacochtli, anoço çoqujnacochtli: auh in iequene qujcentzacuja oaquauhnacochtli in jnacoch: anoço acanacochtli.

In cioa in oc pipiltotonti in oquateçonoaia: auh in ie ueue in, in ie ichpopochti, motzonquentiaia, iece mjxquatequj: auh in omacic cioatl, in anoço iece iconeuh maxtlaoa, no monacochtiaia: ioan mjcujloa in jnmac in jmelpan, vel moxtic, vellamomoxolti in jnnecujlol vel xoxopaleoac, iuhqujn matlali, vel qualli.

In jntlaqual iehoatl in tonacaiotl, in cjntli, in etl, in chilli, in jztatl, in tomatl. Oc cenca vel intonal, ma anoço iuh njqujto y, vel inpac in xocotamalli, in epaoaxtli, in chichi, in toçan, in maçatl.

Izcatquj in jmjtlacauhca, in jmaqualtiliz in Otomj. Amo môozcalia, amo vmpaêeoa: iuhquj ic neaio, manoço ic teaio, ic aio in amozcalia, mohuja: ie vn totomjtl, ie vn totompol, otomjtle quenmach in amo ticcaquj? cujx totomjtl? cujx ça uel totomjtl, amo çan ticmotlâtlalili in totomjtl, vel mellelacic totomjtl, otompol, quaxoxopol, quatilacpol, cuexcochchichicapol, otontepol, otonpixipol.

Injn mochi ic teaio, tepinauhtilo: itech mana itech moqujxtia in ainnezcaliliz otomj.

In otomj cenca ihicome: qujtoznequj, cenca tlatlaelevianj, mjhicultianj: in tlein qualtoton mochi qujcoa, mochi qujnenequj, in maca nel cenca monequj.

In otomj: cenca topalme, xacanme, qujtoznequj: in tlein tilmatli, tlaquemjtl tetonal: mochi qujcuj, mochi intech qujtlalia injc xacanme, amo moiectlal-

---

40. Corresponding Spanish text: "chalchivites fingidos." Foshag, op. cit., p. 9, suggests metadiorite, serpentine, muscovite.

41. Derived from momotzoa? Cf. also corresponding Spanish text: pintada en la misma carne cortandola con vna nauajuela. — Use of tlamomoxoltic in Book XI of the Florentine Codex suggests the possible meaning of "varicolored" or "intricately colored": cap. xi, fol. 222v. Ninepapantlacujloa, nepapan tlacujloli njcchiva, nicqualnextia tlamomoxoltic njcchiva, cujcujlchampotic, cujcujlchampochtic njcchiva, njqujcujloa; cap. viii, § 5, [Quetzalatzcalli (shellfish)] in quemâ iuhqujnma aiauhcoçamalotl, in queman iuhqujnma icpitl moiava, nepapan tlacujlolli, nepapan tlapallo, vellamomoxoltic, vel moxtic.

42. Villa, op. cit., lists several species of the genus Thomomys, others of the genus Cratogeomys.

43. The Acad. Hist. MS adds vel moyolacic totomitl.

they wore all, to be vain people. It was not worn in good taste; thus of them was said: "Hath it possibly been said that someone called thee an Otomí? Is it true that thou art an Otomí?"

Likewise the women, who also bought up all the skirts, [all] the shifts,[44] did not wear the skirts well; they did not wear the shifts well. Such gaudy dressers [were] the young girls [that] they pasted their legs, their arms, with red feathers. Faces were smeared with yellow ochre, and teeth were darkened. Faces were covered a fine brown.

And as gaudy dressers, as vain as the [other] Otomí, were the old women, who still also cut the hair over the forehead; who still also cut the hair on one side, leaving the other side long; who still also darkened their teeth, still painted their faces, still pasted themselves with red feathers; who still also put on the embroidered skirts, the embroidered shifts.

The Otomí were lazy, shiftless, although wiry, strong; as is said, hardened; laborers. Although great workers of the land, they did not apply themselves to gaining the necessities of life. When they had worked the land they only wandered.

Behold what they did: they went catching [game]; they went catching rabbits, spearing rabbits, snaring rabbits in nets, shooting rabbits with reed arrows, hunting rabbits with balls;[45] they went catching quail with snares; they went catching game with snares, catching game with a throw-net, catching game with a lasso; they went shooting deer with arrows, catching deer in nets; they went setting traps; they went setting dead-falls;[46] they went boring the maguey plant, becoming drunk; there they went whiling away their time.

And when to a certain degree our lord had pity in his heart, when already they went to look upon the maize, the tender maize ears, the tender maize ears which sprouted therefrom, they began to eat them, to buy things with the tender maize ears, to buy stinking things. They became drunk on tender maize ears. They sold all the gourds, the green chili. And when the maize was already firm, the better ones they sold to make purchases for themselves. And they cooked green maize ears, they made tortillas, they

pilia, ic intech mjtoa. Can mach mjto, ac mach mjtztocaioti in totomitl ca nel noço totomjtl.

No iuhque in cioa, çan no tlacentoca in cueitl, in vipilli: amono moieccuetia, amo moiecvipiltia: injc cenca vel topalme in ichpopuchtotonti: tlapalivitica mopotonjaia, in jmjcxic, in jnmac, tecoçauhtica moxaoaia: auh motlamjaoa mjxtlapalhoatzalhujaia:

auh injc topalti, injc xacanme, injc otomj: in jlamatoton oc no mjxquatequj, oc no moxoxocolxima, oc no motlamjaoa, oc moxaoa, oc mopotonja in tlapalivitica, oc no intech qujtlalia in tlamachcueitl, in tlamachvipilli.

In Otomj: tlatziuhque, aimel, maçivi in jchtique, in tlamolhoatique, in mjtoa: chicaoaque, tlainj, macivi i cenca elimjqujnj, amo qujcelia in netlaiecultiliztli, in oonelimjque ça nenemj.

Izca in qujchioa: ahantinemj, tochantinemj, tochtzopinjtinemj, tlatochmatlavitinemj, tlatochacavitinemj, tlatochtapaiolhujtinemj, çoltzonvitinemj, tlatzonvitinemj, tlatlapachioazvitinemj, tlatlaçalhujtinemj, maçamjntinemj, maçamatlavitinemj, tlatlâpeoalhujtinemj, tlatlachictinemj, tlaoantinemj, tlatlapevitinemj, vncan nenqujztinemj:

auh in oquenteltzin in tlaocux iiollotzin totecujo, i ie iixco onjtztivi tonacaiotl, xilotl, in jtech maiavi, xilotl in qujpeoaltia qujqua, ic motlacovia in xilotl, ic moxoqujiacacovia, qujtlaoana in xilotl, mochi qujnamaca in aiotetl, in chilchotl: auh in ie tetzaoac tonacaiotl, oc tlapanavia qujnamaca, ic motlacovia: auh qujmelopaoaxia, qujmoxantlaxcalhuja, qujmoxantamalhuja, ic moccovia.

44. Seler, *op. cit.*, p. 412: *Sie ziehen ebenso die Hüfttücher, die Hemden übereinander an.*

45. Possibly bolas are meant. — The *Acad. Hist.* MS adds *tlaçolmatlavitinemj, tlaçolcolovitinemj:* they go catching quail in nets, they go encircling quail.

46. *Tlatlachictinemj, tlacantinemj, tlatlapevitinemj.* Since the context favors this word order, the passage has been so translated.

made tamales of green maize to make purchases for themselves.

There was not much more to harvest of the maize, of their ripened ears. They gathered it without care; they ate it; they sold it. Especially when they harvested, or when they had harvested, they began the buying of turkey hens, of dogs. Tamales were made; there was eating; guests were invited. And then [came] their wine to moisten the food. Thus swiftly they used up their harvest.

They said: "The maize is quickly ended. We shall eat the greens, the sweet roots, the roots, the *nopal*." They said: "Our forefathers said that there are times of plenty and of want." Thus of one or to one who ate much or who quickly consumed his possessions, his goods, it was said: "Thou destroyest thyself just like an Otomí."

The Otomí ate skunks,[47] serpents, squirrels,[48] forest mice, field mice, house mice. They ate all the kangaroo rats,[49] gila monsters, weasels, large lizards. They ate chameleon, lizards, black beetles, dung beetles. They ate grass grasshoppers, mist grasshoppers, rubber grasshoppers.

And also many of the Otomí women [were] weavers of designs. They wove; they made the wonderful capes with designs, the skirts with designs; they wove the gauze weave, the so-called ocelot cape, the woven design skirt, the woven design shift. But all the Otomí women concerned themselves only with maguey fiber. [The green leaves] were toasted, dressed, scraped. They pressed the water [out of the fiber], treated it with maize dough, spun it, placed it over the shoulder, wove it.[50]

Neither was the value great of what they made. They wove the diagonal central motive,[51] the turkey with mat-designed interior, the violet colored,[52] the cape of twisted weave, the good-for-nothing, the useless weave, the glossy maguey weave; the maguey fiber cape, the one of single maguey threads, the net-

Aocmo quexqujch in qujpixca, in ie cintli in jntonacaiouh, amo quitlamachcuj in qujqua, in qujnamaca: oc cenca iquac in pixca, in anoço oonpixcaque, peoa in mototolcovia, in motzcujncovia, motamalhvia, tlatlaqua, mococoachioa: auh njman ie imoc, inic capachoa, ic iciuhca qujtlamja in jnpixquj,

qujtoa, ma iciuhca vntlamj in tonacaiotl, toconquazque in qujlitl, in cimatl, in tlanelhoatl, in nopalli, qujtoa: ca conjtotivi in tocolhoan tatacaputzveli in tlalticpac: ic ipan mjto, anoço ilhujloc, in aqujn cenca tlaqua, anoço iciuhca qujpoloa in jaxca, in jtlatquj, çan timotompoloa.

In otomj. qujqua in epatl, qujqua in coatl, qujqua in mototli, in quauhqujmjchi in tlalqujmjchi, in calqujmjchi: mochi qujqua in veçalotl, in acaltetepon, in coçamatl, in mjlquaxoch, qujqua in tapaiaxi, in cuetzpali, in temoli, in cujtlatemoli, qujqua in çacachapoli, in aiauhchapuli, in olchapoli

Auh in otonçioa, tel mjequjnti in tlamachchiuhque, qujqujti, qujchioa, in maviztic tlamachtilmatli, tlamachcueitl, qujqujti in nepanjuhquj, in mjtoa Ocelotilmatli, tlamachcueitl, tlamachvipilli: ie ce in mochinti Otoncioatzitzinti, çan ichtli in qujmaviltia, tlachichinoa, tlacima, tlaoaçoma, tlaaqujxtia, tlatexvia, tzaoa, tlatlaquechtlampavia, hiqujti:

amono quexquich ipatiuh in qujchioa, qujqujti, in jtichicoio in iollo, in totolitipetlaio, in cacamoliuhquj, in jlacatziuhquj, in nenjuhquj, in nemjquitquj, in ichpetztli, in jchtilmatli, in ce ichtli, in aiatl, in nopalaiatl, in çanjtli: iece amo tle ipatiuh, çaçan quenjn patiio.

47. Cf. Villa, *op. cit.*, pp. 457–465, and Martín del Campo, *op. cit.* (1941), p. 499. Genera *Mephitis, Conepatus, Spilogale* — Striped skunk, Hagnosed skunk, Spotted skunk, respectively, according to Durrant.

48. Villa, *op. cit.*, p. 372: *Citellus mexicanus mexicanus* Erxleben.

49. *Veçacotl* in the *Acad. Hist. MS.* For *ratón*, Molina, *op. cit.*, has *veçacotl;* for *lirón* (dormouse), *viçacotl.* In Book XI, Sahagún describes *uicacotl,* which, according to Martín del Campo, *op. cit.*, p. 504, is of the genus *Dipodomys.*

50. For information on weaving in this passage and in chaps. x and xiv, we are indebted to Irmgard W. Johnson, and to Guy Stresser-Péan and Luis Reyes, who together analyzed techniques currently practised in Otomí and other indigenous areas. Hence such descriptive terms as "woven design skirt" for *tlamachcueitl,* "gauze weave" for *nepaniuhqui,* etc. — Personal communications, Nov. 1, 1958; July 11, 1959.

51. *La parte interior del centro sesgado (ibid.); con gallinas en vuelo* (Sahagún, Garibay ed., IV, p. 360).

52. Or "[ornamented like] coverlets." See *cacamoliuhqui* in Molina, *op. cit.*

like cape,[53] the netlike *nopal* cape, the netlike shift.[54] However, they were worthless, of little value.

The Otomí greatly honored two as gods. The one was Otontecutli; this one had become their first leader. The name of the second one was Iocippa. And only for this one did they observe the principal feast day; to Iocippa, when they celebrated a feast for him, they said: "Totopainalo, Iocippa Totoco." In the grass land they slept, they ate; for four days they lived in the grasslands. They prepared all manner of food, of drink. Not a little was consumed of fruit tamales, of honey tamales[55] ... This happened only when it was the great feast day of the Otomí. They said they named [the feast day] Totopayna, and, they said, Iocippa totoca.

The very important gods of the Otomí were two: the name of the first [was] Iocippa, the name of the second [was] Otontecutli. Then followed one called Atetein. Their important places of worship, their places of prayer, were on the tops of the mountains.

Behold still other ways of the life, of the qualities, of the Otomí. Boys married very young. For the especially infantile, the quite immature, the not yet pubescent, the young boys somewhat grown, they then sought out just such young girls. And the daughters of the lords, the rulers, the leaders, however, were requested. And so that it might not be said that [their daughters] strayed, many times they gave them to any one; they presented them to someone. And also many times they sought out a man for them. And it is said that, when the youth had attained manhood, if he did not mount ten times, so they remained apart; they remained separated. And likewise when the woman did not respond to him with passion, if her mate came to her perhaps eight times — ten times — so they remained separated.

This is all which is to be told here of the way of life of the Otomí.

The Quaquata, the Matlatzinca, the Toloque

The name of the Matlatzinca comes from their manner of work. To shell maize they only placed it in a net; they only beat it. And to carry it on the back, they did not use a bag; they likewise placed the maize kernels in a net called a grass sling. In the bottom they carried grass to form a base.

In otomj: vmentin in cenca vel qujmoteutiaia, injc ce otontecutli: iehoatl in achto inteiacancauh mochiuh: injc vme iehoatl in jtoca Iocippa: auh çan icel, in cenca vel qujlhujchiviliaia in Iocippa: in jquac qujlhujquixtiliaia, qujtoa totopainalo, Iocippa totoco, çacatla in cuchi, in tlaqua: navilhujtl in çacatlanemj, ixquich qujcencaoa in tlaqualli, in atl: amo çan quexqujch in polivi xocotamalli, necutamalli, nenepanolli, coiotli. Injn in jquac y, vel çan iio in jnveiilhujuh Otomj: qujtoa, qujtocaiotia: totopaina, ioan qujtoa, Iocippa totoca,

in cenca veueintin inteuoan otomj, vmentin. Injc ce itoca Iocippa. Injc vme itoca; Otontecutli: njman ie oallatoqujlia, o, in mjtoa, Atetei. Cenca vel inneteuchioaia intlatlatlauhtiaian in tepeticpac

Oc izca centlamantli in jnieliz, in jnnemjliz Otomj. cenca pipiltotonti, in tlapaliuhcati, oc cenca cocone, oc cenca atzitzinti: njman aiamo tlalticpac, vel pipiltotonti, in ie qualton oqujchpilpil: njman noce cioapilpil qujtemolia: auh in tecuti, in tlatocati, in teiacana. Ca tel îtlano, in jmjchpuchoan: auh injc amo çan mjtoa, quauhtlamelaoaz. mjecpa çan qujntemaca, qujntetlauhtia: auh no mjecpa qujmoqujchitlanja, auh qujlmach intlacamo matlacpaeoaz, in telpuchtli, in jquac tlalticpac tlamati, no ic mocaoaia, no ic motlalcaviaia: auh no iuhquj in cioatl, in jquac amo qujhiionamjquj, in aço chicuexpa, matlacpa itech aciz in jnamjc: no ic motlalcaviaia.

Can cuel ixqujch y, njcan onmjtoa, in Otomj inieliz.

QVAQUATA: MATLATZINCA, TOLOQUE.

In matlatzinca: itech qujça in jntoca, in jntlatequjpanoliz, Injc coia cintli, çan qujmatlatema, çan qujvitequj: ioan injc tlamamaia, amo xiqujpilli qujtitlanja: çan no qujmatlatema in tlaolli, mjtoa: çacatematl, ococacatl tlanj qujvica qujxpechia.

---

53. Often referred to as "netted," which is a different weave. Valley of Mezquital Otomí weave very fine *ayates* of one or two *ixtle* fibers; Stresser-Péan reports a *gasa* of cotton (locally called *de nopal,* however) for the Huaxteca. Open-mesh, plain-weave fabric, or a gauze weave (both done on the loom) would give the impression of a "netted" fabric. — Irmgard W. Johnson, *op. cit.*

54. See Spanish text, fol. 133*v*: "*çanjtli: que es vipilli como de red.*"

55. After *necutamalli*, the *Acad. Hist.* MS has *tzopelic tamalli.*

Also especially were they named Matlatzinca [because] they were adept with the sling. The boys always went carrying the sling. Just as the Chichimeca always went carrying the bow, these also always went carrying the sling,[56] always hurling stones with it. Especially were they likewise named Matlatzinca [because], when they made an offering of a commoner, when they sacrificed him before their image of the devil, they did not kill him with something; they only crushed him to death in a net.

And their name was Quaquata: a single one, Quatatl; many, Quaquata. They were named Quatatl because they always carried, they always went with the sling tied about the head. *Qua*[*tatl*][57] is as if to say, "one who wears a sling about the head." The *qua* means "head"; the *tatl* means, "sling"; as much as to say, "one who wears a sling about the head." Or it means *quate, quatetl*, "their heads like stones," which means "one with head of stone."

The home, the land, of these Quaquata, the place by the name of Matlatzinco, is very cold; therefore these Quaquata were also very strong, rugged, hard, sinewy. And also, since from a great distance they sent sling shots which wounded, they thus provided little tranquility in the land and in war. And of one who was presumptuous, disrespectful, one said — one was named — Quatatl; and it was said, "He is like the Quata."

The good wine the good maguey wine, the very strong because it quickly took effect, quickly made one drunk, quickly destroyed one, was also named Quatatl. It was said: "This [is] the real Quatatl; it is considered the real Quatatl."

And the Matlatzinca were also named Toloque[58] — one alone,[59] Tolo; many, Toloque. By [the city of Tolocan] lies their mountain; there it is. It is said its name is Tolotzin [or] Tolotepetl. Some say — furthermore the Toloque also say — that because many reeds grow there the city is Tolocan, and the people Toloque.

These Toloque — along with them those named Matlatzinca — spoke a barbarous tongue, but there were those who spoke Nahuatl. The way they pronounced their language made it somewhat unintelligible; in their language was the letter *r*.

Oc cenca no ic motocaiotia, matlatzinca, vel itech momatia in tematlatl, in pipiltotonti ça cen qujtqujtinemj in tematlatl: in iuh chichimeca in mochipa qujtqujtinemj tlavitolli: no mochipa qujtqujtinemj, in tematlatl, in chichimeca, mochipa ic tlatlamotlatinemj. Oc cenca ic iequene motocaiotia matlatzinca: in jquac tlacatl, maceoalli qujvenchioaia, im jxpan qujmjctiaia diablo iixiptla: amo itla injc qujmictiaia, çan qujmatlapatzcaia:

ioan intoca Qvaquata, in ça çe Quatatl, in mjequjntin Qvaquata, injc quatatl motocaiotia: ipampa in mochipa qujtqujtinemj, in çan mochipa ic moquailpitinemj, in tematlatl in Qua iuhqujn qujtoznequj, quatematle, in Qua, qujtoznequj, tzontecomatl, in tatl, qujtoznequj, tematlatl, iuhqujn qujtoznequj quatematle, anoço qujtoznequj quate quatetl, iuhqujn tetl intzontecon, qujtoznequj tetl itzonteco.

Injque in Qvaquata, in inchan, in jntlalpan, in jtocaiocan Matlatzinco cenca ceoa, ic cenca no chicaoaque, tlapaltique, oapaoaque, ichtique in iehoantin quaquata: auh no in jpampa tematlatl, qujtitlanj in veca tequa: ic cenca no amo tlatlamatcachioa, in tlalticpac, ioan in iaoc: auh in aqujn âtlatlamati, in teixco eheoa, mjtoa, motocaiotia Quatatl, ioan mjtoa, iuhqujn quata.

In qualli vino, in qualli vctli, i cenca ihiio, in jpampa iciuhca tetech qujz, in iciuhca teivinti, in jciuhca tepolo: no motocaiotia Qvatatl, mjtoa, vel quatatl y, vel quatatl momati.

No ioan motocaiotia toluca, in matlatzinca: in ca ce tolo, in mjequjn toloque, ytech mana in vmpa ca intepeuh qujl itoca Tolotzin, tolotepetl cequjn qujtoa, tel no iehoan qujtoa in toloque: in altepetl ca toluca, auh toloque in tlaca: ipampa in cenca vmpa mochioa tuli.

Injque in toluque injoan intoca matlatzinca, ca popoloca, tel vncate in naoatlatoa auh in jntlatol, cequj qujpolonja injc qujtenqujxtia, in jntlatolpan, vnca in letra. R.

---

56. *In chichimeca* appears to be intrusive. The words are not in the *Acad. Hist. MS.*

57. *Quatatl* in the *Acad. Hist. MS.*

58. *Toloque* in *ibid.*

59. Read *ça ce.*

182

Nothing grew in the land of these Quaquata; only maize, beans, amaranth; no chili, no salt. The principal foods of these were tamales, beans; also their principal drink was fruit *atole*. Popcorn was produced right there in their land. Their clothes, their capes, were of maguey fiber; theirs were maguey fiber capes; theirs were the maguey fiber breech clouts. These also occupied themselves with, they enjoyed, the bewitching of people, the blowing of evil upon people.

The name of the god of the Toloque was Coltzin. They showed him honor in many ways. No others knew of him; no others glorified him; by themselves they celebrated the feast day. The Mexica, the Tepaneca helped them not.

When they sacrificed a person they merely crushed a poor commoner in a net. They placed him in a net; they crushed him. His arm bones, his leg bones, his ribs came out from the net; also there [before the image] the blood dripped.

Their virtues

[They were] great workers of the land, very sinewy, great bearers of burdens. They were bathers in the early dawn.

HERE A LITTLE IS TOLD of those who are the Ocuilteca.

Those called Ocuilteca also have their homes there in the land of Tolocan. Their way of life is also like the way of life of the Toloque, only their language is not like the language of the Toloque. They are much given to bewitching others.

THE MAÇAUAQUE

The Maçauaque are a distinctive people. They live here at a place named Xocotitlan. They occupy the same land as the Toloque; however, their language is distinctive. But their way of life is the same as the way of life of the Toloque. However, in still another way they are similar: they are not well reared. The old women paint their faces with yellow ochre or with red. They even paste their arms, their legs with feathers. Also the gourd rattle rests in their hands; also they dance with it. And the men always carry[60] their gourd rattles. When they do something they bind their heads [and] set their gourd rattles on the top of their heads.

Also [they are] great workers of the land; also [therefore] very sinewy. And in their land it is ex-

Injque in quaquata: amo tle mochioa in jntlalpan, çan iio in tlaolli, in etl, in oauhtli, atle chilli, atle iztatl. Injque in, cenca intlaqual in tamalli, in etl: no cenca intlail in xocoatolli vel vmpa mochioa in jncha, in momochitl. In jntlaquen, in jntilma catca, ichtli, imjchtilma catca, imjchmaxtli catca. Injque in, no qujmotequjtia, no qujmaviltia in texoxaliztli, in tehipitzaliztli.

In jnteouh in toloque, itoca Coltzin: mjec tlamantli inic qujmaviztiliaia, aiac quen ipan, amo tepan qujtecaia, nonqua ilhujtlaia, amo qujnpaleviaia in mexica, in tepaneca:

in jquac tlacamjctiaia, çan qujmecapatzcaia in maceoaltzintli, matlac contlalia qujpatzca in jmatzopaz, in jqueztepul, in jomjcicujl: matlacopa oalqujqujça, vncan no oalmotetepeoa, in eztli.

In jnqualtiliz

Cenca elimjqujnj, cenca ichtique, cenca tlamamani oc iooac in maltianj.

NICAN ACHI VNMJTOA: in aqujque ocujlteca.

In mjtoa ocujlteca: çan no vmpa inchan in tolocatlalpan: çan no iuhque in jnieliz, toloque inieliz: iece amo çan no ie in jntlatol toluque, oc centlamantli, ca cenca vel qujmotequjtiaia in tetlachiviliztli.

MAÇAOAQUE

In maçaoaque: centlamantin tlaca, njcan nemj in jtocaioca xocotitla: çan ic centlaleque in toluque, iece centlamantli in jntlatol: auh çan tel no iuhquj, in jnieliz, in jnieliz toluque: iece çan oc ceppa ie iuhqujn amo ozcalia, in jlamatoton, moxaoa tecuçauhtica, anoço tlapaltica: oc noma no mopotonja in jnmac, in jmjcxic: no inmac onoc, no ic mjtotia, in aiacachtli: auh in oqujchtli, ça ce imaiacach ietineca, in jquac itla ai, moquailpia imjcpac qujquetzaia, in jmaiacach.

No cenca elimjqujnj, no cenca ichtique: auh cenca tlapanavia ceoa, in jntlalpa: ipampa ca ceio in jtech

---

60. Read *ietinenca*.

ceedingly cold, because it is cold near where they live, though they dwell at the foot of a mountain named Xocotepetl. And their name Maçauaque comes from him who was their first leader, Maçatl tecutli. And these also called themselves Chichimeca.

THE TOTONAQUE; SINGULAR, TOTONAC

From here the Totonaque lived to the north, to one side, a little to the east. In their appearance these resemble the Huaxteca a little. They are long-faced, with column-shaped faces, because they are broadheaded.

It is hot in their land. There are all kinds of food, all kinds of fruit; but cacao, aromatic herbs never grow. From there comes the liquidambar. And now the fruits which came from Spain are produced there in abundance. There is cotton;[61] from there come the red reed mats, the red reed seats; therefrom come the cotton bearing trees.

To these corresponded a humane, civilized life. The men clothed themselves; they wore capes, breech clouts, sandals,[62] arm bands, necklaces, quetzal feather devices; they bore fans; they had trinkets.[63] They cut their hair, arranged their hair-dress well, looked at themselves in mirrors. The women wore skirts, shifts—embroidered skirts, embroidered shifts. They were quite elegant. And since these wove like Huaxteca women, they were wearers of varicolored skirts, varicolored shoulder shawls. Their shoulder shawls were of netting.

And all the commoners wore blue skirts. Their hair strands were braided with varicolored [strips of cloth] wrapped with feathers. In the market place they were well bedight with flowers.

And these women were good embroiderers, skilled in cotton work. And the men and women were beautiful, fair, tall, slender, firm. Their language was a barbarous tongue, although some spoke Otomí, some spoke Nahuatl, some spoke also the Huaxteca language. They were quite skilled in song; they were very able in the dance.

And they were skilled in their food; from there came (what they called) tamales, meat tamales. Their specialty was their tortilla, which was an ell in circumference. Their staff of life was the chili. Thus did they eat: the tortillas came from a pottery grid-

TOTONAQUE: IN ÇA CE TOTONAC.

In totonaque, njpa in onoque mjctlampa, tlanacaztla: achi tlapcopa. Inique in, achi mocuextecanequj, in jntlachializ ixmelactique, ixmjmjltique: ipampa in quaoacaltique,

in jntlalpan tona, ixqujch vnca in tonacaiutl, ixqujch vnca in xuchiqualli: tel ie aic omochiuh in cacaoatl, in veinacaztli, vmpa vitz in xuchiocutzutl: auh in axcan, vel vmpa motlaelchioa, in castilla vitz xuchiqualli, vnca in jchcatl, vmpa vitz, in ezpetlatl, in ezpetlaicpalli, vmpa vitz in quavichcatl.

Injque in, vel intech ca in tlacaiotl, in tlacanemjliztli: motlaquentia in oqujchtli motlalpiliaia, momaxtlatiaia, mocactia, mocactia, momacuextia, mocozcatia, moquequetzaltia, êcaceoaceque, tecuecuexeque: moxima, qujiectlalia in jnnexin, motezcavia: in cioa cueieque, vipileque tlamachcueie, tlamachvipile, vel mjmati: auh injc cuexteca ic iuhque, injque y, cioa, in tlatlapalcue catca, quechquemeque catca, tlatlapalli, çanitli in jnquechque in toveliecaoa in pilchioa,

auh in ie ixquich maceoalli texocueie: auh in ie mochintin, in jntzonjpilhoaz, tlatlatlapalpoalli, hivitica qujlacatzoaia in tianqujzco vellaxuchimanca:

auh in iehoan y, cioa vellamachchiuhque, vel mocpaimati: auh in oqujchti, ioan in cioa, quaqualti, chipaoaque, pipiaztique, cujllotque, oapaltia: in jntlatol popoloca, tel cequjn otontlatoa, cequjntin naoatlatoa, cequjntin no qujcaquj in cuexteca tlatolli: vel mjmati in jpan cujcatl, vel motlaqujmati, in jpan netotiliztli:

auh mjmati in jntlaqual, vmpa vitz (in qujlhuja) tlapictli, nacatamalli, in tetonal: in jntlaxcal, cenmolicpitl catca injc iaoaltic, vel innacaio in chilli injc tlaquaia, comalcopa oalqujztiuh in tlaxcalli, chiltitlan qujoallaça, çan qujmochicavia.

---

61. Following *jchcatl*, the *Acad. Hist. MS* has, crossed out, *vmpa mochiva yn olli*.

62. In the *Florentine Codex*, *mocactia* is repeated.

63. Corresponding Spanish text: "*se ponen otros dixes.*" Seler, *op. cit.*, p. 422, translates *mit Schellen besetzte Knöchelringe*.

dle; they dipped them in the chili; they simply brought them together.

The Huaxteca

In addition, their name [is] Toveiome, and Panteca, or Panoteca. Their name comes from the land, the place, named Cuextlan. Those who dwell in this land, it is said, are named Cuexteca. The name of only one is Cuextecatl. And their name is Toueiome; one alone is called Toueio. This name Toueio means "our neighbor." And their name is Panteca or Panoteca. This name comes from Pantla or Panotla, for Pantla is also the name of the place where they dwell. Pantla or Panotla means "where the water is crossed," for this is on the sea coast.

Hence is it given the name, "where the water is crossed": they say those who arrived, who reached the land — those who settled here in the land called Mexico, now called the West Indies — came in boats; they crossed over the sea. And there, the coast on which they came to land, so it is said, is given the name Pantla. Earlier it was called Panotla, that is to say, "where the water is crossed."

And there it is very hot; there is much suffering from the heat. And there are all kinds of food; many different kinds of food grow there, none of which appear here, [such as] the one named *quequexquic*. Many other wonderful [plants] grow there; the sweet potato every month. There are all different kinds of cotton. It is called the land of food, the land of flowers.

Behold their array: [they were] wide-headed, broad-headed; they colored, they dyed their hair diverse colors — some yellow, some red. They parted it. It is said that the men wore the hair over the ear lobes; they let it hang over the ear lobes;[64] they left a tuft of hair over the back of the head. They filed the teeth; their teeth were like gourd seeds.

These [wore] arm bands, leather bands about the calves of their legs, bracelets of green stones, quetzal feather devices carried on the back, circular devices of palm leaves, circular devices of arara feathers,[65] arara feather fans.

These used the slender arrow, the bow; and they called it the tipped arrow. On the end was flint, or an obsidian flake, or a broad obsidian blade. And when one came to overpower his enemy, he cut off his head,

Cuexteca:

ioan intoca toveiome, ioan intoca panteca, anoço panoteca. In jntoca in, itech qujça in tlalli: in jtocaiocan cuextla, in jpan onoque y, tlalli: mjtoa, motocaiotia Cuexteca: in ça ce itoca cuextecatl, in jhoan intoca Toveiome: in ça ce mjtoa Toveio: injn tocaitl toveio, qujtoznequj tooampo, ioan intoca panteca, anoço panoteca: itech qujça injn tocaitl pantla, anoço panûtla: ca no itoca pantla, in vmpa onoque, in pantla, anoço panutla: qujtoznequj, panuoaia, ca ie ilhuicaatenco y.

Inic motocaioti panooaia: qujlmach in aqujque, in acique, in tlalmaceuhque, in njcan mopixoco, in mjtoa: mexicatlalpan, in axcan mjtoa india occidental: acaltica in oallaque, injc qujoalpanavique ilhujcaatl: auh in vncã qujçaco, atenco, ic mjto, ic motocaioti pantla, mjtoaia in ie nepa panutla, qujtoznequj, panuoaia:

auh in vmpa y, cenca tona, cenca tlacacaoaca: auh ixqujch vnca in tonacaiotl, oc mjec tlamantli, in vmpa mochioa xuchiqualli, in atle njcan neci, in jtoca, quequexqujc: oc mjec in maviztic, vmpa mochioa, in camotli, in jxqujch in metztli: mochi vnca in nepapan ichcatl, in xuchitl, mjtoa Tonacatlalpan, xuchitlalpan

Izcatquj in jnnechichioal: quaoacaltique, quapatlachtique: in jntzon qujtlatlapalpoaia, qujpaia, cequj coztic, cequj chichiltic catca, qujtlatlamantiliaia: mjtoa, mochampuchtiaia, mochonpilichtiaia, mopiochtia, tlãtziquatique, in oqujchti, iuhqujn aiooachtli intlan catca.

Injque y, matemequeque, cotzeoaoaque, chalchiuhmacuexeque, quetzalmanaleque, çoiatlaçooaleque, cuecallaçooaleque, cueçalecaceoaceque.

Injque y, qujtitlanj in mjtl, in pitzaoac, in tlavitolli: ioan qujlhuja tzaptopilli, tecpatl in jiacac îcac, anoço itztapalcatl, anoço itztilactli: auh in oqujtopeoato iiaouh, conquechcotona, qujtlaztiqujça in jtlac: çan

64. Read *champilichtiaia*; cf. Seler, *op. cit.*, p. 424.
65. Read *cueçallaçooaleque*.

casting his body aside. He carried off only his head; he tied it [on a stick].[66] If he seized four or five in war, he tied on as many heads.

The clothes, the capes, the large cotton capes of these were all of good quality. There were made those called capes of many colors,[67] large capes of many colors, large varicolored capes.[68] From there came the capes with the serpent face design;[69] the capes painted with bloodied faces;[70] indeed they were adept in many [capes]. They used many jewels, green stones, turquoise, fine turquoise; their ear pendants [were] of green stones.

The women dressed themselves very well in skirts, in shifts; they covered themselves very well. Their hair braids [had] varicolored [strips of cloth] wound with feathers.

The defects of the Huaxteca: the men did not provide themselves with breech clouts, although there were many large capes. They perforated their noses with palm leaves. And when they were enlarged, they inserted there a gold palm leaf stem, or a reed from which emerged a red arara [feather]. They filed their teeth; they darkened them with red or with the *tlamiaualli*[71] herb.

TLALHUICA

The Tlalhuica. These are the dwellers of the hot lands. They speak Nahuatl; they speak the Nahuatl language. Cotton, chili, maize, grow well. Now the fruits of Spain are produced in abundance.

These Tlalhuica dwelt there to the south, and the Totonaque, the Toueiome, dwelt there to the north. And this name Tlalhuicatl — or Cuextecatl, Totonac, Toueio — is from the characteristic of imprudence. They say to one who is untrained, "Art thou indeed a Totonac? Art thou indeed a Toueio?" And they say to one, "Crude Cuextecatl, crude Totonac, crude Tlalhuicatl!" And also they were reckoned among the Otomí people. It is asked, "Art thou indeed a crude Otomí?"

Their defects: they appeared pompous as they tied on capes, as they went carrying flowers. And they were untrained; they were very cowardly.

jio in jtzontecon qujtquj, qujmotzonoatzaltia, intla navi, macujlli caçi iavc, izqujtetl qujtzonoatza in tzontecomatl.

Injque y, muchi qualli in intlaquen, in jntilma, in jnquach: mochi maviztic, vmpa mochioa in qujlhuja: centzontilmatli, in centzonquachtli, in tlatlatlapalquachtli: vmpa vitz in cooaxaoacaio, vmpa vitz in jxnextlacujlolli, vel mocentzonjmati: qujtitlanj in cozcatl in chalchivitl, in xivitl, in tevxivitl, inchalchiuhchampuch.

In çioa: cenca vel mocuetia, movipiltia, cenca vel motlapachoa: in jntzonjpilhoaz, tlatlatlapalpoalli, hivitica tlailacatzolli.

In jmjtlacauhca Cuexteca: in oqujchtin amo momaxtlatiaia, maçonelivi in cenca vnca quachtli: moiacavicoltiaia, çoiatica in qujcoiaoa in jniacavicol: auh in ocoiaoac, vncan caqujaia teocujtlaçoatl anoço acatl, cueçali iiticopa qujquixtia motlantziquatiliaia, motlamjaoa tlapaltica anoço tlamjaoaltica.

TLALHUJCA

In tlalhujca: iehoantin in tonaian tlalpan onoque. in naoatlatoa, naoatlatolli injc tlatoa: vel mochioa in inchan, in jntlalpan, in ichcatl, in chilli, in tonacaiotl: in axcan cenca motlaelchioa in castillan xuchiqualli.

Injque y, tlalhujca: ie njpa in onoque amjlpampa, vitztlampa: auh in totonaque in toveiome ie njpa in onoque, ie mjctlampa: auh inin tocaitl tlalhujcatl, anoço cuextecatl, totonac, toveio: itech ca anezcalicaiotl. In aqujn amozcalia, qujlhuja: cujx titlalhujcatl, cujx titotonac, cuix ticuextecatl, cujx titoveio: ioan qujlhuja, cuextecapul, totonacapul, tlalhujccapul: ioan no intech tlacaleoalo in Otomj, mitoa: cujx totompul?

In jmjtlacauhca: çan mototopalquetza injc motlalpilia, inxoxuch iuh ietinemj: auh amo mozcaliaia, vel mauhque catca.

---

66. Seler, *op. cit.*, p. 425, derives the term from *uatza*, to dry. In order to follow the corresponding Spanish text, we derive it from *tzonuaztli* or *tzonuia*.

67. Literally, "four hundred." Corresponding Spanish text: *"mantas de mill colores, y diferencias."*

68. We have consistently translated *tilmatli* as cape and *quachtli* as large cape. Molina, *op. cit.*, defines both as *manta*. In Clark, *op. cit.*, II, pp. 109, 122, the translations are "mantle" and "large cotton mantle." There is evidence that the *quachtli* was also a measure of cloth used as a medium of exchange. See Dibble and Anderson, *op. cit.*, Book IX, p. 48.

69. Corresponding Spanish text: *"mantas que tienen vnas cabeças de mostros pintadas."*

70. Cf. Sahagún (Garibay ed.), IV, p. 339. Corresponding Spanish text: *"pintadas de remolinos, de agua enxeridos vnos, con otros."*

71. Cf. *supra*, chap. xxviii, § 1, n. 83.

COUIXCA, TLAPPANECA

The Couixca, whose name [is] also Tlappaneca — the singular [is] Couixcatl: these are the people of Tepequacuilco, Tlachmalacac, [and the province of] Chilapan. They are not speakers of a barbarous tongue; they speak Nahuatl. These are very rich.

YOPIME, TLAPPANECA

The Yopime, whose name [is] also Tlappaneca; these are the inhabitants of Yopitzinco. The [term] Yopime is taken from their home [land], which is a place called Yopitzinco. And they are Tlappaneca because they paint themselves with red ochre, and because the name of their god was Totec, the red Tezcatlipoca. His array [was of] red ochre. Likewise were his priests and all the commoners; all painted themselves with red ochre.

These were rich. These were speakers of a barbarous tongue. The names of these were Tenime, Pinome, Chinquime, Chochontin; the singular [forms] are Pinotl, Chinquitl, Chochon.

The common name of these was Tenime, because they spoke a barbarous tongue. These were completely untrained; they were just like the Otomí; yet they were really worse. These also suffered affliction.[72] They dwelt in a land of misery; but nevertheless, [they were] knowers of green stones; [they were] people of wisdom.

OLMECA, UIXTOTI, MIXTECA

These, all of these, all were the people from the east. They were also named Tenime, because they spoke a barbarous tongue. These, according to the tradition, were Tolteca — a branch, a remnant, of the Tolteca. These were rich; their home, their land, was really a land of riches, a land of flowers, a land of wealth, a land of abundance . There was all manner of food; there grew the cacao bean, and the "divine ear" spice, and wild cacao,[73] and liquid rubber. There the magnolia and all different kinds of flowers grew. And there were the beautiful feathers, the precious feathers, [the feathers of] the troupial, the red spoonbill, the blue cotinga, the white-fronted parrot,[74] the Mexican parrotlets;[75] the resplendent trogonorus was

COVIXCA, TLAPPANECA

In covixca, ioan intoca tlappaneca: in ça ce covixcatl. Injque y, covixca: iehoantin in tepequacujlca, in tlachmalacac tlaca, in chilapaneca, in amo popoloca, in naoatlatoa, injque y, vel mocujltonoa.

IOPIME, TLAPPANECA

In iopime, ioan intoca tlappaneca: iehoantin in iopitzinca, injc iopime, itech mana in jnchan ca, itocaiocan Iopitzinco. Auh injc tlappaneca: ipampa in tlavitl ic moçaia, ioan ipampa in inteouh, itoca catca totec: tlatlauhquj tezcatlipuca, yn jnechichioal tlavitl: no iuhquj catca in jntlamacazcaoan, ioan in jxqujch maceoalli, mochintin tlavitl injc moçaia.

Injque y, mocujltonoa. Injque y, popoloca, ieiehoan in jntoca Tenjme Pinome, chinqujme, chochõtin, in ça ce, pinotl, chinqujtl, chochon.

Inique y, incentoca tenjme: ipampa in popoloca, ic motocaiotia Tenjme. Injque y, njman amo mozcaliaia, vel iuhqujn Otomj catca oc nel qujnpanaviaia. Injque y, çan no tetolinj ca, çan no cococatlalpan in onoque: auh iece no chalchiuhiximatinj, tlaiximatinj.

OLMECA VIXTOTI, MJXTECA

Injque y, muchintin, iehoantin in jxquichtin tonatiuh iixco tlaca: no motocaiotia tenime, ipampa in popoloca. Injque y, iuhca nenonotzalli ca tolteca: ca inxeliuhcaiooan, ca innecauhcaiooan in tulteca Injque y, mocujltonoa in jnchan, in jntlalpan, vel tonacatlalpan, xuchitlalpan, necujltonoloian, netlamachtiloia: vnca in jxqujch tonacaiotl, vmpa mochioa in cacaoatl, ioan in teunacaztli, ioan quappatlachtli, ioan olli: vmpa mochioa in iolloxuchitl: ioã in ie mochi in nepapan xuchitl, ioan vmpa nemj, in qualli hivitl, in tlaçotli, in çaquan, in tlauhquechol, in teuquechol, in xiuhtototl, in cochotl, in qujlito: no vmpa nemj in quetzaltototl: no vmpa vitz, no vmpa neçi in chalchivitl, in teuxivitl: no vmpa neçi in coztic, in jztac

---

72. *Itolinicā* in the *Acad. Hist. MS.*

73. Corresponding Spanish text: *"otro genero de cacao, que llaman quappatlachtli."* Seler, *op. cit.*, p. 428, n. 3, defines it as *Theobroma bicolor*.

74. *Amazona albifrons albifrons.* Cf. Martín del Campo, *op. cit.* (1940), p. 391, and Herbert Friedmann, Ludlow Griscom, and Robert T. Moore: *Distributional Check-List of the Birds of Mexico*, Pts. I and II (Alden H. Miller, ed.; Pacific Coast Avifauna, Nos. 29, 33; Berkeley: Cooper Ornithological Club, 1950, 1957; hereafter referred to as Friedmann *et al.*), I, p. 129.

75. *Forpus cyanopygius* (Souancé) in *ibid.*, p. 127. Aztec parrakeet, *Aratinga astec* (Souancé) is also given on p. 126. Martín del Campo, *op. cit.*, p. 391, suggests *Psittacula cyanopygia* or *Eupsittula astec.*

also there. Also green stones, fine turquoise were found there. Also gold, silver were found there. It was a good, a beautiful place.[76] The old people gave it the name of Tlalocan, which is to say, "place of wealth."

The array of these was of many kinds: some tied on capes, some wore sleeveless jackets, some wore bark paper breech clouts. And the women were great embroiderers, skilled in work with cotton thread, artisans, well trained; they were verily inhabitants of Anauac, women of Anauac, dwellers of the land of flowers. Each of the arm bands of the women was as much as a hand in width. They wore arm bands of green stones; they put on plaited necklaces provided with pendants. Also the women wore sandals. The sandals of the men were very precious; also, they walked in rubber sandals.

Because they were rich, because there was such abundance in their homes, it was said of these in times past that they were sons of Quetzalcoatl. It was said that he who was rich, who was wealthy, belonged to — was a son of — Quetzalcoatl. These always went bearing the bow, the copper hatchet, because of the abundance of wild beasts in their land. Many of these spoke Nahuatl.

MICHOAQUE, QUAOCHPANME

The singular [form] is Michoa, Quaochpa.

These are called Michoaque; their name comes from the fact that fish in plenty come from there. And And the Quaochpanme are given the name because they never let their hair grow. All shaved their heads; the men, the women, even all the old women shaved their heads. An occasional one wore the hair long.

In their land is all manner of food: ears of dried maize, amaranth, beans, *chía,* gourds, fruit.

Their array was [thus]: the men wore sleeveless jackets; they always went with their bows; their woven reed quivers,[77] their quivers, they went bearing upon their backs. [For] that which was their clothing, they used wild animal skins, ocelot skins, wolf skins, lynx skins, fox skins, deer skins; there were their yellow fan-shaped devices, their garlands of squirrel skins, their shoulder devices of *ayoquan*[78] feathers. Good were their houses, although all were straw huts where they lived. They were real artisans,

teocujtlatl, vel qualca, iecca: qujtocaiotitivi in vevetque Tlaloca. q, n, necujltonoloia.

Inique, y, mjec tlamantli in jnnechichioal, cequjntin motlalpiliaia, cequjntin moxicoltiaia, cequjntin mamamaxtlatiaia: auh in çioa, vel veveintin tlamachiuhque, mocpaimati, tulteca, vel mozcalianj: ca nel noço anaoaca, anaoacaçioa xuchitlalpaneca. In çioa: vnca inmaqujz, quen cecen macpalli, injc patlaoac: mochalchiuhmacuextiaia, cozcapetlatl contecaia, pipiloleque, no mocactia in cioa: in oqujchti vellaçotli in jncac, no qujcçaia in olcactli.

Injque y, injc mocujltonoa, injc atle tlaçotli inchā: mjtoaia in ie nechca Quetzalcoatl ipilhoa. Qujl in aqujn mocujltonoa, in motlamachtia: qujl itech pouhquj, qujl ipiltzin. Injque y, çan mochipa qujtqujtinemj in tlavitolli, ioan jn mactepuztli: ipampa tequantla in jnchan, ynjque in, mjequjntin in naoatlatoa.

MICHOAQUE, QUAOCHPANME:

in ça ce michoa, quaochpa.

Injque y, injc mjtoa, michoaque: itech qujça in intoca y: ipampa in vmpa tlaquauhqujça in mjmjchti: auh in quaochpanme, ic motocaiotique: ipampa aiac motzontiaia mochintin maioichiquja, in oqujchtin, ioan in çioa in manel ilamatzin, mochtin maioichiquja: çan aca in motzonquentiaia.

In jntlalpan, y, mochi vnca in tonacaiotl, in cintli, in oauhtli, in etl, in chian, in aiotli, in xuchiqualli.

In jnnechichioal catca: moxicoltiaia in oqujchti, ça cê in intlavitol ietinenca, inmjpetl, inmjcon qujmamatinenca: qujtitlanja intlaquē catca in tequaneoatl, in oceloeoatl, in cujtlacheoatl, in ocotocheoatl, in oztoeoatl, in maçaeoatl, incoçoiaoalol catca, intetechaloxuchiuh, imaioquanmanal: quaqualli in jncal, tel çan mochi xacalli injc onoca: vel tolteca, vel amanteca: quauhxinque, tlaxinque, quauhtlacujcujque, tlacujloque, tlatecque.

---

76. *Vel qualca yeccā* in the *Acad. Hist. MS.*

77. Seler, *op. cit.,* p. 430, reads the *Acad. Hist. MS* as *mipotl, die Pfeile.*

78. According to Martín del Campo, *op. cit.,* pp. 388 *sqq.,* this is the *Cassiculus melanicterus* or the *Agamia agami;* according to Friedmann *et al., Mexican cacique* (II, p. 277) or *agami heron* (I, p. 31).

real feather workers, carpenters, cutters, wood-workers, painters, lapidaries.

The Michoaca women understood well the working of cotton thread; they were good [cloth] cutters; many were good embroiderers; they made the cross-weave capes. The men made very wonderful sandals.

In this manner they prepared food: they prepared, all at once, what they would eat for two days, for three days, or for a week.

Behold the faults of the Michoaque: they wore no breech clouts, but went bare, covering themselves only with their *cicuilli,* the so-called sleeveless jacket. They wore it just like a shift. And the perforations in their lips, in their ears, were much enlarged. Their lip-plugs were very big. The women wore only a skirt; they lacked a shift. Their skirts were neither full nor long; they reached only to above their knees. The women [and] the men were unskilled with food.

The name of the god of these [people] was Taras; hence they are now named Tarascos. This Taras is called Michoacatl in the Nahuatl language. He is the god of the Chichimeca. Serpents, birds, rabbits were sacrificed before him. They did not sacrifice people; they let their captives live; they were as their slaves.

To him who was their ruler, they paid heed; they paid honor. In all places he was shown obedience. All the rulers of the surrounding cities obeyed him; all paid him tribute, heeded him. He was the equal of him who was the ruler of Mexico.

The Mexica or Mexiti

One alone is called Mexicatl; many are called Mexica. This comes from the name Mecitli: *me,* that is to say, maguey; *citli,* rabbit. It should be pronounced Meçicatl. Hence it is a corruption when Mexicatl is said.

According to tradition, the name of the priest who led the Mexica was Meçitli. It is said that when he was born they named him Citli. And they placed him in a maguey leaf, where he grew strong; wherefore was he named Mecitli. And this one, when he matured, became a priest, a keeper of the god. It is said that he spoke personally with the devil, wherefore they revered him greatly; and all obeyed the one by whom they were led. And since he led his subjects, therefore they were given the name Mexica.

These Mexica, according to the account, came the very last from the land of the Chichimeca, from the desert lands. Behold the story which the old people

In mjchoaca çioa: vel mocpaimati, vellatecoaque, vel centzonme, vellamachchiuhque: qujchioa in nepaniuhquj tilmatli: in oqujchti vel quaqualli in cactli qujchioa.

Injc tlaqualchioa: çan qujcenchioa in omjlhujtl, eilhujtl qujquazque, in aço ce semana.

Izca in jmjtlacauhca, in mjchoaque: amo momaxtlatiaia, çan maxauhtinenca: çan iehoatl ic motlapachoaia in jnçicujl, in mjtoa inxicol: çan vel iuhquj in vipilli conmaqujaia: auh cenca cocoiaoac catca in jntenco, in jnnacazco, vel vevey in jntenteuh catca. In çioa: çan iio mocuetiaia, atle invipil catca: amo no vei, amo no viiac, in jncue catca: çan intlanquaticpac âcia, in cioa. In oqujchti amo motlaqualimatia.

Injque y, in jnteouh catca, itoca taras: ic axcan ic notzalo tarascos. Injn taras: iehoatl in naoatlatolpan mjtoa, Michoacatl: in chichimeca inteouh Coatl, tototl, tochi, im jixpan qujmjctiaia, amo tlacamjctiaia: in jnmalhoan, çan qujnnemjtiaia: iuhqujnma intlacaoan catca.

In jntlatocauh catca: vel qujcemjttaia, vel qujmaviztiliaia, vel novian tlacamachoia: mochintin qujtlacamatia, in novian altepetl ipan tlatoque: mochintin qujtlacalaqujliaia, vel qujcemjttaia, qujnamjcticatca: in mexico tlatoanj catca.

Mexica, anoço mexiti.

In ça çe mjtoa mexicatl: in mjequjn mjtoa, mexica. Injn tocaitl mexicatl: itech qujça in tocaitl Mecitli. me, q. n. Metl, citli, in tochin, citli: mjtozquja meçicatl, ic onjxpolivi in mjtoa Mexicatl:

in iuhca nenonotzalli, in tlamacazquj, in qujnoaliacan mexica, itoca catca Meçitli: qujl injc tlacat, qujtocaiotique Citli: auh memac in qujtecaque, in vncan tetzaoac, ic motocaioti mecitli: auh injn in ooapaoac tlamacazquj teupixquj mochiuh, qujl qujtlacanotzaia in diablo: ic cenca qujmaviztilique, ioan mochintin qujtlacamatque, in iacanaloni: auh in qujniacan in jtlapacholhoan, ic motocaiotique Mexica.

Injque in, mexica: in iuhca nenonotzalli, ça oallacentzacutiaque in chichimecapan, in teutlalpan. Izca in tlatolli in qujtotivi in veuetque. In jqujn in canj, in

told. In the distant past, which no one can still reckon, which no one can still remember, those who came here to disperse [their descendants] — the grandfathers, the grandmothers, those called the ones who arrived [first], the ones who came [first], those who came sweeping the way, those who came with hair bound, those who came to rule in this land, those of the same name, those who seemed to form their [own] little world — came over the water in boats; [they came] in many divisions.

And they drew along the coast, the coast to the north. And where they came to beach their boats is named Panotla, which means "where they crossed over the water." Now it is called Pantla. Then they followed along the coast line; they went looking at the mountains, especially the [snow-]white mountains and the smoking mountains. Going along the coast line, they went to reach Quauhtemallan.

And these did not go of their own volition, for their priests led them. [The priests] went counseling with their god. Then they came — they arrived — at a place named Tamoanchan, which is to say, "We seek our home." And there they tarried.

And these were wise men called Amoxoaque.[79] The wise men remained not long; soon they went. Once again they embarked and carried off the writings, the books, the paintings; they carried away all the crafts, the casting of metals. And when they departed, they summoned all those they left behind. They said to them: "Our lord, the protector of all, the wind, the night, saith you shall remain. We go leaving you here. Our lord goeth bequeathing you this land; it is your merit, your lot. Our lord, the master of all, goeth still farther, and we go with him. Whither the lord, the night [and] the wind, our lord, the master of all, goeth, we go accompanying him. He goeth, he goeth back, but he will come, he will come to do his duty, he will come to acknowledge you. When the world is become oppressed, when it is the end of the world, at the time of its ending, he will come to bring it to an end. But [until then] you shall dwell here; you shall stand guard here. That which lieth here, that which spreadeth germinating, that which resteth in the earth, is your merit, your gift. He maketh it your birthright. For this you followed him here. But we go with him:[80] we go following him whither he goeth."

aocac vel compoa, in aocac uel conjlnamjquj, in aqujque njcan qujnchaiaoaco in coltin in çitin, in aqujque in mjtoa in âcique, in êcoque, in ochpanaco, in tlatzonjlpico, in tlatepachoco, in njcan tlalpan in çan jc mocenteneoa: in iuhqujma centetl cemanaoatontli mochiuhticatca. Atlan: acaltica, in oallaque, mjec tlamanti:

auh vncan atenqujçaco in mjctlampa Atenco: auh in vncan cacanaco imacal, motocaioti Panutla, qujtoznequj, panuoaia: axcan mjtoa Pantla: njman ic atentli qujtocatiaque, qujtztiuj in tepetl: oc cenca iehoan in iztac tetepe, iôan in popocatetepe, haçito in quauhtemalla catentocatiuj:

auh injn amo çan moiocoia in vi, ca qujniacana in jntlamacazcaoan: auh qujnotztivi, in jnteouh: njman ic oallaque, vncan âçico, in jtocaiocan tamooanchan. q. n. temooa tocha: auh vncan vecaoaque,

auh injque y, vncatca in tlamatinime, in mjtoa: amoxoaque. Auh amo cenca vecaoaque, in tlamatinjme, njman iaque: oc ceppa macalaqujque, auh qujtqujque in tlilli, in tlapalli, in amoxtli, in tlacujlolli: qujtqujque in jxqujch tultecaiotl, in tlapitzalli: auh in jquac vnpeuhque, qujnnonotztiaque in ixqujchtin qujncauhtiaque, qujmjlhujque. Qujmjtalhuja in totecujo, in tloque, naoaque, in iooalli, in ehecatl: njcan anmonemjtizque, njcan tamechtocaujlico injn tlalli: amechmomaqujlia in totecujo amomaceoalti, amolhujlti: oc nachca in motlamachititiuh in totecujo, in tloque, naoaque; auh in jca oc ietivi ca tictoviqujlitivi, in canjn motlamachititiuh, in tlacatl, in iooalli, in ehecatl in totecujo, in tloque, naoaque, ca movica, ca mocueptzinoa: tel vitz, moqujxtiquiuh, amechmatiqujuh in oîçiuh tlalli, in ie tlaltzompa, in ie itlamjan, iehoatl tlatzonqujxtiqujuh: auh in amehoan njcan annemjzque, njcan antlapiazque, amolhujl, amonemac, y, in njcan onoc, in jxoatoc, auh in tlallan onoc, amechmomaceoaltilia, iehoatl in anqujoaltocaque: auh in jnca oc ie toniativi, tictoujqujlitiuj: in canjn motlamachititiuh.

---

79. Corresponding Spanish text: "sus sabios, o adeujnos, que se dezian Amoxoaque, que quiere dezir: hombres entendidos en las pinturas antiguas."

80. In ica oc ye tiui, in Acad. Hist. MS.

Thereupon departed those who carried the god on their backs; they carried him wrapped — wrapped in a bundle. It is said that their god went advising them. And as they went, they traveled to the east. They carried the writings, the books, the paintings. They carried the knowledge; they carried all — the song books, the flutes.

But four remained of the old men, the wise men: one named Oxomoco, one named Cipactonal, one named Tlaltetecui, one named Xochicauaca. And when the wise men had gone, then these four old men assembled. They took counsel; they said: "The sun will shine, it will dawn. How will the common people live, how will they dwell? He is gone; they carried away the writings. And how will the common people dwell? How will the lands, the mountains be? How will all live? What will govern? What will rule? What will lead? What will show the way? What will be the model, the standard? What will be the example? From what will the start be made? What will become the torch, the light?"

Then they devised the book of days, the book of years, the count of the years, the book of dreams. They arranged the reckoning just as it has been kept. And thus was time recorded[81] during all the time the Tolteca, the Tepaneca, the Mexica, and all the Chichimeca reign endured. No longer can it be remembered, no longer can it be investigated how long they were left in Tamoanchan, which is to say, "We seek our home."

The history of it was saved, but it was burned when Itzcoatl ruled in Mexico. A council of rulers of Mexico took place. They said: "It is not necessary for all the common people to know of the writings; government[82] will be defamed, and this will only spread sorcery in the land; for it containeth many falsehoods." [83]

And they departed from there, from Tamoanchan. Offerings were made at a place named Teotiuacan. And there all the people raised pyramids for the sun and for the moon; then they made many small pyramids where offerings were made. And there leaders were elected, wherefore it is called Teotiuacan.[84] And

Niman ic iaque, in teumamaque: in qujmilli, in tlaqujmjlolli qujtqui: quil qujnnotztiuh in jnteouh: auh injc iaque, ie tonatiuh yixcopa itztiaque, qujtqujque in tlilli, in tlapalli, in amoxtli, in tlacujlolli qujtqujque in tlamatiliztli: mochi qujtqujque in cujcaamatl, in tlapitzalli:

auh in mocauhtiaque, in veuetque, in tlamatinjme, navintin ce itoca Oxomoco, ce itoca cipactonal ce itoca tlaltetecuj, ce itoca xuchicaoaca. Auh in jquac oiaque y, in tlamatinjme: njman mononotzque, mocentlalique, y, in navintin veuetque qujtoque. Tonaz, tlatviz: quen nemjz, quen onoz in maceoalli: ca oia, ca oqujtqujque, in tlilli, in tlapalli: auh quē onoz in maceoalli, quen manjz in tlalli, tepetl, quen onoaz, tlê tlatqujz, tlê tlamamaz, tleh tlavicaz, tlê tlaotlatoctiz, tlê machiotl, tlê octacatl iez, tlê neixcujtilli iez, tlê itech peoaloz, tlê ocutl, tlê tlaujlli mochioaz.

Niman ic qujiocuxque, in tonalpoalli, in xioamatl, in xippoalli, in temjc amatl. Qujtecpanque in iuh omopix: auh ic otlaotlatoctiloc in jxqujch caujtl omanca tolteca tlatocaiotl, tepaneca tlatocaiotl, mexica tlatocaiotl: ioan in jxqujch chichimeca tlatocaiotl, aocmo vel molnamjquj, aocmo vel onmocxitoca in quexquich cavitiloc tamooanchan, in qujtoznequj: temooa tocha, ca mopiaia in jtoloca,

ca iquac tlatlac in tlatocat Itzcoatl, in mexico: innenonotzal mochiuh in mexica tlatoque, qujtoque: amo monequj mochi tlacatl qujmatiz, in tlilli, in tlapalli, in tlatconj, in tlamamalonj, avilqujçaz: auh injn, çan naoalmanjz in tlalli, ic mjec mopic in jztlacaiutl.

Auh in vncan jn tamooancha, vncan oneooaia, in vntlatlatlauhtiloia in jtocaioca teotioaca: auh in jxqujch tlacatl, vmpa qujtzaqualtique in tonatiuh ioan in metztli: njman ic mjec in qujchiuhque tzaqualtotonti. Vmpa vntlatlatlauhtiloia, auh vmpa vnnetachcauhtlaliloia: injc mjtoa teutioaca. Auh in jquac mj-

81. In the *Florentine Codex*, otla- is repeated.

82. Cf. Horacio Carochi: *Arte de la Lengva Mexicana* (Mexico: Imprenta del Museo Nacional, 1892), p. 448 (De los verbales en *oni*, que significan instrumento); cf. also Angel Ma. Garibay K.: *Llave del Náhuatl* (Otumba: Imprenta Maylí, 1940), p. 47. In some circumstances, the meaning is adjectival (e.g., the governable). See also *Florentine Codex*, Book VI, fol. 103v (*In jtconj, in mamalonj*).

83. After *iztlacayotl*, the *Acad. Hist.* MS contains the following, which is crossed out: *in quitoque ca valpachi yoā miequintin neteutiloque. No quexquichcauh tlatloc in xomiltepec. Auh ōpa valevaloc ȳ vilovac teutiva in axcā itocayoca san juā. Inic mitoa teutivaca vel mochintin ōpa cēquizque.*

84. Corresponding Spanish text: "*Y En este pueblo, se elegian: los que aujan de regir a los de mas: por lo qual se llama, teutioacā: que qujere dezir, vey tioacā: lugar donde hazian señores.*"

when the rulers died, they buried them there. Then they built a pyramid over them. The pyramids now stand like small mountains, though made by hand. There is a hollow where they removed the stone to build the pyramids.

And they built the pyramids of the sun and the moon very large, just like mountains. It is unbelievable when it is said they are made by hands, but giants still lived there then. Also it is very apparent from the artificial mountains at Cholollan;[85] they are of sand, of adobe. It is apparent they are only constructed, only made. And so they named it Teotiuacan, because it was the burial place of the rulers. For so was it said: "When we die, it is not true that we die; for still we live, we are resurrected. We still live;[86] we awaken. Do thou likewise."[87] In this manner they spoke to the dead when one had died; if [it were] a man they spoke to him — they addressed him — as the god Cuecuextzin.[88] And if [it were] a woman, her they addressed as Chamotzin: "Awaken! It hath reddened; the dawn hath set in. Already singeth the flame-colored cock, the flame-colored swallow; already flieth the flame-colored butterfly."

Thus, the old men said, he who died became a god. They said, "He hath become a god"; that is, he hath died. And thus [the ancients] deluded themselves so that those who were rulers would be obeyed. All were worshipped as gods when they died; some became the sun, some the moon, etc.[89]

And when they had lived at Tamoanchan a long time, they departed therefrom; they abandoned the land. There they left behind those named the Olmeca Uixtotin. These were magicians,[90] wise men. The name of their leader, their ruler, a sorcerer, was Olmecatl Uixtotli. They brought along sorcery and still other divinations. So, it is said, they followed those who went to the east. And they went to come upon the sea coast. It is said they were those now called Anauaca Mixteca, because they went there. Their ruler was a wise man who showed them the good land.

quja tlatoque: vmpa qujmontocaia: njman impan qujntlaliliaia, centetl tzaqualli: in axcan onoc in tzaqualli: iuhqujn tepetotonti, ca ça iê matica tlachioalli, ca coiontoc, in vncan qujqujxtique tetl, injc qujtlalique tzaqualli:

auh injc cenca vevei qujtlalique, in tonatiuh itzaqual, ioan in metztli, iuhqujnma çan tepetl: ca njman amo neltoqujztli, in mjtoz, matica tlachioalli: ca oc qujnamêti nenca in jquac. No cenca vel itech neci, in cholollan ca tlachioaltepetl ca xanio, ca tlaqujllo, ca neztica, in çan tlatlalilli, in çan tlachioalli: auh injc qujtocaiotique teutioaca, ipampa in jnnetocaian catca tlatoque. Ca iuh mjtoaia: in jquac timjquj, ca amo nelli in timiquj ca ie tiioli, ca ie titozcalia, ca ie tinemj, ca tiça: itech xicmanjli, injc qujnotzaia mjcquj: in iquac oonmjc, intla oqujchtli ca qujlhuja in qujteunotza Cuecuextzin: auh intla çioatl ca qujlhuja Chamotzi ma xiça ca otlacueçaleoac, ca otlaujzcalli moquetz, ca ie tlatoa in cueçalpaxitl, in cueçalcujcujtzcatl, ca ie nemj in cueçalpapalutl.

Ic qujtoque in vevetque: in aqujn oonmjc oteut, qujtoaia: ca oonteut, q, n, ca oonmjc. auh injc motlapololtique, in aço ic tlacamachozque in tlatoque catca: mochintin moteotocaque, in jquac mjcque. Cequjntin qujnmjxiptlatique tonatiuh: cequjntin metztli. Etc.

Auh in ie quexqujch cavitl onooac: in tamooancha, vncan eoaque tetlalcaujque, vncan tecauhtiaque. Olmeca, vixtoti, in jntoca olmeca, vixtoti. Injque y, nonotzaleque: tlamatinj catca, naoalli in jnteiacancauh, in jntlatocauh, itoca catca: Olmecatl, vixtotli qujtqujque in naoallotl: ioan in oc cequj ixtlatiliz, iuh mjtoa, qujnteputztocaque in tonatiuh, iixco iaque: auh çan atentli ic vnmotzotzonato: qujl iehoantin in axcan mjtoa Anaoaca, mjxteca, ipampa in vmpa iaque, ca tlamatinj catca in jntlatocauh: iehoatl in qujmottili, in qualli talli.

85. *Cholollaca* in the *Acad. Hist. MS.*

86. Seler, *op. cit.*, p. 437, reads the *Acad. Hist. MS* as *yelitinemi.*

87. Seler, *loc. cit.*, reads the term in the *Acad. Hist. MS* as *xicmauili.*

88. See Angel Ma. Garibay K.: "Veinte Himnos Sacros de los Nahuas," *Fuentes Indígenas de la Cultura Náhuatl: Informantes de Sahagún* (Mexico: Universidad Nacional Autónoma de México, 1958), p. 124.

89. The *Acad. Hist. MS* contains the following, which is crossed out: *Auh in otlatziuhque tamovāchā nimā ōmiquanique xomiltepec.*

90. Sahagún (Garibay ed.), III, p. 222: *"Una gente que eran como asesinos, los cuales se llamaban nonotzalique, era gente usada y atrevida para matar."*

And there[91] occurred the boring of the maguey. They discovered the good maguey, from which comes the unfermented maguey juice. The name of the woman, who for the first time discovered the boring of the maguey, was Mayauel; but the name of the one who discovered the stick, the root, with which wine was made, was Patecatl. And [as for] those who made, who prepared wine when it excelled, the name of one [was] Tepuztecatl; of one, Quatlapanqui; of one, Tlilhoa; of one, Papaiztac; of one, Tzocaca.

And they prepared the wine there at Mount Chichinauhia, and because the wine foamed up, they named [the mountain] Poçonaltepetl. There they prepared the wine and there they drank it. And when wine had been prepared in abundance, very many were summoned; all the rulers, the leaders, the old men, the experienced men. They went there to Mount Chichinauhia, where they arranged themselves as guests.

And so very[92] god-fearing were the old people in that which they said, in that which they did, [that] all performed the libation to the god.[93] Thus did they do. Then they gave food to each one; they placed wine before each one — in four bowls or four jars, which each one drank. It was about four each that they drank; this they all drank.

And, it is said,[94] the ruler of a group of Huaxteca people who were of one language, not only drank four, [but] when he had drunk four, demanded still another. Thus he drank five, with which he became well besotted, quite drunk; he no longer knew how he acted. And there before the people he threw off his breech clout.

And since (they said) he showed no respect for divinity, then a conference was held about him. For he had offended when he had cast away his breech clout, when he had been quite besotted. And with shame the Huaxteca abandoned the land; they took all his people with him. All who understood the language moved together; they moved in a body. They traveled there from whence they came, to Panotla, now called Pantla. And as they went with great misgivings of the water, the sea, they settled there. These are called Toueiome, which means "our neighbors." And the name comes from their ruler, named Cuextecatl. They are called Cuexteca.

Auh izca ie mochioa: ie tlachiquj, ie oqujttaque in metl, in qualli itech qujça, in tlachic, in achtopa qujttac tlachiqujliztli, itoca Maiauel, ca cioatl: auh in quittac tlacotl, tlanelhoatl, injc mochioa vctli, itoca Patecatl: auh in qujchiuhque, in qujtlalique vctli, in jquac tachcauhtia, ce itoca Tepuztecatl, ce Quatlapanquj, ce Tlilhoa, ce Papaiztac, ce Tzocaca:

auh inj octli qujtlalique, vmpa in tepetl chichinauhia: auh in jpampa popoçonjnj vctli. qujtocaiotique poçonaltepetl, in vmpa qujtlalique vctli, in joan vmpa qujque: auh in jquac omoveitlali vctli, in ie cenca ie mjec: monotzque in jxqujchtin tlatoque, in teiacanque, in vevetque, in ixtlamatinj: vmpa iaque, in tepetl chichinauhia, vmpa mocooatecaque:

auh can oc injc ca inneteumavilil in ie vecauhtlaca, in tlein qujtoa, in tlein qujchioa: muchi teunappa, iuh qujchiuhque: njman tetlamamacaque, mooctlalique, nanauhcaxitl, manoço nanauhtecomatl in qujque in cecenme, in aço tlein ic qujque, nanavi in qujque mochinti:

auh mjtoa, Cuextecatl in jntlatocauh centlamantin tlaca, in no çe intlatol, amo çan navi in qujc, in oconjc navi, oc qujmjtlanj oc ce, ic macuilli in qujc, ic vel ivintic, vel xocomjc, aocmo qujma in quenjn nen: auh vncan teixpan qujtlaz in jmaxtli:

auh in oqujqujz (qujlhuja) teuiotl: njman ica necentlaliloc, ca otlapinauhti in qujtlaz imaxtli, in vel ivintic: auh çan pinaviztica, in tetlalcavi in Cuextecatl: qujnvicac in imaceoalhoan in jxqujchtin motencaquja, motqujtiaque, ololiuhtiaque: ie vmpa itztiaque, in vmpa oallaque in panutla in axcan (mitoa) pantla: auh çan ic vnmotzotzonato in atl, in ilhujcaatl, vncan motecaque: iehoan in mjtoa toveiome, q, n, tooampooan: auh in itech qujça tocaitl, in jntlatocauh in jtoca, Cuextecatl: motocaiotia cuexteca.

91. Read *nizca,* as in the *Acad. Hist. MS.*
92. Read *çan oc.*
93. See Dibble and Anderson, *op. cit.,* Chap. III.
94. *In itoca* in the *Acad. Hist. MS.*

These, they say, took entertainment, flutes with them, because they amused themselves in many ways. They practised deceit in many ways; thus they made believe that the hut burned, that they made water appear, that they dismembered themselves. They did many kinds of things. But they abandoned not their shameful conduct, their drunkenness. They were much given to wine. And thus they imitated the father, the leader, of the Huaxteca; for the men always went about naked. They never provided themselves with breech clouts until the true Christian faith came. And because he had become besotted, because he had drunk the fifth wine [jar] there at Poçonaltepec, the Huaxteca always went about as if drunk; they were always as if they had gone eating *Datura stramonium.*

And of him who is untrained, who goeth about as if drunk, these words are said: "He is the image of a Huaxteca. Hast thou perchance finished the fifth wine [jar]? He drank the fifth wine [jar]. He drank not only the four wine [jars], he finished the fifth wine [jar]."

And when the reign had endured a long time in the place named Tamoanchan, then the seat of power passed to a place named Xomiltepec. And there at Xomiltepec the rulers, the old men, the priests conferred. They said: "The master of all hath called us; he hath called each one of those who worship him as a god." They said: "We shall not live here, we shall not dwell here, we shall go in search of land. The night [and] the wind, the master of all, hath traveled beyond."

Then they set themselves in motion; all moved — the boys, the old men, the young women, the old women. They went very slowly, very deliberately; they went to settle together there at Teotiuacan. There law was established, there rulers were installed. The wise, the sorcerers, the *nenonotzaleque* were installed as rulers. The leading men were installed.

Then they departed; they moved very slowly. Their leaders accompanied them; they went leading each [group. The members] of each group understood their own language. Each had its leader, its ruler. To them went speaking the one they worshipped.[95] And the Tolteca [were] the ones who took the very lead.

Injque y, qujl qujtquique, in ahavillotl, in tlatlapitzalli: ipampa miec tlamantli, injc omaujltitia, mjec tlamantli injc oteixcuepaia, ic teixcuepaia in qujtlatia xacalli, in qujchioa atl: in motetequj, mjec tlamantli in qujchioaia: auh amo qujcauhque in jnpinaviz, in jvintiliztli: cenca qujmotequjtiaia in vctli: auh injc qujtlaieiecalhujaia in jnta, in jnteiacancauh in Cuexteca. Ca mochipa omaxauhtinenca in oqujchti: aic omomaxtlatique, in jxqujchica ooalla nelli tlaneltoqujliztli, in xpianoiotl: auh in jpampa tlaoanquj, macujloctli qujc in vmpa poçonaltepec: çan no mochipa iuhqujn oivintitinenca in cuexteca: iuhqujn mochipa mjxitl, tlapatl, oqujjquatinen:

auh in aqujn amo mozcalia in iuhquj tlaoanqujnemj: izca tlatolli ipan mjtoa, itech tlaqujxtilli in Cuextecatl: cujx tictlanj in macujloctli, ca macujloctli qujc: ca amo ma çan navi qujc vctli, ca qujtlamj in macujlvctli.

Auh in omoteneuh tamooancha: in ie ixqujch caujtl otlatoloc: njman omjquanj in tlatocaiotl, in jtocaiocan Xomjltepec: auh vncan y, in Xomjltepec monanotzque in tlatoque, in veuetque, in teupixque, qujtoque: ca otechnotz, in tloque, naoaque: qujl ceceiaca qujnnotz, in qujmoteutiaia, qujtoque ca amo njcan tinemjzque, ca amo njcan tonozque: ca titlaltemotivi, ca nachca in tlamattiuh in iooalli, in ehecatl, in tloque, naoaque:

njman ic olinque, ixqujch olin in piltzintli, in veventzin, in cioatzintli, in jlamatzin: cenca ivian, cenca iocuxca in iatiaque, vncan mocentecaco in teotioaca: vncan nenaoatiloc, vncan netlatocatlaliloc: iehoantin in motlatocatlalique, in tlamatinj, in nanaoalti, in nenonotzaleque, vel netachcauhtlaliloc:

njman ic vmpeuhque, olinque cencan iiolic, qujvivica, qujiaiacantivi in jnteiacancaoa, in mocaquj: injc cecentlamantli intlatol, cecenme inteiacancaoa, intlatocaoa. Auh injque y, qujnnotztiuh in qujmoteotia: auh in tulteca, iehoantin cenca vel tlaiacana:

---

95. Following *quimoteutia*, the *Acad. Hist.* MS contains this statement, which has been crossed out: *yehoā tlayacana ȳ tolteca ca yxq̄uich yca in acico ȳ chichimecatlalli ipā aocmo vel molnamiq' ȳ quezqui xivitl nenēque. Acito in teutlalli yitic ȳ texcalli ytzala onca quitlaque chicōtetl oztotl. Auh jnin oztotl in iteucal quichiuhque in itlatla.*

And the leader of the Otomí left [the others] at Coatepec. He introduced his people into the forest. It is said that since they lived there, they always made their offerings on the mountain tops. And they sought out only the mountain slopes to build houses there.

And then these different people went [on]: the Tolteca, the Mexica, the Nahua. All the people, as they sought land, encountered the plains, the deserts. The one they worshipped accompanied them; he went speaking to them. No more could they recall how long they had wandered; for a long time they traveled over the desert. They went to settle at a place in the desert, in a valley among the crags, a very dangerous place. And the people wept; they were saddened, they suffered affliction; there was no more to eat, no more to drink.

And at this place there were, or as one said, there are,[96] seven caves. These different people made them serve as their temples; they went to make their offerings there for a long time. No longer is it remembered how long they resided there.

Then the one whom the Tolteca worshipped spoke to them; he said to them: "Turn back. You shall go from whence you came."

Then they went to make offerings at the cave there at Chicomoztoc. Then they departed. First they came to arrive at a place called Tollantzinco. Then they passed over to Xicocotitlan, called Tollan. And then the Chichimeca, those called the Teochichimeca followed them. And then the Michoaque followed them. They departed; their ruler, named Amimitl, led them. They traveled there to the west, where they dwell today, toward the setting sun. They also first went to make offerings at the cave, Chicomoztoc.

Then the Nahua, the Tepaneca departed; then those called Acolhuaque, then the Chalca, then the Uexotzinca, the Tlaxcalteca. Each one set forth; they returned here to this place (as was already mentioned), the land of the Mexica.

And the god of the Mexica spoke to them; he said to them: "We go still farther."

Then they went to the east. And as they departed, all of them — all — went to make offerings at Chicomoztoc.

[It is] for this reason that all the different people glorify themselves; they say that they were created at Chicomoztoc, that from Chicomoztoc they came

auh in otomjtl, iteiacancauh: çan vncan tecauh in cooatepec, quauhtla qujncalaquj in jmaceoalhoan: qujl ipampa, injc onenque: çan mochipa tepeticpac in ontlatlatlauhtiaia, ioan ça cen tepeixtli in oqujtztinen. in vncan mocaltiaia:

auh njman ic vi, in jquac y, nepapan tlaca, in tulteca, in mexica, in naoatlaca: in ie ixqujch tlacatl teutlalli, ixtlaoatl qujnamjqui, in tlaltemoa: qujnvica, qujnnotztiuh in qujmoteutia: aocmo vel molnamjquj, in quexqujch caujtl nenenque, vecauhtica in jxtlaoatl qujtocatinenque. Cecca ixtlaoacan tepetzala, texcalla, motecato, cenca ovica: auh chocaque, tlaocuxque in maceoalti, in ie tlaihiiovia, in aoc tle qujqua, in aoc tle quj.

Auh in vncan y, vncan catca: manoçiuh mjto, vnca chicontetl oztotl, qujmoteopantique, in iehoantin nepapan tlaca: vncan tlatlatlauhtitinenque quexqujch caujtl, aocmo uel molnamjquj in quexqujch vncan onoca.

Niman qujnnotz in tulteca in qujmoteutia, qujmjlhuj. Ximocuepaca, tiazque: in vmpa oallaque,

njman ie ic vî, tlatlatlauhtizque in oztoc: in vncan chicomoztoc: njman ic oaleoaque, achtopa vmpa acito, in mjtoa tullantzinco: njman oalmjquanjque, in xicocotitlan, in mjtoa tulla: auh njman qujnoaltoqujlique, in chichimeca, in mjtoa teuchichimeca: auh njman qujnoaltoqujlique in mjchoaque: in oaleoaque in qujnoaliacan in jntlatocauh itoca Amjmjtl: vmpa qujmjtztiltitia in cioatlampa: in axcan ie vmpa onoque, in tonatiuh icalaqujampa: oc no achto oallatlatlauhtiteoaque in oztoc, chicomoztoc.

Niman ic oaleoaque, in naoatlaca, in tepaneca: njman ie iehoantin, in mjtoa Acolhoaque: njman ie chalca: njman ie vexotzinca, tlaxcalteca: ceceiaca oalpeuhtimanque, oalmocuepque in njcan, ie vncan y (in ie mjtoa) Mexica tlalpa:

auh in mexica qujnnotz in jnteouh qujmjlhuj: oc nachcan tivi:

njman iatiaque, in tonatiuh icalaqujampa: auh injc ompeuhque y, in ie mochintin: mochintin ontlatlatlauhtitiaque in chicomoztoc.

Ic ipampa in mochintin: ic mochachamaoa, in nepapan tlaca, in qujtoa: ca chicomoztoc iocoleque, ca chicomoztoc oalqujzque: ca amo chicomoztoc oalquj-

---

96. Ōcan ca in the Acad. Hist. MS.

forth. But there was no emerging from Chicomoztoc; [it was] merely that offerings were made at Chicomoztoc when they lived in the desert. And thereupon there was departing, there was returning. Here and there [the people] were granted land; boundaries were established.

But the Mexica traveled farther on; they went seeking land. And according to the traditions of the old people, it is said that the name of the place where they turned back was Colhuacan, Mexico. And how long they lived there at Colhuacan, how long they lived on the desert, no more does one know.

And then the Mexica returned. Their god addressed them; he said to them: "Go. Return whence you came. I will lead you; I will show you the way." Then they set forth; they came here. The [places] by which the Mexica passed, exist, are painted, are named in the Mexican accounts.

And when the Mexica came (for it is true they wandered a long time), they were the last. As they came, as they followed their course, nowhere were they welcomed; they were cursed everywhere; they were no longer recognized. Everywhere they were told: "Who are the uncouth people? Whence do you come?"

Thus they could settle nowhere; in no other place was repose accorded them; they were pursued everywhere.[97] They went passing Tollan, Ichpuchco, Ecatepec, then Chiquiuhtepetitlan, then Chapultepec, where they went all together to settle. And then there was rule at Azcapotzalco, at Coatlichan, at Colhuacan. There was no Mexico; where Mexico now is, was still patches of reeds, of rushes. And when there at Chapultepec the Mexica were attacked, war was made against them. And the Mexica moved to Colhuacan, where they remained some time.

Then they came to the place which is now called Tenochtitlan. Where they went to settle was within the limits of the cultivated fields of the Tepaneca, where they border the Acolhuaque. They went to settle among the reeds [and] rushes, because they came to settle in the land of another. Entry was impossible; there was no vacant land. They became the vassals [and] subjects of those of Azcapotzalco.

These different people all called themselves Chichimeca. All boasted the Chichimeca estate, because all had gone into the Chichimeca land where they went to live; all returned from Chichimeca land. But the

xooac: çan vncan tlatlatlauhtiloia, in chicomoztoc, in jquac ixtlaoacan onooaca. Auh njman ic oalhujlo-oac, oalnecuepaloc, in njcan ie vncan y, tlalmaceoa-loco, nequaquaxochtiloco.

Auh in mexica ie nepa itztiaque in tlaltemoto: auh in jnnenonotzal vevetque: qujl canjn oalmocuepato in jtocaioca Colhoaca Mexico: auh quexqujch cavitl in vmpa nenque, in Colhoaca, quexqujch cavitl in jx-tlaoacan, nenque, aocmo iac qujmati:

auh njman ic oalmocuepque, in mexica: qujnnotz in jnteouh, qujmjlhuj: xivia, ximocuepaca in ompa anoallaque namechiacantiaz, namechittitiz in vtli: njman ic oalpeuhque, oallatiaque: vnoc, icujliuhtoc, tocaietoc, in vncan oalqujqujztiaque Mexica: in jpan mexica tlatolli:

auh in oallaque in mexica (ca nel noço iê nepa itztiaca) ça oaltetzacutiaque injc oallaque, injc qujoaltocatiaque in jmovi, aoccan celiloque: ça noviian aioque, aocmo iximachoque: novian ilhujloque, ac ameoa, campa anvitze:

ic acan vel motlalique, aoccan vellaçaloque: ça novian oaltotocoque, qujçaco in tulla, qujçaco in jchpuchco, qujçaco in hecatepec: njman chiqujuhtepetitlan, njman chapultepec motecato, ololiuhtivi: auh in ontlatolo in azcaputzalco, in coatl ichan, in colhoaca: aiaca mexico: oc tulla, acatla: in axcan ie mexico: auh in vncan y, chapultepec: vncan peoaltiloque in mexica, in iaochioaloque: auh njman ic unmjquanjque in mexica, in colhoaca: vmpa quexqujch cavitique:

njman ic oallaque in axcan ie vncan mjtoa, tenuchtitlan mexico: in onmotlalico, çan tequaxuchco, tepaneca inmjlco: vncan moquaxuchnamjquj, in aculhoaque: tultzalan, acatzalan unmotlalico: ipampa in ça tetlalpan, onmotlalico, ca oâacoac, ca aoccan veli, temaceoal mochiuhque, tetlaiecultique in azcaputzalco.

Injque y, nepapan tlaca: mochintin qujmotocaiotia, chichimeca: mochintin ic mochachamaoa, in chichimecaiotl: ipampa in mochintin, chichimecatlalpan via, in nemjto, in mochintin chichimecatlalpan, oal-

---

97. *Valtocoque* in *ibid.*, followed by *quiçaco ỹ covatepec*.

name of the place is not Chichimeca land; the name of the place is only the desert lands, the house of darts,[98] the north. It is only named Chichimeca land because there live the Chichimeca who eat [and] drink from hunting. It is said the Mexica called themselves Chichimeca, [but properly] it is said they called themselves Atlaca Chichimeca.[99]

The different Nahua peoples also are called Chichimeca, because they returned from the Chichimeca land, they returned from the so-called Chicomoztoc. They are the Tepaneca, the Acolhuaque, the Chalca; the people from the hot lands, the Tlalhuica, the Couixca; those beyond [the mountains], the Uexotzinca, the Tlaxcalteca; and still other Nahua peoples. They also go bearing their equipment, the arrow, the spear.

The Tolteca are also called Chichimeca; they are called Tolteca Chichimeca. The Otomí are also called Chichimeca — Otonchichimeca. The Michoaque are also called Chichimeca. The people to the east are not called Chichimeca; they are called Olmeca, Uixtotin, Nonoualca.

END OF THE TENTH BOOK

mocuepato: tel amo itocaiocan chichimecatlalpan, çan itocaiocan Teutlalpan, tlacochcalco, mjctlampa: çan ic motocaioti chichimecatlalpan: ipampa in vmpa nemj chichimeca, in tlamjnaliztli qujqua, quj: injc mjtoa, mochichimecaitoa, Mexica: mjtoa, motocaiotia, atlaca chichimeca.

In naoatlaca, in nepapan tlaca: no mjtoa, chichimeca: ipampa in chichimecatlalpan oalmocuepato, in mjtoa, chicomoztoc oalmocuepato: iehoantin Tepaneca, Aculhoaque, Chalca, Tonaiantlaca, Tlalhujca, Covixca, Tlateputzca, Vexutzinca, Tlaxcalteca: ioan-in oc cequjntin naoatlaca: ic no intlatquj ietinemj, in acatl, in tlacochtli.

In tulteca no mjtoa, chichimeca, mjtoa tulteca chichimeca. In otomj no mjtoa, chichimeca, otonchichimeca. In mjchoaque: no mjtoa, chichimeca. In tonatiuh iixco tlaca: amo mjtoa chichimeca: mjtoa, Olmeca, Vixtoti, nonooalca.

FIN DEL LIBRO DECIMO

---

98. Corresponding Spanish text: *"aunque a la verdad no se llaman tierras de chichimecas, por donde ellos anduujeron, sino teotlalpan, tlacochcalco mjctlampa, q̃ qujere dezir: campos llanos, y espaciosos, que estan hazia el norte."*

99. Literally, "Chichimeca who live on the water." The corresponding Spanish text reads: *"pescadores, que vinjeron de lexas tierras."*